VITA

VITA
Life in a Zone of Social Abandonment

João Biehl

Photographs by Torben Eskerod

University of California Press

Berkeley   Los Angeles   London

University of California Press
Berkeley and Los Angeles, California

University of California Press, Ltd.
London, England

Library of Congress Cataloging-in-
Publication Data

Biehl, João Guilherme.
    Vita : life in a zone of social abandonment /
João Biehl ; photographs by Torben Eskerod.
        p.   cm.
    Includes bibliographical references and
index.
    ISBN 0-520-24277-7 (cloth : alk. paper) —
ISBN 0-520-24278-5 (pbk. : alk. paper)
    1. Vita (Asylum : Porto Alegre, Brazil)   2.
Institutional care—Brazil—Porto Alegre.   3.
Marginality, Social—Brazil—Porto Alegre.
I. Title.

HV63.B6B54   2005
362'.0425'098615—dc22   2005041745

Manufactured in Canada
14   13   12   11   10   09   08   07   06   05
10   9   8   7   6   5   4   3   2   1

For Adriana and Andre

Contents

Introduction: "Dead alive, dead outside, alive inside" *1*

PART ONE. VITA

A Zone of Social Abandonment *35*
Brazil *46*
Citizenship *56*

PART TWO. CATARINA AND THE ALPHABET

Life of the Mind *71*
Society of Bodies *75*
Inequality *82*
Ex-Human *85*
The House and the Animal *92*
"Love is the illusion of the abandoned" *99*
Social Psychosis *102*
An Illness of Time *108*
God, Sex, and Agency *111*

PART THREE. THE MEDICAL ARCHIVE

Public Psychiatry *123*
Her Life as a Typical Patient *126*
Democratization and the Right to Health *130*
Economic Change and Mental Suffering *138*
Medical Science *146*
End of a Life *151*
Voices *159*

Care and Exclusion *163*
Migration and Model Policies *171*
Women, Poverty, and Social Death *179*
"I am like this because of life" *187*
The Sense of Symptoms *192*
Pharmaceutical Being *199*

PART FOUR. THE FAMILY

Ties *209*
Ataxia *218*
Her House *229*
Brothers *235*
Children, In-Laws, and the Ex-Husband *240*
Adoptive Parents *248*
"To want my body as a medication, my body" *257*
Everyday Violence *265*

PART FIVE. BIOLOGY AND ETHICS

Pain *271*
Human Rights *274*
Value Systems *278*
Gene Expression and Social Abandonment *282*
Family Tree *292*
A Genetic Population *297*
A Lost Chance *307*

PART SIX. THE DICTIONARY

"Underneath was this, which I do not attempt to name" *313*
Book I *321*
Book II *322*
Book III *327*
Book IV *327*
Book V *330*
Book VI *331*
Book VII *333*
Book VIII *334*
Book IX *335*
Book X *335*
Book XI *336*

Book XII *337*
Book XIII *339*
Book XIV *340*
Book XV *341*
Book XVI *342*
Book XVII *343*
Book XVIII *346*
Book XIX *348*

Conclusion: "A way to the words" *353*
Postscript: "I am part of the origins, not just of language, but of people" *359*

Acknowledgments *363*
Notes *367*
Bibliography *377*
Index *395*

Backyard, Vita 2001

"Dead alive, dead outside, alive inside"

"In my thinking, I see that people forgot me."

Catarina said this to me as she sat pedaling an old exercise bicycle and holding a doll. This woman of kind manners, with a piercing gaze, was in her early thirties; her speech was lightly slurred. I first met Catarina in March 1997, in southern Brazil at a place called Vita. I remember asking myself: where on earth does she think she is going on this bicycle? Vita is the endpoint. Like many others, Catarina had been left there to die.

Vita, which means "life" in Latin, is an asylum in Porto Alegre, a comparatively well-off city of some two million people. Vita was founded in 1987 by Zé das Drogas, a former street kid and drug dealer. After his conversion to Pentecostalism, Zé had a vision in which the Spirit told him to open an institution where people like him could find God and regenerate their lives. Zé and his religious friends squatted on private property near downtown, where they began a makeshift rehabilitation center for drug addicts and alcoholics. Soon, however, the scope of Vita's mission began to widen. An increasing number of people who had been cut off from family life—the mentally ill and the sick, the unemployed and the homeless—were left there by relatives, neighbors, hospitals, and the police. Vita's team then opened an infirmary, where the abandoned waited *with* death.

I began working with people in Vita in March 1995. At that time, I was traveling throughout several regions of Brazil documenting how marginalized and poor people were dealing with AIDS and how they were being integrated into programs based on new control measures. In Porto Alegre, I interviewed human rights activist Gerson Winkler, then coordinator of the city's AIDS program. He insisted that I visit Vita: "It's a dump site of human beings. You must go there. You will see what people do to people, what it means to be human these days."

I had grown up in an area outside Porto Alegre. I had traveled through and worked in several poor neighborhoods in the north and south of the country. I thought I knew Brazil. But nothing I had seen before prepared me for the desolation of Vita.

Vita did not appear on any city map. Even though the existence of the place was acknowledged by officials and the public at large, it was not the concern of any remedial program or policy.

Winkler was right. Vita is the end-station on the road of poverty; it is the place where living beings go when they are no longer considered people. Excluded from family life and medical care, most of the two hundred people in Vita's infirmary at that time had no formal identification and lived in a state of abject abandonment. For the most part, Vita's staff consisted of residents who had improved their mental well-being enough to administer care to newcomers and to those considered absolutely hopeless. Lacking funds, training, and the proper equipment and medication, these volunteers were as ill prepared as the institution itself to deal with Vita's residents.

Some fifty million Brazilians (more than a quarter of the population) live far below the poverty line; twenty-five million people are considered indigent.[1] While in many ways a microcosm of such misery, Vita was distinctive in some respects. A number of its residents came from working- and middle-class families and once had been workers with families of their own. Others had previously lived in medical or state institutions, from which they were at some point evicted and thrown onto the streets or sent directly to Vita.

Despite appearing to be a no-man's-land cut adrift, Vita was in fact entangled with several public institutions in terms of its history and maintenance. On many levels, then, Vita was not exceptional. Materially speaking, Porto Alegre contained more than two hundred such institutions, most of which were euphemistically called "geriatric houses." These precarious places housed the abandoned in exchange for their welfare pensions; a good number of the institutions also received state funds or philanthropic donations.

I began to think of Vita and the like as zones of social abandonment.[2]

—

Catarina stood out from the others in Vita, many of whom lay on the ground or were crouched in corners, simply because she was in motion. She wanted to communicate. Adriana, my wife, was there with me. This is the story Catarina told us:

"I have a daughter called Ana; she is eight years old. My ex-husband gave her to Urbano, his boss. I am here because I have problems in my legs. To be able to return home, I must go to a hospital first. It is very complicated for me to get to a hospital, and if I were to go, I would worsen. I will not like it because I am already used to being here. My legs don't work well. Since I got here, I have not seen my children.

"My brothers and my brother-in-law brought me here. Ademar, Armando. . . . I exercise . . . so that I might walk. No. Now I can no longer leave. I must wait for some time. I consulted a private doctor, two or three times. When it is needed, they also give us medication here. So one is always dependent. One becomes dependent. Then, many times, one does not want to return home. It is not that one does not want to. . . . In my thinking, I see that people forgot me."

Later, I asked the volunteers whether they knew anything about Catarina. They knew nothing about her life outside Vita. I repeated some of the names and events Catarina had mentioned, but they said that she spoke nonsense, that she was mad *(louca)*. She was a person apparently lacking common sense; her voice was annulled by psychiatric diagnosis. Without an origin, she had no destiny other than Vita.

I was left with Catarina's seemingly disjointed account, her story of what had happened. As she saw it, she had not lost her mind. Catarina was trying to improve her condition, to be able to stand on her own feet. She insisted that she had a physiological problem and that her being in Vita was the outcome of various relations and circumstances that she could not control.

Catarina evoked these circumstances in the figures of the ex-husband, the boss, the hospitals, the private doctor, the brothers, and the daughter who had been given away. "To be able to return home, I must go to a hospital first," she reasoned. The only way back to her child, now living with another family, was through a clinic. The hospital was on the way to a home that was no more.

But adequate health care, Catarina suggested, was impossible to access. While seeking treatment, she had learned about the need for medication. She also implied that medicine had worsened her condition. This form of care operated in Vita as well: "When it is needed, they also give us medication here." She was referring to a *pharmaceuticalization* of disarray that made persons in Vita "always dependent."

Something had made it impossible for Catarina to return home. But the desire was still there: "It is not that one does not want to."

——

The reality of Vita and this initial encounter with Catarina left a strong impression on me. As I wrote my dissertation on the control of AIDS in Brazil (1999b), I was constantly reminded of the place of death in family and city life, and of this person who was thinking through her abandonment. Over the years, Vita and Catarina became key figures for me, informing my own thinking about the changing political and medical institutions and new regimes of personhood in Brazil's urban spaces. The AIDS work I was chronicling included heroic governmental and nongovernmental attempts to contain the epidemic's spread through daring prevention programs focused on safe sex and efforts to halt mortality by making AIDS therapies universally available. Along with this formidable work and the establishment of new institutions to care for vulnerable and poor populations not routinely slated for intervention, I also saw zones of social abandonment emerging everywhere in Brazil's big cities—places like Vita, which housed, in inhuman conditions, the mentally ill and homeless, AIDS patients, the unproductive young, and old bodies.

Neither legal authorities nor welfare and medical institutions directly intervene in these zones. Yet these very authorities and institutions *direct* the unwanted to the zones, where these individuals are sure to become unknowables, with no human rights and with no one accountable for their condition. I was interested in how the creation of these zones of abandonment was intertwined with the realities of changing households and with local forms of the state, medicine, and the economy. I wondered how life-enhancing mobilizations for preventing and treating AIDS could take place at the same time that the public act of allowing death proliferated.

Zones of abandonment make visible realities that exist through and beyond formal governance and that determine the life course of an increasing number of poor people who are not part of mapped populations. I was struggling to make sense of the paradoxical existence of places like Vita and the fundamentally ambiguous being of people in these zones, caught as they are between encompassment and abandonment, memory and nonmemory, life and death.

Catarina's exercise and her recollections, in the context of Vita's stillness, stayed in the back of my mind. I was intrigued by the way her story commingled elements of a life that had been, her current abandonment in Vita, and the desire for homecoming. I tried to think of her not in terms of mental illness but as an abandoned person who, against all odds, was claiming experience on her own terms. She knew what had made her so—but how to verify her account?

As Catarina reflected on what had foreclosed her life, the degree to which her thinking and voice were unintelligible was not determined solely by her own expression—we, the volunteers and the anthropologist, lacked the means to understand them. Catarina's puzzling language and desires required analytic forms capable of addressing the individual person, who, after all, is not totally subsumed in the workings of institutions and groups.

Two years passed. I had begun to do postdoctoral work in a program on culture and mental health. At the end of December 1999, I returned to southern Brazil to further observe life in Vita, fieldwork that was to result in the text for a book of photographs that Torben Eskerod and I were planning on life in such zones of abandonment.

With the recent availability of some government funds, Vita's infrastructure had improved, particularly in the recovery area (as the rehabilitation center was called). The condition of the infirmary was largely unchanged, although it now housed fewer people.

Catarina was still there. Now, however, she was seated in a wheelchair. Her health had deteriorated considerably; she insisted that she was suffering from rheumatism. Like most of the other residents, Catarina was being given antidepressants at the whim of the volunteers.

Catarina told me that she had begun to write what she called her "dictionary." She was doing this "to not forget the words." Her handwriting conveyed minimal literacy, and the notebook was filled with strings of words containing references to persons, places, institutions, diseases, things, and dispositions that seemed so imaginatively connected that at times I thought this was poetry. These were some of the first excerpts I read:

Computer
Desk
Maimed
Writer
Labor justice
Student's law
Seated in the office

Law of love-makers
Public notary
Law, relation
Ademar
Ipiranga district
Municipality of Caiçara
Rio Grande do Sul

. . .

Hospital
Operation
Defects
Recovery
Prejudice

. . .

Frightened heart
Emotional spasm

I returned to talk with her several times during that visit. Catarina engaged in long recollections of life outside Vita, always adding more details to what she had told me during our first meeting in 1997. The story thickened as she elaborated on her origin in a rural area and her migration to Novo Hamburgo to work in the city's shoe factories. She mentioned having more children, fighting with her ex-husband, names of psychiatrists, experience in mental wards, all told in bits and pieces. "We separated. Life among two persons is almost never bad. But one must know how to live it."

Again and again, I heard Catarina conveying subjectivity both as a battleground in which separation and exclusion had been authorized and as the means through which she hoped to reenter the social world. "My ex-husband rules the city. . . . I had to distance myself. . . . But I know that when he makes love to other women, he still thinks of me. . . . I will never again step in his house. I will go to Novo Hamburgo only to visit my children." She spoke elusively about giving and getting pleasure. At times, she began a train of associations that I could not follow—but at the end, she always brought her point home. Catarina was also writing nonstop.

I had not planned to work specifically with Catarina, nor had I intended to focus on the anthropology of a single person.[3] But by our second meeting in 1999, I was already drawn in, emotionally and intellectually. And so was Catarina. She told me that she was happy to talk to me and that she liked the way I asked questions. At the end of a visit, she always asked, "When will you return?"

I was fascinated by what she said and by the proliferation of writing. Her words did not seem otherworldly to me, nor were they a direct reflection of Vita's power over her or a reaction against it, I thought. They spoke of real struggles, of an ordinary world from which Catarina had been banished and that became the life of her mind.

Dentist
Health post
Rural workers' labor union
Environmental association
Cooking art
Kitchen and dining table
I took a course
Recipe
Photograph
Sperm
. . .
To identify
Identification
To present identity in person
Health
Catholyric religion
Help
Understanding
Rheumatic

Where had she come from? What had truly happened to her? Catarina was constantly reflecting on her abandonment and physiological deterioration. It was not simply a matter of transfiguring or enduring that unbearable reality; rather, it allowed her to keep the possibility of an exit in view. "If I could walk, I would be out of here."

The world Catarina recalled was familiar to me. I had grown up in Novo Hamburgo. My family had also migrated from a rural area to that city to look for a new and better life. Most of my fifty classmates in first grade at the Rincão dos Ilhéus public school had dropped out by the fifth grade to work in local shoe factories. I dreaded that destiny and was one of the few remaining who continued to sixth grade. My parents insisted that their children study, and I found a way out in books. Catarina made me return to the world of my beginnings, made me puzzle over what had determined her destiny, so different from mine.

This book examines how Catarina's destiny was composed, the matter of her dying, and the thinking and hope that exist in Vita. It is grounded in my longitudinal study of life in Vita and in Catarina's personal struggles to articulate desire, pain, and knowledge. "Dead alive, dead outside, alive inside," she wrote. In my journey to know Catarina and to unravel the cryptic, poetic words that are part of the dictionary she was compiling, I also traced the complex network of family, medicine, state, and economy in which her abandonment and pathology took form. Throughout, Catarina's life tells a larger story about the integral role places like Vita play in poor households and city life and about the ways social processes affect the course of biology and of dying.

—

Those early conversations with Catarina crystallized three problems I wanted to specifically address in our work together: how inner worlds are remade under the impress of economic pressures; the domestic role of pharmaceuticals as moral technologies; and the common sense that creates a category of unsound and unproductive individuals who are allowed to die. As Catarina elliptically wrote: "To want my body as a medication, my body." Or, as she repeatedly stated: "When my thoughts agreed with my ex-husband and his family, everything was fine. But when I disagreed with them, I was mad. It was like a side of me had to be forgotten. The side of wisdom. They wouldn't dialogue, and the science of the illness was forgotten."

According to Catarina, her expulsion from reality was mediated by a shift in ways of thinking and meaning-making in the context of novel domestic economies and her own pharmaceutical treatment. This forceful erasure of "a side of me" made it impossible for her to find a place in family life. "My brothers are hard-working people. For some time, I lived with Ademar and his family. He is my oldest brother; we are five siblings. . . . I was always tired. My legs were not working well, but I didn't want to take medication. Why was it only me who had to be medicated? I also lived with Armando, my other brother. . . . Then they brought me here."

I wanted to find out how Catarina's subjectivity had become the conduit through which her "abnormality" and exclusion had been solidified. What were the various mediations by which Catarina turned from reality and was reconstructed as "mad"—what guaranteed the success of these mediations? As I understood it, new forms of judgment and will were taking root in that extended household, and these transformations affected suffering as well as people's understanding of normalcy and the pathology that she, in the end, came to embody. Psychopharmaceuticals seem to have played a key role in altering Catarina's sense of being and her value for others. And through these changes, family ties, interpersonal relations, morality, and social responsibility were also reworked.

Why, I asked Catarina, do you think that families and doctors send people to Vita?

"They say that it is better to place us here so that we don't have to be left alone at home, in solitude . . . that there are more people like us here. . . . And all of us together, we form a society, a society of bodies."

Catarina insisted that there was a history and a logic to her abandonment. As I tried to find out how her supposedly nonsensical thoughts and words related to a now vanished world and what empirical conditions had made hers a life not worth living, I found Clifford Geertz's work on common sense illuminating. "Common sense represents the world as a familiar world, one everyone can, and should, recognize, and within which everyone stands, or should, on his own feet" (2000a:91). Common sense is an everyday realm of thought that helps "solid citizens" make decisions effectively in the face of everyday problems. In the absence of common sense, one is a "defective" person (91).

"There is something of the purloined-letter effect in common sense; it lies so artlessly before our eyes it is almost impossible to see" (2000a:92). That is unique to the anthropological endeavor: to try to apprehend these colloquial assessments and judgments of reality—that are more assumed than analyzed—as they determine "which kinds of lives societies support" (93). Work with Catarina helped to break down this totalizing frame of thought, which envelops the abandoned in Vita in unaccountability. After all, common sense "rests its [case] on the assertion that it is not a case at all, *just life in a nutshell. The world is its authority*" (93; my emphasis).

For me, Catarina's speech and writing captured what her world had become—a messy world filled with knots that she could not untie, although she desperately wanted to because "if we don't study it, the illness in the body worsens." Geertz is well aware of the physiological dimensions of common sense. As stories about the real, he writes, common sense is first and foremost grounded in ideas of naturalness and natural categories (2000a:85).

In Catarina's case, the soundness or unsoundness of her mind was the nature either presupposed by her kin and neighbors or mastered by pharmaceuticals and the scientific truth-value they bestow. Familial and medical deliberations over Catarina's mental state and the actions that resulted made her life practically impossible, I speculated. Here, the familial and the medical, the mental and the bodily, must be perceived as existing on the same register: tied to a present common sense. Following the words and plot of a single person can help us to identify the many juxtaposed contexts, pathways, and interactions—the "in-betweenness"—through which social life and ethics are empirically worked out, that is, "to remind people of what they already know . . . the particular city of thought and language whose citizen one is" (Geertz 2000a:92).

—

During my 1999 visit, Catarina gave me her oral and written consent to be the subject of this work. I had no structured method in the beginning, other than continuing to return and engage Catarina on her own terms. She refused to be seen as a victim or to hide behind words: "I speak my mind. I have no gates in my mouth." Clearly, it was not up to me to give her a voice; rather, I needed to find an adequate understanding of what was going on and the means to express it.[4] The only way to the Other is through language. Language, however, is not just a medium of communication or misunderstanding but an experience that, in the words of Veena Das and Arthur Kleinman, allows "not only a message but also the subject to be projected outward" (2001:22).

In the essay "Language and Body," Das (1997) observes that women who were greatly traumatized by the partition of Pakistan and India did not transcend this trauma—as, for example, Antigone did in classical Greek tragedy—but instead incorporated it into their everyday experience. In Das's account, subjectivity emerges as a contested field and a strategic means of belonging to traumatic large-scale events and changing familial and political-economic constellations. Inner and outer states are inescapably sutured. Tradition, collective memory, and public spheres are organized as phantasmagoric scenes, for they thrive on the "energies of the dead" who remain unaccounted for in numbers and law. The anthropologist scrutinizes this bureaucratic and domestic machinery of inscriptions and invisibility that authorizes the real and that people must forcefully engage as they look for a place in everyday life. In her work on violence and subjectivity (2000), Das is less concerned with how reality structures psychological conditions and more with the production of individual truths and the power of voice: What chance does one have to be heard? What power does speaking have to make truth or to become action?

In Vita, one is faced with a human condition in which voice can no longer become action. No objective conditions exist for that to happen. The human being is left all by herself, knowing that no one will respond, that nothing will crack open the future. Catarina had to think of herself and her history alongside the fact of her absence from the things she remembered. "My family still remembers me, but they don't miss me." Absence is the most pressing and concrete thing in Vita. What kind of subjectivity is possible when one is no longer marked by the dynamics of recognition or by temporality? What are the limits of human thought that Catarina keeps expanding? As the work progressed, I tried to help Catarina reconnect with her family and access medical care. But I was faced at every step with the terminal force of reality. This terminal reality requires an anthropological name for its condition.

Why did I choose to work with Catarina and not someone else? She stood out in that context of annihilation; she refused to be reduced to her physical condition and fate. She wanted to engage, and I had a gut feeling that something important for life and knowledge was going on that I did not want to miss. Her words pointed to a routine abandonment and silencing, and yet, in spite of all the disregard she experienced, Catarina conveyed an astonishing agency. Once I found myself on her side, we were both up against the wall of language. Language was not a point of separation but of relating—and comprehension was involved.

The work we began was not about the person of my thoughts and the impossibility of representation or of becoming a figure for Catarina's psychic forms. It was about human contact enabled by contingency and a disciplined listening that gave each of us something to look for. "I lived kind of hidden, an animal," Catarina told me, "but then I began to draw the steps and to disentangle the facts with you." In speaking of herself as an animal, Catarina was engaging the human possibilities foreclosed to her. "I began to disentangle the science and the wisdom. It is good to disentangle oneself, and thought as well." This remark meant the world to me. I wanted this work to be of value to Catarina. Working with her, as she looked for a way back to a familiar world, was also an anthropological *bildung* for me. Yes, a pedagogy of fieldwork is hierarchical, but it is also mutually formative, as Paul Rabinow notes: "As it is hierarchical, it requires care; as it is a process, it requires time; and as it is practice of inquiry, it requires conceptual work" (2003:90).[5]

Here, anthropology had to do something more than simply approach the individual from the perspective of the collective. Treated as mad, Catarina was presumed to operate outside memory, and in fact there was no evidence whatsoever to determine whether Catarina's recollections were true or false, no one nearby to confirm her accounts, no information available concerning her life outside Vita. How to enlarge the possibilities of social intelligibility that she had been left to resolve alone? I had to find ways to decipher the real in her life and her words and to relate those words back to particular people, domains, and events of which she had once been a part—an experience over which she had no symbolic authority.

An immense parceling out of the specific ways communities, families, and personal lives are assembled and valued and how they are embedded in larger entrepreneurial processes and institutional rearrangements comes with on-the-ground study of a singular Other. Still, there was always something in the way Catarina moved things from one register to the other—past life, Vita, and desire—that eluded my understanding. This movement was her own language of abandonment, I thought, and that forced my conceptual work to remain in suspense and open as well.

I visited Catarina many times over the past four years, seeing her last in August 2003. I listened intently as she carried her story forward and backward. In addition to tape-recording and taking notes of our conversations, I read the volumes of the dictionary she continued to write and discussed them with her. I greatly enjoyed working with Catarina—looking into her eyes; speaking openly of things one does not understand; searching and finding, with someone else, not a perfect form but the means of knowing. And one must also search for ways to make the knowledge of singularity and immediate history that one finds in the field contribute to the care of self and others (Rabinow 2003; Fischer 2003). Talking extensively to friends and colleagues about my conversations with Catarina led the study—and also Catarina and her writing—into new contexts and possibilities. I am thinking not solely of the force of her poetic imagination to reach other lives but also of the thoughtful ways in which some health professionals and administrators interacted with Catarina, with her social and medical condition, and with her critical thinking as this investigation progressed.

At times, I began to act like a detective, seeking out the concrete trajectory of Catarina's exclusion from everyday life, the acceleration of her physiological deterioration, and the roots of her language-thinking. Taking Catarina's spoken and written words at face value took me on a journey into the various medical institutions, communities, and households to which she continually alluded. With her consent, I retrieved her records from psychiatric hospitals and local branches of the universal health care system. I was also able to locate her family members—her brothers, ex-husband, in-laws, and children—in the nearby industrial town of Novo Hamburgo. Everything she had told me about the familial and medical pathways that led her into Vita matched the information I found in the archives and in the field. Through return visits, patience, proximity, the laborious production of data that was not meant to exist, and the thick description of a single life, a certain block of reality came into view.

In tracing Catarina's passage through these medical institutions, I saw her not as an exception but as a patterned entity. That is, she was subjected to the typically uncertain and dangerous mental health treatment reserved for the urban working poor. Medical technologies were applied blindly, with little calibration to her distinct condition. Like many, she was assumed to be aggressive and thus was overly sedated so that the institution could continue to function without providing adequate care. The diagnoses she received varied from schizophrenia to postpartum psychosis to unspecified psychosis to mood disorder to anemia. I interacted with health professionals who had overseen her treatments as well as with human rights activists and administrators who were involved in efforts to reform these services. I was attempting to directly address the various circuits in which her intractability gained form, circuits that seemed independent of both laws and contracts (Zelizer 2005).

After talking to all parties in Catarina's domestic world, I understood that, given certain physical signs, her ex-husband, her brothers, and their respective families believed that she would become an invalid, just as her mother had become. They had no interest in being part of that genetic script. Catarina's "defective" body then became a kind of battlefield on which decisions were made within local family/neighborhood/medical networks, decisions about her sanity and ultimately about whether "she could or could not behave like a human being," as her mother-in-law put it. Depersonalized and overmedicated, something stuck to Catarina's skin—the life-determinations she could no longer shed.

But this work was not only about finding "the truth" of Catarina's story. It also precipitated events. With the help of several doctors, we scheduled medical examinations and brain-imaging, and we discovered that Catarina's cerebellum was rapidly degenerating. We then embarked on a medical journey to identify her ailment and determine what could be done to improve her condition. She was fighting time, and there was a real urgency about the knowledge being generated. As fieldwork linked Catarina to Vita, Catarina to her past, and her abandonment to her biology, it also occasioned Catarina's reentrance, if all too briefly, into the worlds of family, medicine, and citizenship. These events in turn led to a familiarity with the machinery of social death in which Catarina was caught and an understanding of the effort it takes to create other possibilities. As the *realpolitik* of abandonment came into sharp relief, questions of individual and institutional responsibility were addressed in new and different ways.

As fieldwork came to a close, Oscar, one of Vita's volunteers on whom I depended for his insights and care, particularly in regard to Catarina, told me that things like this research happen "so that the pieces of the machine finally get put together." In our conversations and in her writing Catarina was constantly referring to matters of the real. Had I focused only on her utterances within Vita, a whole field of tensions and associations that existed between her family and medical and state institutions, a field that shaped her existence, would have remained invisible.[6]

Catarina did not simply fall through the cracks of these various domestic and public systems. Her abandonment was dramatized and realized in the novel interactions and juxtapositions of several social contexts. Scientific assessments of reality (in the form of biological knowledge and psychiatric diagnostics and treatments) were deeply embedded in changing households and institutions, informing colloquial thoughts and actions that led to her terminal exclusion. Following Catarina's words and plot was a way to delineate this powerful, noninstitutional ethnographic space in which the family gets rid of its undesirable members. The social production of deaths such as Catarina's cannot ultimately be assigned to any single intention. As ambiguous as its causes are, her dying in Vita is nonetheless traceable to specific constellations of forces.

Once caught in this space, one is part of a machine, suggested Oscar. But the elements of this machine connect only if one goes the extra step, I told him. "For if one doesn't," he replied, "the pieces stay lost for the rest of life. Then they rust, and the rust terminates with them." Neither free from nor totally determined by this machinery, Catarina dwelled in the luminous lost edges of a human imagination that she expanded through writing. By exploring these edges alongside a hidden reality that kills, we have a way into present human conditions, ethnography's core object of inquiry.

—

One reads many books and borrows from their languages to understand the world one lives in. One also takes them into the field, where their propositions might not always work that well but are nonetheless helpful in generating figures of thought. This is one of the many good things about anthropology and the knowledge it produces: its openness to theories, its relentless empiricism, and its existentialism as it faces events and the dynamism of lived experience and tries to give them a form. In this book, I integrate theory into the descriptions of what I found in my work with Catarina, the medical establishment, and her family. In a similar vein, I relate her ideas and writing to the theories that institutions applied to her (as they operationalized concepts of pathology, normality, subjectivity, and citizenship, for example) and to the general knowledge people had of her. Rationalities play a part in the reality of which they speak. They form part of what Michel Foucault calls "the dramaturgy of the real" (2001:160) and become integral to how people value life and relationships and "enact the possibilities they envision" for themselves and others (Rosen 2003:x). I want this book to convey the active embroilment of reason, life, and ethics—as human existences are shaped and lost—that fieldwork captures.

One set of ideas that I initially brought to this work and that I briefly explore here concerns a person's "plastic power." "I mean," wrote Friedrich Nietzsche in *The Use and Abuse of History*, "the power of specifically growing out of one's self, of making the past and the strange one body with the near and the present, . . . of healing wounds, replacing what is lost, repairing broken molds" (1955:10, 12). Rather than speaking of an essential individuality or of an all-knowing subject of consciousness, Nietzsche calls our attention to modifications in subjective form and sense vis-à-vis historical processes and the possibilities of establishing new symbolic relations to the past and to a changing world.

Such plasticity—whether we think of it as the capacity for being molded or the adaptability of an organism to changes in its environment—is a theme moving through readings of anthropology, psychoanalysis, psychiatry, and cultural history. It appears in the "allo-plastic" capacity of Sigmund Freud's neurotic patients to alter reality through fantasy (in contrast to "auto-plastic" psychotics) (1959b:279); in Bronislaw Malinowski's argument about the "plasticity of instincts" under culture (as an alternative to the notion of a mass psyche) (2001:216); in Marcel Mauss's ensemble of the social, the psychological, and the biological, "indissolubly mixed together," in "body techniques" (1979:102); in the intrasocial and intersubjective debate that Gananath Obeyesekere regards as the "work of culture" (1990); in Arthur Kleinman's reading of patterns of social and moral upheaval in individual symptoms of distress (1981; Kleinman and Kleinman 1985); in Nancy Scheper-Hughes's account of the medicalization of the bodily common sense of "nervoso" alongside hunger (1992); in the

body of the old person becoming an "uncanny double" in the liminal space between households and the science of old age, as evidenced by Lawrence Cohen
(1998:269); and in the self-empowerment afforded to the subjected by ambiguity, as Judith Butler (1997) argues in *The Psychic Life of Power*. The notion of
the self as malleable material runs through these otherwise divergent argu-
ments; it is central to our understanding of how sociocultural networks form
and how they are mediated by bodily affect and the inner world.[7]

A related literature expands this theme of malleability, finding it not so
much in particular persons as in the plasticity of reality as such—that is, syn-
thetic frameworks mediate social control and recast concepts of a common
humanity. Theodor Adorno, for example, politicizes Freud's group psychology model and argues that the peculiarity of modern authoritarian ties
lies not simply in the recurrence of primordial instincts and past experiences
but in their *"reproduction in and by civilization itself"* (1982:122; my emphasis). According to Adorno, Nazi science and propaganda created new mechanisms of identification that bound German citizens together, and against
outsiders, in a state of moral blindness. Modern subjective reassemblage
goes hand in hand with rational-technical politics and state violence.

In "Colonial Wars and Mental Disorders," Frantz Fanon (1963) identifies
and critiques the colonized subjectivity of the Algerian people under French
imperialism. From Fanon's perspective, the locus of imperial control is not
necessarily the political and economic institutions of the colonizer but the
consciousness and self-reflective capabilities of the colonized.[8] Subjectivity
is a material of politics, the platform where the agonistic struggle over being
takes place. He states: "Because it is a systematic negation of the other person and a furious determination to deny the other person all attributes of humanity, colonialism forces people it dominates to ask themselves the question, constantly, 'In reality, who am I?'" (1963:250). Fanon's answer is one
of deconstruction: whose reality?

Fanon rethinks Freud's characterization of psychotic experience as being cut
off from reality and being incapable of achieving transference.[9] Rather than ex-
cising the psychotic from the possibility of treatment, Fanon is concerned with
the mechanisms by which the reality that the psychotic patient appears unable
to grasp has been effected. In dealing with psychosis, Jacques Lacan also urges
psychiatrists and psychoanalysts to question their own trust in the order of reality (1977:216), to halt diagnosis, and to let patients define their own terms.

"There is intuitive intelligence, which is not transferable by speech," said a
patient in a conversation with Lacan. "I have a great deal of difficulty in *logify-
ing*. . . . I don't know if that is a French word, it is a word I invented" (1980:27).
We are here faced with the patient's making of meaning in a clinical world that

would rather assign such meaning (see Corin 1998; Corin, Thara, and Padmavati 2003). We are also faced with Lacan's important insight (drawn not only from intellectualization but also from his psychoanalytic practice)[10] that the unconscious is grounded in rationality and in the interpersonal dimension of speech: "It is something that comes to us from the structural necessities, something humble, born at the level of the lowest encounters and of all the talking crowd that precedes us . . . of the languages spoken in a stuttering, stumbling way, but which cannot elude constraint" (1978:47, 48). For Lacan, subjectivity is that failed and renewable and all too human attempt to access the truth of oneself.[11] As I listened to Catarina, I saw a picture of social life emerging as agonizing and uncertain, as order and chaos, as it was actually lived.

Through and beyond subjective recollection and archival representations, my ethnographic work approached the stubborn (though ambiguous), concrete, and irreducible experience of Catarina's being in relation to others, to what was at stake for them in her vanishing from reality, and to what counted for her now (Kleinman 1999; Das 2000). In her own words:

I know because I passed through it
I learned the truth
And I try to divulge what reality is

It was not a matter of finding a psychological origin (a thing I don't think exists) for Catarina's condition or solely of tracking down the discursive templates of her experience. I understand the sense of psychological interiority as being ethnological, as the whole of the individual's behavior in relation to his or her environment and to the measures that define boundaries, be they legal, medical, relational, or affective. It is in family complexes and in technical and political domains, as they determine life possibilities and the conditions of representation, that human behavior and its paradoxes belong to a certain order of being in the world.[12]

How does one become another person today? What is the price one pays? How does this change in personal life become part of memory, individual and collective? By way of her speech, the unconscious, and the many knowledges and powers whose histories she embodies, there is the plastic power of Catarina as she engages all this and tries to make her life, past and present, real, both in thought and in writing.

In working with Catarina, I found Byron Good's study of epidemic-like experiences of psychoses in contemporary Indonesia particularly illuminating (2001). While directing attention to how the experiences of acute brief psychoses are entangled with the country's current political and economic turmoil, the ghostliness of its postcolonial history, and an expanding global psychiatry, Good emphasizes the ambiguities, dissonances, and limitations that accompany all attempts to represent subjectivity in mental illness. He suggests three analytic moves: the first, working inward through cultural phenomenology to discover how the person's experience and meaning-making are woven into the domestic space and its forceful coherence; the second, bringing to the surface the affective impact and political significance of representations of mental illness and subjectivity; and the third, inter-preting outward to the immediate economic, social, and medical processes of power involved in creating subjectivity.[13] Good unremittingly resists clo-sure in his analysis, challenging us to bring movement and unfinishedness into view.

As Catarina and I disentangled the facts of her existence, both the ordi-nariness of her abandonment and the ways it was forged in the unaccounted-for interactions of family, psychiatry, and other public services came into view. In the process, I also learned that the overpowering phenomenology of what is generally taken and treated as psychosis lies not in the psychotic's speech (Lacan 1977) but in the actual struggles of the person to find her place in a changing reality vis-à-vis people who no longer care to make her words and actions meaningful. Catarina's human ruin is in fact symbiotic with several social processes: her migrant family's industrious adherence to new demands of progress and eventual fragmentation, the automatism of medical practices, the increasing pharmaceuticalization of affective break-downs, and the difficult political truth of Vita as a death script. Adopting a working concept, I began to think of Catarina's condition as social psychosis. By social psychosis, I mean those materials, mechanisms, and relations through which the so-called normal and minimally efficient order of social formations—the idea of reality against which the patient appears psy-chotic—is effected and of which Catarina is a leftover.

Catarina was constantly recalling the events that led to her abandonment. But she was not simply trying to make sense of them and to find a place for herself in history, I thought. By going through all the components and sin-gularities of these events, she was resuming her place in them "as in a be-coming," in the words of Gilles Deleuze, "to grow both young and old in [them] at once. Becoming isn't part of history; history amounts only to the set of preconditions, however recent, that one leaves behind in order to 'be-come,' that is, to create something new" (1995:170–171). As Catarina rethought the literalism that made possible a sense of exclusion, she de-manded one more chance in life.

This is a dialogic ethnography, and the book's progression mirrors the progression of our joint work. Both Catarina's efforts, as desperate as they were creative, to write herself back into people's lives and the anthropologist's attempts to support her search for consistency and demands for a possibility other than Vita are documented here. The narrative is constructed around my conversations with Catarina and the many people with whom we interacted as the study and related events unfolded—the other abandoned persons and the caretakers in Vita, Catarina's extended family, public health and medical professionals, and human rights activists. I personally conducted all the interviews that compose the main body of the text and translated them to the best of my ability; they appear chronologically and have been edited only for the sake of clarity and conciseness.[14] I wanted the book's texture to stay as close as possible to Catarina's words, to her own thinking-through of her condition, and to the reality of Vita, which envelops Catarina and her words.

Fieldwork and archival research further addressed the circuits and actions—the verbs, if you will—in which those words and thoughts were entangled, illuminating their worldliness and that of the social practices that affected Catarina. The book follows a logic of discovery. Throughout the narrative, I provide glosses on the history and scale of the various forces impinging on her abandonment. Just as I would like Catarina to talk to the reader, I also would like the reader to become increasingly intimate with the broader social terrain in which her destiny was configured as nonsensical and valueless. The book is written in a recursive mode, to convey the messiness of both the world and the real struggles in which Catarina and her kin were involved. At each juncture, a new valence of meaning is added, a new incident illuminates each of the lives in play. Long-term ethnographic engagement crystallizes complexity and systematicity: details, often dramatically narrated, reveal the nuanced fabric of singularities and the logic that keeps things the same. This ethnographic sense of ambiguity, repetition, and openness collides with my own sensibility in the way I have tried to portray the book's main characters: as living people on the page, with their own mediated subjectivities, whose actions are both predetermined and contingent, caught in a constricted and intolerable universe of choices that remains the only source from which they can craft alternatives.

Tracking the many interconnections of Catarina's life also allowed the tentative untangling of the puzzling strings of words that compose her dictionary, the book's touchstone. The selection presented in Part Six is just a small sample of the richness of her creation. The more I learned of the literal conditions of Catarina's life, the more I seemed able to decipher some of the raw poems in her writing. I hope that this ethnographic rendering of Catarina and her life will also help the reader to hear the desperation lying within her words and to respond to her unique capacity to transfigure that desperation into a form of art.

As the ethnographer and interpreter, I am always present in the account. Every time I went one step further in knowing Vita and Catarina and their symbiotic world, I was faced with anthropology's unique power to work through juxtaposed fields and particular conditions in which lives are—concurrently, as it were—shaped and foreclosed. I find this ethnographic alternative to be a powerful resource for building social theory. The book weaves various theoretical debates through the human and ethnographic material. Throughout the book, as layers of subjectivity, reality, and theory open up, the figure and thought of Catarina provide critical access to the value systems and often invisible machineries of making lives and allowing death that are indeed at work both in the state and in the home. The book thus also represents the anthropologist's ethical journey: identifying some of the ordinary, violent, and inescapable limits of human inclusion and exclusion and learning to think *with* the inarticulate theories held by people like Catarina concerning both their condition and their hope.

Vita is a progressive unraveling of the knotted reality that was Catarina's condition—misdiagnosis, excessive medication, complicity among health professionals and family members in creating her status as a psychotic—and the discovery of the cause of her illness, which turned out to be a genetic and not a psychiatric condition. It charts the domestic events and institutional circumstances through which she was rendered mentally defective and hence socially unproductive and through which her extended family, her neighbors, and medical professionals came to see the act of abandonment as unproblematic and acceptable. Psychopharmaceuticals used to "treat" Catarina mediated the cost-effective decision to abandon her in Vita and created moral distance. Zones of abandonment such as Vita accelerate the death of the unwanted. In this bureaucratically and relationally sanctioned register of social death, the human, the mental, and the chemical are complicit: their entanglement expresses a common sense that authorizes the lives of some while disallowing the lives of others.

Catarina embodies a condition that is more than her own.[15] Her life force was unique, but the human and institutional intensities that shaped her destiny were familiar to many others in Vita. In the dictionary, Catarina often referred to elements of a political economy that breaks the country and the person down and to herself as being out of time:

Dollars
Real
Brazil is bankrupted
I am not to be blame
Without a future

By tracking the social contexts and exchanges in which Catarina's abandonment and pathology took form, this book reflects on the political and cultural grounds of a state that keeps playing its part in the generation of human misery and a society that forces increasingly larger groups of people considered valueless into such zones, where it is virtually guaranteed that they will not improve. The book demonstrates that, through the production of social death, both state and family are being altered and their relations reconfigured. State and family are woven into the same social fabric of kinship, reproduction, and death. Catarina's body and language were overwhelmed by the force of these processes, her personhood unmade and remade: "Nobody wants me to be somebody in life."

In many ways, Catarina was caught in a period of political and cultural transition. From his inauguration in 1995, President Fernando Henrique Cardoso worked toward state reform that would make Brazil viable in an inescapable economic globalization and that would allow alternative partnerships with civil society to maximize the public interest within the state (Cardoso 1998, 1999).[16] But in the process and on the ground, how are people, particularly the urban poor, struggling to survive and even prosper? And what is happening to the polity and social relations?

Scholars of contemporary Brazil argue that the dramatic rise in urban violence and the partial privatization of health care and police security have deepened divisions between the "market-able" and the socially excluded (Caldeira 2000, 2002; Escorel 1999; Fonseca 2000, 2002; Goldstein 2003; Hecht 1998; Ribeiro 2000). All the while, newly mobilized patient groups continue to demand that the state fulfill its biopolitical obligations (Biehl 2004; Galvão 2000). As economic indebtedness, ever present in the hinterland, transforms communities and revives paternalistic politics (Raffles 2002), for larger segments of the population, citizenship is increasingly articulated in the sphere of consumer culture (O'Dougherty 2002; Edmonds 2002). An actual redistribution of resources, power, and responsibility is taking place locally in light of these large-scale changes (Almeida-Filho 1998). Overburdened families and individuals are suffused with the materials, patterns, and paradoxes of these processes, which they are, by and large, left to negotiate alone.

The family, as this ethnography illustrates, is increasingly the medical agent of the state, providing and at times triaging care, and medication has become a key instrument for such deliberate action.[17] Free drug distribution is a central component of Brazil's search for an economic and efficient universal health care system (a democratic gain of the late 1980s). Increasing calls for the decentralization of services and the individualization of treatment, exemplified by the mental health movement, coincide with dramatic cuts in funding for health care infrastructure and with the proliferation of pharmaceutical treatments. In engaging with these new regimes of public health and in allocating their own overstretched and meager resources, families learn to act as proxy psychiatrists. Illness becomes the ground on which experimentation and breaks in intimate household relations can occur. Families can dispose of their unwanted and unproductive members, sometimes without sanction, on the basis of individuals' noncompliance with their treatment protocols. Psychopharmaceuticals are central to the story of how personal lives are recast in this particular moment of socioeconomic transformation and of how people create life chances vis-à-vis what is bureaucratically and medically available to them.[18] Such possibilities and the foreclosures of certain forms of human life run parallel with gender discrimination, market exploitation, and a managerial-style state that is increasingly distant from the people it governs.

I need to change my blood with a tonic
Medication from the pharmacy costs money
To live is expensive

The fabric of this domestic activity of valuing and deciding which life is worth living remains largely unreflected upon, not only in everyday life, as Oscar, the infirmary coordinator, mentioned, but also in the literature on transforming economies, states, and civil societies in the contexts of democratization and social inequality. As this study unfolded, I was challenged to devise ways to approach this unconsidered infrastructure of decision-making, which operates, in Catarina's own words, "out of justice"—that is, outside the bounds of justice—and which is close to home. Fieldwork reassembled the decision-making process at various points and in various public interactions.

This ethnography makes visible the intermingling of colloquial practices and relations, institutional histories, and discursive structures that—in categories of madness, pharmaceuticals, migrant households, and disintegrating services—have bounded normalcy and displaced Catarina onto the register of social death, where her condition appears to have been "self-generated." Throughout this chain of events, she knows that the verb "to kill" is being conjugated; and, in relation to her, the anthropologist charts and reflects on what makes this not only possible but ordinary. This is also, then, a story of the methodological, ethical, and conceptual limits anthropology faces as it goes into the field and tries both to verify the sources of a life excluded from family and society and to capture the density of a locality without leaving the individual person and her subjectivity behind.

From the perspective of Vita and from the perspective of one human life deemed mad and intractable, one comes to understand how economic globalization, state and medical reform, and the acceleration of claims to human rights and citizenship coincide with and impinge on a local production of social death. One also sees how mental disorders gain form at the personal juncture between the afflicted, her biology, and the technical and political recasting of her sense of being alive.

—

How to restore context and meaning to the lived experience of abandonment? How to produce a theory of the abandoned subject and her subjectivity that is ethnographically grounded?

Catarina is subjected
To be a nation in poverty
Porto Alegre
Without an heir
Enough
I end

In her verse, Catarina places the individual and the collective in the same space of analysis, just as the country and the city also collide in Vita. Subjection has to do with having no money and with being part of an imaginary nation gone awry. The subject is a body left in Vita without ties to the life she generated with the man who, as she states, now "rules the city" from which she is banished. With nothing to leave behind and no one to leave it to, there remains Catarina's subjectivity—the medium through which a collectivity is ordered in terms of lack and in which she finds a way to disentangle herself from all the mess that the world has become. In her writing, she faces the limits of what a human being can bear, and she makes polysemy out of those limits—"I, who am where I go, am who am so."

Catarina's subjectivity is discovered in her constant efforts to communicate, to remember, to recollect, and to write—that is, to preserve something unique to her—all of which take on new and special import in the zone of abandonment where she and I encountered each other. In a place where silence is the rule, and the voices of the abandoned are regularly ignored, where their bodies are politically useful only in the publicity of their dying, Catarina struggled to transmit her sense of the world and of herself, and in so doing she revealed the paradox and ambiguity of her abandonment and that of others. The human condition here challenges analytic and political attempts to ground ethics or morality in universal terms, or in the exceptions who stand outside the system. As I had to grapple with the ways Vita creates a humanity caught between visibility and invisibility and between life and death—something I came to call, sadly, the ex-human—I also had to find ways to support Catarina's efforts to make feasible her own way of being.

In Vita, then—beyond kinship, the right to live, and the taboo against killing—emerges the social figure of Catarina. Her language, bordering on poetry, autopsies the human and grounds an ethics:

The pen between my fingers is my work
I am convicted to death
I never convicted anyone and I have the power to
This is the major sin
A sentence without remedy
The minor sin
Is to want to separate
My body from my spirit

The book brings forth the reality that hides behind this "I," coming to a final line in Vita. It also transmits the struggle to produce a dialogic form of knowledge that opens up a sense of anticipation in this most desolate environment. How can the anthropological artifact keep the story moving and unfinished?

Vita 1995

Vita 1995

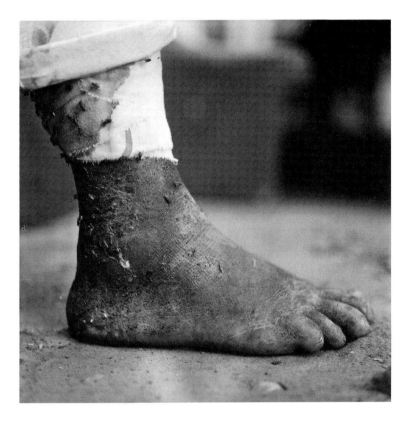

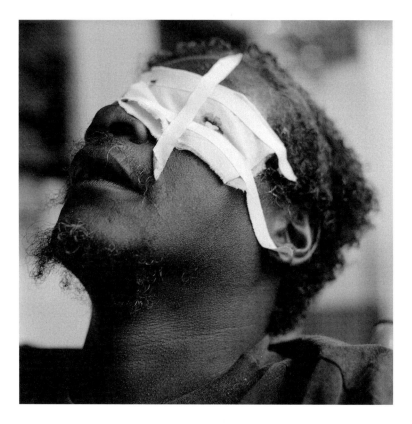

Vita 1995

Vita 1995

Vita 1995

Part One

VITA

A Zone of Social Abandonment

Vita sat on a hill of absolute misery. Gerson Winkler, a human rights activist, took me there in March 1995, along with Danish photographer Torben Eskerod. We were greeted by Zé das Drogas, Vita's founder. "Vita is a work of love," he told us. "Nobody wants these people, but it is our mission to care."

The place was overcrowded and covered with tents. The few permanent buildings included a wooden chapel and a makeshift kitchen with no hot water. Some two hundred men lived in the recovery area, and two hundred additional people stayed in the infirmary. Each of these areas contained only one bathroom facility. The infirmary was separated from the recovery area by a gate, which was policed by volunteers, who made sure that those who were the most physically or mentally disabled would not move freely around the compound. These individuals wandered around in their dusty lots, rolled on the ground, crouched over or under their beds—when there were beds.

Each one was alone; most were silent. There was a stillness, a kind of relinquishment that comes with waiting, waiting for the nothingness, a nothingness that is stronger than death. Here, I thought, the only possible abstraction is to close one's eyes. But even this does not create a distance, for one is invaded by the ceaseless smell of dying matter for which there is no language.

Like the woman the size of a child, completely curled up in a cradle and blind. Once she began to age and could no longer work for the family—"and worse," explained Vanderlei, the volunteer who guided our visit, "she was still eating the family's food"—relatives hid her in a dark basement for years, barely keeping her alive. "Now she is my baby," said Angela, a former intravenous drug user, who most likely had AIDS. Angela had long ago lost custody of her two children and now spent her days caring for the old woman. "I found God in Vita. When I first came here, I wanted to kill myself. Now I feel useful. To this day, I have not discovered the grandma's name. She screams things I don't understand." Yes, it was all horrific. Yet there seemed to be something ordinary and familiar in the ways these lives had been ruined. How to retrieve this history? And how to account for the unexpected relations and care emerging here? What is their potential, and how is it exhausted time and again?

A little later, words of salvation were everywhere. Loud, they emanated from the chapel that was now overcrowded with men undergoing rehabilitation, their heads bent as they quietly listened to several pastors of the Assembly of God. "You are fighting against God, but His words will give you victory over the world and the temptations of the flesh." Improvised loudspeakers amplified these words of God and saturated the environment. In order to receive food, the men had to attend such sermons each day; they also had to give testimonies of conversion and memorize and recite Bible verses.

Seu Bruno spoke from the pulpit: "Brothers, faith in God will make you win over the world. I came here in bad shape. I did the worst things in the world. At sixteen, I left home, and I tried to be free. I was involved with alcohol and drugs. I was destroying myself. I am forty-eight years old. I lost my family. My three children want nothing to do with me. When I began to beg, my friends also left me. Vita was the only door open to me, and here the word of God opened my mind . . . and I began to see that I have value."

Many of the men who had already passed through the recovery area took over a nearby spot of land, where they built shacks. A slum, known as the village (vila), formed on the outskirts, as if Vita were radiating outward. The economy of the streets persisted there. Although Vita was presented as a rehabilitation center, drugs moved freely between the facility and the village. I was told that criminals used the village as a hideout from the police. And there was a consensus among city officials and medical professionals that nobody actually recovered at Vita. How could they? Vita means life in a dead language. There were rumors that Zé das Drogas and his immediate assistants were embezzling donations, and even talk of a clandestine cemetery in the woods.

For Zé, Vita, despite all its disarray, was "a necessary thing. . . . Someone has to do something." State and medical institutions as well as families were complicit in its existence, and they continued bringing bodies of all ages to die in Vita. Zé's rhetoric was filled with outrage. He quoted the Old Testament and made a case for himself as a prophet: "While we are struggling, others are sleeping and not doing anything. One sees so much injustice that there are no words to express it."

Stories about the tragedies of Vita were heard in millions of households. Much of the charity that kept Vita functioning was channeled through the work of Jandir Luchesi, a state representative and a famous radio talk-show host. With more than twenty local affiliated stations, his "Rádio Rio Grande" reached nearly 50 percent of the province's population (some nine million people). During his morning show, Luchesi often put *abandonados* on the air, pleading with and scolding his radio audience: "Does anyone know this person? Who on earth could have done this to him?" Voicing moral indignation over the fate of the abandoned, Luchesi attracted donations of food and clothing while also carrying out his own political campaigns. Yet in spite of this impressive publicity, Vita was visited mostly by *crentes* (believers), poor volunteers from nearby Pentecostal churches who brought donations and tried to convert the abandoned. There were also sporadic visits by a few health professionals, such as Dr. Eriberto, who spent two hours a week administering donated medications and writing medical reports.

Only a few of the abandoned looked at us as we entered the infirmary. As they moved around or were moved, their bodies seemed passive, most likely an effect of drugs. Still, we thought, they must plan to leave this place. But we were told that when some manage to escape, they return, humiliated, begging to be allowed back. There is no other place for them to go. Who will hear their stories on the radio and "recognize that that is me"?

A middle-aged man was screaming, "*Sou capado!*" (I am castrated). As we approached, he stretched out his left arm and pretended to inject himself. "Who knows what has happened to him?" a volunteer shrugged. The man kept screaming, "*Sou capado, sou capado!*" They belong to Vita: simple people who still recollect being fathers, mothers, sons, daughters, uncles, aunts, grandparents—unclaimed lives in terminal desolation. If anthropologist Robert Hertz is right in arguing that the deceased is not only a biological entity but also a "social being grafted upon the physical individual" (1960:77), one wonders what kind of political, economic, medical, and social order could allow such a disposal of the Other, without indicting itself.

During the first day that Torben and I spent in Vita, we came upon a middle-aged woman sitting on the ground; she crouched over a stream of urine, her genitals matted with dust. As we approached, we could see that her head was full of small holes: worms burrowed in the wounds and under the scalp. "Millions of *bichinhos* [little animals], generated from her own flesh and dirt," said Oscar, a former drug user, now being trained by Zé to become one of the infirmary's coordinators. "We tried to clean it." Torben could not bear to look. Momentarily paralyzed, he kept saying, "It is too much, it is too much." The reality of Vita had overwhelmed picture-taking, too. This was a socially authorized dying, ordinary and unaccounted for, in which we participated by our gazing, both foreign and native, in our learned indifference and sense of what was intolerable. Yet rather than remaining paralyzed by moral indignation, we felt compelled to address life in Vita and the *realpolitik* that makes it possible. Not to represent it would equally be a failure.

Marcel Mauss, in his essay "The Physical Effect on the Individual of the Idea of Death Suggested by the Collectivity," shows that in many supposedly "lower" civilizations, a death that was social in origin, without obvious biological or medical causes, could ravage a person's mind and body. Once removed from society, people were left to think that they were inexorably headed for death, and many died primarily for this reason. Mauss argues that these fates are uncommon or nonexistent in "our own civilization," for they depend on institutions and beliefs such as witchcraft and taboos that "have disappeared from the ranks of our society" (1979:38). As we saw in Vita, however, there continues to be a place for death in the contemporary city, which, like Mauss's "primitive" practices, functions by exclusion, nonrecognition, and abandonment. In the face of increasing economic and biomedical inequality and the breakdown of the family, human bodies are routinely separated from their normal political status and abandoned to the most extreme misfortune, death-in-life.[19]

Where had this woman come from? What had brought her to this condition?

The police found her on the streets and took her to a hospital that refused to clean her wounds, much less to take her in. So the police brought her to Vita. Before living in a downtown public square, she had had legal residence in the São Paulo Psychiatric Hospital, but she had been released as "cured"—in other words, overmedicated and no longer violent. And before that? No one knew. She had passed through the police, through the hospital, through psychiatric confinement and treatment, through the city's central spaces—and in the end she was putrefying even before death. It is clear that dying such as hers is constituted in the interaction of state and medical institutions, the public, and the absent family. These institutions and their procedures are symbiotic with Vita: they make death's job easier. I use the impersonal expression "death's job" to point out that there is no direct agency or legal responsibility for the dying in Vita.

What happened to this nameless woman was far from an exception—it was part of a pattern. In a corner, hunched over a bed in the women's room sat Cida, who seemed to be in her early twenties. Diagnosed with AIDS, she had been left at Vita by a social worker from the Conceição Hospital in early 1995. During her early days at Vita, the volunteers began calling her Sida, the Spanish word for AIDS. Later, I was told that they had replaced the "S" in her new name with a "C"—"like in Aparecida, so that people would stop mocking and discriminating against her." I was surprised to learn that the volunteers believed that Cida and a young man were the only AIDS cases in Vita. Too many of the wasted bodies I saw also had skin lesions and symptoms of tuberculosis. Oscar told me that Cida came from a middle-class family, but that no one ever visited her. She spoke to no one, he said, and sometimes did not eat for three or four days. "We have to leave the food in a bowl in the corridor, and sometimes, when nobody is watching, she comes down from her bed and eats," explained the volunteer, "like a kitty."

Here, animal is not a metaphor. As Oscar argued: "Hospitals think that our patients are animals. Doctors see them as indigents and pretend that there is no cure. The other day, we had to rush old Valério to the emergency. They cut him open and left surgical materials in there. The materials became infected, and he died." What makes these humans into animals not worthy of affection and care is their lack of money, added Luciano, another volunteer: "The hospital's intervention is to throw the patient away. If they had sentiment, they would do more for them . . . so that there would not be such a waste of souls. Lack of love leaves these people abandoned. If you have money, then you have treatment; if not, you fall into Vita. *O Vita da vida* [the Vita of life]."

As I see it, Oscar and Luciano were not using the term "human" in the same way human rights discourses do, with a notion of shared corporeality or shared reason. Neither were they opposing it to "animal." Rather than referring to the animal nature of humans, they spoke of an animal nature of the medical and social practices and of the values that, in their ascendancy over reason and ethics, shape how the abandoned are addressed by supposedly superior human forms. "There was no family; we ourselves buried old Valério. The human being alone is the saddest thing. It is worse than being an animal." Although they emphasized the "animalization" of the people in Vita, Oscar and Luciano conveyed a latent understanding of the interdependence of the terms "human" and "animal" and of a hierarchy within the human itself. The negotiation over these boundaries, particularly in the medical realm, allows some human/animal forms to be considered inappropriate for living.[20]

In the face of the First World War, Sigmund Freud wrote an essay entitled "Thoughts for the Times on War and Death." Freud spoke of a generalized wartime confusion and disillusionment that he also shared and of people being without a glimmer of the future being shaped. "We ourselves are at a loss as to the significance of the impressions which press in upon us, and as to the value of the judgments which we form . . . the world has grown strange to [us]" (1957b:275, 280). This sense of an ethical and political void experienced by "helpless" citizens had been provoked by "the low morality shown by states which pose as the guardians of moral standards" and by the brutality demonstrated by individuals who, "as participants in the highest human civilization, one would not have thought capable of such behavior" (280). At stake, in Freud's account, was not the citizen's failure to empathize with the suffering of fellow humans but his or her estrangement from imaginaries gone awry. This anxiety over the discredited imaginaries of the nation-state and of supposedly inexorable human progress stood for people's actual incapacity to articulate the function of the Other's death in the organization of reality and thought.

We moderns—this is how I read this melancholic Freud—operate with an instrumental idea of the human and are time and again faced with a void in what constitutes humanness. One's worthiness to exist, one's claim to life, and one's relation to what counts as the reality of the world, all pass through what is considered to be human at any particular time. And this notion is itself subject to intense scientific, medical, and legal dispute as well as political and moral fabrication (Kleinman 1999; Povinelli 2002; Rabinow 2003; Asad 2003). It is in between the loss of an old working idea of humanness and the installment of a new one that the world is experienced as strange and vanishing to many in Vita. I do not refer here to the universal category of the human but rather to the malleability of this concept as it is locally constituted and reconstituted, with semantic boundaries that are very fuzzy. Above all, the concept of the human is *used* in this local world, and it cannot be artificially determined in advance in order to ground an abstract ethics.[21]

Vita is the word for a life that is socially dead, a destiny of death that is collective. "These people had a history," insisted Zé. "If the hospitals kept them, they would be mad; in the streets, they would be beggars or zombies. Society lets them rot because they don't give anything in return anymore. Here, they are persons." Zé was right on many counts: disciplinary sites of confinement, including traditionally structured families and institutional psychiatry, are breaking apart; the social domain of the state is ever-shrinking; and society increasingly operates through market dynamics—that is, "you shall be a person there, where the market needs you" (Beck and Ziegler 1997:5; see also Lamont 2000).[22] Yes, treating the *abandonados* as "animals" might release individuals and institutions from the obligation of supplying some sort of responsiveness or care. But I was also intrigued by the paradox voiced by Zé: that these creatures—apparently with no ancestors, no names, no goods of their own—actually acquired personhood in the place of their dying. The idea that personhood, according to Zé, can be equated with having a place to die publicly in abandonment exemplifies the machinery of social death in Brazil today—its workings are not restricted to controlling the poorest of the poor and to keeping them in obscurity. But the idea of "personhood in dying" also challenged me as an ethnographer to investigate the ways people inhabited this condition and struggled to transcend it.

Though no money circulates in Vita's infirmary—there is nothing to be bought or sold—many inhabitants hold something: a plastic bag, an empty bottle, a piece of sugar cane, an old magazine, a doll, a broken radio, a thread, a blanket. Some nurse a wound or simply count their fingers. One man carries garbage bags with him day in and day out. They are his sole property. He bites people who try to take the trash away. "Sometimes there is food rotting in these bags, even feces," said Luciano. "Then we give him a tranquilizer, put him to sleep, and replace the things in the bags." The volunteer added, "Any institution needs control in order to exist," without explaining where the prescriptions for the tranquilizers came from.

At first, I saw the objects carried by the abandoned as standing for their lack of relationship with the world outside Vita as well as for their past experiences, impossibly distant but remembered. In this sense, the objects are a defense against everything that banishes these people from the field of visibility and planning, everything that establishes them as already dead. As I kept returning to Vita, I also began to see the objects as forms of waiting, as inner worlds kept alive. Words, too, though powerless to alter conditions, are still a source of truth here. Both objects and disjointed words sustain the sense of a search in these people, their last attachment to the possibility of rediscovering a tie or of doing something with what is left of their existence. This desire is something that one does not give up, though it might be taken away.

The photographs Torben Eskerod took during our first visit to Vita in 1995 and on a later visit in December 2001 give us a sense of the persons who were facing this kind of abjection.[23] "Photographs are a means of making 'real' (or 'more real') matters that the privileged and the merely safe might prefer to ignore," writes Susan Sontag (2003:7). It would be too much to say that Eskerod's photographs make real the abandonment in Vita. They are at most an initial approximation, a sincere attempt to render visible this tragic experience. They are his personal testimony to the abandonment in their bodies and to a wakefulness that accompanies social death.

If these photos are shocking, it is because the photographer wants to focus on our learned indifference and provoke some ethical response. If they are haunting, it is because this is an enduring reality, not so far from us. We manage not to see the abandoned in our homes and neighborhoods, rich and poor. How are our self-perceptions and our priorities for action dependent on this blindness?

Arthur and Joan Kleinman argue that the globalization of images of suffering commodify, thin out, and distort experience. This process corroborates our epoch's dominating sense that "complex problems can be neither understood nor fixed," fostering further "moral fatigue, exhaustion of empathy, and political despair" (1997:2, 9; see also Boltanski 1999). The key verbs here are "to understand" and "to hope"—so that people's destinies might be different. For the Kleinmans, the challenge is to ethnographically chart how large-scale forces relate to local history and biography, and thereby to restore context and meaning to the lived experience of suffering captured by the artist.

How to bring into view the reality that ruins the person?

Signaling a shift from the artistic to the political function of artwork, Walter Benjamin (1979) suggested that captioning would become the most important part of photography, the foundation of meaning.[24] For some time after our first visit to Vita, I thought that these photos were enough, that they did the work of bringing this reality out of concealment and into the public eye. The photos stayed with me and fueled a desire to return to Vita—not to find a caption but to try to further engage some of the abandoned, to listen to and record what they thought of their plight, who they once had been. By hearing them and tracing their trajectories, I hoped to prevent them from remaining merely depictions of powerlessness and to address the routine domestic and public interactions that foreclosed the possibilities of their lives. Ethnography helps to disentangle these knots of complexity, bringing into view the concrete conditions and spaces through which human existences become intractable realities. And yet, as I began to know these people better, I was challenged to think of life in Vita also in terms of anticipation and possibility.

Before we went back to Vita in December 2001 to conclude the photographic work, I briefed Torben on what my research had found in Vita and beyond. Learning about Catarina's life history and having clues to the lives of some of the other abandoned affected his approach to the photography. In his earlier pictures of life in Vita, he mostly photographed fragments of people's bodies, conveying their death-in-life and overall detachment from a larger social body. This time, with some of their fragmented histories in mind, Torben pictured the abandoned at a certain distance, I would say. Enclosure, adjacency to others, and introspection are shown. Older than their bodies tell and yet with time left, the people of Vita appear more familiar to us than before, left with their own intimacy and a way to fold into themselves and reflect.

Infirmary, Vita 2001

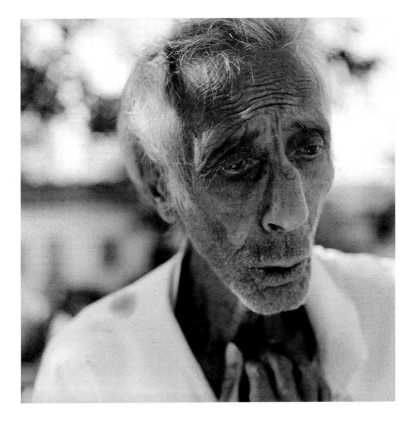

Pedro, Vita 1995

Brazil

Consider the old man whose eyes were cast downward, his hands shaking, his body skeletal. Family members had left him at Vita's gate. I asked him his name even though the volunteers told me that he did not know it. He muttered, "Pedro," and smiled. He also knew where he had once lived: "Charqueadas." He then grabbed his throat. "Grrrahaaa . . . hhhrhrraaahh-grrrrss . . . ahhrgaaahgrqqaa . . . " I could not understand. It was not the absence of words but the speaking of *nonwords*.

Oscar and other volunteers told me that Pedro probably had throat cancer, although they did not know for sure. When they brought him to a nearby hospital, the doctors would not see him—a document was missing—and told him to return in three months. The clinic will not refuse to see him, but it will put him in line, make him return to schedule appointments, and when the doctors finally have time for Pedro, it will probably be too late. Then the clinic can claim, as it does with too many others, that nothing can be done.

The residents of Vita are not simply isolated individuals who, on their own, lost the symbolic supports for their existence. Rather, the *abandonados* are the carriers and witnesses of the ways in which the social destinies of the poorest and the sickest are ordered. The experience of individuals who live in such a dead space/language is traversed by the country's structural readjustment, unemployment, malfunctioning public health system, and infamously unequal distribution of wealth.[25]

Historically, Brazil's welfare system has been structured so that state intervention varies according to the segment of the population claiming social protection. "Citizenship" has been deemed universal for the minority who are rich, regulated according to market forces for the working class and the middle class, and denied to the multitudes who are poor and marginalized. According to Sônia Fleury, the "noncitizens" might be entitled to some minimum form of social assistance and charity in exchange for their votes—this is their "inverted citizenship" (quoted in Escorel 1993:35). Those occupying the upper strata of society not only live longer; their right to do so is ensured through bureaucratic and market mechanisms.

As I talked to city administrators, public health officers, and human rights activists, I was able to identify some of the institutional networks through which Vita emerged and was integrated into local forms of governance as well as some of the everyday practices that help to constitute the residents' nonexistence. With the adoption of Brazil's democratic constitution in 1988, health care had become a public right. "Health is a right of every individual and a duty of the state, guaranteed by social and economic policies that seek to reduce the risk of disease and other injuries, and by universal and equal access to services designed to promote, protect, and recover health," stated the new Brazilian constitution (Constitution of the Federative Republic of Brazil 1988). The principles of universality, equity, and integrality within health services (Fleury 1997) were supposed to guide the new Brazilian health care system (Sistema Único de Saúde, or SUS). In practice, however, efforts to implement these principles collided with historically entrenched forms of medical authoritarianism (Scheper-Hughes 1992) and the realities of fiscal austerity, decentralization, and community- and family-centered approaches to primary care, amid the rapid encroachment of private health care plans. In 1989, for example, the federal government spent eighty-three dollars per person on health care, but in 1993 this amount plunged to only thirty-seven dollars (*Jornal NH* 1994b).

Many of the country's discourses and practices of citizenship in the 1990s were related to guaranteeing the universal right to health care as the economy and the state underwent a major restructuring.[26] The activism of mental health workers was exemplary (Tenorio 2002). They actively engaged in making laws that shaped the progressive closure of psychiatric institutions and their replacement by local networks of community- and family-based psychosocial care (Amarante 1996; Goldberg 1994; Moraes 2000).[27] This deinstitutionalization of the mentally ill was pioneered in the state of Rio Grande do Sul (Porto Alegre is its capital), where it was well under way by the early 1990s. In reality, however, the demands and strategies of the mental health movement became entangled in and even facilitated local government's neoliberalizing moves in public health: the mad were literally expelled from overcrowded and inefficient institutions, and little new funding was allocated for the alternative services that had been proposed.

On the one hand, this local psychiatric reform confirmed the role of the Workers' Party as a representative of a novel politics of social inclusion—PT, the Partido dos Trabalhadores, was already in power in the capital. It also occasioned a few exemplary services that treated "citizens burdened by mental suffering" and realized, if all too partially, a socialized form of self-governance. On the other hand, it shifted the burden of care from state institutions to the family and communities, which failed to live up to their idealized representations in the reform movement's discourse. People had to learn new techniques to qualify for services and to live with what were, by and large, the limitations of new ideologies and institutions. Increasing numbers of mentally ill people began to live in the streets, along with the other leftovers of the country's unequal and exclusionary social project. Many ended up in places like Vita.

Everyday life in the 1980s and 1990s in that region was marked by high rates of migration and unemployment, the rise of a drug economy in the poorest outlying areas, and generalized violence (see Ferreira and Barros 1999). As police forces increasingly engaged in erasing signs of misery, begging, and informal economies from the city, pastoral and philanthropic institutions took up the role of caregiver, albeit selectively. Simultaneously, families frequently responded to the growing burdens posed by new responsibilities for care and narrowing employment options by redefining their functional scope and value systems. As a corollary to all these institutional, economic, and familial processes, unemployed health professionals began opening their own care centers (modeled after Vita) for patients who had welfare benefits or some remaining assets. Around 1976, some twenty-five "geriatric houses" operated in Porto Alegre (Bastian 1986). There are now more than two hundred, about 70 percent of which operate as clandestine businesses hosting the elderly, the mentally ill, and the disabled in the most problematic of conditions (Ferreira de Mello 2001; Comissão de Direitos Humanos 2000).

That so many are regarded as superfluous testifies to the further dissolution of the country's moral fabric. The Brazilian middle class, for instance, has historically acted as a buffer between the elite and the poor, as both guardian of morality and advocate for progressive politics. But in the wake of the country's democratization and fast-paced neoliberalization, this vein of moral sensitivity and political responsibility has been largely replaced by sheer contempt, sociophobia, or sporadic acts of charity like the ones that sustain Vita (Freire Costa 1994, 2000; Kehl 2000; Ribeiro 2000; Caldeira 2002).

The abandoned in Vita know of death, and, when listened to, they offer insights into its fabrication. Their abandonment is part of a larger human life-context—it was realized in many domestic and public sites and through intricate medical transactions coexisting with already entrenched strategies of nonintervention. It is this apparently unknown relation of letting die to the constitution of private lives and public domains that an ethnography of Vita helps to illuminate.[28]

"A man is no longer a man confined but a man in debt," writes Gilles Deleuze as he elaborates his idea of the fate of *anthropos* within the development of late capitalism. Deleuze speaks of the erosion of disciplinary and welfare institutions and the concurrent emergence of new forms of control in affluent contexts—"controls are a modulation, like a self-transmuting molding continually changing from one moment to the next, or like a sieve whose mesh varies from one point to another" (1995:178). Family, school, army, and factory are increasingly "transformable coded configurations of a single business where the only people left are administrators" (181). He explains: "Open hospitals and teams providing home care have been around for some time. One can envisage education becoming less and less a closed site differentiated from the workspace as another closed site, but both disappearing and giving way to frightful continual training, to continual monitoring of workers-schoolkids or bureaucratic-students" (174, 175). According to Deleuze, "we're no longer dealing with a duality of mass and individual. Individuals become '*dividuals*' and masses become samples, data, markets, or 'banks'" (180).

The market, however, keeps generating both wealth and misery, movement and immobility. "One thing, it's true, hasn't changed—capitalism still keeps three quarters of humanity in extreme poverty, too poor to have debts and too numerous to be confined: control will have to deal not only with vanishing frontiers, but with mushrooming shantytowns and ghettos" (Deleuze 1995:181). There are too many people to include them all in the market and its flows. The question of what to do with these surplus bodies, with no apparent value and no way to survive and prosper, is no longer at the core of sovereignty and its outmoded populist welfare rhetoric. Their destinies are now determined by a whole new array of networks, and, as formal institutions either vanish or face ruin and governmental distance is crystallized, the household is further politicized.

As I traveled throughout the country, I could see signs of Vita everywhere: death and dying in the midst of Brazil's big cities, Vita as a social destiny. True, statistics were showing important improvements in areas such as infant mortality and literacy, and the Cardoso administration was experimenting with significant new forms of governmentality whereby patient groups could mobilize within the state and have their demands for life-extending treatments realized (AIDS programs are by far the most visible and successful story of the reforming state).[29] But even though the poorest could now also access medication and basic medical care in local (and often poorly functioning) branches of the universal health care system, I found an immense distress among these individuals over lack of housing and jobs, safety, and growing police violence. People I interviewed conveyed an overall sense that they had failed their children and themselves.

José Duarte, his wife, and four little children lived in a hut made of plastic bags, on the outskirts of the northeastern city of Salvador. I met him at a breakfast meeting for the homeless that had been organized by a group of Catholic volunteers. José had come to get food for his family. They had been evicted from the city's historic district, which was being remodeled as a tourist center.

"The government kicked us out. The little compensation they gave us was only enough to buy this little piece of land next to a swamp. I worked downtown, sold ice cream, but now it takes me two hours to get there by bus. Winter is tough. How can I make money? What will the children eat?" He began to weep.

"The kids are all sick; rain passes through the plastic. Who has health? Health nobody has. . . . Every day we are ill, all kinds of illnesses, it is never good. There is no medical aid. Only if one has money for the bus and gets in line early in the morning and waits till late at night. But then one loses the day of work. To waste time, that is all there is. At home, wasted, looking at the children, hungry, lacking sandals, clothing. . . . I am so enraged"—he had no words to account for his failed struggles as a worker and his desperation as a father.

"The government says it wants to help. But you end up talking to so many people in this and that office, signing forms—and they don't get back to you. They don't listen. They do nothing. They have made the life of the poor even more difficult. Only the president can solve the problem of Brazil. He is the only one who could do something. But people like me can't talk to him, and he does not know what is happening in the city. The only way to reach the president's ears is if I were to go to TV. But to be on TV, you must have resources, and we all have the same story that people don't want to hear. To do what?"

José's words echoed philosopher Renato Janine Ribeiro's strong critique of Brazil's political-economic culture: "In Brazil it is actually possible to imagine a discourse that aims at the end of the social in order to emancipate society." The categories *social* and *society* do not pertain to the same people and worlds of rights: "social refers to the needy, and society refers to the efficient ones" (2000:21). State and marketing discourses transmit the conviction that society is active as economy and passive as social life. "The objects of social action are assumed not to be able to become an integral and efficient member of society" (22). In sum, according to Ribeiro, dominant discourses "have privatized society" (24).

José's troubled existence was caught in ceaseless contact with governmental services, but to no avail. He knew quite well that he and his family were part of a repetitive machine that spoke a language of accountability, while in practice the citizen faced indifference and his voice was lost. Meanwhile, José has learned to use his anguish and subjectivity to evoke moral sentiments in order to procure at least minimal objective help, which is so desperately needed.

This is an example of what people still outside Vita and similar institutions must do in order to survive as they are driven further into poverty and despair: some twenty homeless persons, including children, invaded an abandoned zoological garden in a city near Porto Alegre in the late 1990s. The squatters made their rooms in the cages. "Luiz Carlos Apio is one of the new residents of the Zoo," wrote the newsletter *Jornal da Ciência*. "He is handicapped and an unemployed auto worker. Luiz made his house in the place formerly set aside for the rabbits. In order to enter, he has to go through a small door no more than half a meter high" (Sociedade Brasileira para o Progresso da Ciência 1998:24). For those who have no money, social life is the physiological struggle to survive. This plight is intrinsic to an economy thriving on an image of action, efficiency, and modernity, concludes Ribeiro—"we live a kind of schizophrenia" (2000:24).

In the bodies of the abandoned—such as those residents of Vita—political and social forms of life and thereby subjectivity have literally entered into a symbiosis with death without those bodies belonging to the world of the deceased.[30]

Consider Clifford Geertz's chilling reflections on the technically and politically engineered demise of the Yanomami people as well as on our own blindness to this modern form of life/disappearance: "Now that their value as control group, a (supposedly) 'natural,' genetically 'ancestral popula- tion'—the 'last major primitive tribe . . . anywhere on earth,' is diminished or disappeared and the experiments upon them have ceased and the experi- menters departed, what sort of presence in our minds, what sort of whatness, are they now to have? What sort of place in the world does an 'ex-primitive' have?" (2001:21, 22).

Vita is a place in the world for ex-humans. I use this concept reluctantly as I try to express the difficult truth that these persons have been de facto terminally excluded from what counts as reality. I first thought of the term "ex-human" as Catarina told me, "I am an ex," and constantly referred to herself as an "ex-wife" and her kin as "my ex-family." It is not that the souls in Vita have had their humanity and personhood drawn out and are now left without the capacity to understand, to dialogue, and to keep struggling. Rather, when I say ex-human, I want to highlight the fact that these people's efforts to constitute their lives vis-à-vis institutions meant to confirm and ad- vance humanness were deemed good for nothing and that their supposed in- humanness played an important role in justifying abandonment. In the end, too many people "too poor to have debts"—even perhaps too poor to have families—are reduced to struggling without being able to survive on their own. As an extension and a reflection of the country's political-economic and domestic readjustments, zones of abandonment such as Vita emerge. They make the regeneration of the *abandonados* impossible and their dying imminent. Before biological death, there comes their social death.

—

Social death and mobilization of life coexist in Brazil's political and medical institutions, and the process of making decisions about who shall die and who shall live and at what cost has increasingly become a domestic matter (Biehl 2004).[31] Against an expanding discourse of human rights and citizen- ship, we are confronted with the limits of infrastructures that help to real- ize these rights, biologically speaking, but only on a selective basis. As the reality of Vita reveals, those incapable of living up to the new requirements of market competitiveness and profitability and related concepts of nor- malcy are included in the emerging social and medical orders only through their public dying—and as though these deaths had been self-generated.

By "self-generated," I mean that these noncitizens remain by and large untouched by governmental and nongovernmental interventions and become partially visible in the public health system only when they are dying. Without legal identification, they are marked as "mad," "drug addicts," "thieves," "prostitutes," "noncompliant"—labels in which their personhood is cast and which are meant both to explain their dying and to blame them for it. In the end, no records of their individual trajectories remain. The families or neighbors who disposed of them are also not to be found. The overall poverty and the complex social and medical interactions that seem to have exacerbated infections and weakened immunity remain unaccounted for. Moreover, Vita's environment is so charged that the sickest are constantly exchanging diseases with the mad, so to speak, leaving them no possibility but "to die each other." I do not know precisely what I mean by this expression "to die each other," but I have seen the complexity of what happens in Vita, both in institutional and experiential terms, and I struggle to understand the matter of dying and what makes life and death so intimate with one another. No one mourns the abandoned, cast into oblivion.

Unknown man, Vita 2001

Unknown woman, Vita 2001

Citizenship

I returned to Vita in March 1997, two years after my first visit with Gerson Winkler, the human rights activist, and Torben Eskerod, the photographer. This time, I could see an incipient citizenship being generated along with social death. Some of Vita's residents were now being effectively rehabilitated and given the possibility of a future. In the recovery area, men were developing discipline, becoming drug-free, and being retrained as potential workers; a few of them even had access to state-funded AIDS disability pensions, specialized medical care, and free antiretroviral therapies. People in the infirmary, however, continued to live in utter abandonment, Catarina now among them—waiting with death.

The previous November, Zé das Drogas had been evicted from the establishment by a philanthropic coalition called Amigos do Vita (Friends of Vita), headed by Representative Luchesi. Captain Osvaldo, a police officer working for the state of Rio Grande do Sul, began to administer Vita. The volunteers working there were more reserved now and generally refused to talk about what had led to the coup. Over time, I learned that Zé had become consumed by his cocaine addiction and that he and his immediate associates had used Vita as their source of income. "The more rundown the place, the more donations they got," an insider told me, reluctantly. A local human rights coordinator alluded to the political interests of Luchesi and his associates: Vita would now be their base for denouncing the ruling government and advertising their own paternalistic politics.

In addition to his responsibilities for Vita and the police department, Captain Osvaldo attended to Representative Luchesi's personal security and took night courses in law. He proudly considered himself the mayor of Vita.

"Here, we work with finances, health, the provision of food, building maintenance. . . . It is a city of sorts." This population, the captain noted, "does not pay taxes, so how to sustain this work?" He explained that Vita had taken advantage of new state legislation encouraging civic responsibility for welfare functions and had officially become what is called an "entity of public utility." Given this new status, the institution could now receive state funds to build its infrastructure as well as accepting tax-exempted industry donations.

Vita was indeed undergoing impressive structural changes—"an environmental transformation," as the captain described it. Much construction was going on in the recovery area (though not in the infirmary): houses and shacks for lodging were replacing the tents, new administrative offices had been built, and space had been allocated for a pharmacy, a medical and dental clinic, and a large building for state-funded job training. Monthly contributions from Friends of Vita and various industries provided for daily living. Vita was also raising money through its bakery, producing some fifteen hundred small loaves of bread for its inhabitants' daily consumption as well as four hundred sweet breads sold in nearby neighborhoods. Individual donations were still pouring in, mainly from Luchesi's radio listeners.

"Privileged society does not contribute. Their only contribution is to call the radio and say, 'There is a homeless person in front of my building, making the sidewalk dirty.' I say, bring the person here, and he says, 'No, he will fill the car with smells and dirt.' Can you imagine if we were to bring in all the cases that are called in?" The captain stressed that "we are now overpopulated." Before the change in administration, some ten to fifteen people showed up every week needing some form of help. Now, however, a triage system was in place to keep Vita's population "stable," in the words of the institution's secretary.

Such triage was the job of Dalva, a social worker and the captain's wife. Previously, she had worked at the Santa Rita Hospital, but after changes in the universal health care system, she was sent to the emergency service. "My role was to decide who would receive treatment and who wouldn't. Terrible, right, to decide who will go on and who will not?" She had been volunteering for more than a year at Vita, "but Zé das Drogas always created barriers to my work. He seemed to be afraid of what I could do." She suggested that there had indeed been an intricate plot to change the course of the institution. "Vita was not rehabilitating. But now it has changed. In order to do good work, we must diagnose and know our clientele. This is a very diversified population. We must have a group and an individual approach, work on all questions, and try to bring the family into the rehabilitation process."

Both the captain and his wife were excited about building a model program of human regeneration. As the captain put it: "I don't believe that people recover in hospitals with more medication. Throwing the person in here and filling him with religious doctrine doesn't solve the problem, either. The most important things are food, work, and housing. If these three things coexist, then there is a 'why' for the person to live. We will rescue their citizenship." The city of Vita was now a rescue operation. I kept wondering what the immediate economic and political gain of such planned change would be and how this work would affect the lives of its residents in the long term.

Several inhabitants of the recovery area referred to what was going on as "modernizing." Luis asserted: "We eat as human beings. Before, we had big bowls and ate with our hands. Now we have trays." A former drug addict, Luis had first come to Vita in 1987, when he was just eighteen. "See these scars? I injected wherever I could find a vein," he acknowledged, pointing to his arms, legs, and forehead. "Even in my head. See, my throat, I pierced it. I was so mad." Luis ran away from Vita several times but always returned. His family in the nearby city of Canoas wanted nothing to do with him. "I began when I was twelve years old. I did not respect my mother anymore. I robbed the family, I lost my character, I became garbage. Then they brought me here."

Luis said that under Zé's administration there was "too much liberty," no control at all: "We were allowed to come back even if we were drunk or high. Now it is much more rigorous. This is very good for those of us who are addicted and sick." In former times, the residents "never saw the donations. The tents were rotten, filled with roaches and rats. Now we see the building going on."

Outside Vita, Luis was a petty thief. In 1990, he was caught shoplifting and sentenced to two years in the Porto Alegre Central Prison. "I saw the worst. But I was cool and endured it. Once, they stuck a broom in a guy's ass, up to the mouth. I was quiet and survived." In 1992, Luis decided to take the HIV test. Three of his friends from the drug circle had already died of AIDS. He was found to be seropositive and was "hit hard by the news." But he decided to face it. "If I was man enough to do it to myself, I had to be man enough to face it." In 1993, at Luchesi's radio station, Luis met his wife, Nair, then fifteen but already the mother of a little girl. Zé das Drogas allowed them to live together in a tent in Vita. Soon they had two more kids, both HIV-positive: "It was natural, and welcome." Luis observes that many people in the recovery area are HIV-positive, "but they don't want to admit it."

Because of his good behavior, Luis has been guaranteed Vita's support in his efforts to ensure access to medical and welfare aid for himself and his family. Vita, he says, "is my family now." As I heard from several residents, the para-state institution now providing for them had replaced the biological family and had become a temporary place of work. "I am weak. I like being dependent here. My thinking is always in here. Here, I feel safe. I work, I am learning to make chairs. The social worker will register me to get an AIDS pension. I hope I can stay here the rest of my life."

During Zé das Drogas's administration, daily life in the recovery area had been structured around worship and Bible studies. Now the emphasis was on personal hygiene, civic values, eating well, total abstinence from smoking and drinking, work therapy, and group self-reflection. After dinner, a general meeting was held, and a log of daily events was read. According to the captain, "This is the time of justice. To call someone by his name rescues personhood, makes that person feel important, part of something. We mention the working shifts for the next days as well as internal promotions. When there are faults and wrongdoings, we report them and punish them harshly. Three strikes mean that you're out for good—no return. That's the platform of our work: they are useful, they are important. They must rescue themselves." Now there was a deadline: "We expect them to recover in six to eight months. We will help them find a place in the market—it is there that they belong. Then, afterward, it is their life."

Part of this new regimen involved constantly checking Vita's residents for drugs and sexual behavior (even though the captain insisted that "alcohol has annulled their sexuality"). The daily logs of the first month under the new administration (mid-February to mid-March 1997) were filled with references to catching people smoking, using cocaine and alcohol. Illicit sexual activities were euphemistically referred to by describing people caught in an "inappropriate position and place." Social regeneration also meant being part of the broader legal system. Several notes reported that residents had been summoned by the police to address warrants. Other notes were from the newly constituted "Tutelage Councils" (Conselhos Tutelares). These councils were citizens' associations whose task it was to advocate for human rights within families and communities and to monitor state and medical institutions. They worked in conjunction with the Public Ministry—the citizenry's legal forum for challenging the state. The logs also reported that three deaths had been registered in the infirmary in twenty-four days.

—

I asked the captain about his vision for the infirmary and its residents. "It is very difficult," he replied. "It represents the putrefaction of the street. They don't exist as a juridical fact. They have AIDS, tuberculosis, all these things that don't exist in statistics." He told me that there were some fifteen cases of AIDS in the infirmary alone, nearly 10 percent of that population, and that treatment was available to these patients only on an emergency basis.

"There, you also have the mentally ill, the elderly, the abandoned. They don't have anything to give anymore. What does one expect from them? Nothing. Simply put, they will be that which they are now. It is a depository of human beings. We cannot bring them back to society. As horrible as it is, here one sees a truth."

As the captain denounced the intractability of the abandoned, his words subtly suggested that the *abandonados* themselves were unable to anticipate anything but death and had no purpose but to die: "In their thinking, they have more in terms of dying than living. What does a normal person want? To move up in life, to reach another plateau. . . . What can they expect for themselves? Nothing." As the captain critiqued the condition of Vita as "a thermometer of the political unimportance of human life" to the outside world, he participated in the process of letting die inside Vita with his "realistic" conception of the abandoned: "Their future is dead; they will stay behind."

The social worker had a more optimistic take on the situation, though I wondered whether and how her view would be put into practice. "An old man was fasting for three days, protesting his abandonment by the family," she sighed. "There are days when I leave this place crazy." Horror stories abounded, like that of Vó Brenda, a seventy-five-year-old wheelchair-bound "grandma." Rats had eaten her toes. "Our shack was too old," she told me, after Dalva introduced us. "The rats came under the blankets and gnawed my feet." She insisted that her alcoholic husband was a good man. "We spent fifty years happily together." But he never took her to the hospital. "He had to work, he had no time," the woman sadly explained. When the husband died, Vó Brenda's son, unable or unwilling to care for her, left her at Vita.

"They all have a history, a name," Dalva said. She was beginning to catalog all the cases, trying to identify the nameless people in local registries and hospitals and, whenever possible, attempting to contact their families. Many times, she explained, "families use hospitalization in Porto Alegre as an opportunity to abandon." Dalva was referring to about forty mentally ill patients in the infirmary who were not receiving psychiatric care. "They shouldn't be here." The majority of infirmary cases involved people who "once had a dignified life."

They all have "the same pattern," she argued, and, as the captain did, she emphasized the active involvement of these individuals in the process of their own abandonment. "They are the ones who were always drunk or took drugs, couldn't work anymore, and then came the time when the family didn't give them another chance and closed the doors. . . . They moved from one place and job to the next, began to age, to sleep in the streets. All because at some point they decided to abandon the family. And, all alone, they needed the favor of a stranger or the police to get to a hospital or to be dropped here."

What sustains them?

"Some have the expectation that a family member will come and take them out of here. They make the family into their ideal, which in fact it never was." I was told that families showed up only when they needed the abandoned person's signature to settle inheritance issues or to keep his or her welfare benefits flowing into the household. Vó Brenda's son visits her to guarantee that he will receive her shack when she dies, Dalva reported. Working amid a "lack of legal documentation and lack of memory," the social worker was mapping the population and trying to build partnerships with psychiatric and general hospitals as well as to mediate welfare claims. The immediate goal, however, was to get beds for those in the infirmary and to keep the place sanitized.

Oscar was now the infirmary's coordinator. He was a rare person, I thought, because he was always there, and he cared. Other volunteers appeared only irregularly, and, as I learned, there was much abuse of the abandoned. Oscar had come to Vita in the early 1990s from the state of Santa Catarina, leaving behind his wife and two teenage daughters. He had recovered from his intravenous drug addiction, converted to Pentecostalism, and found a new wife in the village surrounding Vita. He adopted his wife's two sons, and they had a daughter of their own. They made Vita their home.

Although Oscar was not paid to coordinate the infirmary's work, he was happy to have shelter, free food, and access to a car—"I even have a cell phone." He was also euphoric about the changes under way. "The new co-

Vó Brenda, Vita 2001

ordinators have many projects. They have very good ideas and are trying to solve things in the quickest way. But it takes time. Things are developing." This altruistic and hard-working man was always there to welcome me in the following years as I charted Vita's development and, particularly, Catarina's history. Over time, I became very fond of him. "We are friends," we both said.

Oscar had taken his father, sick with advanced cirrhosis, to a special room in Vita. "I am feeding him. He is not here because of family abandonment, but because I can take better care of him. My siblings are helping out with the food." Oscar *was* the institution. He had a vision of care that he had no power to implement, although he spoke of it openly: "People need better and more varied kinds of food, also some kind of therapy, like you offer when you listen to them. . . . If families came at least once a month and left some special food, I would prepare it for the grandpas and grandmas with much joy."

But instead, he continued, "they just stay here, and when something bad happens to them, we take them to the hospital, and they are immediately sent back. We do the back-and-forth, and in one of these back-and-forths, they will die." Oscar was specifically thinking of the AIDS cases. "I don't think they have much time." The captain's rationality and the social worker's commitment both collapsed in the face of the truth that, as Oscar saw it, "there is no return."

As I learned at the city's epidemiological surveillance service, there was no means of tracking deaths in places like Vita, although the deaths of Vita's residents were now at least registered at local hospitals. In the end, the deaths of these individuals could not be traced back to their abandonment. And the clinic and the state were symbolically acknowledged as having cared.

The dilemmas voiced by the captain—particularly his emphasis on Vita the place, rather than the people—were revealing for what they suggested about the complex politics of death at work here: "We ask ourselves, if we know the problem, why don't we solve it? This is a paternalistic view of things. Even if the institutions that are supposed to do the work of caring don't do it, we still cannot let these creatures rot in the streets. . . . So, should we be paternalistic or let these creatures die?"

That said, the captain became pragmatic in pondering the future of Vita. "We shall not turn this place into a hospital. At most, the infirmary can be a place where people who leave the hospital and have nowhere to go can recuperate for a while." In this view, people in the infirmary would eventually die out, except for those few whose families might rescue them after being pressured by the social worker.

I began to realize the strategic value of not framing Vita as a health-enhancing site. By officially registering Vita as an "entity of public utility" at a time when the Workers' Party administration in Porto Alegre was re-defining the system of public health inspection, the coordinators were pre-venting the city administration from interfering in their management of the institution. Defining Vita as a clinic or hospital might have invited city in-terference in the form of enforcing sanitary regulations or conducting legally required visits by city health professionals. In other words, the coor-dinators were keeping Vita to themselves. Here, we understand the function of conceiving the destiny of the abandoned as self-generated, irreversible death. The few who recover set the limits of who is considered worthy of having a biological existence—and this measure informs the public health institutions and pastoral extensions of a local triage state (Biehl 1999b; 2004).

After many visits, I also saw that the *abandonados*—with their daily rations of bread and bean soup and hot water—were not being kept alive in vain. While dying in Vita, they still had a final social function. Under the new re-gime, everyone admitted for rehabilitation had to spend a few days in the in-firmary as part of their initiation into Vita. Additionally, throughout their stay, men in rehabilitation had to come up to the infirmary and take care of some of the abandoned, dispose of their wastes, and move their bodies back and forth. As one of Vita's new coordinators explained, the infirmary served as "a platform of information for the ones down here. It is useful for getting the addicts to fall back into reality, for if they don't change, that's their end." The captain was more straightforward. He described the abandoned as "*cobaias* [experimental guinea pigs]. Their life is over. They show the young ones what will happen to them."

Oscar and Luciano had once told me that medical and familial circum-stances had made the *abandonados* in the infirmary inappropriate for living. It was now evident that the negotiation over the human/animal boundary that had produced them had become a subjective technique. Lauro had been in Vita for three weeks when I met him. The thirty-year-old man sat next to Lucas, formerly known as Vaquinha (Little Cow), about whom nothing was known. Lauro said that he had adopted and baptized "the poor thing" as Lucas. "Now he has a name. He talks little. He is mentally retarded. I am responsible for him. He is like my child now—we play." Lucas looked the same age as his new caretaker, and there was a warmth to their relationship.

Lauro said that he had been a factory worker, but he had been fired. "I became dependent on alcohol and drugs and descended to hell. I was even sleeping in the streets." He lost contact with his wife and daughter. "I finally realized that either I stopped or I would end up dying. . . . So I asked God to give me the chance to change my life, and He partly fulfilled this. The first step has been taken, which is to be here . . . to be far away from drugs and alcohol." As part of his initial rehabilitation therapy, he has to take care of Lucas, bathe him, change his clothes, watch him as he crawls around, sit silently next to him. This human relation has filled a void in him. "I help him, so automatically he helps me too."

How so?

"By helping him, I am helping myself." Lauro then spoke of Lucas and himself in the plural, as belonging to two distinct collectives: "*They* give force to *us*. Only to look at them already helps *us* to walk forward, to not stay in the same condition *they* are in." He voiced an impersonal feeling: "One develops a tenderness toward him. He is a well-behaved guy, right?"

Lauro claimed that as he followed these people's deterioration and inescapable destiny, he developed a new appreciation for health and a resolve to retain it. "Yes . . . seeing this situation is one more force keeping me from plunging deeper into a well, till there is no return. Thank God, I found this place. I feel good just being able to help, to still have the health. When I look around, I see people who don't have this health, disabled—this helps me a lot." He then asked Lucas to speak: "Show him that you can talk." In that most disturbing encounter, the man became a spectacle, not meant to be heard or addressed. His worth as a human socially and medically devalued, Vaquinha/Lucas remained the animal form through which the salvageable human constituted himself.[32]

The new pedagogical role of these abandoned men and women stems precisely from their alleged inability to produce anything more than bodily infections, parasites, and silent suffering. Their social death is the negative image of the future. In the end, the negative ones are object lessons for potential citizens—or, better, they provide a ground for the appearance of a distinct concept of citizenship. I say "concept of citizenship" because local governments do not provide the means needed for this regenerated citizenship to become a structural possibility. Philanthropic sites like Vita make the personal regeneration of a marginal individual possible and livable either for a limited period or in the form of fiction. This concept of citizenship enlivens the image of the state as universal and life-enhancing. Yet, empirically, citizenship remains a matter of triage and, of course, money. As some are being healed in that simultaneously "militarized" and philanthropic setting, they wake up next to those who are socially dead, blind, without name, without origin, without ties. Like Cida, the nameless young woman with AIDS who, according to volunteers, "now and then asks us to tie her to her bed. She does that when she feels like killing herself. . . . Then, a few hours later, she mumbles to be untied. How do you understand such a person?"

In Vita one sees how life is achieved through death—the ambiguity and violence involved in this process. The negotiation over the human and non-human forms part of a complex set of relations through which individuals are linked to each other and to the political body. The Other's dying makes it possible for one to belong to a family-like institution, to a new population and subjective economy. The ethnographic challenge is to find these empirical relations and linkages—technical, political, conceptual, affective—and to bring them out of thoughtlessness. The random encounter with Catarina and the events it precipitated made it possible to retrieve a world deemed to be lost.

Catarina, Vita 2001

Part Two

CATARINA AND THE ALPHABET

Life of the Mind

As we passed through the gate of the infirmary, my eyes immediately turned to a woman seated in a wheelchair in the shade. She was writing. "It's Catarina," I told my wife, Adriana. This time, Catarina was no longer riding her bicycle. Death was coming upon her, I thought.

With her head down, Catarina held a pen and scribbled with much effort. We greeted her by name, and she looked up, recognizing us. "João and Adriana," she said.

Catarina seemed dazed; she spoke slowly and with great difficulty, as if she had suffered a stroke. We asked how she was doing. "My legs don't help anymore," she replied, adding that this problem was a result of "rheumatism," although she was not taking any medication for it. "Sometimes the volunteers give me pills, but I don't know what they are."

What are you writing?

"This is my dictionary," she said. "I write so that I don't forget the words. I write all the illnesses I have now, and the illnesses I had as a child."

Catarina handed me her book. Her handwriting was uneven. The words were composed in block letters, with no cursive writing, and with few verbs or full sentences. I was amazed by the force of the words, by her ragged poetry:

Divorce
Dictionary
Discipline
Diagnostics

Marriage for free
Paid marriage

Operation
Reality
To give an injection
To get a spasm
In the body
A cerebral spasm

Why do you call it a dictionary?

"Because it does not require anything from me, nothing. If it were mathematics, I would have to find a solution, an answer. Here, there is only one subject matter, from beginning till the end. . . . I write it and read it."

I perused the dictionary, as Adriana spoke with Catarina. "In the womb of pain," she had written. "I offer you my life." "The present meaning." Amid recurring references to medical consultations, hospitals, and public notaries, she wrote of a working woman and wanderer, of sexual emotion and mental disturbance, of medication and food for a baby, of poverty and abundance, of officers and indebtedness, and of things being "out of justice."

Blended with allusions to spasms, menstruation, paralysis, rheumatism, paranoia, and the listing of all possible diseases from measles to ulcers to AIDS were names such as Ademir, Nilson, Armando, Anderson, Alessandra, Ana. Here and there, she wrote of motherhood; of divorce; of a rustic life with sows and insects, veterinarians and a Rural Workers Association; and of desire. Striking statements from a world that was no more.

Question, answer, problem to solve, the head
Who contradicts is convicted
The division of bodies

Then there were expressions of longing:

Recovery of my lost movements
A cure that finds the soul
The needy moon guards me

With L I write Love
With R I write Remembrance

Catarina writes to remain alive, I told myself.[33] These are the words that form her from within. What are the ways of these words? How to tell it all, and what are we to do with it?

DIVOKCIO DICIONAKIO   j J

DICIPLINA DIAG-NOSTICO

CAZAMENTO PAGO

CAZAMENTO GRATIS

CAZAMENTO GRAÇA

ENGINTARIO BEN PAGO

MASCADUZEN

MATRIMONIO

MATRIZ

IGREJA GUARIOR   RMOR

CAPELA   CONFORTO

STATO KATAKINA INKIS   j J

Dictionary

Society of Bodies

I returned to Vita a week later, this time alone. With neighborly care, Catarina immediately asked, "Where is Adriana?" She remarked that she had enjoyed talking to both of us the other day. I sensed in her words an integrity that neither forgot bonds nor envied the bonds of others, the character of a time when one earned respect, if not from governmental institutions and employers, then at least from family members and neighbors. As simplistic as it may sound, this sociality was a life-giving force.

The left side of Catarina's face was bruised. "I fell from the chair when I tried to reach the bathroom." A volunteer overheard and contradicted her, claiming that she had thrown herself to the ground in a fit of rage.

Why aren't you writing today?

"I already filled the dictionary."

I asked if I could take another look at it. Catarina called India, a silent, twenty-something woman of Indian descent who was sitting on a bench nearby, and asked her to fetch the notebook, which was wrapped in a plastic bag inside a suitcase under her bed. She assured India: "It's not locked." As the story goes, India is "mentally retarded." Her brother, they say, is a Pentecostal pastor who speaks about her on a radio program but never comes to see her.

I asked Catarina if she wanted to keep writing. When she responded, "Yes," I ripped out several pages of scribbled field notes from my own notebook and gave the empty book to her. "Write your name and address here," she asked.

"I want to leave, I want to leave," a young black man named Marcelo broke into the conversation. Like the majority of those in Vita, his true name and origins were either unknown or did not matter. He kept looking straight into my eyes, his hands grasping a small suitcase: "Take me, take me with you."

Many *abandonados*, like crippled Iraci, have no formal identification but recall a home, a family, a childhood, or simply freedom in the streets. "I also want to leave," he told me. "I came from Lages, state of Santa Catarina. I was raised in the interior and like it better than the city. I lost my father and my mother. We had cows and pigs and planted corn and beans. I have ten siblings, all scattered. My sister put me on a bus to Porto Alegre. Nobody wanted to take care of me. I was already paralyzed. I got paralyzed when I was one-and-a-half years old. I lived in the streets for five years. Now I am forty-one years old and have been here for more than five years. Better to live in the streets than in a place like this for the rest of life."

Vita "makes me nervous." Iraci said. "Here one dies." He has seen too many pass away. "During winter, it is pretty bad. I lost count of how many died this past year. It's serious. This place is a sadness. I want to get out of here. This is not life. It's the end of life. The one who is ill gets even more ill, and one gets nervous. I am a nervous man."

What happens to the dead?

"When someone dies, the administration calls the morgue. They pick up the body and put it in the machine."

What do you mean?

"They throw oil over the body and set the body on fire. Then it becomes ashes, and the ashes are thrown into the Guaíba River. If one is buried, it is only for a few days, for they need the grave for other people. That's what I heard."

During the long days in Vita in which nothing happens, Iraci and his friends, including India, whom he says he is dating, "keep track of time. . . . We tell each other which day of the month and which year it is, the year that passed and the year that will begin. One reminds the other. Today is December 30, 1999; tomorrow is December 31, 1999, right? See how smart I am? Thank God, my head works very well. I am not ill."

I asked Iraci what was inside the plastic bag over his lap.

"The words of God."

So you know how to read?

"No, but I understand them."

What do the words of God say?

"They say, 'The Lord is my shepherd, and I will lack nothing.' "

What else do you carry in here?

"Bread. I keep the crumbs I find so that I can eat during the day. Sir, I enjoyed talking to you very much. Do you have a pen?"

Yes.

"So, I want you to write my name in your book. It's Iraci Pereira de Moraes. My name comes from my deceased mother. Her name was Dormíria Pereira de Moraes. The name of my deceased father was Laudino Pereira de Oliveira."

Why didn't you get your father's name?

"I don't know why. I was pushed to the side of the deceased mother. I think it's good like this."

Were you registered at birth?

"Yes, but I lost my documents in the streets. I must do them all over again."

Iraci then again summed up his fate: "I tell you the truth, I have no father or mother. I have ten siblings. We were eleven; one died. We are scattered in the world. So I wanted to see if I could return to the interior. I have an acquaintance, a good friend of the family. He lives near the town of Arvelino Carvão."

Catarina was listening. We resumed our conversation. Why, I asked her, do you think families, neighbors, and hospitals send people to Vita?

"They say that it is better to place us here so that we don't have to be left alone at home, in solitude . . . that there are more people like us here. And all of us together, we form a society, *a society of bodies*." And she added: "Maybe my family still remembers me, but they don't miss me."

Catarina had condensed the social reasoning of which she was the human leftover. I wondered about her chronology and about how she had been cut off from family life and placed in Vita. How had she become the object of a logic and sociality in which people were no longer worthy of affection, though they were remembered? And how was I to make sense of these intimate dynamics if not by trusting her and working through her language and experience?

India could not find the dictionary, so she brought the whole suitcase. A strong smell of urine, moisture, and also a kind of sweetness wafted out as I opened it. The contents of the suitcase were all that Catarina had in life: a few pieces of old clothing, some carefully assembled candy wrappers, fake jewelry, a bottle of cheap powder, a toothbrush, and a comb as well as several plastic bags containing magazines, books, and notebooks. "My worker's identity card was kept by the hospital," she noted.

I picked up the dictionary and read aloud some of her free-associative inscriptions.

Documents, reality
Tiresomeness, truth, saliva
Voracious, consumer, saving, economics
Catarina, spirit, pills
Marriage, cancer, Catholic church
Separation of bodies, division of the estate
The couple's children

The words indexed the ground of Catarina's existence; her body had been separated from those exchanges and made part of a new society.

What do you mean by the "separation of bodies"?

"My ex-husband kept the children."

When did you separate?

"Many years ago."

What happened?

"He had another woman."

She shifted back to her pain: "I have these spasms, and my legs feel so heavy."

When did you begin feeling this?

"After I had Alessandra, my second child, I already had difficulty walking. . . . My ex-husband sent me to the psychiatric hospital. They gave me so many injections. I don't want to go back to his house. He rules the city of Novo Hamburgo."

Did the doctors ever tell you what you had?

"No, they said nothing."

Denial or resistance to the verdict "psychotic," I thought. But what was the heaviness in her body that she repeatedly described? Just as they had the first time we met, in March 1997, Catarina's words suggested that something physiological had preceded or was related to her exclusion as mentally ill, and that her condition worsened in medical exchanges. "I am allergic to doctors. Doctors want to be knowledgeable, but they don't know what suffering is. They only medicate."

Oscar, the infirmary's coordinator, stopped by. Every time the good man saw me, he called me *"O vivente"*—"O living creature"—an expression I found eerie in that context. As we moved aside, Oscar explained that, as far as he knew, a hospital had sent Catarina to Vita because her family did not want to care for her. But he had no specific information to back this up.

"She is very depressed. Like the others, she feels rejected and imprisoned here. They are placed here, and nobody visits them." He linked Catarina's paralysis to a complicated labor, "a woman's problem. She lost the child, it seems. We don't know which hospital it happened in; we have no reports. These are things people say, but nobody truly knows. The fact is that people make pacts to get rid of the person, and that's why we have institutions like Vita. That's how things work these days."

Oscar emphasized that probably 80 of the 110 people now in the infirmary (the population had significantly decreased since the time of Zé das Drogas's administration) were "psychiatric cases." But he agreed that Catarina was "a lucid person." A person that no one listens to any longer, I added.

"When my thoughts agreed with my ex-husband and his family, everything was fine," Catarina recalled, as we resumed the conversation. "But when I disagreed with them, I was mad. It was like a side of me had to be forgotten. The side of wisdom. They wouldn't dialogue, and the science of the illness was forgotten. My legs weren't working well. The doctors prescribe and prescribe. They don't touch you there where it hurts. . . . My sister-in-law went to the health post to get the medication for me."

According to Catarina, her physiological deterioration and expulsion from reality had been mediated by a shift in the meaning of words, in the light of novel family dynamics, economic pressures, and her own pharmaceutical treatment. Her affections seemed intimately connected to new domestic arrangements. "My brothers brought me here. For some time, I lived with my brothers . . . but I didn't want to take medication when I was there. I asked: why is it only me who has to be medicated? My brothers want to see production, progress. They said that I would feel better in the midst of other people like me."

But Catarina resisted this closure, and, in ways that I could not fully grasp at first, she voiced an intricate ontology in which inner and outer state were laced together, along with the wish to untie it all: "Science is our consciousness, heavy at times, burdened by a knot that you cannot untie. If we don't study it, the illness in the body worsens. . . . Science . . . If you have a guilty conscience, you will not be able to discern things."

Catarina said that she wrote in order "to know afterward," as if she could not have been present in the circumstances that determined the course of her existence. Her spoken accounts and her writing contain the confused sense of something strange happening in the body—"cerebral spasm, corporal spasm, emotional spasm, scared heart." Along with all those people coming in and out of her house, and her moving from house to hospital to other houses, it seemed there was a danger of becoming too many, strange to herself. "One needs to preserve oneself. I also know that pleasure in one's life is very important, the body of the Other. I think that people fear their bodies."

Writing helped her to endure the days in Vita, Catarina added. "Now and then, we also talk to each other. But the toughest are the nights, for then we are all alone, and one desire pushes the other. I have desire, I have desire."

When I approached Iraci to say good-bye, he repeated that he and India were dating. "We take care of each other. Last night, I dreamed it was our wedding, and we were eating the cake. Then I woke up . . . and I was so hungry." But the story is much more complicated. I learned that volunteers sometimes actually tied India to her bed to prevent her from masturbating in public. I also heard rumors that volunteers from the recovery area whose task it was to bathe the women had forced themselves sexually on India.

As I bade Catarina farewell, I asked to borrow the dictionary, for I wanted to study it. She consented. I told her that I would bring it back in August, and we would continue the conversation. She smiled and said that she had run out of ink. "I need another pen."

I read the word she was trying to finish writing: CONTACT.

Iraci and India, Vita 2001

Inequality

"A maimed statue." *Estátua entrevada.* That is how Catarina described her condition in her dictionary. *Entrevada* means to be paralyzed; it also means to become dark or obscure, to grow clouded. The associations that follow this description are striking—in the eyes of the maimed statue, there is Catarina, along with her son, confronting officers and looking into the eyes of a machine:

Birth certificate
Catarina and Anderson
To be present in person
Policeman
Electoral officer
Eye to eye
Machine
To make meaning

On the next page of the dictionary, Catarina repeats the word "statue" and, writing in the imperative, demands to be addressed: "Call my address: *Brasil, Brancil, Brecha, Brasa.*"

Vita is Brazil's address or destination. *Brancil* is a word Catarina made up; to me, it sounds like the name of a prescription drug. *Brecha* is a fissure, a wound, as well as the void that Catarina became. *Brasa* is a burning coal. It also suggests anxiety, wrath, and sexual tension.

The notebook in which Catarina wrote her dictionary had been distributed a few years earlier by the municipal government of Porto Alegre, considered a model of popular administration both domestically and internationally (Pont and Barcelos 2000; Abers 2000). The site of the World Social Forum, the city has become famous for its policies of social inclusion, most notably its "participatory budget-making." The inside covers of the notebook outlined the consciousness-raising philosophy of the Workers' Party under the title "Writing (Dis)Organizes Life": "You, the people, are the main actors in the work we carry out. . . . Information invades our lives without asking for permission. All forms of the written word are a daily part of the city, but citizens are increasingly excluded from the content. This reality is in constant flux, blurring the conceptual lines between literacy and illiteracy. How much time is needed before we learn to critically engage with the written word?"

In this official text, the city's secretary of education observed that at least twenty million people in the country were illiterate (some 15 percent of the population) and added that access to literacy and education was "a political project that questions the neoliberalism being implemented in the country and in our province. The democratic and popular government of Porto Alegre, in partnership with civil society, ensures the high quality of education and also guarantees access to health care, employment, leisure, sanitation, and housing." The secretary concluded by explaining that this project, called "totalities of knowledge," took its central inspiration from Paulo Freire's argument that *reading the world precedes reading the word*: "Our literacy program develops critical citizens who have a choice, with the capacity to transform their own lives and the realities of the world."

Catarina's use of this discarded educational material to compose her dictionary ironically exposes the imaginary and selective quality of what is described here as social change. The truth is that Catarina and the residents of Vita remain excluded from this particular popular project as well as most others.

"Citizens are those who search for services," explained Mariane Gross, a journalist and human rights activist working in the city's security office, who was critical of what the policies of social inclusion have meant in practice. She argued that the Workers' Party administration had been highly effective in creating novel "service counters," which address various medical and social needs, within a limited capacity. This in turn generated a new culture of citizenship and "democratic experts," as she put it. "Those who want access have to get registered, wait in line, and participate. But what if you don't read the folder, if you don't have friends who tell you about these possibilities? Individuals have also learned to use this structure to accumulate power in their communities." Meanwhile, "on the way to the counter, others, particularly the young and unemployed, are recruited by parallel forms of commerce and government—that is, organized crime."

In 1997, I presented some of my initial ethnographic findings from Vita at an AIDS workshop organized by Porto Alegre's municipal government. I suggested that there were signs of a hidden and untreated AIDS epidemic in Vita, which could well be an indication of what was happening in Porto Alegre's streets and ghettos (Biehl 1999b). At the time, a representative of the Ministry of Health voiced indignation about "such a degree of dehumanization" and asked the local officials present to consider "closing Vita in the name of public health." The city's health secretary promised that her office would definitely investigate.

But, as another top city administrator admitted, the pressure to produce quick results for this progressive administration too often led to the creation of commissions and the writing of reports: "In truth, problems are identified, but things are not solved." The poorest urban inhabitants, by and large, remained in a "vacuum of response." And, in this vacuum, new social units and economic activities emerged to care for the invisible. This was tragically apparent in the so-called geriatric houses that mushroomed throughout the city to shelter the elderly, the mentally ill, and the disabled—the "unproductive and useless," as Mariane Gross described them. "We used to say that in each street of Porto Alegre there was a clandestine hospice, operating without legal authorization."

In 1998, Gross began a campaign to publicize the tragic conditions in these institutions. "People are confined and have no adequate care. Some of these businesses are surrounded by barbed wire, like camps." On July 2, 1999, for example, a fifty-eight-year-old man was bitten to death by dogs in a geriatric house in Porto Alegre. "Bits of skin were all over the ground," Gross and her colleagues wrote in the annual report of the state's Human Rights Commission (Comissão de Direitos Humanos 2000:108).

But human rights rhetoric was not strong enough to close down Vita and similar institutions. The city's public health inspection service had also begun to investigate these businesses but was having difficulty finding judges who would support shutting them down, according to health professional Jaci Oliveira. "The judges tell us that these houses are doing good. After all, where would these people go if they were freed?"

Even if Vita had been shut down, it would most certainly have reemerged elsewhere in the city. For Vita is indeed symbiotic with various levels of government, and people like Catarina now have their destinies forged by a set of forces and a logic of exceptions that operate, in her words, *"out of justice."*

Ex-Human

"I finished writing the book you gave me," Catarina reported when we met again in early August 2000. "I left the book in the pharmacy with Clóvis, the nurse, but he threw it away. I was sad. I kept thinking that one day João and Adriana will come back, and they will want to read the book, and I don't have it anymore." I told Catarina I trusted that her writing would resume. She then confided: "Clóvis and I are dating."

She quickly changed the subject: "My little suitcase was also thrown away. The volunteers said that it was getting moistened."

I handed Catarina another empty notebook. She smiled, with a seemingly sedated face: "I have been at a standstill. . . . My head was full, full of nonsense. . . . So I stopped writing."

"My gums are inflamed. It aches a lot. Clóvis told me that they would take me to the dentist." Catarina added that he was giving her vitamins and pills, a white and a blue one, for pain. "Clóvis gives medication to each one of us. He puts the pills in the little cups with our names and the dose, the right dose . . . and distributes it to all of us." Catarina looked very tired.

How did you sleep?

"I woke up in the middle of the night because of Lili, my bedmate. She talks in her sleep. It took me a long time to fall asleep again."

Do you recall any dreams you had?

"I dreamed that I was . . . no . . . suddenly a man came and hit me and pulled my hair. I don't know. I felt bad and began to scream, asking for help. Then Lili was there. I don't recall more. It was a nightmare."

It sounded like it had really happened, I thought. I asked whether she had recognized the man in the dream, but she said she had not.

I mentioned that sometimes, after waking from a dream, I would scribble down the things I recalled.

"Yes," she replied, "dreams help us to understand the fears we have. A nightmare can also be a desire. If one doesn't study what one has dreamed, then the dreams stay in the life that was dreamed. And, as one returns to life, one keeps thinking that everything is normal."

I was confused. Are you saying, I asked, that if we don't interpret a dream, then the dream stays present during the day, as if we lived in a dream-state?

"No, that's not what I am saying. A little remnant of the dream is transmitted to us . . . the rest is up to us to channel and decipher. If we don't decipher, we will not be able to remember what actually happened, what was and what wasn't."

What was and what wasn't. In Catarina's conception, the workings of the unconscious did not simply substitute for reality.[34] Rather, the unconscious seemed to be a storehouse of ciphers that one must assemble and decode in order to understand *what actually happened*—the truth of losing one's way of being in the world.

A cipher is an arithmetic symbol—zero—of no value by itself, used to occupy a vacant place in decimal numeration. A cipher is a person or thing that fills a place but is of no importance, a nonentity. A cipher is also a secret or disguised system of writing, a code used in writing; or a message written in this manner; or a key to such a system.

According to Catarina, that which truly happened continues to exist in the lost and valueless, in nonentities such as herself. Our grammars, George Steiner writes, make it difficult, even unnatural, to phrase a radical existential negativity, "but the failure of the human enterprise makes the doubt inescapable" (2001:39).

How did you learn to decipher your dreams?

"By myself," answered Catarina, "when I was little. As I woke up, I kept thinking about what I had seen in the dream. I kept it to myself. I learned that it is good to dream, to think, the mind . . . "

But the time came when the borderline between the I and the Other had to be drawn more clearly. The fragile and forceful birth of writing and of the social person was what she described next.

"My father, he taught me the alphabet. We sat at the kitchen table, and he wrote 'a,' 'b,' 'c' in my notebook. I had to memorize the letters. But at first they didn't stay in my mind. My father kept saying, 'Catarina, you must keep this in your mind. If not, you will know nothing, and you won't be a person.' It was difficult. I wept a lot, but I learned the a, the b, and the c."

That is what her dead father, she said, had left her with. A vital supplement, I thought.

Without knowing why, I changed the subject. Reminding Catarina that she had once told me that the doctors could not understand her pain, I asked her when she had first visited a doctor. She took my question literally, not letting me divert the conversation from where her thinking was taking it: "I think I was five years old. . . . I came down with something on my body that itched a lot. So my father took me to the pharmacist, and I healed. As a child, I only went to pharmacies. Real doctors who wrote prescriptions, that was later, the psychiatrists."

She was telling me more than I could comprehend at the time about a painfully learned symbolic order and a personhood, both of which were no longer of any value (like her discarded book). As she alluded to them, the pharmaceutical identifications were another kind of writing that seemed to stand for her estrangement from the world.

"My ex-husband first took me to the psychiatrist, Dr. Gilson, in Novo Hamburgo, for him to help me, to discover the illness. But he lied to the doctor, saying that I was aggressive, that I beat the children. I got so mad that I actually hit him in front of the doctor. The doctor only prescribed. The nurse gave me an injection. I always had some medication to take. They said that they wanted to heal me, but how could they if they did not know the illness? . . . If I will count on doctors to tell me what I feel, I will remain incapacitated, because they don't know the reason of what I am, of my illness, of my pain. They don't know a thing."

At that point, a woman who had been observing us for a while at a distance finally approached.

"This is my friend Lili," said Catarina. "She speaks at night."

"Yes, I am her friend," replied Lili, looking straight into my eyes, with a wide-open smile and a copy of the New Testament in her hands.

Before I could ask Lili anything, she asked me: "Do you know what 'not to live by the desire of the flesh any longer' means?"

Stunned by her question, I failed to answer. I stayed on the surface of her words and mentioned that, as far as I knew, this was a statement by the Apostle Paul and that I would look into it further. I asked Lili where she was from, a question I grew up learning to ask in that world where mobility, both geographic and social, was all too rare.

"I am from Canoas, but now I am living here. I used to be Catholic, but then I converted to the Assembly of God. I used to leave home and run to the church. My husband hit me. I lived in the streets for some time, but then I went to live with my son. My son brought me here. My daughter-in-law wanted to kill me. I did nothing wrong. She called him 'daddy,' and I told her that I did not like that. She then tried to kill me with a kitchen knife."

I was again faced with a condensed account of what the "mad person" thought had happened to her in life. I had heard similar accounts from Catarina when I first met her in 1997 and from Iraci during my previous visit. In their initial statements, all three had described being banned from the family and suffering the rupture of relations as well as the dangerous and now impossible desire for homecoming. These were not illness narratives channeling a search for meaning (Kleinman 1988; Good 1994; Mattingly 1998). Nor were they the "schizophrenic recording codes" that Deleuze and Guattari saw as opposing or simply parodying social codes, "never giving the same explanation from one day to the next" (1983:15). Neither were they the "diffuse and external rain of distractions" that marked the being-in-the-world of the homeless in the Boston shelter chronicled by Robert Desjarlais (1994:897).

As I came to realize over time, the accounts of many of the so-called mad in Vita were not ever-shifting. Rather, these narratives maintained an impressive steadiness and contextuality (as I would learn by tracking Catarina's history), in spite of caretakers' repeated insistence that they were "nonsense." Instead of seeing these condensed accounts as proof of "a retreat from the world" (Desjarlais 1994:897), I began to think of them as pieces of truth—let me call them life codes—through which the abandoned person attempted to hold onto the real. As I listened, I was challenged to treat the accounts as evidence of the reality from which the abandoned had been barred and their failed attempts to reenter it. In this sense, these pieces ultimately gave language to the exclusion that was now embodied. Moreover, for the abandoned themselves, these accounts were spaces in which destinies were rethought and desires reframed.[35]

Consider the old black man standing barefoot against a wall and how he transformed social dying into speech. As I passed by, again and again he called me *senhor* (master) and, with downcast eyes, begged: "*Senhor*, can you, please, loan me your wife so that I can take her with me to see God, who has descended there in Porto Alegre?" I knew that he had seen me with Adriana, but I did not have a clue as to what he meant.

One day, I asked him about this epiphany.

"God is near the bus station," the old man replied.

How do you know?

Osmar, Vita 2001

"I don't know. People tell me. I also heard it on the radio. I have heard it for some time. Yes, *senhor*, I just want to go there and see God—and if you were to loan me your wife, I could go and see God."

Why do you want to see God?

"It's good to see God, to see and to get to know God."

After a silence, I asked where he had come from.

"I am here now."

How long have you been here?

"My family does not want me to see God, who has descended there at the bus station."

Did your family leave you here?

"My family does not want me to see God. They say that I am not worthy of anyone. That I am worth nothing, that I am a very bad nigger. Truly, that's what they say."

Why did they leave you here?

"I don't know; I didn't wrong anyone."

What did you do before getting to Vita?

"I always worked in a plantation . . . to sell for the market."

How old are you?

"I don't know. I have no birth certificate."

He did recall his name: "Osmar de Moura Miranda." Osmar said that he had always been a single man, that since he was a child he had known "nothing" of his parents. Later, a volunteer told me that Negão—"Big Nigger," that is what they call him in Vita—had actually been brought there by "his boss."

Now Osmar is a useless servant, so to speak; his family is that which never existed; and God (as I interpret it) is the dignity and liberty he never knew as a man of African descent in Brazil. "They brought me here where there is no work to do, and they never let me free. . . . *Senhor*, could you arrange things for me to leave?"

I explained that I could not, but I asked him where he would go if he left.

"To the streets, for I don't have a place to live."

Why is living in the streets better than here?

"In the streets, there is nobody to order me around."

The accounts of Catarina, Osmar, and their neighbors represent agency. As these bits and pieces give language to a lived *ex-humanness*, they also work as the resources and means through which the abandoned articulate their experience. According to the *Oxford English Dictionary*, the adjective "ex" means "former, outdated"; the preposition "ex" is used to mean "out of" in reference to goods; and the noun "ex" refers to "one who formerly occupied the position or office denoted by the context," such as a former husband or wife. "Ex" also means "to cross out, to delete with an x," and stands for the unknown.

I spent the months of August and December of 2000 working with Catarina in Vita. We talked for hours and hours, and I continued interviewing her neighbors and caretakers. During and between these visits, Catarina finished two more volumes of the dictionary, and I was increasingly amazed by her capacity to give form to her interior life, despite the crumbling of all hope. "I desire to be present"—that is what I heard her saying, time and again.

How to methodologically address her agonistic struggle over belonging? In the simplest of terms, for me it meant first to halt diagnosis, to find time to listen, to let Catarina take her story back and forth, to take her voice as evidence of a relatedness to a now-vanished lifeworld, and, throughout, to respect and to trust.

The House and the Animal

"Even if it is a tragedy? A tragedy generated in life?"

Those were Catarina's words when I asked her for the details of her story the next day.

"I remember it all. My ex-husband and I lived together, and we had the children. We lived as a man and a woman. Everything was as it should be; we got along with the neighbors. I worked in the shoe factory, but he said that I didn't need to work. He worked in the city hall. He used to drink a bit after work when he played billiards in a bar. I had nothing against that.

"One day, however, we had a silly fight because he thought that I should be complaining about his habits and I wasn't. That fight led to nothing. Afterward, he picked another topic to fight about. Finally, one day he said that he had gotten another woman and moved in with her. Her name was Rosa.

"What could I do? Anderson said, 'Mom, father has another woman. Aren't you going to do something about it?' What could I do? 'Alessandra and I must have a destiny,' he said. 'If this woman wants my father, he should stay there, because it is impossible for a man to have two homes, two families. . . . He is making a cancer here.' I kept wondering what to do. . . . He wanted to divide himself between both of us."

I remembered the phrase "the separation of bodies" in Catarina's dictionary, and it seemed to me that her pathology resided in that split and in the struggles to reestablish other social ties.[36] In Vita, out of that lived fragmentation, the family was remembered. Her associations continued on the theme of the changing family, which was the cause of much pain and confusion.

"My mother was living with us. I had to take care of my mother. She couldn't walk anymore; she had rheumatism and wanted treatment. I also have rheumatism. My father had had another family since we were kids; he stayed in the countryside. My father also wanted to heal, for he got poisoned planting tobacco. My ex-husband wanted to do the same as my father did, but I said 'no' to that kind of arrangement. So the marriage ended. During my last pregnancy, he left me alone in the hospital. He didn't go there to see if the baby had been born or not. I had to be mother and father at the same time."

According to Catarina, her husband repeated what her father had done. In marriage, she found herself once more in a fatherless family. Her father had been poisoned; he worked for a big company and for another family. Her mother lived with the young couple. The disease that paralyzed her was also emerging in Catarina's body. When it was time for her to give birth to her last child, Catarina was left alone in the hospital, to be both mother and father to an unwanted child. All these references resonated with a fragment in the dictionary in which a breathless child was said to suffocate the mother:

Premature
Born out of the schedule
Out of time, out of reason
Time has passed
The baby's color changes
It is breathless
And suffocates
The mother of the baby

Nothing could account for what was happening. "Out of time, out of reason," she was feeling untimely. As our conversation continued, Catarina again emphasized her agonistic effort to adhere to what was "normal" and behave the way a woman was supposed to in that world. She alluded to the occlusion of her thinking as if it were daydreaming and to an urge to leave the home in which she was locked. The house and the hospital doubled as each other, and she was left childless:

"I behaved like a woman. Since I was a housewife, I did all my duties, like any other woman. I cooked, and I did the laundry. My ex-husband and his family got suspicious of me because sometimes I left the house to attend to other callings. They were not in agreement with what I thought. My ex-husband thought that I had a nightmare in my head. He wanted to take that out of me, to make me a normal person. They wanted to lock me in the hospital. I escaped so as not to go to the hospital. I hid myself; I went far. But the police and my ex-husband found me. They took my children."

When was the first time you left home?

"It was in Novo Hamburgo. In Caiçara, I didn't leave the home; it was in the countryside. One always has the desire to leave. I was young then. But pregnant and with a child, I wouldn't leave. . . . When we first got to Novo Hamburgo, we rented a place at Polaco's. I left home and ran because . . . who knows? Because . . . he was late in coming home from work. . . . And one day he left work earlier and rode the motorcycle with girls. I went to the bar and asked for a drink. I was pretty courageous and left. I was kind of suffocating inside the house. Sometimes he locked us in, my son and I, and went to work. I kept thinking, 'How long will I remain locked?' I felt suffocated. I also felt my legs burning, a pain, a pain in the knees, and under the feet."

Did he find another woman because you left home? Or why did it happen?

"No."

After a silence, Catarina answered a question I had not asked: "He didn't leave me because of my illness either. . . . That didn't bother him." Yet it struck me that her statement affirmed the very thing she sought to deny: the key role played by her physiology within the household, of which she was both conscious and unconscious. She then added that jealousy was her husband's basic state of consciousness.

"He was jealous of me. He used to say how ugly I was. He wanted me to stay in the wheelchair . . . so that he could do everything as he wished. He found another woman because he wanted to be a true macho. One day, he came back and said, 'I don't want you anymore.' I said, 'Better for me. I want a divorce.' We separated from bed, bath, table, home, and city. I wanted a divorce. Divorce is mine, I asked for it first."

This man's virility was dependent on negating and replacing her. And the doctors, according to Catarina, helped to objectify the new family arrangement, making it impossible to truly reflect about what was going on.

"The doctors listened only to him. I think that this is wrong. They have to listen to the patient. They gave me pills. A doctor shouldn't have contempt for the patient, because he is being unjust. He only writes prescriptions and doesn't look at the person. The patient is then on a path without an exit. At home, people began to call me 'mad woman'—'Hey, mad woman, come here,' that's what they used to say."

The psychiatric aura of reality.

You seem to be suggesting that your family, the doctors, and the medications played an active role in making you "mad," I said.

"Instead of taking a step forward, my ex-husband took life backward. The doctors he took me to were all on his side. I will never live in Novo Hamburgo again. That's his land; he rules that territory. Here in Vita, at least I can transmit something to people, that they are somebody. I try to treat everybody with simplicity. He first placed me in the Caridade Hospital, then in the São Paulo—seven times in all. When I returned home, he was amazed that I recalled what a plate was. He thought that I would be unconscious of plates, pans, and things and conscious only of medication. But I knew how to use the objects."

This is how I was interpreting Catarina's account: her condition was the outcome of a new family complex that was given agency within everyday economic pressures, governing medical and pharmaceutical practices, and the country's discriminatory laws. These technical procedures and moral actions took hold of her: she experienced them as a machine with no exit in which mental life was taken backward.[37]

Through her increasing disability, all of the social roles Catarina had forcefully learned to play—daughter, sister, wife, mother, migrant, worker, patient—were being annulled, along with the precarious stability they had afforded her. To some degree, these cultural practices remained with her as the values that motivated her memory and her sharp critique of the marriage and extended family who had amputated her as if she had only a pharmaceutical consciousness. Yet this network of relatedness, betrayals, and institutional arrangements seemed to have affected Catarina profoundly, leaving her able to symbolize her condition only through the dilemmas and certainties of the world of infancy. As she put it: "When I was a child, I used to tell my brothers that I had a piece of strength that I kept to myself, only to myself."

Catarina continued: "My ex-husband's family got mad at me. I have a conscience, and theirs is a burden." Interestingly, as she reconstructed the actions of her ex-family, she described something that, speaking as an amputated being, she could not perceive as a plot against her.

"One day, Nina—she is my ex-husband's sister—and Delvani, her husband, came to my house, and I began to tell them what I thought. He said, 'Catarina, we have put our shack for sale. If you want, we can simply trade places, and you can get out of here.'"

The goods that had been left to Catarina after the separation from her husband were now taken as well by these relatives. In this transaction, disguised as a fair exchange, the misery of one became good business for the other. Catarina quoted the brother-in-law, who pretended not to know the business aspect of the trade: " 'This idea just came to mind now; Nina and I have not discussed this before,' he said. So they kept my house, and I moved into theirs. I recall when I took the little girl and we went into the moving truck. I had such a pain in my legs, such a pain. . . . My legs felt so heavy. I was nervous."

What happened in the new house?

"I went to live alone. Anderson and Alessandra stayed with their grand-mother. She took care of them; she could walk. At first, Ana was with me, but then Tamara kept her for longer and longer. She liked to prepare her birthday party. They are well-off people. She took my little daughter, adorned her, and took photographs. And I stayed in the house."

And next? I kept pushing the recollection.

"My shack burned down. The fire began in my neighbor's shack—her TV set exploded. There was a short-circuit, and it was all on fire. Divorce is fire. It all burned down. I stayed a few weeks with my brothers. A week in the house of one and a week in the house of the other. Ademar looked at me and said, 'We progressed on our own . . . and now this woman lying here.' My brother wants to see production, he wants one to produce. . . . He then said, 'I will sell you.' "

I had to stop her for a moment. I don't understand, Catarina.

From that point, her account became more and more elliptical, oscillating between what I understood as a fantasy that equated production with the brothers' demand that she procreate and the account of a pharmaceutically mediated form of fraternal cruelty. Catarina, however, insisted that the siblings respected her and that they were not ex-brothers: "They liked me and wanted me to stay in the house. They didn't demonstrate it, but they wanted us to remain together." This image of the brothers, I thought at the time, was what remained of the house of infancy. What happened in that space that was left? What in life made that space remain?

"I fell sick while I was in my other brother's house. It was such a bad flu—it was a cold winter. They gave me such strong medication that I couldn't do anything but sleep. Day and night were the same for me. My brother told me that I had to go. He said that he already had four children, that I only had three, that I was obligated to have five or six kids, like my mother. He didn't realize that he demanded from me what he asked from himself. He married twice. The first woman died giving birth to a son. To do what? So he got another woman and now has three children with her.

"Like Altamir, he also has an auto repair shop. He always has money . . . but, here, I don't have money. Here, we live from donations. The important thing is not to have money and things but one's life. That is very important—life and to give opportunity to whoever wants to be born. . . . My brother used to say that we, my husband and I, had too few children, too little sexual relation."

The demands for economic progress made by the brothers and the changing value of kinship ties became entangled in a battle over the discarding of Catarina's body. In order to endure being left to die in Vita, Catarina has recomposed the ruined fraternal tie, I thought. Desire finds lost objects. Yet the men in Catarina's account—the brothers, the ex-husband, and the brother-in-law—seemed beyond the tragic mode. Their actions were guided by other interests: getting rid of Catarina before she became an invalid like her mother, taking her house, having another woman. In reality, Catarina could not be the human that these men wanted.

"After my ex-husband left me, he came back to the house and told me he needed me. He threw me onto the bed, saying, 'I will eat you now.' I told him that that was the last time. . . . I did not feel pleasure, though. I only felt desire. Desire to be talked to, to be gently talked to."

In abandonment, Catarina recalled sex. There was no love, simply a male body enjoying itself. No more social links, no more speaking beings. Out of the world of the living, her desire was for language, the desire to be talked to. I reminded Catarina that she had once told me that the worst part of Vita was the nighttime, when she was left alone with her desire.

She kept silent for a while and then made it clear that seduction was not at stake in our conversation:

"I am not asking a finger from you."

She was not asking me for sex, she meant.

Catarina looked exhausted, though she claimed not to be tired. At any rate, it seemed that she had brought the conversation to a fecund point, and I also felt that I could no longer listen. No countertransference, no sexual attraction, I thought, but enough of all these things. The anthropologist is not immune. I promised to return the next day to continue and suggested that she begin to write again.

But my resistance did not deter her from recalling her earliest memory, and I marveled at the power of what I heard—an image that in its simplicity appeared to concentrate the entire psyche.

"I remember something that happened when I was three years old. I was at home with my brother Altamir. We were very poor. We were living in a little house on the plantation. Then a big animal came into the house—it was a black lion. The animal rubbed itself against my body. I ran and hugged my brother. Mother had gone to get water from the well. That's when I became afraid. Fear of the animal. When mother came back, I told her what had happened. But she said that there was no fear, that there was no animal. Mother said nothing."

This could have been incest, sexual abuse, a first psychotic episode, the memory of maternal and paternal abandonment, or a simple play of shadows and imagination—we will never know.

The image of the house, wrote Gaston Bachelard, "would appear to have become the topography of our intimate being. A house constitutes a body of images that give mankind proofs or illusions of stability" (1994:xxxvi).

In this earliest of Catarina's recollections, nothing is protecting the I. It is in Vita that she recalled the animal so close to the I. This story speaks to her abandonment as an animal as well as to the work the animal performs in human life. In this last sense, the animal is not a negation of the human, I thought—it is a form of life through which Catarina learned to produce affect and which marks her singularity.

When I told her it was time for me to leave, Catarina replied, "You are the one who marks time."

"Love is the illusion of the abandoned"

Crawling on the cement ground, a man was shouting: "O devil, eat shit! O devil, stick this bread in your ass!"

Most of the people in the infirmary sat quietly against a wall, absorbing the weak warmth of the winter sun on that late morning, August 5, 2000. Some moved around the body of the cursing man and, holding their sole possessions, wandered through the courtyard undisturbed. Inside of me, the man's voice named the place: Inferno. He kept shouting the same thing.

Does he shout all day?

"It's the spirit of the sufferers," replied Catarina.

Do you believe in spirits?

"Yes," she said, "in spirits, in a person passing desire to the other. . . . Like in the church, the priest transmits sexual tension." Catarina added that she had been calm for the past three days, that her tooth was aching less, and that she had been writing "nonstop." Her new volume began: "My dictionary, my name."

On the next page, Catarina wrote: "Clóvis Gama, Catarina Gomes, Catarina Gama."

She again told me that she and Clóvis, the nurse I had not yet met, were "together." After Clóvis's name, she first wrote her maiden name (her husband's family name was Moraes) and then took up Clóvis's last name, Gama—*gamado* means "very attracted to" and "sexually aggressive." Catarina wrote the divorce into her name, I thought. She first identifies with the dead father's name, as if she did not need to belong to another man, but then imagines that she belongs to the nurse who medicates her.

There was now an openness to her name as well. In the dictionary, the

"R" in CATARINA was often replaced by an invented character similar to the letter "K" (which is not part of the Portuguese alphabet)—CATAKINA. She explained, "If I didn't open the character, my head would explode."

These names were followed by an accurate recollection of the Ten Commandments. Then, among a long list of diseases, she had written the statement "rheumatism in the nerves, in the muscles, in the flesh, in the blood" and a reference to *"mal de parto"* (a complication of childbirth) and "amnesia." The next two pages were filled with references to money: "millions of cents, of *reais*, of dollars; Brazilian bank, credit union, savings account." A long list of professions followed, beginning with "doctor and nurse."

The next page, after references to religion, medicine, money, and the body, contained an acknowledgment of sexual enjoyment. She wrote of the discovery of love in sexual tension:

Sexual tension, pleasure, fuck
I discovered that I love you
In every kiss, in every hug
I feel that I want you ever more

In searching for love in the Other's body, she is left with incompleteness and a surplus of desire.

In the next fragment, Catarina wants sperm and confounds the substance with the man:

I desire sperm
Viscous mucus
Now I know you

Love, sex, and the fantasy of both are not distinguishable in Catarina's writing:

Love, fuck, masturbation
Making love with the fingers
Love among two is potency
For then man and woman
Don't feel despised and abandoned

Without social ties, I thought, Catarina was left with sex as if it were love in Vita. Or perhaps she was knowingly writing that one is alone in love, in sex. One can also read this fragment as suggesting that a sexual relationship writes itself. The spirit of two lone sufferers and sexual tension meet in the discovery of love: an energy or potency, as she put it, to fight abandonment. "We don't know what it means to be alive except for the following fact, that a body is something that enjoys itself" (Lacan 1998:23). In love, in sex, in writing, Catarina approached the reality of being a thing left to die:

To live masturbating and things
Things in life
To alleviate the penis
To be a thing of resurrection

How to be a thing of resurrection? Catarina knows the hatred of which the despised man is made and what he does to the Other as he eases the penis that he is.

Man without God, man without family. The despised man hurts.

Love for Catarina was a vital enjoyment. The dramatic effect of love, she wrote, was a point of suspension in her "nonexistence" in Vita, a path both out of and back into abandonment.

To feel love
Lonely love
To follow desire in lonesomeness
Love is the illusion of the abandoned

Social Psychosis

"Shut up. I am ordering you to shut up." A volunteer wearing a white coat approached the cursing man and threatened to lock him up.

The man on the ground was undeterred: "O devil, eat shit! O devil, stick this bread in your ass!"

As the volunteer turned, he saw me talking to Catarina and walked toward us. It was Clóvis, the nurse. He said he had heard a lot about me, and he apologized for all the noise. "Only medication makes this poor thing shut up. We have to sedate him. But he spits it out. What to do?" Clóvis also apologized for being unshaven. "I really don't have time. Work here begins at 5 A.M. and continues nonstop till 9 P.M."

"Clóvis gives me the vitamins," interjected Catarina.

"Yes, I am the one who medicates . . . when there is medication to be dispensed," added the fifty-four-year-old man. "I give injections, take care of wounds, bathe the grandmas—everything here happens with me." Clóvis said he had been doing this work for almost a year "out of charity. I don't get paid."

He explained that he had learned all these nursing skills while working as a volunteer in Porto Alegre's major psychiatric hospitals. In an association that sounded strange to me and that linked his work to Catarina's, Clóvis alluded to a "pharmaceutical dictionary" he used to read at the São Paulo Hospital, which gave him "the knowledge to now manage Vita's pharmacy." Clóvis was also the man who had thrown away the second volume of the dictionary that Catarina had entrusted to him.

"But let me tell you the truth," stated Clóvis. "I have been an alcoholic for almost my entire life." He began drinking as a teenager. At the age of fifteen, he left his mother's home in Porto Alegre, becoming a vagabond and a migrant worker. He made brief references to having lived in Uruguay, Paraguay, and Venezuela. For a while, he said, he had a family of his own in Rio de Janeiro, but his only son had died in a car accident.

As we talked, Clóvis disclosed that he had in fact been an inmate in the psychiatric institutions where he had learned about medications and that in the early nineties he had also lived in Vita. "This time, I came back by myself. São Paulo's social worker is my friend; she wanted to rent a place for me, but I decided to come here. My treatment there had ended, and I was afraid that I would go back to drinking and living in the streets. It's tough—alcoholism is a bad disease." This man's history held much more than his words were ready to tell, I thought.

Like many of the other volunteers and inhabitants of Vita's recovery area, Clóvis saw the dying creatures in the infirmary as important material for shaping the citizen he wanted to become: "I can see the inhuman conditions here. So I can tune in, find myself again, and forget drinking. Working with the abandoned is a therapy one does with oneself. I still want to get some more years of work outside here so that I can retire and get my social security benefits. We don't get paid anything here."

As the man on the ground continued to call out to the devil, Clóvis insisted that we move to the pharmacy. He tried to joke with Catarina, saying, "She fights with me. If I don't give her attention, she cries like a cat." Catarina nodded and mentioned something I could not understand.

The infirmary's small pharmacy was indeed well organized now. More medications were on the shelves, mostly donations (many of them expired, as I later verified), and labels were everywhere. On the table, little plastic cups marked with patients' names or nicknames contained the various doses to be consumed throughout the day. Clóvis's services were in high demand. Many men from the recovery area, as well as mothers and children from the village surrounding Vita, knocked at the pharmacy's door, asking him to fill prescriptions or provide medical advice.

"Before I ran the pharmacy, many more people died in here," Clóvis asserted.

How so?

"Wrong medication. I guess that some twenty people died here in one month about three years ago. The police even investigated. It was during the time Vita's administration changed." According to Clóvis, many of his predecessors in the pharmacy "couldn't even read and simply put pills in the cups and distributed them to the dirt poor. Many had heart failure."

Things in Vita changed under the new administration, Clóvis observed. "There are fewer *abandonados* in the infirmary. I shouldn't say this, but I will: Vita now works more like a business. There are still some people from the time of Zé das Drogas, but they are dying out. They accept fewer people into the infirmary now, and the new inmates are mostly elderly women who have pensions. Some of them even get three minimum monthly salaries."

Vita had an organized triage system these days, coordinated by social worker Dalva. "Before," explained Oscar, the infirmary coordinator, "people who came in here had no identity. We didn't know whose children they were or whether they were parents. . . . Many came alone. Now at least they have to have an ID card, and the triage makes it possible for us to contact the patient's family if we have to."

Captain Osvaldo was straightforward about the institution's current modus operandi when I spoke to him later that day: "We are not taking in injured persons anymore. . . . We want to reach a level of zero confinements in the infirmary. We are not a hospital. We are basically a rehabilitation service, so that people can return to society and work."

I asked Oscar to elaborate on the rationale for this shift in policy. Tired of having his pledge to improve the infirmary dismissed, he reluctantly spoke his mind: "Today, the people who administer the institution have their own private interests. This is a political game. They are not interested in the social good of the persons. They are more interested in the visibility the institution has to the outside world. Given all the donations, life in the infirmary should be much better than it is, in terms of food and treatment. I am tired of fighting. . . . They are concerned with the image of Vita outside, while the reality in here is completely different."

As for the future of the infirmary and its inhabitants, he said, "the vision of the administration that the captain passed on to me is that these people will be terminating themselves until we have zero of them. . . . Perhaps in a few years, none of these people you have been talking to will be left." As if it had all been self-generated, I noted, and with no accountability for their suffering. Oscar made an affirmative gesture. "How else? This is the social reason: these people don't produce, they don't vote."

Oscar told me that I was standing in front of "a shattered man," but that he "would move onward with life, with the help of our Lord." He had recently found out that that he was HIV-positive. "AIDS was not the thing I feared most," Oscar said. "I was scared to death that my wife and child would be infected as well. They didn't do anything wrong, like I did, all those years of injecting drugs. But maybe I got infected here in the infirmary as I handled AIDS patients. I finally had the courage to tell my wife, and she was tested. Thank God, she and the child don't have the virus. She told me that she would not leave me, that she would face it with me."

With the help of Vita's social worker, Oscar was learning to navigate the local medical AIDS world. He was being seen by an infectious-disease specialist and had his CD4 levels checked regularly. "The doctor said that I am healthy, that I don't need the cocktail yet, and I will do whatever I can to postpone using it. But thanks to the government, we now have hope." Oscar was referring to the free distribution of antiretrovirals by the Brazilian government.

For the abandoned, however, medical assistance remained minimal. A doctor-philanthropist was still visiting Vita once a week, basically spending one or two hours signing disability reports for the inmates of the recovery area. Depending on the availability of transportation and the good will of volunteers, some of the diseased in the infirmary found immediate treatment at a nearby public health post. Specialized treatment—for cancer or diabetes, for instance—"is a lottery," explained Alencar, a volunteer who, along with hundreds of other people, stood in line from 5 P.M. to 8 A.M. at the university hospital every week, waiting for a ticket to schedule an appointment. "And it generally takes a few more months to see the doctor," he added.

At the local health post, automatic prescription was the rule, and continuity of care was nonexistent. As Clóvis put it: "The psychiatrist prescribes for us. If the medication does not work, I change the dosage and try other combinations." In other words, the man Catarina was attracted to played the doctor, the pharmacist, the nurse, and the caretaker. I wondered who else the man was. "I have a whole bunch of psychotics here," said Clóvis, pointing to all the psychiatric medications he dispensed: "Haloperidol, levomepromazine, chlorpromazine, prometazine, biperiden, diazepam, imipramine." In this utterance, the psychotic was the medication itself.

During my first visits to Vita in 1995, I had heard no talk about "psychotic patients." At the time, the abandoned received no specific diagnoses at all. As Catarina's own account hinted, the widespread availability of psychiatric drugs on the market and through the universal public health service had increasingly framed these creatures as "mental" in family and neighborhood circles as well as in Vita.

As I interpreted the captain's words that day, the rhetoric of mental health also suited the current management priorities of the institution: "As I mentioned before, we try not to bring injured people in, so that we might reach a patient list of zero. But we cannot throw the patients we have back onto the streets. These dependent beings, the mentally ill, are an obstacle for their families, a financial obstacle, a shame, a social obstacle. But, ultimately, they are not our responsibility. There are specific institutions for that kind of treatment. We don't have adequate personnel for that."

I am concerned with how novel conjunctions of kinship, public institutions, psychiatry, and medication work, if not to make people psychotic, then to give a certain form and value to their experience as psychotic, thus recasting intersubjectivity and mediating abandonment. This is what I mean by social psychosis. I am not saying that mental illness is not real or that psychopharmaceuticals do not carry potential benefits for the afflicted. My point is simply that ethnography can help us to resituate and rethink psychopathology within these various circuits and struggles over belonging, agency, and care. In doing so, it can give us a clearer understanding of the concrete instances in which lives are scripted as otherworldly and out of time and of the work that is needed to give the afflicted and their kin—or, for that matter, health professionals and public officers—another chance and a sense of possibility rather than exclusion. As mentioned earlier, I am particularly interested in assessing the process by which medication becomes a social tool, as this process was recounted by Catarina and the volunteers at Vita: from the doctor's use of medication in treating the working poor at local health posts and in total psychiatric institutions to the role of drugs in the family's recasting of its ties and values, to the individual's chemical and subjective alterations, to Vita's recycling of leftover medication to ensure the removal of the abandoned from reality.

As Oscar described: "I recently hospitalized a grandpa at the Caridade Psychiatric Hospital. He had been here for six years. I don't know where he came from. I stand and look at him: where did he originate? He mentions that he had a family, that he raised cattle. What if all that he says is true? Anyway, he was aggressive and we hospitalized him, but they almost killed him there. If I look back, I don't think he had psychiatric problems. They filled him with medication."

At public psychiatric institutions, added Oscar, the use of medication is indeed undifferentiated and tentative. Idiosyncratic experimentation with new drugs and dosages and oversedation (ostensibly to prevent aggression) becomes the rule, creating a passive patient population that makes it easier for the institutions, with typically weak infrastructures, to continue functioning. In these familial and medical exchanges, pharmaceuticals substitute for the lack of social links. Moreover, pharmaceuticals make this loss of links irreversible and legitimate the disposal of unwanted persons.

One can argue that in their deployment, psychopharmaceuticals constitute the register of the true and the normal and are integral to the shaping of identity. Biomedically known, Catarina was left without the choice to live her life as she had known it. She was now, in her own words, "on a path without an exit."

As Clóvis left to attend to an injury, Catarina expressed a remarkable understanding of her condition. "I am not a pharmacist," she said. "I cannot say which medication heals an illness, I cannot say the name of the *fármaco*, but the name of my illness I know. . . . How to say it?"

Say it.

"Mine is an illness of time."

I don't understand, I said.

"Time has no cure."

An Illness of Time

Later, when Clóvis returned, I pulled him aside and asked him how he thought Catarina was doing.

"I am treating her for toothache, but her real problem is the nervous system," he said. "I have already asked her a few times, but she has never told me her full life history. She is very confused. . . . She suffers, thinking about her children. She says they took the children from her and then left her at the Caridade Hospital. . . . They probably told the children, 'We cannot have your mom at home because she is mad.'" Alluding to my work with Catarina, Clóvis added, "I probably do not have enough time to listen to her stories."

He continued: "I don't know where her paralysis comes from. It seems like she had a stroke, that she lost strength in her legs and that her tongue got stuck. . . . But her real problem is depression. I am taking care of it now." In a low voice, he explained that the "vitamins" Catarina was taking were in fact the antidepressant imipramine. "Two pills in the morning and two pills in the afternoon. She stopped crying. She was always fighting; now she is calmer." He quickly added, "The doctor prescribed it."

Why was she fighting?

"I came to the following conclusion: in here, the person lacks affection; then she gets attached to whoever gives her attention. She gets jealous and doesn't like me to be kind to anyone else but her."

What was really going on?

When we approached Catarina, Clóvis again joked with her: "This woman is full of manias and beauty concerns; she is too spoiled. If one doesn't do what she wants, she cries nonstop. If I don't go there and take her out of her bed, she stays there in the room. There are several grandmas that let only me bathe them."

Why was he telling me that?

Catarina interjected: "He caresses us . . . then pretends that he doesn't understand."

"But I cannot treat you badly. When I bathed patients at the São Paulo, I never mistreated any of them."

Such a defensive speech.

To this point, I had interpreted Catarina's words as this: "I have become mentally disordered to the family, to the doctors, to the world. Abandoned in Vita, everything that I sustain as a social link is dying with me." But, as she insisted, this was not all her subjectivity was reduced to: there was love in Vita. And where there is love, there is a sexual relation that "does not stop not being written" (Lacan 1998:94).

I now began to work with the following interpretation: since Catarina ultimately could not say "I do" to life, through her relationship to Clóvis—imagined or real—she was stating: "I now love the person who knows how to know me, the person who handles the medication." In pharmaceutical abandonment, Catarina surrendered her body to that man. "To be sincere," she wrote in her new dictionary, "I want to offer my love to Jesus, the gynecologist, the pediatrician, the pharmacist, the masseur, the psychiatrist, the nurse."

"I do it all," repeated Clóvis, "bathing, injections, bandaging, everything. With many of them up here, you must open the wounds and take the worms out." He offered a description that was medicine as perverse craft.

"One of our inmates had little animals in his left eye. It was a cancer, I think, and I began to take care of it. I had to take whole balls of pus out. One day, Cobrinha, that woman who is tied up against the tree, escaped and hit his eye. There was blood flowing everywhere. Oh, God, we had to do the cleaning. He didn't take care, and flies got in there. A few days later, I took some twelve animals out. We couldn't get them all out with tweezers. So I prepared a kind of medication. . . . I got the disinfectant that we use to clean the toilet, put a few spoons in a glass, added serum and flour and prepared a plaster, put it over his eye, and wrapped it. The next day, when I took it off, you should have seen, most of the animals inside the hole were glued there; the rest came out the next. I kept applying that plaster for a few more days, then put morphine in his eye, cleaned it, and again applied disinfectant. It seemed like it was going into his brain. . . .

"That night, when I went to bed, I prayed for God to have mercy on him, to take him and not let him suffer, or else to finally heal him. In the morning, when I opened the wound, I couldn't believe it. . . . I called the other volunteers, come and see Bastião's eyes. The hole had closed. It was like he had had reconstructive surgery. He is still alive."

Clóvis wanted me to believe, so he took me to see the disfigured creature. "He doesn't talk," I was told.

God, Sex, and Agency

Why do people convict me because of words?
Saddened flesh
Muscles in agony
I don't have to pay for a bill I didn't incur
I don't have to suffer for a crime I didn't commit
It is not easy to stay the whole day in the same place

I returned that afternoon. Catarina had written a few more pages. As she indicted the laws of her destiny, she also wrote of her powers under a new name, sex in abandonment, and a certain sightlessness that comes with the body of the Other:

I am the driver
I speak magic and I conquer man
Clóvis Gama
We do what is in our reach
Pleasure in the bones
Desire in the nerves
Rheumatic woman
Acute spasm, secret spasm
Acute pang, pang in the chest
The servant of the Lord
Love
I served a man not a toy

Catieki Ikeni Gama
Abandoned
Padding
Closed pussy open
Angel, if you have a body
Come close
Mask me

We toast, I recall love, relation, a hug, a kiss,
Cataract, conjunctivitis, eye drops
The voice that is too loud
Shatters the heart, the body
Sterilizes desire
Angels fear the loud voice

Catarina, I said, this morning you began speaking of how pleasure is passed to the other person, of sexual tension.

But she did not let me finish recollecting where our conversation had left off and instead began talking about the medication she was taking. Medication, I thought, is the instrument through which she understands her experience and recounts the psyche.

"Now I take a capsule and two small vitamins. . . . I think so. . . . It is because my mouth is inflamed and to gain weight, to preserve the body."

How do you feel when you take the medication?

"The vitamins make me hungry."

And your mind?

"I sleep the whole night . . . when Lili does not wake me up. Poor Lili, she wakes up and asks, 'Do you know who God is?'"

Who is God?

"It is much love."

Catarina then began repeating things she had mentioned before, and the account became increasingly elliptical and confused.

"When I and my ex-husband were together, God gave me three children. I consider many parts in the human. . . . Sex is the part that transmits desire. I always want my partner to feel well. My thought at the moment of sex is without limits. In the act, the person alleviates my and his drive. I know this. The proof is that my brothers are very calm. They talk and say what they feel. I have a side of the brain that does not work well because of the others . . . because of my ex-husband. He was illiterate. He did not like to hold a pen, but I did. I taught my children to read and to write for the school. . . . He refused."

You said that one side of your brain did not work well?

"Yes, because of him. When we were together, there was a side that I had to forget. It was the side of wisdom, the science of the illness. . . . If we don't study it, the body grows worse."

Catarina, I replied, you told me this before. You also told me that you write in the dictionary all the illnesses that you had as a child and that you have now. Is this writing your own way of doing science?

"I think that when one is at home and is suffering, then one must make a medication according to what one is feeling. . . . Like Lurdinha, when she had a pain in her stomach, she didn't know what to do. I then told her to scramble some eggs and to smear them over her navel. Her pain disappeared . . . it was *mal de parto*. Did you ever notice that within the light part of the egg you can see the beak of the little hen? Many times I think that when we break an egg . . . good-bye . . . because it will no longer generate."

Is that why one smears the creamy eggs over the navel—so that the person doesn't continue to generate?

"Yes," she said.

Why didn't Lurdinha want to have more children?

"No . . . in fact, she couldn't have children. One breaks the eggs to God."

What does all this have to do with writing the names of the illnesses?

"One knows. . . . For anemia, there is Haldol."

And for amnesia?

"*Biotônico*, for not losing the memory of it all."

Catarina had mentioned smearing the eggs, a domestic practice that I suspected was used to induce abortion, followed by the antipsychotic drug haloperidol (Haldol), which did not correspond to the bodily ailment she mentioned, anemia. Then she alluded to a life tonic *(biotônico)*, an alternative medicine that I recall from my own childhood and that is still widely consumed by the poor to strengthen the minds of their children. Catarina wanted to move out of forgetfulness. This hole in reality that she was, a kind of living nonmemory, was revived through the constant signifying of the events that excluded her from genealogy and through precise and intense recollections of sex.

"When I was a child, I had sex on the plantation, with Sérgio and Oli. They were siblings and our friends. One was my mother's godson. I was flirtatious. I was seven years old. The oldest of the boys was twelve. I was taking squash home, and they stopped me. . . . I faced them and said, 'I will not run away from you.' They surrounded me and were afraid that I would escape. I kept walking, and before getting out of the plantation, I said, 'If you want, it's here, now.' . . . He said, 'I want.' . . . So we did it."

Catarina continued speaking of childhood sexuality.

"I knew of sex because once we visited my aunt Lira's farm. My cousins were very curious, and we saw two pigs fucking. We wanted to see . . . and that pig, I don't know, drew a desire in us. This stayed forever in my mind. So I was already aware of sex before I did that with Sérgio and Oli."

After this story of farm animals evoking desire, Catarina paused and then said something that, in my mind, resonated with the story of the black lion coming into the house during her mother's absence: "I only did it because mother was not with us." If, in that earliest of recollections, the animal's proximity had provoked fear, here a certain human agency seemed to have emerged from a movement toward the animal.

"That first time I didn't bleed. I bled with my husband. We did it when we were engaged. Since I was certain that we would get married, I surrendered to him. We made love. It was good. Sometimes I felt pleasure. I know that desire and pleasure are very important for one's life, the body of the other, of the other person. . . . These things then go to the heart, and one can achieve many things—did you know that? The woman's menstruation is a regulator . . . not to get pregnant. If a person wants to have relations with a person with the regulator, there must also be pleasure for the one who gives the body and not just the one who writes the prescription."

Prescribed medication had mediated Catarina's expulsion from the world of exchanges (as if she were ignorant of the language she spoke) and was now the lens through which she recounted withering. This was what she was left with: "enjoyment enjoying itself" (*se goza gozo*), as she wrote in her new book. "Pleasure and desire are not sold, cannot be bought. But have choice." The opportunity to "restart" and a human choice were all she wanted. This was what Catarina affirmed in her love stories.

"I dated a man who volunteered as a security guard here. He bought me a ring and a bracelet, shampoo, many things. We met at night and had sex in the bathroom. But people were trying to separate us. Vera began to say that he was her boyfriend, too. So I gave back the ring. He refused to take it back. I said, 'I will not throw this into the garbage,' so I put it in my suitcase. After we split, he had other women here. . . . But as far as I am concerned, I was not his prey. I didn't fall to him. I wanted it. I have desire, I have desire. I am with Clóvis now."

Catarina refused to depict herself as a victim. "Clóvis and I have sex in the bathroom . . . and in the pharmacy," she confided. "It is a secret, but not so well kept." For her, desire and pleasure were gratifying, "a gift that one feels." During sex, she said, "I don't lose my head, and I don't let my partner lose his head. If it is good for me, I want to make it good for him, too." She was, in her own words, "a true woman."

Female reproducer
Reproduces
Lubrication
Anonymous reproducer
To fondle the aggressive lust
And manias

Doctor reproducer
Catieki Ikeni
Nurse, doctor
Private
Nurse on call

Scientific decadence
Kiss, electricity
Wet
Mouth kiss
Dry kiss
Kiss on the neck
To start from zero
It is always time
To begin again
For me it is time to convert
This is salvation day
Clóvis Gama
Catieki
Catakina Gama
Ikeni Gama
Alessandra Gomes
Ana G.
To restart a home
A family

The spirit of love
The spirit of God
The spirit becomes flesh inside

———

I was deeply disturbed by Catarina's reference to a continuing history of consensual sex in the infirmary. I again asked the captain about the reality of sex in Vita. He reiterated that "this doesn't happen here, and were it to happen, we would have ways to know it and stop it." Oscar also denied it but left room for doubt. "The truth is that we don't know what happens at night in the infirmary. It's easy for people to sneak in. . . . Now and then, I also hear rumors that my volunteers touch women's genitals when they bathe them. But if I have not seen it, how will I punish someone?" Oscar also admitted that once a security guard was caught having sex with a woman in the infirmary, "but he is no longer here."

I had also heard this story from Sassá, who spent her days walking endlessly throughout the infirmary, back and forth from the gate to her room and to the yard, where she smoked leftover cigarettes. On one of those days, Sassá asked me to photograph her. She told me that, a few weeks before, she had been dragged to the woods and raped by a volunteer who was also working as a security guard in the infirmary.

Sassá was from the northeastern part of the country and had worked as a maid before living in the streets. She did not know her age. She got to Vita "a little by foot, a little by hitchhiking." A truck driver dropped her off there. As for life in Vita, she commented, "Here, I do nothing. Here, nobody does anything."

How do people treat you here?

"Well. . . . But sometimes they tie us to our beds. They get enraged when I talk back to their orders. It's not only me, though, but almost everyone here. Verinha was also tied for many days. The only one they don't tie is Catarina. They untie us so that we can eat. They are bad. I don't know what they think, I only know they tie us."

What happened to your face, I asked.

"I cut it, with a blade."

And your arms, too. Why would you do this? I knew that cutting was a tactic commonly used by prostitutes to scare away unwanted clients and the police by displaying their supposedly HIV-infected blood.

"I drank too much and mixed alcohol with pills. I cut the legs, the arms. I liked it. I had the desire to do it. . . . Every time I cut, I had the desire to cut

Sassá, Vita 2001

even more. I didn't feel any pain. The more I cut, the more I wanted to cut. Now I stopped for a while. I was very crazy."

Sassá then told me that her rape had not been an exception and that what had been done to her was beyond legal action.

"João Pedro, Maria's husband, grabbed me and took me to the woods. I was not the first. He also took another woman who was here. He is in prison now, but not because he did that to me or to her. It was because he raped a guy who is in a wheelchair. . . . That's when people wanted to kill him. He hid in the school in the village, but people found him and cut his leg with a sickle."

As she described the lynching, Sassá painted a picture of Vita's recovery area as a true extension of local organized crime networks and as a haven for psychopaths.

"Some guys in the village went after him. They wore masks. They are dangerous. But the police came and took him before they killed him. The police had come here before—they took a man who had escaped from prison who was hiding here. I already saw much drug dealing in Vita. . . . Down there, cocaine, pot, crack. . . They have, they take. . . Up here, too. . . . There was a guy who brought cocaine up here and got pretty crazy. Oscar expelled him. Do you know that guy I was talking to at the gate? He said he is a psychopath, that he will spend some time here to see if he can rehabilitate."

I asked her the question I posed to everyone: why do families leave people here?

"They dump us here to die and don't come back."

In her newest notebook, below her new name—CATIEKI—Catarina wrote of the "legalization of bodies," bodies doing "a check-up of their cadaveric state and head," forgotten persons who "don't lose their sense of things."

Marked off as mad and left to death, yet claiming understanding and desire, Catarina signifies the circuits in which her experience took form and suggests that life is potentially inexhaustible. By tracking the many interconnections of Catarina's story, I hoped to achieve an understanding of her condition and of Vita as complex wholes comprising of relations among sets of relations, overdetermined and also always open. Catarina's subjectivity here is a complex symbolic, social, and medical artifact-in-the-making that illuminates the conditions of life, thought, and ethics in contemporary Brazil and beyond.

"When will you come back?" asked Catarina.

Tomorrow, but why do you ask?

"I like to respond to what you ask. . . . You know how to ask questions. Many people write, but they don't know how to get to what matters . . . and you know how to make the account."

I thanked her for her trust and told her that in order to make the account, I would try to find her medical files in the São Paulo and Caridade Hospitals, where she said she had been treated. Catarina agreed.

"I want to know what they wrote of me."

Lurdes, Iraci, Catarina, and João, Vita 2001

Part Three

THE MEDICAL ARCHIVE

Public Psychiatry

What caused Catarina?

After many frustrating calls to the Caridade Psychiatric Hospital, I got in touch with a social worker, who was kind enough to search the medical files thoroughly. When I anxiously called back, she told me, "Catarina had several admissions here and at the São Paulo Psychiatric Hospital. She has a history of mental illness in the family. A maternal uncle committed suicide." That was supposed to explain Catarina's condition: a madness that ran in her blood.

"More, I cannot tell you," she added. The rules could not be broken. The hospital would release the records only if Catarina requested them in person.

Catarina was brave enough to come along on a trip to the hospital to request a copy of her records. On the way back to Vita, she was quiet. When I asked why, she admitted, "I was a little afraid." Of what? "That you would leave me there."

Catarina Gomes Moraes was first hospitalized at the Caridade in April 1988. The records said that she was born the daughter of Dario and Ilda Gomes, on December 1, 1966, in the town of Caiçara, in the province's northwestern region. Married to Nilson Moraes, she was described as a housewife and as having finished elementary school. (In fact, as I learned from her, she had studied only until the fourth grade.) The couple lived in Novo Hamburgo, a town known for its large-scale, if troubled, complex of shoe factories.

Catarina returned to the Caridade in March 1989, was admitted a third time in December 1992 (this time referred by the Novo Hamburgo mental health service), and was briefly hospitalized in August 1993. Her last admission to the Caridade was in March 1994.

At the São Paulo Hospital, the province's most notorious total institution (it is the country's second oldest psychiatric institution, founded in 1884), officers let me access her records without even asking for my identification card or Catarina's letter of consent. There, she had been hospitalized in March 1992 (referred by the Novo Hamburgo service) and in January 1995. Most of Catarina's crises had occurred between 1992 and 1994, when she gave birth to her third child and her marriage broke up. All the people, places, and events to which she had alluded in our conversations appeared in the archive.

As I charted Catarina's encounters with these institutions, they seemed to be part of a pattern. She had been subjected to the inadequate mental health treatment reserved for the masses—the urban working poor. It was evident that the thoroughly routinized local psychiatry (caught up in its own struggle for deinstitutionalization, a push to implement alternative mental health treatments, and the proliferation of new classifications and treatments) had failed to account for her singularity, her social condition—or her biology, for that matter.

As a psychiatrist who once worked at the Caridade put it: "In practice, the public health care system does not pretend to treat singular individuals, and psychiatric institutions make patients' conditions chronic. The illness starts to be the person. In most cases, the patient acquires such a 'mad' identity that she cannot leave it behind anymore."

Doctors in the two psychiatric institutions had assigned varied diagnoses to Catarina: schizophrenia, postpartum psychosis, psychogenic psychosis, unspecified psychosis, mood disorder, and depression. I was intrigued. If Catarina's mental condition had remained by and large undefined and her diagnosis had softened over the years into an affective disorder (reflecting broader psychiatric trends), why had she ended up in such an extreme situation in Vita—paralyzed, categorized as severely mentally ill, and lacking social ties? How had this happened at a time when the state's psychiatric reform was under way?

According to the records, no real effort had ever been made to medically assess or treat what Catarina experienced as rheumatism. Why did she insist that her paralysis was acquired and not inherited? Some would call this insistence medical ignorance or denial. But, for me, her line of reasoning emphasized the work of time on her body.

In reading the file reports, I saw the signifiers of Catarina's dictionary coming to life. In its many volumes, she continually referred to medical institutions and professionals, diseases, diagnostics, and medications—all of it mixed with references to work and family life, politics, advertisements she heard on the radio in Vita, the national anthem, the Lord's Prayer, and more, as well as repetitive allusions to desire and pain. As her interlocutor and anthropologist, I tried to sift through all this, finding meaningful connections and poetic associations to the fragmented stories she was telling me.

But this was only one part of my search. I knew that if I stayed only with the dictionary and Catarina's apparently disconnected reflections, it would be easy to reify and dismiss them as psychotic symptoms. How had her "other possibilities of speech [been] silenced?" In Catarina's medical records, I saw something similar to what Roma Chatterji, in her work with dementia patients, calls the "file self" (1998). Notes on Catarina's treatment and discussions with family and health professionals allowed me to retrieve the patient's voice and, more important, the narrative of its alteration and the conditions of its present intractability.

As I mapped the various relational, medical, and institutional networks and practices that had mediated her abandonment, I identified a complex transitional field between the deinstitutionalization of psychiatry and its reinstitutionalization in a "typical" family. Caught in a moment of transition, Catarina was a subject bridging these two regimes. My interviews with doctors and public health administrators captured a generalized optimism shared both by privatizers and by people who advocated universal access to and decentralization of state services. Meanwhile, Catarina's psychiatric records narrated the pharmaceuticalization of care and her successive abandonment to the family and by the family, working in the end as proxy-psychiatrists. Thus, what began as an ethnography of social abandonment and then of madness evolved into an ethnography of transition. The enduring inhumane realities are indeed most visible in times of transition, but so also are the new materials and values of the forms of life and experience that, for better or worse, are being remade.

In what follows, the juxtaposition of archival and ethnographic materials exposes the instrumentality of a social and medical field that no longer anticipated anything from Catarina or for her. Excluded from a jointly created common sense, she was increasingly enveloped by a "deadening" language with a force of its own, which, as such, turned Catarina and her words into dead objects.

Her Life as a Typical Patient

Catarina was twenty-one years old when she entered the Caridade Hospital on April 27, 1988. Since she had a valid worker's ID, she was entitled to state-sponsored treatment. She was brought in by José Aníbio Lima, who identified himself as "self-employed" and her *compadre*. The term *compadre*, which literally means "co-father," usually refers to a close family friend; most likely, this man was the godfather of one of her two children, a two-year-old son and a four-month-old daughter. Even though Catarina was still married and living with her husband in a city district of Novo Hamburgo, the admission records do not mention him.

At that time, anyone—a family member or even a neighbor—could attempt to hospitalize an individual. A psychiatrist told me: "By law, you could deny hospitalization for clinical reasons but not for psychiatric reasons. It was common for people to go to psychiatric stations and say, 'This person is impossible to handle,' ordering us to take that person, leaving the person there. How many times we hospitalized when it was not needed!"[38]

Catarina's first admission reflects this common practice and also reveals that her own family was absent at the beginning of her psychiatric journey. Like all other psychiatric patients, she had to leave her possessions and clothes at the admission office, so that she could not use them to harm herself and so that she would not be robbed. From then on, she had to submit to the institution's rules and temporality. The records show that she did not speak. Her life as a typical patient began.[39]

The doctor on call recorded what he heard from her *compadre:* "Patient experienced behavioral changes in the past weeks, and they worsened two weeks ago. Patient doesn't sleep well, speaks of mystical/religious matters, and doesn't take care of herself and the house. She says that God gives signs to her when people mock or doubt her, and that she has received a gift of transmitting her thoughts to people." The doctor reported that the patient "had no clinical ailments and no psychiatric history." He summarized her psychiatric symptoms as "affective hypomodulation, hallucinations, grandiose delusion, thought broadcasting."

Given her "affective rigidity," several psychiatrists who read the files with me speculated that Catarina could have been experiencing postpartum psychosis or clinical depression. Her inner life and social existence, however, seemed to be of no medical concern, and she was, according to the psychiatric modus operandi of the times, immediately diagnosed as schizophrenic.

A psychiatrist working at the Caridade explained: "As doctors, we have to see the mental situation. Very few places do the social evaluation. Generally, the social analysis is done to verify whether or not the patient will be abandoned at the hospital." Indeed, one does not exclude the other. She could have had hallucinations as a result of a basic mental/biological problem and simultaneously been suffering from a debilitating social situation. But the fact is that as Catarina entered the world of public psychiatry, her personal existence was not simply disregarded—it was made hollow. Whatever she was expressing through her mistrust was dismissed as having no objectivity, no objects, no reference to reality—and this failure to explain her condition became the basis for shackling her to a diagnosis of schizophrenia.

Catarina was placed in Unit 3B, a female unit for chronic patients, and given combinations of medications at maximum doses, aimed at sedating her, controlling her aggressiveness, and alleviating the supposed psychotic episode. The doctor prescribed the antipsychotic haloperidol (Haldol), the antipsychotic and sedative levomepromazine (Neozine), the hypnotic benzodiazepine nitrazepam (Mogadon), and biperiden (Akineton) to control side effects of the antipsychotic medications. Catarina had entered the precarious but powerful psychiatric reality of the times, with its highly stigmatizing diagnostics and routinized overmedication.

Dr. Daniela Justus, who once worked at the Caridade, told me that this diagnosis and the subsequent treatment were quite common. "At that time, everybody who came in was considered schizophrenic, was diagnostically undifferentiated and treated as aggressive. Today, it is quite common to diagnose a mood disorder in a person who ten or fifteen years ago would have been locked into a diagnosis of schizophrenia. That's the way to work with an overloaded unit: sedate and do not particularize. Most likely, there was no lithium available, no laboratory exams, no ways to make dosage adjustments, so everything had to be done clinically, by trial and error."

A similar pattern played itself out during the rest of Catarina's two-month stay at the Caridade, as evidenced in the negligible weekly psychiatric evaluations and the daily nurses' reports. The two sets of reports were kept separately, as though they were unrelated. The psychiatrist met only once a week with the patient and then in a public space, either in the unit or in an office accompanied by nurses, with doors left open (patients were presumed to be aggressive, a threat to either their own lives or the lives of others). As the former Caridade doctor recalled: "This was an institution with persecutory anxieties. Never was a tie of trust established." The rest of the time, patients were left to the nursing personnel; sedation was a way of making things work. In short, there was no attempt to engage with whatever Catarina had to say, no assessment of her family life, no psychological follow-up.

If one can speak of any form of patient agency in these reports, it is present in Catarina's refusal to take medication and in her attempts to escape the compound. Paradoxically, these acts conferred truth-value on her diagnosis and her fate, marking her as agitated, aggressive, verbally nonmanageable, and psychotic. After her escape attempts, Catarina was restrained to her bed by force.

The only person allowed to take her out of the hospital was her husband, and he did eventually take her home. As the same former Caridade doctor put it: "To leave the hospital well meant being calm, sedated, back to the family—but not necessarily with inner conflicts resolved."

Psychiatric Notes:
28/4: Delirious interpretations with mystical content, history of recent birth. Lucid.
03/05: Psychiatric condition is worsening.
10/5: Patient is improving but is confused and disoriented.
17/5: Patient wants to leave.
24/5: Discrete improvement.
31/05: Patient is better, wants to leave.
6/6: Patient is well. Acute period is over. Patient can be discharged.
16/6: Patient left with her husband.

Nursing Notes:
27/4: Patient calm, slept well.
28/4: Patient calm, slept well.
29/4: Patient confused but calm.

30/4: Patient confused but calm.

01/05: Patient confused.

2/5: Patient calm and confused, slept well.

2/5: Patient agitated, refusing medication, aggressive with patients and nurses, restrained to her bed, sedated.

3/5: Patient agitated, weeping, wants to leave, using force and aggression, not accepting verbal management, was tied to her bed with male help, to liberate after sedating. Supervisor ordered patient to be out of restraint. Patient calm but confused.

4/5: Patient calm but confused.

6/5: Patient didn't accept medication, is verbally aggressive, does not respond to verbal management.

The reports for the next two weeks were basically the same. As of May 25, Catarina began to participate regularly in group activities, and the reports reiterate: "Patient calm, slept well." Notes for the month of June refer to a throat infection and a certain agitation because she did not receive visitors. Finally, on June 16, Catarina left with her husband, Nilson Moraes. Dr. João Renato, who had seen her weekly, discharged her with the note "improved," prescribing a continuation of the drug regimen she was already on. This was typical for the treatment of schizophrenia at the time.

Paradoxically, the doctor seemed to have realized that Catarina was not a case of schizophrenia, at least not a typical one, because upon her discharge he suggested a different diagnostic hypothesis: "acute paranoid reaction." This shift, one can argue, however, may reveal less about Catarina's condition than about the psychiatry of that day, marked as it was by a fluctuation between the closed diagnosis of schizophrenia and the diagnosis of affective disorder. The limited resources for treatment available in public institutions also narrowed the possibility of a carefully considered diagnosis.

Democratization and the Right to Health

Brazil's progressive constitution of 1988 proclaimed health the right of all and asserted that it was the duty of the state to provide it. During the following years, the country debated and struggled over the issue of how that right could be guaranteed amid the restructuring of the country's economy and state institutions. In the early 1990s, health assistance was municipalized through the universal health care system, Sistema Único de Saúde (SUS). New primary health care policies were designed to empower families and communities, and new partnerships were established among the federal, provincial, and municipal governments. But the everyday reality of primary care was, by and large, marked by inappropriate physical conditions, inadequate human resources, and high and unmet demand for specialized treatments—not to mention the bureaucratization of local community health councils and the proliferation of private health care plans among the middle and upper classes (Biehl 1995; Bosi 1994).

The state of Rio Grande do Sul pioneered the deinstitutionalization of psychiatric patients and the creation of a network of comprehensive mental health care services under the slogan "To Care: Yes. To Exclude: No."[40] The mental health care system began to change in this direction in 1988, the year Catarina entered it. The province's psychiatric reform law, proposed by a Workers' Party representative, was approved in 1992. Besides legislating the progressive closure of psychiatric institutions and creating a network of alternative services in all municipalities, the law protected the civil rights of those experiencing mental suffering, particularly regarding compulsory hospitalization.[41] A similar law, which had been circulating in the national House of Representatives since 1989, was eventually approved by the Senate in January 1999. These prominent discourses on human rights and the practices of citizenship as related to health coincided with two other developments: the reduction of public health funding as a result of the country's economic and political transformations; and the widespread availability of new biochemical mental health treatments through the "pharmaceutical basic basket," a set of basic medications freely dispensed to users of the rapidly decentralizing universal health care system.

In addition to talking to psychiatrists who worked at the Caridade and São Paulo Hospitals and reading Catarina's records with them, I also interviewed the coordinators of the mental health programs of the province of Rio Grande do Sul and the city of Porto Alegre (run by the Workers' Party) and the leaders of the state's leading mental health activist group, called Fórum Gaúcho. While tracking the various institutional linkages of this mental health reform, I also inquired into local alternative services and spoke to mental health workers (psychologists, social workers, nurses), particularly in Novo Hamburgo, where Catarina had been treated at one point.

Catarina's files contain a history of both psychiatry and the country's movement toward social change (see Freire Costa 1976; Tenorio 2002; Almeida-Filho 1998). The files attest to a neoliberal undoing of a supposedly universal public health care system, to the entrenchment of a global psychiatry amid local struggles to provide comprehensive care for "citizens burdened by mental suffering," and to the use of these developments by poor urban families as the laws of the household were being rewritten (see Duarte 1986). As I investigated these changes in mental health policy and in the types of assistance available beyond the hospital, I found that emergent forms of social control also projected changes in subjectivity. Within these networks, interactions, and fluxes, a double of Catarina emerged—the typical and anonymous mental patient—that stuck to her voice and skin.[42] What follows describes some of this history and the political ideas involved.

In the late 1970s, Brazilian mental health workers began to mobilize politically around the definition and treatment of schizophrenia. Inspired by the anti-psychiatry movement led by Franco Basaglia (Trieste, Italy) and the Lacanian-inspired institutional psychotherapy program of La Borde (France), these Brazilian professionals, associated with various democratic, trade union, and socialist-leaning politics, began to orchestrate the anti-asylum struggle *(luta anti-manicomial)*. They harshly criticized psychiatry's support of military repression and its political role as "the science of order."

As psychologist Janete Ribeiro, coordinator of the Fórum Gaúcho, described it to me: "The history of madness is not disconnected from the history of people's struggle for liberty. When we began the movement, we were living in a military dictatorship, and we fought for all possible forms of freedom, one of which was to take people out of asylums. The hospital had been used to confine the mad and the ones who were seen as revolutionary, as a source of public disorder. To engage in the anti-asylum struggle was not just a technical decision and a concern for health; it was politically motivated. People with political consciousness began to fight this type of exclusion."

The Fórum Gaúcho is composed of patients, family members, and health professionals. Ribeiro was proud of its interdisciplinary, community-based, and democratic character: "We share decision-making power equally. The Fórum stands for social representation, for the community's participation and decision-making within the state. Throughout the years, we have been able to influence regional policy as well as help to build the national anti-asylum movement."

In this activist concept, the sociomedical figure of the "mad person" *(louco)* epitomized the basic lack of citizenship experienced by the Brazilian masses, seen as revolutionary *in potentia:* "the mad [are] denied the possibility of inscription in the space of the city, the world of rights, the practices of citizenship" (Amarante 1996:16). A 1934 mental health assistance law still in place at the time stipulated that any person could be hospitalized against his or her will. As of 1992, there were reportedly more than half a million "anonymous and silent psychiatric hospitalizations in Brazil" (*Jornal NH* 1992a; see Russo and Silva Filho 1993). The psychiatric reform movement campaigned for the extinction of psychiatric hospitals and their replacement by alternative family- and community-based treatments, the demedicalization and destigmatization of madness, the search for its socioeconomic roots, and the social regeneration of patients as "full citizens."

The 1988 postmilitary constitution gave legal language to the movement's demands: universal access to mental health care; comprehensive public health interventions; decentralization of political and administrative decision-making; stratification of health care planning (city, province, country); community-based decision-making. This movement had links to other democratic initiatives in the Southern Cone, exemplified by the work of Rubem Ferro, an Argentinian psychiatrist who helped to conceptualize local mental health services for the state of Rio Grande do Sul. "Mental health is not a problem for psychologists and psychiatrists," he argued, "but for the whole community." Ferro highlighted the recovery of the mental patient's citizenship as "the beginning point of a democratizing proposal" (cited in Moraes 2000).

I asked Ribeiro, the Porto Alegre–based activist, how the mental health workers' struggle had shifted from freedom of expression to health as the most important political right. Was this a way of forcing the neoliberal state to assume a social responsibility?

"The new constitution stated that health is a public good," she replied. "It is the right of all and a duty of the state—it posits the state as the one who has the obligation to promote health and quality of life. The background to our struggle is any form of exclusion, and health is a key to garnering people's solidarity. There is a tendency for people to support any action on health. We used health as an instrument for political alliances and as an instrument to pressure the government to guarantee social inclusion. We made the right decision. Health politics is one of the few places within the government where there is some form of social representation."

In Ribeiro's account, the representatives of the people, operating through the instruments of elected government and legislation, were forcing the state to honor its biopolitical obligations. In the effort to imagine a form of mental health that could be supported practically, the movement had to constitute a certain subject, a community, and a will. As we will see, other concepts and practices of health and subjectivity that accompanied new technologies and institutional arrangements would eventually undermine these ideals, and, in the process, unexpected "space-times" would emerge. According to Gilles Deleuze, space-times are spontaneous and fleeting windows of opportunity that emerge as dominant forms of knowledge/power take shape. Like events "that can't be explained by the situation that gives rise to them, or into which they lead," space-times "appear for a moment, and it's that moment that matters, it's the chance we must seize." Deleuze emphasizes the inherent "real rebelliousness" and creativity of space-times as minorities seize them and resist control (Deleuze 1995:176). In my ethnographic work within this local mental health transition, I saw how people, particularly health professionals and families, took emerging space-times less as a means to an alternative "becoming" and more as a strategic chance to buttress everyday forms of rule that were tentatively in course (thus practically redirecting both old and new forms of knowledge/power).

A new mental health concept was in the making: *debiologize pathology and sociologize suffering*. Ribeiro stated: "People are getting poorer, and we know that all forms of social and economic exclusion promote mental suffering." While government created new pathways of differential access to public health and welfare, the mental health reform movement understood that the market was a constant determining factor and argued that citizens should see themselves as potential mental sufferers whose task was to revolutionize state care.

"At that time, we had a medical concept of illness and health, and since policies were framed according to specific diseases, there was a dispute among the sufferers about which condition had more status. So we created this concept of *citizens burdened by mental suffering*, which includes all people who identify themselves as experiencing mental suffering. . . . It does not matter if the person is schizophrenic, neurotic, alcoholic . . . that person will receive dignified treatment without the label of the disease."

The reform movement challenged confinement, emphasized new democratic and legal institutions, and established channels through which citizens could claim their rights. As Ribeiro asserted: "The psychiatric hospital should not be anybody's home. The movement began to work with the Public Ministry. As a result, psychiatric hospitalizations today have rigid criteria. All hospitalizations must be communicated to the Public Ministry within twenty-four hours. The ministry has a team that goes to the hospitals and verifies whether patients were involuntarily admitted. They also call on us to check some dubious cases." As a consequence, the psychiatric system is no longer overfilled; "it can now define who its target public is." The family became more visible in these new legal transactions, and, as the state grew more accountable to the citizen, triage of services became an unintended effect, as we will see later.

The reform movement's struggle for comprehensive attention to mental health was locally implemented by new ambulatory services (part of what Basaglia termed "emergency welfare"; see Scheper-Hughes and Lovell 1987) and by the creation of the Centers for Psychosocial Attention (CAPS). The ambulatory services were meant to receive and treat deinstitutionalized patients as well as those who would otherwise be hospitalized. People's expectations had to change, Ribeiro observed: "In people's minds, treatment meant hospitalization. We had to change that. Now people can be treated in outpatient clinics and followed up at home." Psychiatric hospitalizations were to be limited to extreme cases in which ambulatory care and family containment were no longer possible.

A federal decree of January 29, 1992, regulated the interdisciplinary psychosocial treatment offered by CAPS and allowed municipalities to receive federal funds for such treatment (see Goldberg 1994:99–141, 151). At CAPS, questions concerning the true nature of psychosis and the best medical way to treat it were displaced by the problem of how the individual was culturally recognized as psychotic. The choice of therapeutic action was guided by a strategy aimed at restoring the person's temporarily lost normal functioning vis-à-vis his or her environment. A central part of this therapeutic intervention involved helping the person to resume acting as a moral subject (Goldberg 1994:12).

In treating patients, CAPS professionals (psychologists, psychiatrists, social workers, nurses, nutritionists, occupational therapists) considered socioeconomic and psychodynamic aspects of mental suffering as well as family ties. They provided different types of therapy, intended to allow the patient's unique experiences to emerge and be addressed. Several theoretical languages were deployed at the same time: the patient was thought of as a citizen, as a subject of the unconscious, and as an individual who could be neurochemically regulated. The positivist foundation of medical knowledge was replaced by disciplinary reflexivity and "the primacy of the ethical." As psychoanalyst Jurandir Freire Costa writes: "There is no way one can speak of psychotic behavior or subjectivity without bringing to the center of discussion the ethical ideal of the community/tradition to which patients and care professionals belong. Without the explicit acknowledgment of these normative ideals, we would not even be able to know what psychotic conduct would be" (cited in Goldberg 1994:16).

The process of addressing the patient as a social figure was to be mediated by a family contract, in which family members took responsibility for home care. "Before, the family exempted itself completely from treatment, and the state made all the decisions about that subject, over life and death. But today, with this new modality of mental health attention, we begin with a dialogue with the family. We make the family commit itself to care—at least one person must follow the treatment—and we put the family within the treatment itself. So, through this suffering person, we also begin to provide treatment of sorts to the remaining family," stated Ribeiro.

A psychotic's recurring crises do not allow the creation of stable references, a problem, as Jairo Goldberg has noted, that was only exacerbated by the way mental health services had been structured historically: "Constantly differing referrals or nontreatments end up making the symptom something permanent" (1994:113). The services of CAPS were thus conceived as an alternative form of listening and interpreting, of temporality and citizenship.[43] They encouraged group therapy and helped to provide literacy and occupational therapies. These services operated with continuous attention: patients who dropped out were contacted and routines reestablished. Several model services based on the principles and therapeutic strategy of CAPS acquired high profiles in regional and national mental health politics; they were portrayed as collective creations, suggesting a level of community participation that in fact rarely existed. In the province of Rio Grande do Sul, two cities became models of such forms of psychosocial rehabilitation: São Lourenço and Novo Hamburgo—the service where, according to the medical records, Catarina had once been treated.

This new practice of mental health was established as a paradigm in the final report of Brazil's Tenth National Health Conference. This yearly event, established in 1986, brings together representatives of civil society and establishes guidelines for public policy (for example, it was responsible for the approach to universal health care proposed in the 1988 constitution). As the Tenth Conference further politicized this psychosocial approach to mental health, it also, interestingly, highlighted the place of subjectivity in governance:

Comprehensive health assistance to a person burdened by mental suffering should give priority to family and community participation in health delivery. The psychiatric and hospital-centered model should be replaced by treatment offered in local health units, in centers of psychosocial care, transitional housing for sufferers, outpatient clinics, and, when necessary, by short-term hospitalizations in general hospitals. The construction and expansion of psychiatric hospitals [are] prohibited, as is compulsory hospitalization. . . . All spheres of government shall establish plans that guarantee humane, ethical, and rehabilitative assistance founded on the full exercise of citizenship and on the reactivation of the subjectivity of those burdened by mental suffering. . . . *These plans should stipulate the human and material resources necessary to address the epidemiological, cultural, and social characteristics of the local population and submit them for consideration and approval to the local Health Council. . . . Health Councils shall constitute Psychiatric Reform Committees that shall demand from local authorities mental health projects that incorporate this comprehensive care proposal and follow through on its implementation. (Décima Conferência Nacional de Saúde—SUS 1996; my emphasis)*

This manifesto suggests how the mental health reform movement was transformed in the midst of Brazil's neoliberal predicament, becoming a highly bureaucratized ethics committee of newly qualified political actors. They intended to represent mental health user groups and idealized families and communities, which were themselves understood as a society that could "reproduce the market and the state," as Ribeiro put it. Here, ethics necessarily focused on the allocation of increasingly scarce health resources.

Even if the meager funds reached only the model services, the theory ran, this could at least highlight a form of more egalitarian citizenship and thereby confer visibility on an alternative government for the people—specifically, that of the Workers' Party, which had been heralding the psychiatric reforms. The key political battle in this dynamic involved legislation guaranteeing that the new mechanisms for demanding social inclusion would remain open in case of political discontinuity (after new elections).

These ideals and policies, then, formed the background of Catarina's expulsion from reality into Vita, where she remained unaddressed. From this vantage point, such democratic ideas and practices retained only a kind of ghostly texture, integral to the triage process that made Vita her endpoint.

The manifesto also stressed the social need to produce an interior space that coexists with these exterior practices of citizenship. Employing Foucaultian/Deleuzian language, the manifesto introduced the question of subjectivity as a matter of countergovernance: all spheres of government should influence the ways in which individuals and groups constitute themselves as subjects so that citizens might elude both established forms of knowledge and dominant forms of power.

But by tracking the reality of Catarina's words, I came to see that subjectivity is neither reducible to a person's sense of herself nor necessarily a confrontation with the powers that be. It is rather the material and means of a continuous process of experimentation—inner, familial, medical, and political. Always social, subjectivity encompasses all the identifications that can be formed by, discovered in, or attributed to the person. Although identification-making mechanisms are quite difficult to detect, this process of subjective experimentation is the very fabric of moral economies and personal trajectories that are doomed not to be analyzed. I am thinking here of a diffused form of governance that occurs through the remaking of moral landscapes as well as the inner transformations of the human subject. By staying as close as I could, for as long as I could, to Catarina's struggles to articulate desire, pain, and knowledge, I also came to see the specificity and pathos of subjectivity and the possibilities it carries. While her sense of herself and of the world was perceived as lacking reality, Catarina found in thinking and writing a way of living with what would otherwise be unendurable. Thus, subjectivity also contains creativity, the possibility of a subject adopting a distinctive symbolic relation to the world to understand lived experience.

Economic Change and Mental Suffering

In many ways, the demands and strategies of the mental health reform movement became entangled in and gave occasion to the neoliberal government's moves in public health: the mad were literally expelled from the overcrowded and inefficient psychiatric institutions, little new money was allocated for alternative services, and the responsibility of caring for patients was left to communities that did not in fact exist. As Ribeiro recalled: "The process we called 'deinstitutionalization,' the government turned into dehospitalization. For them, it was easy—they said, 'Hey, there's a movement that wants us to take people out of the psychiatric hospitals, so let's do it.' And they did a massive dehospitalization. The government took advantage of the movement, for there was no legislation yet in place and no resources available for these freed patients to be socially reintegrated. There was no structure in the communities to receive them back, nor was there an alternative medical network in place."

Public hospitals such as the São Paulo released thousands of long-time inmates and began limiting admissions. By the early 1990s, the population of that hospital had declined from five thousand to fewer than one thousand. A report published by the province's largest newspaper (*Zero Hora* 1991) read: "Not even families want to take care of mentally ill patients." Although the psychiatric reform law had been approved, "few services [were] established. Some of the mentally ill were sent back to their families and communities, but many had no families anymore and are wandering through the streets, abandoned." "Many died," said Elias Azambuja, former director of the São Paulo. But the dead included not only those on the streets. Ribeiro explained that "the state no longer invested in the infrastructure of these institutions. There was no maintenance, and deaths peaked, either as a result of mistreatment or lack of care."[44]

There were now more mentally ill people on the urban streets than ever, undistinguishable from other leftovers of the country's unequal and exclusionary social project. It was in this context that Vita began to be replicated, in the form of the "geriatric houses" described earlier. In fact, these are "family businesses" or "money-making machines," as Marcelo Godoy, director of Porto Alegre's public health inspection service, describes them. These houses, in which the elderly, the disabled, and the mentally ill are thrown together, are an alternative for families no longer able to easily abandon their relatives at hospitals. Godoy found that "many families who had to care for their own relatives simply added a few more beds to a garage or a room in the backyard and, in the most makeshift conditions, began to make money out of providing care."

Families also learned to use the local mental health units to obtain disability certificates for their relatives, and the coordinators of geriatric houses turned these certificates into pensions once they were in charge of the abandoned. "We heard of several cases in which families simply gave the person to the institution with a pension card and never showed up again."

Around 1997, the municipal administration of the Workers' Party began to conduct public health inspections of these houses. With the help of the province's Human Rights Commission, Godoy and his team identified and raided some of these new commercial units. They estimated that 20 to 30 percent of the people in the more than two hundred geriatric houses were "psychiatric patients." They closed down a few of the houses, but others remade themselves as health institutions, minimally adhering to the city's sanitation demands. Many others became mobile sites—moving from place to place depending on the outcome of the city's inspection. Still others reopened in nearby towns that had no such restrictions. Institutions such as Vita opted to be officially classified as philanthropic sites of social rehabilitation, a classification that did not require inspection by city agencies.

"Neglect by family and by policy is the norm," stated Jaci Oliveira, a health professional who since 1997 has monitored the city's work with the geriatric units. "Even though we and the Human Rights Commission brought this to light, we have not been able to address the key questions: law and morality. This is a very lonesome battle; there are very few people who care about this situation." The public and state institutions have no need to deal with the problem, she commented sadly. "The necessity is something else: to find a depository for useless persons." Overall, these "family businesses" expose a thorough destructuring of kinship ties as well as the fragility of policies promoting social inclusion. "The intentions are good, but that's as far as they go: plans. Mainly they expose a generalized impoverishment—monetary, to be sure—but, above all, the impoverishment of human values."

Throughout the 1990s, the mental health reform movement struggled against the government's fiscal austerity and cuts in social programs, austerity that constantly jeopardized the rhetorical gains of citizenship and health as universal rights. It proved difficult to implement the network for alternative mental health assistance (CAPS), with advocates encountering much local resistance as well as a lack of resources. As a stop-gap measure, a continuous flow of ambulances from the interior began to carry the mentally ill to the shrinking number of increasingly ill-equipped psychiatric hospitals in large urban centers—doctors call this "ambulance therapy."

Private hospitals such as the Caridade suffered greatly from the lack of governmental resources. Although it is currently the sole institution in Porto Alegre offering immediate hospitalization, the Caridade has only about two hundred beds. As a local psychiatrist told me: "SUS was no longer funding these hospitals. In the seventies and early eighties, a psychiatric hospitalization via SUS meant a lot of money. Many administrators and doctors got lots of money; many psychiatrists then didn't need to have a private practice. But this system fell apart, and the impression is that, paradoxically, universal public mental health treatment is now slowly disappearing. The state's daily allocation for a mental health patient is less than the cost of a dog's stay in a veterinary hospital. I was not trained to do animal medicine or charity."

As the services of public psychiatric institutions became limited and institutions like the São Paulo and the Caridade withered, more CAPS units were created (parodies of the São Lourenço and Novo Hamburgo model services), and a few beds were made available for the mentally ill in general hospitals. Although this gave patients access to treatment that was less stigmatizing, general hospitals could not absorb the demand. In practice, the steady flow of people to local mental health services forced the institutions to begin triaging their services. In Novo Hamburgo, for example, three out of five persons who come to the service are likely to be turned away because they suffer from drug addiction or some minor personality disorder, explained psychologist Simone Laux, the coordinator of the House of Mental Health.

I also learned that although people can no longer simply abandon a family member at the hospital and disappear, many continue to request hospitalizations. Families now ask for such authorization directly from the Public Ministry. "The fact is that many public prosecutors simply stamp the authorization," Ribeiro reported. Through all possible forms of dissimulation and argument, relatives also manage to obtain hospitalization referrals from local mental health professionals. When this happens, as it did with Catarina, patients either go to the crumbling São Paulo or Caridade Hospital or are left to their own devices, usually ending up on the streets or in institutions like Vita.

In practice, the mental health reform plan has also faced the widespread availability of new biochemical treatments. As part of the decentralization and rationalization of universal health care, the government began in the mid-1990s to implement a nationwide pharmacy program in which municipalities distributed basic medication (including psychopharmaceuticals) to the general population. In theory, this policy was intended to lower the hospitalization rate and to strengthen family and community participation in therapeutic processes.[45] In reality, as I could see in my fieldwork in the southern and northeastern regions of the country, the program, even today, is marked by discontinuity. The availability of medication is subject to changing political winds, treatments are easily stopped, specialized diagnostics and treatments still have to be sought in the health market or on the system's endless waiting lists, and local services can rarely plan alternative treatments because of their restricted budgets and pharmaceutical quotas. In this study, I am particularly concerned with how the urban and working poor are involved in these developments as they rewrite domestic norms. The family is here a key "means and material" of sociopolitical operations and a central bearer of what emerges as reality.

This pharmaceutical policy has also taken root in the services provided by CAPS. According to psychologist Simone Laux: "People are always looking for more help, for they hear more and more that depression exists, that there is a treatment for it." Many people who seek mental health assistance request the same medication that other family members are taking. They come to group therapy to compare regimens with other patients. As I also learned, psychotropic medication has facilitated the process of excluding disturbed family members. That is, a patient's family members find ways to dictate prescriptions, adjusting the dosage as they see fit. Psychiatrists in private practice are described as regularly telling families, "Try this; if it does not work, double the dosage."

These everyday strategies and practices of "intensified disengagement," both familial and medical, are often not obvious to the mental health activists. Consider Ribeiro's insistence on keeping an idealized family in mind and on psychoanalyzing this moral economy: "We analyze this [exclusion] as being perverse, as something unconscious that is not done by the families on purpose. It's a defensive way of saying, 'This madness has nothing to do with me; it is not a part of me that went crazy.' This is a natural reaction to the psychic movement of the person. As you negate this being who is supposedly crazy, you are in fact negating a part of yourself. 'I will amputate you from my family'—this is an unconscious movement. If this is talked about in the house, the family can realize its own perverse moves of excluding the mad and the drug addicts."

This is not done quite so easily, however. As I learned from the abandoned in Vita, they were not left to die simply because they tarnished the family's social status; worse, they occupied space and consumed an important portion of the family's goods and attention. In spite of deinstitutionalization and progress in psychiatry, the marginalization and devaluing of the sufferer remained intertwined with the diagnosis and treatment of mental health. Moreover, as Catarina had been pointing out, the scientific nature implicit in the pharmaceutical management of her suffering made it easier for families and neighbors to dispose of the nonproductive and the unfit on "reasonable" terms as mad, noncompliant, or beyond repair.

The social dying of patients like Catarina is inseparable from the development of programmed and ideal forms of government and citizenship, community and family life, as well as different modes of structuring subjectivity. Here, the Other's death is linked to people's ways of imagining and practicing their lives—if not according to principle, then guided by priorities of cost effectiveness. In this perverse and crippling process, mediated by new pharmaceutical tools, the state acquires its local form as well (see Das and Poole 2004).

In sum, in the history of the mental health movement's ideas and practices, one sees the intersection of a number of developments that mark Brazil's current transformation: a health-related concept of citizenship guaranteed by new democratic laws and institutions—an imaginary practice, as far as the majority are concerned; a local biopolitics realized in pharmaceutically mediated bodily affects; and novel imbrications of family, medicine, and public organizations. Paradoxically, what is also realized in these configurations is a symbolic order parallel to the law through which, as Catarina put it, the person is "almost killed."

All of these elements were present in the way the Fórum's coordinator read reality and mental suffering as well as how she described the future.

When I asked Janete Ribeiro, "What is next?" she spoke of a model mental health institution, of Vita as an extension of the state-sponsored social change, and of the disappearance of schizophrenia amid a proliferation of market-induced pathologies.

"In the early 1990s, as we began to design new mental health policies, we wrote the *Project São Paulo Citizen*. With the help of organized civil society and progressive health professionals, we wanted the São Paulo Hospital to become a model of comprehensive mental health attention. Today, there are still six hundred chronic patients in the São Paulo, completely abandoned persons, with no family ties. Most of them are old and have been there for more than thirty years. Some are handicapped.

"The state is responsible for these persons. So we proposed constructing a kind of village for them on the hospital's land. These people would have their homes, and itinerant health teams would visit them periodically. They would also have work collectives in which they would learn skills and crafts and generate money. But previous governments never carried out the project—there was no political will to do it. They even threatened to sell that piece of land.

"Since the election of Governor Olívio Dutra [of the Workers' Party] in 1998, we have been lobbying with all that we have to realize the project. The chronic patients at the São Paulo are now being prepared to live outside the walls of the hospital. One hundred and forty houses are under construction. We are also making a great effort to ensure that a network of comprehensive care is created throughout the whole state. Municipalities must take care of their mentally burdened citizens. We are arguing for the legalization of residential therapeutic services . . . houses that can temporarily lodge some eight patients and that are linked to the city's outpatient service.

"So that all this can happen, we made sure that the governor appointed one of our comrades to direct the state's Mental Health Division. All this is very new. We are trying to regain lost time. We are making sure that the state congress approves most of our laws so that if the neoliberal government comes to power again, at least we have legal mechanisms in place to guarantee these public policies."

I could not avoid this thought: the members of the mental health movement make history through their model programs and law-making in order to survive and prosper as the professional citizens of a government committed to the "coming into social being" of "the excluded in general."

"Do you know of Vita?" I asked Ribeiro.

"Yes," she answered. And, to my bewilderment, she added: "Vita is one of those spontaneous initiatives that was generated to attend to society's needs and that succeeded. In the movement, we are not generally against these kinds of services that opened to care for people. Some of them are indeed very good. We are asking the state's Mental Health Division to select the services that are good and to include them as public resources available in the city. Not all assistance has to come from the state. Let us not 'statize' everything; we are not from Cuba. We consider Vita to be fulfilling an important role, and it is not from the state . . . but such services must be under the control of the state."

The vanishing of persons like Catarina occurs within the "coming into being" of Brazil's new regimes of health, normalcy, and citizenship. The death experienced in Vita is symbiotic with projects of economic and social change. In this coexistence, death-in-life as experienced in abandonment is considered nonviolent and self-generated, and thus killing remains unaccounted for.

Near the end of my conversation with the mental health activist, I asked her what mental health looks like after ten years of the province's psychiatric reforms. Interestingly, Ribeiro alluded to an epidemiological fading of schizophrenia and psychosis in the wake of a massive emergence of market-induced mood disorders—a diagnostic movement similar to the one I found in Catarina's medical records.

"Our movement chose schizophrenia and psychosis to begin politicizing mental health, but today we see that they represent only a small group within the spectrum of all mental health pathologies. The epidemiological profile of mental health in the state changed. A few years ago, we had the impression that all was psychosis, but not today. Today, we have a huge number of cases of generalized depression as well as the use and abuse of drugs. It is not that we think chemical dependence is a psychiatric problem, but what does this dependence tell us? That human beings are suffering from searching for relief in the world of objects. The market forces them to anesthetize the conflicts they face. This chemical dependence reflects a social dissatisfaction, an empty psyche."

Ribeiro suggested that schizophrenia might have diminished because of successful treatment and prevention measures, but she noted that further research was necessary to confirm that. She added that the mental health movement "works with the notion of plenitude: fulfillment is definitively included in our desire, utopia, and trajectory, but to reach it is a process. We cannot schedule its arrival."

Meanwhile in Brazil, the world's eleventh largest economy and one of four countries with the most unequal distribution of wealth, practices of citizenship and accountability outside the few model institutions remain family affairs or matters of triage. Sets of connections between a mutating state, economy, medicine, and family—what I call noninstitutionalized ethnographic spaces—work quite efficiently alongside established institutions in generating new forms of exclusion that drown out the person and ultimately determine the course of his or her life. I am interested in the literality and everydayness of this process: the making of life determinations. In what follows, I track how Catarina's physical and mental condition was molded in unconsidered familial and medical practices, how she became a nonsensical thing with no ties to this world.

Medical Science

Seven months after her first psychiatric hospitalization, Catarina was back at the Caridade. On March 2, 1989, her husband, Nilson Moraes, at the time working as a security guard at the Novo Hamburgo city hall, brought her in and asked that she be readmitted. She presented a document that used her maiden name and was duly corrected by the officer on duty: "According to the marriage certificate, her correct name is Catarina Inês Gomes Moraes." Based on information provided by her husband, the psychiatrist on call wrote: "Patient was hospitalized here in April 1988 because of agitation and hallucinations. Ten days ago, she presented the same symptoms and left her home. She was found wandering in the streets of downtown Novo Hamburgo."

The psychiatric symptoms listed were "hypomodulated affect, visual and auditory hallucinations, mystical ideas—she thinks that she has seven gifts of the Holy Spirit." Dr. Nei Nadvorny assigned a general diagnosis of "unspecified psychosis." She was started on the same drug regimen she had received before, although there was no note in the file to indicate whether she had adhered to it at home.

The weekly psychiatric notes during this stay reflected the standard lack of direct engagement with the patient and contained optimistic comments on her improvement. These notes speak of her hallucinations in somewhat contradictory terms. They also suggest that, early on during this two-month hospitalization, Catarina was, in some ways, confronting her doctor's authority.

Weekly psychiatric progress:

3/3/89: When admitted, patient was agitated and had auditory and visual hallucinations. She had left home and was found in the streets.

3/10/89: Patient says that I am not her doctor, that her doctor is somebody else. Confused.

3/15/89: Patient is improving.

3/22/89: Patient keeps improving.

3/29/89: Patient is doing very well, has no complaints. Refers to toothache.

4/5/89: Patient is improving, had dental consultation. At times, she still hears voices and sees persons, but they are distant. She does not explicitly refer to auditory hallucinations.

4/12/89: Patient is better from the hallucinations and is integrated into the unit. She can leave on April 14.

4/18/89: Family was contacted by mail.

4/19/89: Patient is well and waits for the family.

4/22/89: Patient discharged, left with her husband.

A separate entry in her drug regimen file says that on March 7 a doctor was called for her and that "levomepromazine was canceled because patient was suffering from hypotension." This incident suggests that Catarina could have been oversedated. As a former Caridade doctor put it when reviewing her file, "Haloperidol, levomepromazine, and biperiden and nitrazepam could, perhaps, be too much if she were a private patient, with a family member coming along in a specialized clinic . . . but here you had sixty patients in a unit." Yes, it is a matter of discipline in a "total-control institution with more than five hundred patients, with few resources and personnel." But there is more to it. I view this as a routine moment in which medical science is operationalized—treatment begins with a pharmaceutical surplus, which is either scaled down or not, according to individual bodily tolerance. And at what cost?

As I examined the records, the first inscription I had read in Catarina's dictionary came to mind:

Divorce
Dictionary
Discipline
Diagnostics
Marriage for free
Paid marriage

Operation
Reality

To give an injection
To get a spasm
In the body
A cerebral spasm

Thinking through Catarina's references, one can say that her diagnosis and discipline are likely linked to being cut off from her family ties. Without the ties, she is dehistoricized, like words in a dictionary. The reality of her body is the outcome of an "operation": a process, a business, a surgical procedure. This common pattern gains form in the pharmaceutical "injection," which in turn induces the symptom "in the body." Yet this symptom— "a cerebral spasm"—connects the technical and the biological.

I returned to Catarina's files. While medication is supposed to do the job, this pharmaceutically fueled psychiatric automatism has real biological effects beyond those of sedation and "improvement." Typical patients like Catarina often worsen in the course of their passage through psychiatry, by and large remaining unable to do anything with their lives. This is the normal course for those who do not have the funds to be treated as individuals by doctors in private practice, and certain politics, scientific measures, and technicalities are specific to it. "The system," said the doctor who once worked at the Caridade, "has to do with this. . . . This also has to do with the times." My interest is in how the sciences and the practitioners of these times assess the mental and how these interventions influence the individual's physiology.

The work of Ludwik Fleck is illuminating in this regard. In his book *Genesis and Development of a Scientific Fact* (1979), Fleck emphasizes how the making of scientific fact is related to reigning "thought-styles"—shaped by concepts, technologies, and value systems—and how the making of facts also alters social relations and experience. He shows, for example, that in order for syphilis to be perceived as an empirical-therapeutic disease entity—that is, as an undoubtedly "real fact"—certain aspects such as its response to mercury had to come to the fore, and other aspects such as the notion of "carnal scourge" had to be disregarded (5, 6).[46] Fleck writes: "In the course of time, the character of the concept has changed from the mystical, through the empirical and generally pathogenetical, to the mainly etiological. This transformation has generated a rich fund of fresh detail, and many details of the original theory were lost in the process. So we are currently learning and teaching very little, if anything at all, about the dependence of syphilis upon climate, season, or the general constitution of the patient. Yet earlier writings contain many such observations. As the concept of syphilis changed, however, new problems arose and new fields of knowledge were established, so that nothing here was really completed" (19).

The contentiousness over the scientific status of schizophrenia and psychosis makes these diagnoses an everyday site for thought experimentation. It is crucial to hear Catarina's voice in relation to the common sense and the measuring tools that assessed and treated her. Certain ways of proving madness—conditioned and limited though they may be—are further authorized in Catarina's travails.

The Caridade's psychiatric records system does not account for Catarina's social and physical existence and leaves very little room for naming and assessing iatrogenic effects. Only in the nurses' notes do we learn that after Catarina was admitted and sedated, rendering her "calm and noncommunicative," she "referred to pain in her feet, as if they were burning. She also presents wounds on her legs" (March 2, 1989). Because psychiatrists were concerned with the course of otherworldly voices, Catarina was foreclosed from articulating the reality of her body. In the process, the possibility of a neurological condition was never raised, although Catarina herself expressed such a concern. Fleck argues that medical science defines the morbid as an entity by "rejecting some of the observed data" and by "guessing on non-observed relations." That is how the irrational becomes rational in its details, he writes, but that is also how other things are left unaccounted for and remain unexplained (1986:39, 40).

In Catarina's case, much was disregarded or subtracted from clinical reasoning: the normative ideals of her family and neighborhood as well as those of the health professionals; her agonistic struggle for or against moral adaptation—not to mention her references to physical pain. And the "non-observed" was subsumed under the reports from the neighbor and the husband and the automatism of public psychiatry. As I read the psychiatric files, I tried to be attentive to those things that were unaccounted for, and how they confirmed what counted as truth.

On the one hand, for example, I learned that there was no neurologist working at the Caridade at the time of Catarina's stay. On the other hand, as a typical mental patient, she was already locked into a patterned form of diagnosis and treatment.[47] A referral for an outside medical examination would have required the personal intervention of an "idealist," as "good doctors" are now described. Yet, as mentioned before, medication did most of the work in this context. Was Catarina's complaint of burning feet thus taken as hallucination? A local private psychiatrist told me: "The episode of hypotension and pain in her feet could be related to high dosage. We know that the kind of medication she was taking can provoke neurological side effects that we call extrapyramidal effects, such this one." Also, why were the wounds not acknowledged by her doctor? What had caused them? Had she fallen in her escapes from home? Were these marks the result of abuse?

At this intersection of overmedication and negligence, a different disease was emerging; it would not be addressed. The nurses' notes from March 3 to March 7 basically repeat that Catarina slept well and was calm. But on March 7, she was restrained. It all happened because she had wanted to keep a pen. "Patient very aggressive, didn't want to give back the nurse's pen and then threw it in her face. While being restrained, she scratched nurse Leopoldina's arm and hit Mario's back." The nurse supervisor was contacted, and Catarina was physically controlled and sedated.

In the afternoon of that same day, her blood pressure lowered dramatically, and "levomepromazine was suspended until new evaluation." Medication instead of the pen: physical alteration and nonwriting. "Patient slept well, a bit confused." And so it goes in the records until her discharge, back to an unknown and most likely violent and fractured domestic world: "Patient slept well. Confused. Eating. Helping in the kitchen. Patient calm, without alterations."

Catarina's hallucinations, symptoms, and farcical cures sustain common sense: the knowledge and practices this family and the medical institutions produce to uphold their routines and normal functioning—*rituals of depersonalization, the life of medication, and the mortification of the body*. In Catarina's most desocialized state, one sees how human relations and technical and political dynamics become the substance of psychopathological processes. Here, the psychiatric process requires that the plurality, instability, and flux that compose Catarina's environment and experience be ignored and that her inner life be restrained, annulled, even beaten out of her.

As this operationalized medical science speaks, Catarina's voice disappears. Psychosis is treated as if it were the question of an Other that does not concern us. And with the social and subjective grounds erased from the clinical picture, there is nothing to motivate a search for causes. The cause of Catarina's condition is simply assumed by this medical science, as experimentation on all sides—family, public health, institutional, diagnostic, pharmaceutical—gains body. As she is depersonalized and overmedicated, something sticks to Catarina's skin—the life-determinants she can no longer shed. And what comes to mind is the unspoken question posed by Catarina's body of words: Why do I have to die for you to realize the way life is?

End of a Life

To my surprise, the São Paulo Psychiatric Hospital had lengthy records of conversations between Catarina and Dr. Ada Ortiz, a resident psychiatrist. The names, incidents, and dates I had heard repeatedly from Catarina were also recorded there.

Catarina was brought in by her husband on March 6, 1992. This time, she had a referral from the Novo Hamburgo mental health service. The referral stated that she was suffering from "postpartum psychosis and depression" and that "ambulatory treatment was not possible." Catarina was first screened by Dr. Carlos Garcia Viato, who identified an "acute psychotic episode: patient does not sleep, does not eat, escapes to the streets."

Catarina's admission chart had two entries: information provided by her husband and a description of the "social situation." Interestingly, the latter entry repeats almost precisely the husband's account. Catarina did not speak. Here, the husband was portrayed as "cooperative and affectionate"— in stark contrast to the picture Catarina had been painting for me. The doctor's writing endorsed the husband's version, and this portrayal would form the substance of Catarina's treatment there, both medical and human:

Patient lives with husband and children. A month ago, she had a baby, who was born prematurely. At this time, she also lost a sister-in-law. Patient says that the sister-in-law has not died and that the baby has died. She has two older kids. She does not sleep, does not eat, leaves home, and wanders through the city without direction. She says that she has the Holy Spirit in her head and that the family does not understand her. She already had similar episodes in the past and was then hospitalized at the Caridade Hospital. The husband said that he has help from the Novo

Hamburgo city hall, where he works. He is very cooperative and affectionate and said that he will help her to follow the treatment. He said that the patient has mental health problems in the family, that her mother was mentally ill.

A new variable emerges here: Catarina's mental condition can be traced to heredity. How true is this? By this time, the state's psychiatric deinstitutionalization plans were already on course, and families now needed more than their own will to ensure a relative's hospitalization. A new form of knowledge, then, was being introduced to account for Catarina's crisis. "You wouldn't imagine what one family member does to hospitalize another," a local psychiatrist told me. Whether this was true or false, from that moment on, Catarina's episodes would recur ever more frequently, always discursively framed in the form of maternally inherited madness.

That same day, Dr. Ada Ortiz spoke to Catarina; she was put in charge of Catarina's treatment in the month that followed. "Counter-transference is one of empathy," she wrote. According to Dr. Ortiz's initial notes, Catarina "looked her real age" and was dressed "simply, but appropriately." Catarina's intelligence was acknowledged as "average," her language skills as "adequate," and her affect as "hypomodulated." Catarina had some difficulty speaking and walking, Dr. Ortiz noted, "because she is too sedated." The patient was said to have auditory and visual hallucinations: "God speaks to her, and she sees God." Catarina's recent and distant memory was "apparently preserved." According to the resident, Catarina had "persecutory ideas," and her thinking was "predominantly magical."

The first time Catarina spoke, according to the psychiatrist's notes, it was to say that she had literally been misled into the hospital. Catarina claimed she had been told that she was being taken to see her newborn daughter, but instead her destination was the hospital:

Patient comments that she does not know why they brought her here. She says she thought that they were taking her to where her daughter is, but they brought her straight here. She was staying at Seu Urbano and Dona Tamara's house. They are friends and are helping her with the divorce from Nilson. Catarina says that she heard voices in her head. The voices left her confused, for she couldn't understand clearly what they were saying. Sometimes she could hear and talk to God, and God said that things should return to their place, that she should get a divorce from Nilson, and that Valmir de Souza would come from heaven to marry her.

Dr. Ortiz continued with the life history she collected from Catarina:

Catarina is the oldest of five children. When Catarina was eight years old, her mother fell ill and slowly became paralyzed. The father separated from the mother and entered a second marriage. Catarina studied until the fourth grade. When she was eleven, the father took her out of school so that she could take care of the mother and the younger siblings. The family worked in agriculture.

At that time, she met Valmir de Souza. He came with her father's friends to eat watermelons in her house. She liked Valmir as soon as she saw him. He had blond and curly hair and blue eyes. Her mother told her she shouldn't date young men, for they only wanted to use women for sex. She should only date older men. When the patient was eighteen, she met Nilson, her future husband, at a dance. She said that when she noticed Nilson, she told her brother, "I will dance with that guy," and the brother answered, "That guy is no good." Nilson took Catarina to dance, and after one year they got married.

They went to Novo Hamburgo to work in the shoe industry and had four children: Anderson, six years old; Alessandra, four years old; Bibiana, two years old, and Ana, about a month. She wants to get a divorce tomorrow; she will be better off alone, she says. She thinks that the mother will live again if she divorces her husband. Baby was premature.

Though it took place on the same day as her admittance, this second psychiatric review uncovered different elements of Catarina's migrant life. Perhaps Dr. Ortiz's gender and professional training played a role. Most noticeable were the reference to a maternal paralysis rather than the mental illness to which Catarina's husband referred, the association of her marriage's breakdown with her parents' separation, and the desire to reconstruct a past love story. In both psychiatric accounts, however, Catarina's marital conflict was framed as a persecutory idea; no real effort was made to track the couple's conflicts. Her problems with walking were dismissed as the side effects of drugs and, as at the Caridade Hospital, were not checked. A new diagnosis was attempted, however: "other and unspecified reactive psychosis" (a situational form of psychosis, the result of a life event). She was medicated with haloperidol and chlorpromazine (Amplictil).

March 9: Patient is feeling better, dizzy at times. Keeps saying that she needs to sign her divorce so that she can marry Valmir. She says that she is no longer hearing God talking to her. She would like her mother to return to life, but then she retracted this, saying that her mother suffered too much in this life and that she was probably better off up there in heaven. As patient walks, she stumbles and leans against the walls.

March 10: Patient complains of strong pains in her leg. She said she was still hear-ing voices in her head, voices asking for help, but now fewer and quieter. She has not seen or spoken to God and speaks about the divorce that she wanted to have signed yesterday. She wants to leave here well and immediately so that she can get divorced, take the kids from her mother-in-law, and rent a house to care for them. She wants to work, would love to work with clothing. She doesn't know how to sew but knows how to design clothing. She thinks that any work will be okay and that after the divorce things will get back to normal.

I asked her if she had a newborn baby, and she said, "Yes, it's Ana," and began to weep, saying that she would have to give this daughter away. She says that Seu Urbano and Dona Tamara will take care of the baby when she leaves the hospital and that she wants to go back to her first love, Valmir. She says that Valmir is in heaven. I tell her he cannot be in heaven unless he has died. She answered that he hasn't died, that it was her mother who has died and that she will no longer come back.

She speaks again about the divorce and weeps. She wants to divorce because Nil-son beats her and the kids. She says that he is very jealous and that sometimes he locks her at home so that she does not go out. He is addicted to playing pool. I asked if he drank alcohol. She said, "Yes, but not that much, and not always." She wept and said that she pities him. I commented that perhaps she has pity for herself as well. She kept weeping and said that she is mad at him because he beats her and the kids, and that's why she wants a divorce immediately.

At this point, Catarina was evaluated as "still having auditory hallucina-tions." Her consciousness was "lucid," and her thought was "predominantly logical with some magical aspects but without delirious ideas." She was "pre-dominantly sad."

March 11: Patient says that she feels better and that she would like to go home to sign the divorce papers. She says that she is still hearing voices of people calling and that this is like having a telephone in her head. She thinks this is naturally so. I tell her that while this may seem to her like it is really happening, it is because of the illness and is not natural, and when she recovers, this will pass away. Patient says she will work hard to be able to leave soon, but she does not want to return home to Nilson and would like to go to Seu Urbano and Dona Tamara's house.

March 12: Patient was sleeping on a mattress on the floor. I asked why. She an-swered that she liked sleeping that way, that she felt better, and that she wanted to go home to sign the divorce. She is still hearing voices of people and the telephone in her head, wants to get the children and live alone. Says that the name of the new-

born baby is Bibiana and that she must still be in the hospital, for she was born be-
fore the ninth month and was very little when born.

It seems reasonable to assume that Catarina was afraid of falling as she stepped out of bed.

That same day, Catarina's husband came to the hospital, according to a note by the psychiatric resident. A conversation with the doctor ensued:

The husband says that Catarina has already been hospitalized a few times before. This time, she got worse, for she had a premature baby who needed to stay in the hospital. She also worsened because her brother's wife died. After her sister-in-law's death, Catarina began to say that it was her newborn daughter who had died, and she refused to go to the hospital to breastfeed the baby. He said that Catarina never spoke of divorce during the other crisis. And that after a crisis is over, she does not like to speak about what happened and says that "she does not remember anything."

As a psychotic, Catarina was presented as animated by a suffering that had no object and as having no memory. In her own accounts, however, Catarina insisted that various people and circumstances kept her from her child. Yet it was the husband's portrayal of Catarina as not being herself in her denial of motherhood and her demand for separation, with no memory of her currents words and acts, that provided the direction for her treatment. Even though Catarina's words were extensively recorded by the psychiatrist—the physical abuse, the dispute over child custody, her intense desire to legally separate from her husband, and her physical disability—no one followed up on these issues. She was continually medicated, with no integration of previous treatments into her current regimen. The "psychotic process," one can argue, is constituted by the discourses and practices through which Catarina's "delusions" were approached.

There was no appreciation for Catarina's existence whatsoever. This was a male script in which psychiatry was symbiotic with conflicts in working-class households and collectivities. The exclusion of an unwanted family member was being set into motion. The husband and family helped the psychiatric professionals to reify the patient's delirium, receiving in turn a "truthful" frame to legitimize her eviction. As one psychiatrist remarked: "Families keep the patients ill in order for themselves to be healthy." Changing affective and moral economies were being realized. But the abandonment of Catarina must not have been an easy and straightforward process for anyone involved. There were sporadic visits, gifts, promises, returns home. Nilson's and Catarina's roles and obligations as husband and wife withered side by side.

In the records that follow, one can see that Catarina's release from confinement was incumbent on her ability to reestablish a tie with her husband. She learned that the domestic conflict would always be seen as her symptom and that her only way out of confinement was to return home, at least for a while. No one seemed to think that, once discharged, she would in all probability face more abuse and added discrimination as a mental patient.

March 17: Patient says that she dreamed about the children and that she misses them sorely. She wants to go home, is not hearing voices, but still has a noise in her head. Says that the only reason she enjoyed Nilson's visit is because he brought her cigarettes and that she does not want to see him anymore. She clarified that Bibiana is the two-year-old daughter of Seu Urbano and Dona Tamara and that she is not her daughter. Says that her newborn baby is Ana and that she will stay with Seu Urbano and Dona Tamara. Patient is apparently better, although sleepy; plays with a ball. When asked to draw, she always makes the same drawing: she draws a pair of pants, a dress, and a blouse. (*my emphasis*)

March 18: Patient asked whether the person who brought her to the hospital is the only one who can take her out. I asked if she was referring to Nilson. She answered, "Yes," and said that she would not like to go out with him, that she wanted to divorce him, that he hit her when things didn't go well. When do things not go well? I asked. It's when there are things missing in the house, when there is no money to buy food. She wants to divorce and to try to be happy with another person, Valmir. I asked, where is Valmir? She said that she does not know, that he must be around.

She said that she would like to work as a seamstress in a clothing factory and that, with time, she might be able to buy a sewing machine and work autonomously. Patient says that she wants to take the kids to live with her and that Anderson and Alessandra can help to take care of Ana. Sometimes she hears the voices of her children, but knows that this comes from her head. She knows that they are not here.

March 20: Husband visits her, leaving cigarettes and crackers. She treats him well, does not mention divorce, and asks about the children. She behaves adequately with him. After he leaves, she says she liked that he came only because he brought her cigarettes and that she was happy to hear about the kids.

March 23: Patient asked us to contact Nilson so that he might come and bring her cigarettes. Says that today is his free day and that he should come. She weeps and says that she misses the children. I asked her if she is missing Nilson. She says that she will make an agreement with him, that she will stay with him if he promises

not to hit her anymore. If he hits her again, she will divorce him. She hopes they
will be able to get things straight.

March 24: Patient talks about the family and her desire to find a new companion.
Says that she would like to find someone who caressed her and to whom she could be
gentle too. She repeated that she will give Nilson a last chance—if he does not hit
her, she will stay with him.

A medical note in the file requests a neurological examination: "Patient
loses equilibrium while walking; she holds herself against the walls. Patient
using haloperidol." The neurological examination was not performed.

March 31: Patient says that she slept well, that she dreamed about the children, and
then began to weep, saying that she misses them and wants to go home. I told her
that a woman called at Nilson's request to inquire how she was doing. I told her that
during Nilson's next visit we would discuss discharge plans.

Then, on April 1, the psychiatrist summarized what had supposedly been
learned about Catarina's episode and condition. The discharge note reads:

After the birth of her third child, patient began having auditory and visual hallu-
cinations. She saw and heard God, wanting to divorce the husband, and refusing to
see the baby in the hospital, a premature baby who needed to stay incubated in the
hospital. Amid all this, a sister-in-law died, and the patient began saying that the
baby had actually died. She had already been admitted to Caridade Hospital twice,
immediately after her two other children were born. Patient improved from hallu-
cinations; thought became logical, and patient had adequate behavior in the unit.
Diagnostics: short reactive psychosis.

In today's terms, the diagnosis would be called an acute brief psychosis.
Notice, also, the incorrect information alleging that Catarina had been hospitalized twice before following childbirth.

The doctor prescribed haloperidol and biperiden and discharged Catarina
on April 2, 1992. This was a fairly short stay, twenty-seven days, in accord
with the recent dehospitalization policies. In the end, she was domesticated:
"Patient left accompanied by the husband."

As I write this now, I am reminded of a report by Jacques Lacan on a 1976
conversation he had with a psychotic patient, Mademoiselle B. Lacan began
the case presentation by highlighting the general difficulty encountered in
thinking about the boundaries of mental illness and suggested humility and
modesty regarding the limitations of the analyst's knowledge. As for Mademoiselle B., in the conversation with Lacan, she identified herself with a

dress suspended in a wardrobe: "She has no idea of the body she has to put inside the dress. There is nobody to inhabit the garment. She is this cloth. She illustrates what I call semblance. She has no more existing human relations, relations to garments, that's what exists for her" (1993a:30).

Similarly, Catarina drew nothing but clothing and was at the endpoint of human relations. She wanted to transcend a reality in which her body had become a site of aggression and her voice had no familial resonance. Lacan ended his narrative of Mademoiselle B's case by stating: "She already has too many things to occupy herself with. She wants to value herself; she wants other people to value her, if they can" (1993a:31). The psychotic experience is connected to people's unwillingness to listen to and value the afflicted, what is left of the person in terms of human attributes. As for Catarina, she was still able to resort to her roles as a working-class mother and an independent thinker in order to envision something for her fragmented body: not as a semblance, a typical patient, or a subjugated married woman, but as the autonomous worker she wanted to be. She wanted a sewing machine, her children at home, another chance at life.

Voices

On August 12, 2000, the day after I found the São Paulo records, I went back to Vita. I told Catarina that I had retrieved some very interesting notes on her conversations with Dr. Ada Ortiz.

As you were admitted, the doctor wrote, among other things, that you were hearing voices. . . .

"That's true," said Catarina.

Which voices?

"I heard cries, voices weeping. And I was always sad."

Where did these voices come from?

"I think that they came from the cemetery. All those dead bodies. They nicknamed me 'Catacumba.'"

No longer addressed as Catarina, she understood herself as a burial chamber, I thought. What?

"They called me 'Catacomb.' . . . Once, I read in a book that there was a catacomb and that the dead ones were in there, closed up, the dead bodies. And I put that into my head. The mummies were completely wrapped. One mummy wanted to get hold of another one, who was suffering too much at the hands of the bandits. But when she came to help, a big guy came with a chain, and she couldn't get rid of the bandits. Afterward, that mummy was also put into the catacomb."

And how did the story end?

"They imprisoned her there, and the mummy became a corpse."

How do you think these voices got into your head?

"I escaped and read that book. I was sad. I was separated from my ex-husband. He went to live with the other woman, and I went to live alone. . . . Then my house was set on fire."

Dead in name, buried alive, looking for a story line in a book found as she escaped from home.

Was it then, when the house burned down, that you began hearing voices?

"No, it was much earlier—immediately after I separated."

The split of the I. "Separated." Catarina was no longer the person she had struggled to become—just as she had labored to learn the alphabet from her father.

Catarina again told me that "the catacomb is the place where you put the dead ones" and then made an astonishing association: "The cemetery was located on our land. My deceased father bought that land. The original owner made the price very high. My father took out a loan. One day he showed me receipts of the debt."

Back to Caiçara, the landscape of her infancy. She had literally grown up on a cemetery. I wondered whether the profuse allusions to money, banks, documents, public notaries in her dictionary might be references to this familial indebtedness.

You mentioned that your father introduced you to writing. . . . How did he treat you as you grew up?

"All right. But when I deserved it, he got the belt. He was very demanding."

What happened to the land?

"My ex-husband sold it. He never made enough money to pass the land to his name. . . . The public notary . . . there was never money to legalize things. . . . So time passed and debts accumulated, and then he was forced to sell it. . . . So he sold his and my piece of the land."

She had nothing under her name anymore.

I continued: Dr. Ortiz also said that your mom had died and that you were waiting for a Valmir to come, that he was a first love of yours.

"I remember. . . . Valmir was my first boyfriend, a boyfriend of childhood. He was called Alemãozinho. We didn't stay together because I had to take care of my mother. We were all young. It was before I met Nilson, my exhusband. My brothers told me I had to go through life alone."

Why did you say that Valmir would come and stay with you?

"I didn't say that. . . . I said that I dreamed about him. That I liked him more than I liked Nilson, that he was my first love."

So you told the dream to the doctor?

"Yes . . . and she thought it was true."

You mean that you were only telling a dream, and she thought it was a fantasy?

"Yes. But I actually dated Valmir."

Did the voices vanish with the medication?

"Yes, after a few days it cleared. . . . I recall that they also cut my hair very short. I looked like a boy."

This was how I pieced things together: Catarina no longer had a home with Nilson. She wanted to see her newborn baby and go to a friend's house, but she was misled and ended up having to solve the conjugal impasse in the psychiatric ward. There, she was not assessed neurologically and, caught up in a diagnostic fluctuation, was medicated as if she had not been treated before. At the ward, her femininity was symbolically annulled, and she had to relearn domestic servitude. Between her family and the institutions of psychiatry, Catarina was increasingly framed as mad and consigned to an order that was gone.

"He didn't want to give me the divorce. He was wayward. He wanted to have two families, two homes. He couldn't give love and take care of two at the same time. No man can do that. He hit me . . . in the arms, in the legs, too. . . . It got blue, the marks of his boots."

When he hit you, did he take you to the hospital?

"No, he went back to the house of this other woman. He had a kind of fear of me. Because I was always on the side of order. I always said that my way of living was that one, and it would continue to be that one. He kind of feared my way of being."

After a silence, she said, "I am Gama now."

Catarina again referred to what she had written and spoken about: "the separation of bodies." This time, she made it clear that she meant the phrase literally.

"When we separated, . . . the children were all mine. . . . But my mother-in-law went there and said that I was in no condition to take care of them. So she kept two in her house, and the godmother got the little one. We had to go to the judge to pass Ana to Tamara's name. We passed her to Tamara and Urbano and signed the papers, the separation of bodies. Two times, we stopped at the bank, and my ex-husband got money, but I didn't want to take it. Money from our welfare and for children, bonuses. I didn't want to take it. I was stupid, I think that I was beginning to get crazy. I think that if at that time I had picked up that money . . . "

Catarina was left childless and with no money.

So you are saying that he began the adoption process?

"Yes. He was the one who signed first. Then I began to get crazy. I escaped at first, when the kids were small. I didn't leave them alone. . . . I remember I had bad thoughts. . . . I only thought of —I had a melancholy . . . I suffered through my lots."

And now?

"Life is here, it continues. . . . Things go on, according to the moon. And now the moon is moving very slowly."

Care and Exclusion

In December 1992, eight months after her discharge from the São Paulo Psychiatric Hospital, Catarina was sent back to the Caridade Psychiatric Hospital. She stayed for a month and then returned once again, in August 1993. This time, she was hospitalized with a referral signed by a Dr. Gilson Kunz, from Novo Hamburgo.

Catarina had repeatedly brought up Dr. Kunz's name in our conversations. She said that he and the other doctors to whom her ex-husband had taken her had always been "on his side" and did not listen to her: "They said that they wanted to cure me, but how could they if they did not know the illness? If I count on doctors to tell me what I feel, I remain incapacitated . . . because they don't know the cause of what I am—of my illness, of my pain, they don't know a thing. They only prescribe."

I found the psychiatrist's name in the catalog of a local health insurance program, and I soon learned that his private practice was in very high demand. A local psychologist, one of Dr. Kunz's most vocal critics, was up front in his assessment: "He gives the patients' families what they want." I called Dr. Kunz. He politely told me that he did not remember a patient by that name, that it had been very long ago. But he promised to check his records nonetheless. When I called back, he told me that there was no reference to a Catarina Inês Gomes Moraes in his clinic records.

He explained that in the early 1990s he had also seen patients at the city's mental health service, known as Casa da Saúde Mental (the House of Mental Health, or simply "the House"). Dr. Kunz was still employed by the city, but, as his critic pointed out, "given internal conflicts with the House's team, he was reassigned to treat mental patients in the city's general hospital. The most difficult thing is to find him when an emergency comes up." Dr. Kunz bade me farewell and repeated that Catarina might have been a "public patient" and that I might find some reference to her in the *arquivo morto* (the dead archive, the inactive files) of the mental health service.

And there I found her. The House's records show that Catarina was first brought to the service in February 1992 (before the São Paulo hospitalization) when Ana, her prematurely born daughter, was fifteen days old.

Founded in 1989, the House has become a model for interdisciplinary and comprehensive care in the state. Here, health professionals are committed to dehospitalization and the socioeconomic etiology of mental suffering. They critique the possibility of an actual "cure of the mental" and envision treatment alternatives that "do not remove the patient from family and community and from the possibility of subjectivizing," in the words of psychologist Fábio Moraes, one of the House's founders.

The juxtaposition of records from the House and the two psychiatric hospitals is revealing. The interdisciplinary and more socially oriented approach of the House exposes the medical routine at work in the Caridade and São Paulo Hospitals and also brings us closer to the experience of the patient's escape from the ordinary. In the notes recorded by psychiatrists, nurses, and social workers at the House, as well as in what we can read between the lines of these jottings, we see shattered domestic worlds, the imagery of another world, and Catarina's failed attempts to speak of life otherwise. Within the context of the House's comprehensive approach to mental health care, the doctor's right to decide the patient's future is revoked and the family's "therapeutic role maximized," argued Moraes. But Catarina's records also offer glimpses of how the family (or whoever stands for it) interacts with and deploys the House's new dispositive care, often redirecting it away from inclusion.[48] We see, too, how even here psychopharmaceuticals mediate new domestic arrangements and subjective possibilities.

On February 18, 1992, psychiatrist Nilton Borges wrote:

Catarina has visual hallucinations about tragedies with babies. She saw a child hanging on a carousel and a tree trunk that was broken and bleeding. She escapes from home. She has been like this since the premature birth of her baby. She doesn't recall the birth. She is disoriented in time and space and has disaggregated thoughts. She has a history of previous psychiatric hospitalizations. Husband was unable to inform us of which medication she had been using. The child will be taken care of by the wife of the chief of the municipal guard. Diagnostic hypothesis: postpartum psychosis.

As Catarina had told me, her nuclear family was disintegrating at that time, with Nilson already seeing another woman. In his report, Dr. Borges added that "it is the second time that she has had a crisis after giving birth," as if the crisis was related only to becoming a mother. (Interestingly, Catarina's growing paralysis would later also be mistakenly described as originating from the birth of her second daughter, as a complication of labor.) Catarina was sedated with an injection of haloperidol and was prescribed haloperidol and biperiden. Medication stands in for and mediates the broken family dynamics: the husband made it clear that he did not know her previous treatment regimen, but he was nonetheless instructed to administer the new one. Medication was supposed to do the work of cure at home, as if family affection or care could still be relied on. Since Catarina was ill, another woman would replace her in caring for the newborn. Roles had been recast.

The husband was told to bring Catarina back to the House in three days for a follow-up. But the broken household had a different sense of time than the mental health service, and the couple returned a week later, on February 25. This time, Catarina spoke: only the legal action of separation could bring the disorder of the world to an end.

Catarina remains delirious. She has mystical ideas and ideas of grandeur. She says that she is in contact with God and has been chosen by Him. Visual hallucinations—signs of God. She insists on getting a divorce so that the illnesses and the confusion of the world might come to an end. The family situation is unbearable. Patient should keep using the same medication.

This time, surprisingly, Dr. Borges added that "the husband is part of the delirium." Given the problematic family situation and the husband's participation in the delirium, Dr. Borges recommended hospitalization. The family structure was sick and was causing her illness, but only Catarina should be hospitalized and then "return to the service after hospitalization."

A different family constellation came into the clinical picture on February 26: "Catarina and Nilson came to the service with Seu Urbano (chief of the municipal guard) and Dona Tamara. The couple said that they wanted to avoid hospitalizing Catarina and promised to take care of her in their home, with medical supervision."

The extended family was not in sight. Where were the brothers of whom Catarina always spoke in such loving terms? Instead, the migrant couple now had new and powerful connections. An unspoken economics underlay this novel domestic arrangement. Catarina was going to live in the house of people one described with titles—Seu and Dona—as signs of respect: they were her husband's boss and his wife. Who were these people who took in Catarina and her premature child, and why?

Seu Urbano and Dona Tamara reported that the couple's situation is conflicted and that there are signs of aggression on Catarina's body. Catarina says that the husband hit her with chains. She insists on signing the divorce and agrees to stay for some time with Seu Urbano and Dona Tamara. Nilson also agrees.

The doctor backed off the hospitalization plan and stipulated weekly follow-up visits at the House so that "Catarina and the new plan could be evaluated." In case this housing and treatment arrangement did not work, "new procedures would be discussed."

According to the records, the combination of separation from her husband and the medication seemed to be working. That is what Dr. Borges noticed two days later:

Catarina is lucid and oriented in time and space, and her thought is aggregated. She recognizes the newborn baby and is recollecting her personal history. Visual hallucinations? She repeats that Nilson beat her during this crisis and that she wants the divorce. She is thinking about how to reorganize her life.

Temporarily out of an abusive relationship and in a different household, there was no more God-talk. Catarina wanted to reorganize her life, not just to repair her self.

Ultimately, however, she was unable to work through this hope. The structures already in place drowned out her voice. As described in an earlier section, on March 6 Catarina was told that she would be going to see her newborn baby but instead was taken to the São Paulo Psychiatric Hospital, where her husband's account became her "social condition." The Novo Hamburgo mental health service was not notified of this hospitalization.

What made it impossible to keep Catarina at the foster home? Was keeping Catarina for a few days simply part of Seu Urbano and Dona Tamara's plan to take custody of her baby, who would soon be healthy enough to leave the incubator? In retrospect, it seems so. It also seems that the husband and his boss had contacts at the city hall who facilitated finding a vacancy for Catarina at the São Paulo.

Catarina's narrative of life reorganization was discontinued. The failure to socially carry through such a narrative might well be the crisis that is all too often mistakenly thought of as psychosis. Anguished, Catarina faced a new domestic order in which she was dispensable. What was left for her to hold onto?

On April 22, 1992, three weeks after her discharge from the São Paulo, Catarina was brought back to the House of Mental Health.

Catarina is still taking haloperidol and biperiden. She says that she is well. She is already taking care of her children. She is now critical of the things she said while in crisis, such as wanting to divorce her husband. She is lucid, oriented in time and space. Her thinking is logical and aggregated. She speaks little and basically answers yes or no, has no sensorial and perceptual alterations. She is sleepy.

The nervous woman and unfit mother who escaped from home had been transformed into a pharmaceutically domesticated maternal subject, a passive being who basically answered yes and no. The treatment of her psychotic crisis led her to assume the role of the typical patient as well as the role of the woman others wanted her to be. "When my thoughts agreed with my ex-husband and his family, everything was fine," she told me in our August 2000 conversations. In light of the archived records, it is easier to understand what she had been saying all along: "But when I disagreed with them, I was mad. It was like a side of me had to be forgotten. The side of wisdom."

In this process, "the science of the illness was forgotten." At that time, as shown in the São Paulo records, her legs "weren't working well" (as she put it). The way she was treated by the family and by the various health professionals, however, masked her physical ailment. "The doctors prescribe and prescribe. They don't touch you there where it hurts." The root of the bleeding tree trunk. This medical nonknowledge, suggested Catarina, had been brought back to what was left of the family in the form of continuous medication: "My sister-in-law went to the health post to get the medication for me."

During her many hospitalizations, Catarina had learned what she must become in order to leave confinement and reenter her fractured everyday life. In the meantime, her family and neighbors had found in the mental health services the means to codify their distance from her. As Catarina once told me: "When I returned home, he was amazed that I recalled what a plate was. He thought that I would be unconscious of plates, pans, and things and conscious only of medication. But I knew how to use the objects."

Indeed, Dr. Borges ended his report on Catarina's well-being this way: "Medication should be continued." Medication is the tie. And the debate over whether Catarina belonged to reality would be played out on this register: Is she taking the medication or not? Does she want to cure herself or not? As if it had all been self-generated. In Catarina's ostracized wisdom, this scientifically mediated moral economy makes up "a knot that you cannot untie." Science, for her, had become "our conscience." "Science . . . if you have a guilty conscience, you will not be able to discern things." Moral economy is confounded with this science in the body: "If we don't study it, the illness in the body worsens." Catarina was scheduled "to return to the Santo Afonso health post on May 5, 1992." There were no records to check at this local health post, but both Catarina and her family members repeatedly mentioned visits to the *postinho* (as it is commonly called) to procure medication and referrals to see specialists.

The Santo Afonso district is mostly occupied by "victims of the rural exodus," according to Paulo Bassi, Novo Hamburgo's former urban planning secretary (*Jornal NH* 1995b). In the 1980s, Santo Afonso was the end-station for migrants like Nilson and Catarina, who were looking for jobs in prosperous Novo Hamburgo. Wetlands under the city's jurisdiction make up two-thirds of the Santo Afonso district, but clientelism and a lack of policing made it easy for people to squat on the land. Substandard habitations and no adequate sanitary or electric infrastructure are the rule there. During the 1980s, the local newspaper, the *Jornal NH*, reported that the district's population officially grew from 9,260 to 22,000 people—an increase of 130 percent. The average growth for the entire city over this decade was 60 percent (*Jornal NH* 1995b).

A 1995 report on the Santo Afonso health post stated: "Some 120 persons are treated here every day. Ailments range from small cuts to affective needs" (*Jornal NH* 1995a). Most people looked for the social worker's help: "The majority suffer from problems in the family and are in need of emotional support." In 1997, social worker Flávia Ruschel, then the director of the House of Mental Health, was quoted in the *Jornal NH*, deploring the socioeconomic deterioration faced by people there: "There are places in the Santo Afonso district where the healthiest thing to do is to have a psychotic episode" (1997b). At that time, according to Ruschel, her facility could provide specialized and continuous care only to some five thousand people: "This is only a small sample, compared to the very great number of people and ill families that we lack the structure to attend to." The Santo Afonso, Canudos, and Lomba Grande health posts referred patients to the House.[49]

The next time we hear of Catarina within this local network of health services is on August 10, 1993. José Hamilton Bittencourt, the House's nurse, wrote in the file that counselor Lurdes from the Conselho Tutelar, the local branch of the Public Ministry, had called the House, asking about Catarina: "Since 1992, we don't know anything about her, and Dr. Borges is no longer working here. According to counselor Lurdes, Catarina set fire to the husband's clothing and also burned his documents. She has a four-year-old daughter with her. The husband wants to hospitalize her. Lurdes wants to do a home visit. But she wants to go with the municipal guard. In case Catarina is aggressive, she shall be taken first to the general hospital and then brought to the House."

At this point, Catarina's case was being mediated by new social actors and health professionals: the local human rights council, the citizens' representative, the specialized mental health unit, the local health post, the general rather than the psychiatric hospital, the nurse, and the municipal guard. It had now become more difficult to hospitalize the mad. In order to commit Catarina, her husband was now legally obligated to obtain the authorization of the Conselho Tutelar—all in accordance with the province's newly approved psychiatric reform law.

In the Caridade's records, I saw that Catarina had been forcibly hospitalized in December 1992 with the allegation that she was putting other people at risk—a threat that allowed doctors to hospitalize patients. At that time, the House was not contacted. In August 1993, she was hospitalized at the Caridade with a referral by Dr. Kunz and signed a form for "voluntary hospitalization." Is it possible that her husband got the referral from Dr. Kunz at the Santo Afonso health post or in the doctor's private practice? And did Catarina actually know what she was signing?

There is a complex field of operations involving the household, the local health post, the private medical practice, the alternative mental health service, the city hall, and psychiatric confinement. Through these interactions and movements, a reality principle gains form. As Moraes sharply put it: "While producing new possibilities of social existence and subjectivity, the House is also a mechanism that extends and complicates the control of individual bodies and the population's movements." He was analyzing the House's practices through Gilles Deleuze's idea of "machine"—technical, political, and social assemblages that make things visible and produce speech, all the while engendering control.[50]

The nature and strategies of social machines like the House of Mental Health change as they align themselves with other technical and political developments and as they are tinkered with by their users. Through these processes, novel cultures of care emerge along with matrices of normality, making it possible for some people—such as Catarina—to remain unheard and invisible. As she once told me: "One is then on a path without an exit." This woman was caught in unconsidered interstices of this machine's workings, where her chances for reorganizing her life were lost. Before going further into the medical archive, then, let me sketch the history of this city, its public services, and the patient population of which Catarina was once part.

Migration and Model Policies

I went to the Novo Hamburgo city hall, searching for information on the history of migrant workers, their settlement in Novo Hamburgo in the 1970s and 1980s, and how they transformed the city's social and economic landscape. "You will not find anything about those people or the history of those times. There are no registers," explained Rose Lima, the city's cultural liaison and herself a historian.

This statement evoked what I had heard at Vita after first meeting Catarina and inquiring about her: "She speaks nonsense. We don't know where she comes from or what her illness is. She was left here." Rose added that city officers "destroyed all archival materials related to the city's history when they bought the microfilm machine. They thought that was the modern thing to do. The films are boxed but disorganized." Catarina, I thought, is a clue to this migrant population, out of history's sight. She says that she writes her dictionary in order "to not forget the words." Life on paper. "What was and what wasn't."

Novo Hamburgo is known as Brazil's "Shoe Capital." Educational materials and tourist brochures portray the city as industrious, with German origins, mimicking a 1944 history by Leopoldo Petry. Petry highlighted three periods in the city's past. During the first, from 1824 to 1876, German settlers founded the colony of Novo Hamburgo as part of the São Leopoldo General Colony (which was then considered a "laboratory" for Brazil's postcolonial attempt at modernizing its economy and society; see Biehl 1999a).[51] This period was marked by the evolution of Novo Hamburgo into a trading post and by the construction of a railroad that allowed the flow of agricultural and commercial goods between Porto Alegre and the colonies. During the second period, from 1876 to 1900, the colony began to develop leather and shoe products and increased its commercial and cultural ties with Germany. As a result of its economic growth, the Novo Hamburgo colony finally separated from São Leopoldo during the third period, from 1900 to 1927. In the following decades, the independent town of Novo Hamburgo consolidated its economic growth and experienced an impressive urban expansion.

Petry's account contains only scattered and not fully articulated references to the native population, who either were killed or fled the region; to the slaves who kept working (illegally) for a few rich colonists; or to the politics of the fratricidal war that took place among German colonists in that region in 1874 (Biehl 1999a). This city, one can say, represents itself in a unified and nonhistorical mode, and its anthropology is a Germanist fantasy (Biehl 2002b).

There are no official accounts of what followed Petry's imaginary past.[52] In the 1960s, thousands of peasants, still German-speaking, migrated from the nearby colonies to develop the city's periphery and to work in the shoe industry. In the 1970s, shoe companies took advantage of federal government subsidies to further expand production for export. These were the years of Brazil's economic miracle. Novo Hamburgo became an El Dorado of sorts, attracting many in search of work and social mobility. From the province's western region, where Catarina and Nilson were born, city officials recruited an illiterate and cheap labor force. At the end of the 1980s, the city's residents had one of the highest per capita incomes in the province—but at least 20 percent of its growing population lived as squatters. This situation worsened in the 1990s, when the city experienced an abrupt economic decline and acute impoverishment, as Brazil failed to implement a more lucrative export policy in the face of growing competition from China in the global shoe market.

Today, the city presents itself in another way: as a model city. Following the norm for such modern and unequally divided Brazilian cities, Novo Hamburgo issues glossy administration reports highlighting how people's demands for housing, education, health, and security are being met. These reports contain, for example, plenty of statistical data on health (particularly child mortality), though very little, if any, information on living conditions. Policies designed by newly hired specialists and model services such as the House of Mental Health testify to the attempt to guarantee the citizens' constitutionally mandated right to a healthy existence, though in practice they bring to life little more than ideology. What happens to the citizenry when the city is a model/plan?

Although the city's Health Division had existed since the mid-1970s, it did not hire mental health professionals until 1986.[53] At that time, the São Paulo Psychiatric Hospital was beginning to send patients back to their communities. The Health Division hired a psychiatrist, a psychologist, and a social worker to work with this anticipated population and to set up some preventive programs (mostly related to drug addiction) in high schools.

The health secretary at the time recalled a visit to the São Paulo Hospital as she herself joined a patient in the common "ambulance therapy": "When I first took up the job in 1987, mental health assistance simply meant taking the patient to the São Paulo. Once, I went along in the ambulance. As we entered the parking lot, I was terrified. The patients approached the ambulance in throngs, and I ducked so that they couldn't see me. The experience was eye-opening" (Moraes 2000:75). This anecdote conveys the stigma and fear that had traditionally marked mental illness in the eyes of city administrators and health professionals. Significantly, however, the health secretary noted that this had changed, with the establishment of the House of Mental Health.

In 1988, after being trained in health management, several of the local mental health professionals proposed starting an alternative service, in accordance with the province's anti-asylum movement and the country's health reform. This project, which would eventually become the House of Mental Health, initially collided with the incoming mayor's attempt to construct a psychiatric hospital. Quoted in the *Jornal NH* (1988a), he declared: "Novo Hamburgo is completely *unprepared* to deal with the mentally ill, and it is worthless to try to send these people off to hospitals in Porto Alegre, for there is overcrowding there" (my emphasis; see also *Jornal NH* 1988b).

In a populist move, the future mayor suggested that he was solving both family problems and security matters: citizens needed a place to drop off their problem persons, whose burgeoning numbers threatened the city itself. To garner popular support for their cause, the advocates of the alternative service also used the language of risk and fear: "Most people who have a crisis are simply sent to psychiatric hospitals, but, given the high demand, they are refused hospitalization and then come back to the community, where they are exposed to and expose others to risk" (Projeto de Programa de Atendimento em Saúde Mental, 1998, cited in Moraes 2000:76).

Times had changed, and the idea of a city psychiatric hospital never took off. New forms of social control, as well as new concepts of citizenship and mental health, were in the making. The House of Mental Health was inaugurated in September 1989. Its objectives were initially defined as reducing hospitalizations (which would guarantee its institutional survival as a cost-effective health care alternative); promoting family-based psychosocial rehabilitation; developing a community movement to destigmatize the subject and to pressure administrators for quality services; and systematizing experience-based knowledge through partnership with local universities.

In a 1989 open letter to Novo Hamburgo's newspaper, psychologist Fábio Moraes, the House's first director, said that the service was not designed to "clean the city" of unwanted people. A comprehensive approach to mental health care "deals with ethical and moral prejudices and profound individual and social contradictions. It works with culture and people's subjectivity, whether they are ill or not" (*Jornal NH* 1989). The city had to be subjectively addressed and treated.

The service began providing ambulatory aid as well as long-term CAPS-like psychosocial treatment. Several projects were jointly developed: family group therapies, a community garden, an atelier of art and expression, a patients' newsletter. Psychology interns were integrated into local health posts, along with social workers, fostering close work with patients' families. According to Moraes, nonhospitalization was the norm: "We hospitalize only those patients who put their life and the lives of others at risk" (*Jornal NH* 1991). Moraes described the service and its ideas at the time:

In the outpatient clinic, we have people looking for a quick solution. Those are also more technical encounters; there is not too much involvement. In CAPS, it is different. It is not just whether the patient is with or without symptoms, but how he lives, how he relates to people who take care of him or who could care for him, questions of housing, other factors such as violence and drug trafficking. The main thing is not simply decreasing his symptoms. Many times, we see that the symptom is not the patient's main risk factor; rather, it is the whole social basis that is missing.

The mental health service, in Moraes's words, had to deal with the effects of something that no longer existed: the social domain. Treating the citizen's mental burden implied the restoration of this domain. The House brought patients to the city's central square to socialize with passersby in an attempt to destigmatize mental illness. The service also organized public demonstrations and artistic events all over the city to inform people of the House's activities and ideas, in an attempt to create a new public mentality.

The House's first year of operation was indeed successful. The numbers spoke for themselves: reports noted that Novo Hamburgo had one of the lowest psychiatric hospitalization rates in the province, and the House actually had the lowest hospitalization rate among all new mental health services. The service gained significant political visibility. Health officials, professionals, and politicians from other cities visited the House, looking for ways to replicate the service elsewhere in the province. The interdisciplinary team actively participated in the regional and national anti-asylum movements. In May 1992, for example, the Novo Hamburgo service hosted the first regional mental health conference (*Jornal NH* 1992b), bringing in several national and international leaders of the anti-psychiatry movement.

By 1992, the successful service had come to represent the entire city. A full-page political advertisement in the local newspaper read: "Novo Hamburgo is an example . . . also in mental health treatment" (*Jornal NH* 1992c). The service's exemplary quality could be measured in the city's drastic drop in hospitalizations: from one hundred in 1992 to thirty in 1993 (*Jornal NH* 1994a). City administrators were also proud of the project's community pharmacy. Beginning in 1992, it distributed free essential medication to all those who used the city's public health system. Psychiatric medication was dispensed directly at the House until 2000 (*Jornal NH* 1997a). The reconstructed social domain was now also a pharmaceutical domain.

Dr. Gilson Kunz was coordinating the House in 1994 when Catarina passed through the service another time. In an interview with the local newspaper early that year, Dr. Kunz mentioned a growing demand for treatment, praised the work of the local health posts, and described both a Catarina-like general patient and the ways Catarina had always said doctors approached her: "When treated in local posts, people don't incur an additional travel expense and remain in direct contact with the community. The majority of patients are women in a productive age, between twenty and forty years old; chronic illness and psychosis are common. We only medicate the aggressive ones. Yes, at times we still have to forward these patients to specialized hospitals in Porto Alegre" (*Jornal NH* 1994a).

Recall what Catarina once told me: "My ex-husband first took me to the psychiatrist, Dr. Gilson, in Novo Hamburgo, for him to help me, to discover the illness. But he lied to the doctor, saying that I was aggressive, that I beat the children. I got so mad that I actually hit him in front of the doctor. The nurse gave me an injection. I always had some medication to take. . . . Doctors only listened to him. I think that this is wrong. They have to listen to the patient."

The clinical encounter generated an affective state, and this, in part, became the basis of Catarina's designation as aggressive. In the process, according to her, the knowledge of her illness was lost, and she was further removed from family life. But in Dr. Kunz's words, a community was in place. In another interview published in 1994, Dr. Kunz emphasized the need to acknowledge the sociocultural determinants of mental disorders and the importance of sociality as key to healing: "The search for the sociocultural origins of the subject is a key alternative to the evolution of her condition. The best treatment is based on sociality and puts the patient in harmony with her environment. We know that family problems and problems of adaptation can be the origins of much suffering. We are therefore offering support and orientation to the whole family" (*Jornal NH* 1994c).

Rhetorically, the family had to be treated. But, as we know, it was not. Instead, Catarina was again hospitalized. I began to question how this model of supposedly socialized self-governance related in practice to the city's other modes of thought and self-presentation: nonhistoricity and anthropological fantasy. How do people become familiar with these modes? As I was tracking how Catarina had become something besides herself, it seemed that the performance of the household emerged as a central locus of city governance, now a psychosocial politics. How was this model city embodied in family life and in Catarina's casting out?

In December 1994, at the House of Mental Health, Dr. Gilson treated a woman he later forgot about. This is what he wrote in Catarina's file: "Patient brought in by the municipal guard. She was found in the streets with her son. Patient was medicated in the general hospital with Haldol and then taken home." A month and a half later, Catarina was back at the mental health service. In the meantime, she had been hospitalized once more at the São Paulo. Dr. Gilson then wrote: "Patient is back home and is doing well after hospitalization. Same prescription." Medication is the medium through which the household, the model service, and state policies come together and into view. As Catarina was pharmaceutically managed and her life chances withered, she was written into the medical archive as being well in a home that we know was nonexistent.

In *The Divided City*, Nicole Loraux writes that one must "expose the city to what it rejects in its ideological discourse yet live in the time of the event" (2002:61). Overall, Loraux is concerned with the denial of historicity in Greek classical democracy, "the denial of conflict as a constitutive principle, in order to construct the generality 'city'" (61). Civil war is at the core of civic life. Fratricide, she argues, is "ordinary civil war, because the brother is also the paradigm of the citizen" (209). The historian shows how the citizenry's concealment of war generates an affect that works like "the cement of the community." The crime being concealed has been engendered "in a single family" (33). Loraux thus constructs a scenario in which the household is affectively politicized: "Hate would be more ancient than love, in which forgetting can be valued only in terms of the unspeakable joy brought by the wrath that does not forget" (66). The restoration of familial relations becomes paradigmatic of reconciliation in the city. In the end, a false brotherhood conceals the original reality of division (39). For Loraux, the city is the subject that makes the symptom through the family.

While passing through the model mental health service, Catarina was being removed from the family, from medical accountability, and ultimately from social existence. What happened to her was not an exception. A machinery was in place, and an ethos of indifference enveloped her: she was a body not worth governing. With the passage of time, the House's socially committed professionals realized that inside the service old and new forms of treatments oddly coexisted. According to the recollection of Fábio Moraes (2000:89), a certain silence was being generated:

While in one room we had the project "Pathways of Expression," in the other room people were just medicated, and when the social and family resources proved insufficient, they were sent to the old São Paulo. While we were struggling for changes in mental health assistance, we also had the impression that in situations of crises old modes of controlling madness were preserved and that, paradoxically, new institutional arrangements were actually keeping them in place. As madness continued to exist in the streets, our clinic went further inside. Ever more often, encounters took place in closed offices, in private. A certain silence emerged. One could even notice a decrease of note-writing in the patients' charts.

Disputes over medical competence and ethics as well as over personal agendas and political ideologies also marked the mid-1990s at the House. A leading social worker left, and Dr. Kunz was relocated to the general hospital. According to Moraes, the House was becoming "a great public ambulatory, with people coming in at night to guarantee an appointment next day" (Moraes 2000:99). An ill multitude, I thought, and the impossibility of producing a different political body.

Twice set on fire and once flooded, the House was given a new address (with the second most expensive rent in the city) in 1996. Concurrently, it was restructured around four services: ambulatory treatment (people were increasingly triaged in the city's twenty-four local health units); CAPS; occupational therapy (money-generating workshops); and the three local specialized health units (in the Santo Afonso, Canudos, and Lomba Grande districts). By early 1997, the service was treating approximately one thousand patients per month. Two years later, the mental health team was seeing fifteen hundred persons per month, and psychiatric hospitalizations kept decreasing.

As for internal conflicts, Moraes recollects: "One can say that psychologists and psychiatrists, besides being distant from each other, also kind of distanced themselves from the patients. The nurses had to do the dirty work of controlling psychotic patients. Not much was known of family life except for the issues raised in individual and group therapy."

I was trying to break open the reality principle according to which Catarina was not allowed to decide about living. As I entered the public sites and went behind the scenes, where Catarina's destiny had been forged, I began to see her as a truth-speaker to the very processes that had left her socially dead, an absent thing in the household and in the city. In her symptoms, she knows. As Catarina's anthropologist, I focus on motion, putting these ideas and materials, lived experiences and perceptions, back into circulation with and against one another, so as to keep the story unfinished and open through the anthropological artifact.

Women, Poverty, and Social Death

"We have at least five hundred Catarinas in the House right now," said psychologist Simone Laux, the coordinator of the Novo Hamburgo service, after I told her about Catarina and my work with her. Laux affirmed the ordinariness of the story I was reassembling. In the discussion that followed with her and the team at the House of Mental Health, I got a clearer sense of the epidemic quality of the human destiny I was charting as well as the relational and technical dynamics that make it seem inevitable. As Laux aptly put it, the exclusion "always passes through the family."

By "five hundred Catarinas," she meant most of the female clientele of the House. This service was at the time treating around fifteen hundred people a month at its headquarters. Some seven hundred of these clients got free psychiatric medication at the city's community pharmacy: "An average treatment costs thirty-five dollars per month," added Fábio Moraes. "Many of our patients don't have this much to buy food or to pay for transportation."

I asked these thoughtful professionals to tell me more about the profile of the House's clients.

"When the service began, it was meant to deal mainly with schizophrenia and psychosis, but this has changed a lot, both diagnostically and numerically. There is an immense growth of mood disorders," reported psychologist Wildson Souza, who was coordinating the House's first systematic study of mental illness incidence. "We don't have statistics, but we see that the social field is breaking down and that the population is getting sicker and sicker." Catarina, I thought, was recognized as part of a social pattern treated at the House, if only partially, and remaining by and large uncharted.

Souza cited "unemployment, the harsh struggle to survive, no opportunities for social mobility, urban violence" as contributing to this epidemic of mental suffering. The psychologist suggested that the House had become the vanishing social world, the welfare state, and the social medicine that was no more: "Many factories are closed, people don't have jobs or health plans or family support. . . . They need some form of recognition and help, and they demand it from SUS. Nothing is isolated." The mental health service is the imaginary state.

I was introduced to the preliminary findings of a study conducted at the Novo Hamburgo House by sociologist Maralucia Mendes (2000), who profiled those who used the service from March to September 2000. During this time, 7,335 people were seen, the majority of whom came from the districts of Canudos and Santo Afonso, where Catarina once lived. Based on the city's official census, Mendes identified a mental illness prevalence of 13 percent among the city's total population. This sample was biased, however: the service was structured so that people were increasingly triaged out. A potential patient had to first visit one of the city's local health posts or one of the three other specialized mental health units (the Santo Afonso, Canudos, or Lomba Grande unit) in order to be referred to the House. The requirement that families sign a contract and commit themselves to participating in treatment also selected out many "problem persons." In addition, the House did not treat those addicted to illegal drugs. During the period of her data collection, Mendes reported, the city had authorized twenty-six mental health–related hospitalizations: twelve of these were for psychosis, eight for alcoholism, four for acute depression, and two for other causes. Fourteen patients were sent to the Caridade, one to the São Paulo, and eight to psychiatric hospitals in the interior (São Sebastião do Caí and Caxias do Sul).

Working with a sample of one hundred first-time patients, Mendes found that fifteen of them had been identified as psychotic and nine of those had been previously hospitalized. Of the fifteen, "only seven lived with their families; the rest lived alone or were successively hospitalized" (2000:23). She wrote: "By and large, when they come in, they bring clinical exams and medication and say that the local doctors couldn't help anymore. A disarticulated discourse is commonly in place, and family members do most of the talking. The problem that comes to the House under the name of the patient coincides, quite often, with the family's history and patterns of exchange."

What is the state of the family?

"Misery," said Moraes. "They are all very compromised, destructured, and confused, with a traumatic life trajectory. We cannot see these families in ideal terms, as if they could be fully responsible and care for the mentally ill. Responsibility implies conditions, and, objectively speaking, many times these families do not have the minimum conditions to provide care. The family is already suffering from alcoholism, from previous mental illnesses. There is very little information. Sexual violence is also very prevalent. The majority come from the interior. A high number participate in Pentecostal churches."

"We have three women's groups here," continued Laux. "Most of them are not psychotic. But at some point in their lives, they had a crisis or were at risk of committing suicide. All of them have a story that resembles Catarina's." The other health professionals then began to tell tales of "women's historical subjugation," female bodies entangled in realities of migration, poverty, and violence. "Once, a woman came in with a machete cut in her head. The husband of another one had raped all their children. Many report that, according to their husbands, they are always inadequate." The common pattern was that "he is the owner of her life, in all possible ways." I was again struck by how historically entrenched power relations in heterosexual households were woven together with social death.

Consider Maria Helena. The group reconstructed her history as follows:

Her father had abused her, and after some time her "good husband" also began to drink and to beat her. They had five children . . . and the guy set the house on fire with all of them inside. They survived, but lost everything. She had to go on the streets to sell food she was cooking. She saved and bought another shack and then went back to him. She says that he is truly "a great guy." Recently, the youngest son followed the father's path and went into drugs. He died in a motorcycle accident. She is seeing us because of the son's death but cannot make the larger connections.

Catarina always said that her thinking differed from that of her husband and his family, that her husband locked her in, that she wanted to find her worker's ID card. Her records also spoke of her escapes from the home and her wanderings through the city. "Husbands don't like that the women come downtown. They are from the periphery, and women who come to the center of the city by themselves are said to be looking for men—that's what they think," I was told. It was the occlusion of the feminine, I thought, in the name of a threatened virility or the fantasy of it.

There is also the story of Frida:

She came to us with a diagnosis of psychosis. She had six children, and the husband sexually abused all of them. He was the pastor of a Pentecostal church. She had to come to the House secretly, to talk and to take her medication, to be able to minimally differentiate what was right and wrong in the household. She didn't want to have more kids, but the husband prohibited her from taking the pill. She went to the hospital to have her tubes tied, but in the end the doctor canceled the surgery, saying that she had no written authorization from her husband. If a woman is legally married, she needs her husband's consent to get sterilized. The law is on the man's side: it is her body, but he must sign.

Catarina's insistence that she wanted to sign the divorce came to mind. She wanted the law to recognize her name and her will. But it was still unclear why that separation had remained such a pressing question for her in Vita.

"Because of stigma and domestic power dynamics," said Laux, "many women who come here have to lie, have to say that they are going somewhere else. They say things like, 'I can lose my job,' or 'My sister and neighbor will say that I am mad.'" Moraes argued that "a person might also use the illness as a means to look for inclusion, to be something." But in the process, I added, paradoxically she might occasion exclusion. That happened to Catarina. In front of Dr. Kunz, for example, she actually became the aggressive and intractable being who had to be medicated and removed so that the lives of those around her could continue.

Psychiatrist Daniela Justus joined the discussion. She had worked for fifteen years at the Caridade Hospital, was asked to leave, and was now coordinating the House's work with suicidal patients: "Not one of our fifty patients has been hospitalized." In her opinion, the House was the best place for mental health assistance in the region, offering "the possibility of respect for the patient as a person." She described the Caridade as "a hospital that does not permit rehabilitation." For too long—"and in vain"—she had tried to change things: "I wanted to make the patients' life viable, but this idea died, too."

Dr. Justus is the psychiatrist who kindly helped me read and interpret Catarina's records. As I briefed her on Catarina's trajectory, she replied: "Catarina is not searching for a diagnosis, but for life."

Dr. Justus mentioned different outcomes of the same illness: "What a difference there is when a family supports the patient. I have had a schizophrenic patient in my private practice for more than twenty years. He had only one hospitalization and has started his own family. Of course, it is a different social class." I told her that Catarina used to say: "I am allergic to doctors."

"She is right. That's the minimum attitude she could have developed. It is a must to trust the patient. The ideology and politics of a psychiatric hospital are not to trust. Patients are treated like animals. Minimal medical effort and social control through medication."

Catarina's story shows that the patterning of the mass patient and her dying at the crux between abandonment and overmedication are both public and domestic affairs, I noted. I told the group about my work and about the issues in which I was interested. In the discussion that followed, Moraes emphasized that the House's model represented the realm of the possible: "For many families, CAPS is life-altering. The fact that they sign a contract, accept responsibility, and have us to rely on changes the picture. There is an alternative symbolic order in place. We have family members whose relatives have been discharged but who keep coming to meetings because this is an important space for them. These are the educated family members who accept differences and who are patient with the Other's nonproductivity." This well-staffed and caring health service stands for a demand increasingly considered antiquated by the articulators of the country's new modes of governmentality: people's need for some form of institutional accountability.

A distinct mentality and affective state seemed to gain form in the exchange of these subjugated families with the model service. "There are families who try to use common sense and say: 'I am pissed that I have to take care of him and that he will not contribute to the family income, that this person will always be a problem. But it is better to do this with help than to do it all by ourselves.' If there is a subjective change, it is that people feel more included in a plan." Perhaps, Moraes added, "they also show less aggression toward the patient." In such cases, a pervasive hostility is contained and occasions a new collective arrangement. "I still think that in spite of what they suffer in their families, this is less perverse than what the state does. The state has no obligation to keep these people alive and simply wants their elimination. The family still has other kinds of commitments like blood ties and social ties."

As part of her study, Mendes made home visits to a representative sample of eighty-seven patients in the Canudos and Santo Afonso districts. She identified two types of clients: patients who undergo continuous pharmaceutical and psychotherapeutic treatment, and patients who are frequently hospitalized. She wrote, "Light depression and psychosis are now somewhat integrated in the local community, but hospitalizations for psychotic episodes continue and are by and large not referred by the service. There is also a very high level of alcoholism that remains unaddressed by the House." Families play a key decision-making role in whether a patient stays in treatment or is hospitalized. This exclusion happens "according to the productive capacity of the person burdened by mental suffering," Mendes observed (2000:14).

From what I was hearing and reading, it seemed that the acutely depressed and alcoholics now shared the same patterns of exclusion that had long been the social norm for schizophrenics and psychotics. "There is still much stigma," admitted Souza. "The mentally ill person is seen as a criminal, as being responsible for his suffering and that of others." A diagnostic softening does not seem to alter people's destinies. "The bipolar individual," said Moraes, "is kept isolated at home just as the schizophrenic was. I don't think that diagnostics make the differentiation."

What remains constant is the process of casting the person out. "They live off the family's income and are increasingly unwanted," stated Andreia Miranda, the House's occupational therapist. And as the sociologist noted in her home visits: "These patients are badly adjusted to a world in which the temporality of the everyday is caught between a regular working life, the security that guarantees the exact and certain product of this work, and the increasing insecurity of unemployment. As they couldn't sustain normative relations, they now also don't seem to have the capacity to submit to the new norms of a life of treatment." Here, Miranda was highlighting the fundamental question of how to create a therapeutics through which the afflicted can actually build new normative relations to his or her environment.

"The worst scenario," said psychologist Luisa Rückert, moving beyond the hopeful outcomes to which Moraes referred, "is when families don't take responsibility and objectively and subjectively exclude the patient until she ends up in the street. From a psychiatric point of view, most of these patients could live with their families and could do so successfully, for there is no more risk of aggression, and psychotic episodes are under control. But families organize themselves so that they are no longer part of the treatment and care."

At home, the mentally ill person is increasingly spatially individuated. "Many are placed in a room in the backyard or in the garage. Hospitalization becomes a temporary normality, and the patient's isolation is reinforced after each hospitalization," Mendes reported (2000:15). Recall Catarina's account of moving from her house to a shack deeper in the slum and then staying here and there after the fire, eventually moving to the houses of her brothers until she ended up in Vita—literally the dead end. "Some families even change addresses and disappear," continued Rückert. "Others leave a wrong phone number so they cannot be reached. But first they make sure to get the patient's possessions placed under their names." The major exception is when cash is involved. "Many families keep their mentally ill relatives as long as they can manage their disability income," said Miranda.

Dr. Justus pointed out the family's role in fostering illness. "When patients improved—and we saw this quite often at the Caridade—families discontinued treatment, and the person had to be hospitalized again." Crisis situations were constantly induced. The relation between the family and mental illness, I was told, is made explicit in the culture of pharmaceuticals: "In our group sessions, we can see that the fragility of a minimal social integration is revealed in everyone's relation to the medication, the fight over its discontinuation, the lack of money to buy it, or the problems with forgetting to take it."

Families, in fact, come into the service demanding medication. "When I ask them to tell their story," said psychologist Luisa Rückert, "many times they say, 'No, I came here to get a medication for her.'" Rückert added that when she is coordinating an initial group meeting, people often ask, "'Why is the psychiatrist not here?' As if I were not sufficient for a first treatment. They want to leave with a prescription." The House refers all patients to group therapy. But according to psychiatrist Patrícia Silva, "some fifty percent of the patients stay in group therapy, whereas ninety percent stay in medication-based treatments."

As I have argued, medication has become a family tool: to help with adherence, withdrawal, or oversedation. The family crystallizes its way of being in the ways it deals with medication. "Bottom line, the type of ethics the family installs," said Rückert, "serves to guarantee its own physical existence." Moraes agreed that "the family caretaker quite often becomes the state that does not care." The family is thus *a state within the state.* Freud actually used this expression to reiterate the constraining features of neurotic, pathological processes vis-à-vis "external reality" (cited in Loraux 2002:84).

I take the interplay of political power and individual psychology to be more than analogic. The decision to make persons and things work or to let them die is at the center of family life. And science, in the form of medication, brings a certain neutrality to this decision-making process. "In the meetings," added Rückert, "the patient quite often realizes that, given the continuing process of exclusion, she has already structured her own schemes of perception and codification of reality." Rather than psychosis, out of all these processes a para-ontology comes into view—a Being beside itself and standing for the destiny of others.

When Simone Laux first opened Catarina's folder, she read aloud an entry by nurse Lilian Mello from December 12, 1994, that left us all speechless:

I drove Catarina home. But as she now lives alone, I left her at the house of her mother-in-law, called Ondina. Catarina was badly received. The mother-in-law said that Catarina should die, *because she was stubborn and aggressive, didn't obey anyone, and didn't take the medication. The mother-in-law made clear that she will not be responsible for Catarina. I told her that the family should take Catarina to the general hospital for a clinical evaluation. Ondina told me to call Nilson, Catarina's ex-husband. I went to talk to him. My impression is that he really wants nothing to do with her. He only said that, like other times, Catarina should be taken to Porto Alegre and hospitalized.* (my emphasis)

There is much to learn from this responsible health professional as she moved through public institutions and households. She disturbed diagnostic certainties and refused to isolate Catarina's body and voice from her surroundings. She followed her behind the scenes of medicine and model programs, listened to a multiplicity of voices, and registered the modes of affect and social practices that made Catarina a double of sorts and empty of all practical possibilities. The nurse's work did not veil what was truly happening, the concreteness of "the truth" Catarina embodied.

"She died socially," said Laux. "That is the pain that aches in us . . . when we realize this: she cannot opt to live."

A machine in which a tie to others and to living are rendered impossible. If it were not for this archival fragment, the explicitness of these medical and domestic operations would remain lost from history.

Patricia Barbosa, a psychiatrist, named the line that had been crossed: "She was killed."

The ex-human.

"I am like this because of life"

Acute spasm
Secret spasm
Rheumatic woman
The word of the rheumatic
Is of no value

As I finished reading Catarina's medical records and contextualizing them, I perused the five volumes of the dictionary she had written in 1999 and 2000. I wanted to juxtapose what people wrote of her in the records with the way she wrote against that same language. "I made peace with the letter characters," she claimed. Scattered throughout her writings is the desire to render the world as it is.

The dictionary is filled with references to deficient movement, to pain in the arms and legs, to muscular contractions. In writing, as in speech, Catarina refers to her condition, by and large, as "rheumatism." This word is popularly applied to various kinds of painful articular and muscular affections. These affections, Catarina suggests, were acquired over time and are related to her life experience: *"Sou assim pela vida"* (I am like this because of life).

I followed the word "rheumatism" as it appeared throughout Catarina's dictionary, paying close attention to the words and expressions clustered around it. At times, Catarina relates her growing paralysis to a kind of biological and familial marker, alluding to a certain "blood type becoming a physical deficiency," "a blood stroke," "a lesion in the brain," "a cerebral forgetfulness," and an "expired brain and aged cranium" that "impede change, the feet to make the steps." She also recalls the approximate time when the first symptoms appeared: "When I was nineteen, I gave birth to my first son. We lived in the interior. My legs were shaky when we moved to Novo Hamburgo." In another fragment, Catarina sees the "chronic spasms" as related to unconscious workings and as indicators of the history of landless Others:

Nightmare, chronic spasms
Encroached rheumatism
Indian and gypsy prepared fire to heat their feet
Had no covers when they slept
My father said

Most of the time, Catarina speaks of the man-made character of her bodily affections. In the following inscription, for example, she depicts rheumatism as a mangling of the threads people tinker with:

People think that they have the right
To put their hands
In the mangled threads
And to mess with it
Rheumatism
They use my name
For good and for evil
They use it
Because of the rheumatism

Her "rheumatism" ties various life-threads together. It is an untidy knot, a real matter that makes social exchange possible. It gives the body its stature and is the conduit of a morality. It is Catarina's bodily affection and not her name that is exchanged in that world: she becomes a symptom. "What I was in the past does not matter." Catarina disappears, and a religious image stands in her place: "rheumatism, spasm, crucified Jesus."

As I saw it, the "secret" of Catarina's condition stemmed from an unknown biology *and* the unconsidered experience of what had been made of it over time. The acute pain Catarina described and the authoritative story she became in medicine and in common sense—as being mad and ultimately of no value—must be considered and deciphered side by side.

Consider all that is entangled in Catarina's "rheumatism":

Divorce
Religion
Separation
Public notary
Separation of bodies
Marriage license
Civil register
Document
Personal data
Silence does not disturb
The pharmacist disturbs
The thought of the patient
See the prescribing information
To medicate
Rheumatism
Destiny
Personal name
Rheumatic
Desire
Vote by vote
Father
Political party
Workers
Rheumatic
Useless
Convicted

The existence of the ailments Catarina interprets as rheumatism is linked to the separation of legally bound bodies and to personal data becoming public documents. Her destiny has to do with the ways her pains and contractions are medicated. The pharmaceuticals and the work of the experts disturb thinking. In the rheumatic's state, the name of the father, the political party, and the workers are "useless," like her own words, Catarina suggests. In another fragment, she acknowledges that there is a rationality and a bureaucracy to symptom management: "chronic spasm, rheumatism, must be stamped, registered." All of this happens in a democratic context: "vote by vote."

Catarina rarely mentions mental disorders, but when she does, she also describes them as rheumatism-related—as in the inscription "rheumatic in the head"—and with a social etiology: "Cerebral spasm, paralysis, paranoid, rheumatism, unemployment." The perception of persecution that allegedly characterizes the psychotic's hallucination is here tied to the brain, to the lack of movement, and to the economy. The domestic economy makes one crazy: *louca da cabeça, louca da casa* (crazy in her head, crazy in her house). Catarina does not forget the workings of psychiatry—there is a science to her affections:

Mental disturbance
Illness goes to the brain
Reaches the cranium
Takes over the head:
Psychiatrist

Ironically, Catarina writes that in the medical records, she readies herself to vanish into the imaginary, as though she had been merely a collection of easily dismissed subjective symptoms: *prontuário, prontinha para ir ao céu* (protocol, she is all set to go to heaven). There is also a blindness in the making: "I became paralyzed and the others became very blind."

And so goes the manipulation of her ailments and their maintenance, until they are all that remain to Catarina in Vita:

Vita
Rehabilitation center
Politics as it is
Catarina
Spirit
Love before gestation
The vote
Reelected by the people
Rheumatism in the legs

But what one is made of, is not all there is:

The paralyzed woman is not served on a tray
When men throw me into the air
I am already far away
Every woman must keep a secret

As one of "five hundred Catarinas," she is at once in Vita and elsewhere in her thoughts. And since nothing makes her identical to herself, Catarina makes herself a different name: "Reality, Catkini." In her writing, she makes us see things otherwise.

promazine is an antipsychotic and sedating drug that can also decrease the patient's white blood cell count and increase body temperature. Like haloperidol, it can affect extrapyramidal symptoms. Haloperidol can induce muscular rigidity, trembling, constipation, and depression, among other things. Prometazine is used to maximize the sedating effect of other drugs, but it can produce symptoms such as dry mouth, mental confusion, trembling, and various other movement disturbances. Biperiden, which is intended to prevent neurological side effects, can provoke agitation, dry mouth, constipation, disorientation, mood disorders, euphoria, and dizziness.

Catarina's charts were full of such symptoms. As I read the files, I was intrigued and disturbed by how difficult it was to separate the signs and symptoms of the psychiatric illness being treated from the effects of the medications—and by how little doctors seemed to care about differentiating between them. To call this "just malpractice," as a local psychiatrist did, misses the productive quality of this unregulated experimentalism. The effects of pharmaceuticals essentially constituted the body that was being treated, and in the process a real/imaginary/technical affliction that Catarina called "rheumatism" came into existence.

The day after Catarina's hospitalization (December 9, 1992), Dr. Artur Lima, the psychiatrist assigned to see her weekly, wrote that she "has a personality disorder (schizoid with psychogenic reactions), has delirious ideations, wants to divorce her husband. Her general condition is good." He made no reference to her difficulty in walking, and, without any apparent reason, he replaced the drug chlorpromazine with levomepromazine, a stronger and more sedating antipsychotic drug.

Paradoxes abound. Catarina had initially been diagnosed and treated as schizophrenic, then as psychotic and as suffering from postpartum psychosis—all of which seemed to imply some organic etiology for her various states. Now, when her walking difficulties were finally visible and at least medically reported, and as she showed signs of depression, she became a "psychogenic case." Because she had no room to describe her self-understanding, the biological etiology of her condition faded from view. And although her diagnoses were becoming progressively softer, she was still given "the full antipsychotic package," as a local psychiatrist described it. These unconsidered paradoxes gained form in her body. In the records, the voices of the psychiatrist, the psychologist, and the nurses verify the life of the pharmaceutical and the occlusion of Catarina's possibility of becoming something else.

On the first day of confinement, the psychologist intern reported that

Catarina was "euphoric": "She went to the hospital's theater stage, danced, and sang." Three days later, Catarina complained to the intern that she was "dizzy." The nurses initially noted that Catarina was "lucid and oriented" but also "shaky and falling as she walks." On December 10, the morning after Catarina's doctor put her on levomepromazine, a nurse detected very low blood pressure and wrote in the chart: "Is it because of the psychiatric medication?" The nurse withheld the morning dose of levomepromazine, but full treatment resumed that night.

In the following days, the nurses referred to Catarina as "calm," as trying to walk and "constantly falling." She was then restrained in her bed. "Patient complains of dizziness." Only on December 20 did a doctor on call make a full clinical evaluation of Catarina and discontinue the levomepromazine. He noted that she was suffering from "postural hypotension." Because she was oversedated, she was lying in bed too much of the time, and this posture, according to the doctor on call, was occasioning her low blood pressure. It was not a direct effect of the medication per se, he reasoned. Thus, a day and a half later, the full treatment began again.

Catarina's psychiatrist did not acknowledge these signs and symptoms and interventions in his weekly report. "Patient has improved a lot. We will try to schedule a family visit for the holidays." That visit never materialized. In the following weeks, the nurses kept writing that Catarina was "calm," and the psychologists continued claiming that she was "feeling better, more motivated, and participating in recreational activities."

On January 8, the psychiatrist deemed Catarina ready for discharge and judged that her "psychogenic psychosis" could be followed up in local clinics. The hospital's social worker came into the picture and contacted "the family," basically to make sure that the patient would not be left in the hospital. The nurses note: "Patient left with family members, was calm, lucid, and oriented." The imaginary care. A better-informed note from the administration reads: "Patient left with the driver of Novo Hamburgo's municipal ambulance." Amputated from the family, the pharmaceutical subject is the city's patient.

"Haldol" (haloperidol) and "Neozine" (levomepromazine) are words in Catarina's dictionary. In a fragment, she defiantly writes that her pain reveals the experimental ways science is embodied:

The dance of science
Pain broadcasts sick science, the sick study
Brain, illness

Buscopan
Haldol, Neozine
Invoked spirit

Psychiatric truth has played a definite role in Catarina's expulsion from reality. But as the generative figure she is, Catarina here is pushing the anthropology of science and technology a step further. The ordinary workings of medical science are traced to her ailments. She claims that her signs and symptoms are not a subjective indication, as opposed to an objective one. They have not been unintentionally induced; they are not iatrogenic per se. Rather, Catarina's "rheumatism" has been relationally and medically engineered.

An individual history of science is being written here. Catarina's lived experience and ailments are the pathos of a certain science, a science that is itself sick. There has been a breakdown in the pursuit of wisdom, and there is commerce. The goods of psychiatric science, such as Haldol and Neozine, have become as ordinary as Buscopan (hyoscine, an over-the-counter antispasmodic medication) and have become a part of familial practices. As Catarina's experience shows, they also operate over her brain *and* her illness. These pharmaceutical goods—working, at times, like rituals—realize an imaginary spirit rather than the material truth they supposedly stand for: objects are then supposed subjects. There is a science to Catarina's affects, a money-making science. As transmitters of this science, her signs and symptoms are of a typical kind.

In his lecture "The Sense of Symptoms," Freud hinted at the existence of a kind of symptom that could not be traced to an individual's idiosyncratic history and that the science and skills of psychoanalysis failed to satisfactorily explain (1957a:271). He spoke of "typical symptoms of an illness" that are more or less the same in all cases: "Individual distinctions disappear in them or at least shrink up to such an extent that it is difficult to bring them into connection with the patient's individual experience and to relate them to particular situations they have experienced" (270). Freud had in mind, for example, the repetition and doubt that would be common to all obsessional neurotics. Instead of linking these typical symptoms to biology, Freud saw them as another level of experience, reflecting, perhaps, a kind of universal culture: "If the individual symptoms are so unmistakenly dependent on the patient's experience, it remains possible that the typical symptoms may go back to an experience which is itself typical—common to all human beings" (271).

Freud admits that the symptom that makes people similar actually makes the work of medical science possible: "And we must not forget that it is these typical symptoms, indeed, which give us our bearings when we make our diagnosis" (1957a:271). But rather than elaborating on how the expert uses the symptom to produce science, Freud shifts attention back to the individual's tinkering with it. Insightfully, he notes that the typical symptom activates a subjective plasticity: "On this similar background, however, different patients nevertheless display their individual requirements—whims, one is inclined to say—which in some cases contradict one another directly" (270). Through typical symptoms, patients actively project—manufacture, one could say—their own individual conditions and moods. But then, instead of exploring the materiality and historicity of this prosthetic agency, Freud refers to it as a kind of nucleus around which the patient refashions his or her given neurosis.

In the end, not surprisingly, Freud universalizes. He suggests that these affects actually make the individual symptom and the typical symptom one and the same: "I will try to console you, therefore, with the reflection that any fundamental distinction between the one kind of symptom and the other is scarcely assumed" (1957a:271). Thus, the repetition and doubt that are common to obsessional neurotics can be read as "general reactions which are imposed on the patients by the nature of their pathological change" (271). The problem with this interpretation in modern times is that the subject is not simply the reflection of unconscious processes but is literally composed by morbid scientific/commercial/political changes.

In Catarina's writing and thinking, global pharmaceutical goods are not simply taken as new material for old patterns of self-fashioning. These universally disseminated goods are entangled in and act as vectors for new mechanisms of sociomedical and subjective control that have a deadly force. In this sense, it is not the symptom per se that is ahistorical but our understanding of how these scientific identifications became so widely available and how they replace social ties, voiding certain forms of human life in the family and medicine.

We can now more fully understand what Catarina meant when she said that she was writing a dictionary so as "not to forget the words, all the illnesses I had as a child and that I have now." The illnesses she experienced were the outcome of events and practices that altered the person she had learned to become. Words such as "Haldol" and "Neozine" are literally her. The drug named "Akineton" (biperiden) is embedded in the new name Catarina gave herself: "Catkini."

In 1960, Jacques Lacan wrote that the science of his time was already occupying the place of desire in the human: "During this historical period the desire of man, which has been felt, anesthetized, put to sleep by moralists, domesticated by educators, betrayed by academies, has quite simply taken refuge or been repressed in that most subtle and blindest of passions . . . the passion for knowledge. That's the passion that is currently going great guns and is far from having said its last word" (1992:324). The science Lacan had in mind was physics—specifically, the development of the atomic bomb and the nuclear arms race. Political powers, he said, had been taken in by science's propaganda and had provided the money for new machines, gadgets, and contraptions, "as a consequence of which we are left with this vengeance" (325). Abandoned in Vita to die, Catarina writes that her desire has been betrayed. It is now a pharmaceutical thing with no human exchange value:

Catarina cries and wants to leave
Desire
Watered, prayed, wept
Tearful feeling, fearful, diabolic, betrayed
My desire is of no value
Desire is pharmaceutical
It is not good for the circus

Pharmaceutical Being

In the remaining hospital records, we see the inexorable process of Catarina becoming a pharmaceutical being.

On August 16, 1993, Catarina was again hospitalized at the Caridade. Dr. Gilson Kunz wrote the referral requesting her hospitalization. I found the document, written on the letterhead of the Novo Hamburgo Health Division, in Catarina's Caridade chart, but there is no trace of it in the archives of the House of Mental Health or in Dr. Kunz's memory. It seemed to me that shady transactions had made it possible to confine Catarina one more time. In his referral, Dr. Kunz wrote that Catarina was "psychotic" and that she had set the couple's house on fire: "Patient is depressed, anxious, set house on fire, escapes to the streets, and wanders without direction. She has been hospitalized before and is not doing ambulatory treatment."

This time, when other legal requirements were in place, Catarina signed a "voluntary hospitalization form." We do not know what she thought she was signing, but her signature exempted the psychiatrist from the responsibility of reporting her hospitalization to the Public Ministry. Yet there was a kind of agency to Catarina's act: she signed her maiden name.

Her admission report reads: "Patient has been depressed for the past fifteen days, has insomnia and does not eat, has magical and noncoherent thoughts (ideas of ruin and death), is aggressive, and escapes from home. Eight days ago, she burned her husband's things and tried to set the house on fire." The woman was now threatening family life and property. As for her "past condition," she was said to have had "depressive moods since her early twenties." A family history of mental disorders was now considered: "A maternal uncle committed suicide, and two cousins from her mother's side

psychiatric patient" suffering from "malnutrition, dehydration, and anemia" and diagnosed as "anorexic."

Besides haloperidol, levomepromazine, and biperiden, Catarina was given vitamins and was put on a hypercaloric and hyperproteic diet. At some point in the records, a physician referred to "atrophied muscles," but this was left unexamined. In sum, the attitude seemed to be that all medicine could do was help her to gain some weight.

But not even that goal was successfully achieved. On September 3, a nursing assistant recorded Dr. Vera's complaint that Catarina had not received her prescribed parenteral nutrition for two days. On September 18, surveillance increased because she was "trying to escape." Twelve days later, Catarina was discharged with the comment "improved." No family member arrived to pick her up, and a worker from the Caridade signed her out. The decaying physiology belonged to no one.

—

Half a year later, on March 28, 1994, Catarina was back at the Caridade. Again, she had a referral from Dr. Gilson Kunz, describing her "unspecified psychosis": "Patient is delirious and has persecutory ideas, is depressed and agitated. She does not accept ambulatory treatment. Had previous hospitalizations." The Novo Hamburgo House of Mental Health has no record of this referral.

Sedated with haloperidol and prometazine, Catarina was admitted while sleepy and suffering from hallucinations. Under these conditions, Catarina signed a "voluntary" hospitalization form. The doctor who admitted her wrote the date on the form she signed. He assessed her condition in these terms: "For the past three weeks, patient has been physically aggressive, agitated, does not sleep at night, almost does not eat, see things, hears cries, and weeps. She does not let anyone go into the house—the police had to break in. She is throwing her medication away. Patient has suicidal ideation, thinks that people want to mistreat and kill her."

Catarina is described as increasingly dangerous to the family and to herself. She has been left to the care of the police. It is implied that she was actually responsible for her own decay—she throws medication away. It was as though her moods and thoughts had nothing to do with the isolating reality surrounding her. Instead, Catarina's fear and anger were understood as the direct result of nonmedication and thus as having no truth-value. A gene for depression might now explain her mental condition: "Maternal cousins with psychiatric problems, uncle hanged himself."

The doctor who admitted Catarina added chlorpromazine and biperiden to her existing drug regimen. Dr. Irineu Amorin, who would see Catarina twice a week, said that she was suffering from "affective psychosis" and thus added the antidepressant imipramine to the mixture. A local psychiatrist reviewing the record, however, observed that this dose, in combination with Catarina's other drugs, was too low to effectively treat a mood disorder and could eventually occasion "Parkinson-like trembling and an overall bad feeling." During this hospitalization, Catarina was also given the hypnotic flurazepam (Dalmadorm).

On March 29, Catarina complained of a "weakness in her legs." But since delirium seems to be the currency of psychiatry, only her supposed paranoia and aggressiveness were addressed. "Patient improved from hallucinations," Dr. Amorin wrote on March 31. A week later, the psychologist intern commented that Catarina was "apathetic and not critical of herself, didn't join recreation activities, saying that she had to sleep." A week later, the same intern reported that Catarina was "complaining of difficulty walking." Medical common sense should recognize that an antipsychotic drug like chlorpromazine could easily lead to a loss of balance. But medication was to continue.

"Catarina is typical of the psychiatry of the times. She is the very history of it," Dr. Justus reflected. "She stayed without a clear diagnosis, and her neurological condition was never addressed. They took her neurological signs as manifestations of the psychiatric. This differentiation is crucial, however: it is something we do in private practice. But she was at the Caridade. This is Brazil.

"Recently, a patient was referred to me as depressed. She had constant headaches, and I requested an MRI. After a month, a family member came back to the service and said that it would take half a year to do the exam through SUS. I took the woman to a friend of mine who has a private lab. The exams showed that she had a massive brain tumor that was still growing."

On April 20, the hospital's social worker tried to contact Catarina's family, "but the phone number the family gave was incorrect. There was no way to contact them." Catarina was supposed to vanish in these hospitalizations. No one was accountable for her. On April 22, the psychologist intern described a form of understanding and communication that Catarina might have been in touch with: "Patient behaved adequately, talked to the others, spoke about visiting her family. *She had a poetry book in her hands.*"

The nurses continued to chronicle Catarina's sedation, her "calm," and her walking problems. The psychologist intern was highlighting her supposed integration: "Participated in the cosmetic workshop, helped another patient to do her makeup." In early May, Catarina's psychiatrist judged that the "patient is better from the hallucinations, but has delirious ideation about family members, that they want to harm her." What was delirious about her perception that the family wanted her gone?

By May 13, the family had not yet responded, though a letter had been sent informing them that Catarina was "without psychotic symptoms" and could leave. Only a week later, after a successful communication with the Novo Hamburgo city hall, Catarina was picked up by an ambulance and left at her home. After years of medication and with her family disintegrating, Catarina was nearly emptied of possibilities.

Dr. Gilson Kunz, then the coordinator of the House of Mental Health, saw her on June 23, 1994. He basically adjusted medication: "Patient is better, separated from husband, living with small child, keeping treatment: imipramine, the hypnotic diazepam, and the mood stabilizer carbamazepine."

That same year, on December 12, the municipal guard found Catarina wandering the streets and brought her to the mental health service. She was later sedated at the general hospital. As described earlier, nurse Lilian Mello took Catarina home at this point and heard the mother-in-law pronounce a death wish: "She should die." The ex-husband made it clear that she should be left to public medicine and kept at a distance in Porto Alegre.

On December 16, 1994, Catarina was hospitalized at the São Paulo— her last hospitalization before being left in Vita. Her ex-husband brought her in. "She is aggressive, throws stones at the neighbors, has set her house on fire, says disconnected things, refuses to take medication, for no reason says that people want to cause her harm, cannot take care of herself alone. As for her paralysis, husband says that other family members walk like that."

It is not true that Catarina set her shack on fire. But there was little regard for what actually happened here. Catarina's movements were ever more difficult, she was separated from Nilson, the children were in the custody of their father and a third party, she had no money, her parents were dead, and her brothers seldom visited her. According to the ex-husband, "she cannot handle medication by herself."

Dr. Viola, who wrote the admission report, saw a lucid Catarina who could not walk without falling. And perhaps because she was not on medication at the time, she was able to tell the doctor that "the spasms in the legs first emerged when she was some twenty years old, that she had had three normal births, that she never had a fall that traumatized the spine or used anesthesia. She falls with high frequency and denies that she is an alcoholic. Mother had the same problem, died in a wheelchair."

"I am against admission," wrote Dr. Viola. "She should have a neurological evaluation."

Catarina signed her "voluntary admission."

Her final diagnosis was "paranoid schizophrenia." Her supposedly delirious thinking and fears of persecution were heavily medicated: chlorpromazine, haloperidol, biperiden, and also prometazine. The psychiatric evaluation of December 19 reads: "Patient slept last night, mistrusts the therapist and medication."

Doctors wrote that they were working with the patient "to give her data on reality." On December 23, after an episode of diarrhea, she was reported to be "resting, feeling well, and talking to other patients about her ex-husband." After the holidays, on December 28, a psychiatrist reported that "her thinking is aggregated and less delirious. Patient keeps good personal hygiene and participates in occupational therapy activities. She values the progress that has been made." On January 5, she was said to have acquired an "acute self-critique" and was judged "ready for discharge." Her bodily condition was described as "drained." There was no one to be contacted.

A week passed. "Patient has slurred speech. She reported why she decided to leave the husband and the life she was living. Thought is logical and coherent, and affect is modulated and adequate. Social worker has not been able to reach any family member."

As Catarina kept complaining of pain in her legs and joints, a nurse urged her to discuss it with the doctor. That never happened. On January 12, Catarina was sent into the world, to medicate herself: "Patient without acute symptoms. She is ready for discharge. She was advised to take medication at home at the right time, and to stay well."

On January 23, 1995, Dr. Kunz saw Catarina at the House of Mental Health and wrote: "Patient is better after hospitalization." And he kept prescribing the antipsychotics haloperidol and chlorpromazine.

Six months later, on June 5, not even Dr. Kunz could deny her overall physical deterioration: "Patient is psychiatrically better, but has difficulty walking. Should continue on medication." Finally, the House of Mental Health made it possible for her to see a neurologist. Doctor Rosana Bomarech wrote: "Patient has difficulty speaking and walking. Cerebellar and pyramidal clinical picture. She needs hospitalization for adequate neurological examination. I recommend Infirmary 14, at the Santa Casa in Porto Alegre." But who cared?

At the age of twenty-eight, alone, without a home and without legal rights to her children, with no income or welfare, overmedicated, and losing her locomotion, it was too late for Catarina, and no one followed through with the referral. But in Vita, in her writing, Catarina recollected this note by Dr. Bomarech: "Doctor, Novo Hamburgo, neurologist, a woman doctor, specialist in the case, here in Porto Alegre."

Catarina wrote about the effect of the coupling of family-state practices with these medico-scientific (non) interventions and her body over time. In this sense, her symptoms were both a patterned reality and a thing that was being lost. Her dismissed condition gave consistency to an altered common sense. She did not "forget the words" and thought against them: "Die death."

Dr. Kunz wrote two more notes on Catarina.

After seeing her on October 19, 1995, he wrote: "Prescriptions."

After seeing her on December 26, 1995, he wrote: "Prescriptions."

That is the end of Catarina's presence in the city's domain.

Part Four

THE FAMILY

Ties

No matter how much I thought I had already learned about Catarina's life from our long conversations or from detailed readings of the medical records, every time we met and talked I encountered something that kept eluding my understanding. This unknown was not related to novel or contradictory information Catarina brought up, but to the ways in which she repeatedly moved figures from one register to the other: her past life, abandonment in Vita, and what she desired. She seemed to make this movement itself the life of her mind, understanding what was happening to her being in her own terms and keeping herself and the listener in suspense.

I returned to Vita in December 2000. Adriana, my wife, went with me. It was my third visit in a year. Having spoken to Catarina at length and examined her medical records, I could have stopped the work at this point and said, "I have a story to tell." But such an approach would have been too similar to the long history of actions that had time after time discontinued Catarina's possibilities. In participating in the recollection of her life, I had gained a clearer understanding of the ordinariness and representativeness of Catarina's abandonment. But her desire was to reenter the world. As the work moved on, I was becoming more than Catarina's listener and interpreter; our interaction had grown into a means for her to access medicine and the family. The ethnographic work helped both to historicize the apparent intractability of her condition and to propel new events.

The look of Vita was constantly changing. To put it simply, there were now more buildings and fewer people. At the infirmary, the urine-soaked soil had been covered with concrete, and the smells of the day were cleared away with a hose. The population of some two hundred *abandonados* who had been residing in Vita during my first visits in 1995 and 1997 had now been reduced to seventy. In a span of three years, more than half had either died or left. But as I learned at the city's epidemiological surveillance division, there was no way to track the number of people who had died in Vita. Death certificates were written by doctors in nearby hospitals, and the deaths were registered as if they had occurred in those hospitals, making it impossible to map death in abandonment. All we could see was the inexplicable evacuation of unwanted bodies.

Catarina sat outside the pharmacy, writing. She was very skinny and tanned and moved her arms with evident difficulty. She smiled and said that she had been waiting anxiously for us. The notebook was almost full and was packed with candy wrappings, cards, and photos.

Who are these people?

"A neighbor of mine, when he was little," she said. Clóvis, the nurse, had given her the photos.

How are you?

"I want to travel in the coming days. To see my relatives. Oscar said that he had to first talk to Dona Dalva, the social worker, to make plans for us to go to Novo Hamburgo."

Catarina often mentioned an address in Novo Hamburgo—999 Constituição Street—and said that she would like to see her children. Vita's coordinators insisted that they had tried but had not been able to reach her relatives. This time, I would try to find Catarina's family. I had no idea where this work would end.

How is your health? I asked.

"My health is good, but my legs ache. I sit for too long."

Do you try to stand up?

"Sometimes I try, but I fall. The other day, I got mad at the wheelchair. I didn't want it anymore. I tried to stand, and I fell. I wept for a long time. I didn't want anyone to get close to me. Clóvis helped. He gave me medication, and it went to my legs. He did the same thing with Marcelo. Now it passed. But that madness stayed in my legs."

Are you still taking medication?

"Vitamins. Clóvis gives them to me."

Are there new people in Vita?

"No, nobody."

Catarina dropped a few valentine cards from the notebook, cards Clóvis had given her. She said they had been dating for over a year now.

Sassá approached me and asked, "Have you brought it?"

What? I had forgotten something.

"The photos," she said. She wanted the photos I had taken last August.

I found myself participating in the process of forgetting that seemed to rule Sassá's existence. It is not that I had broken my promise, for I had indeed brought the photos to Brazil—they were in my apartment. It was that for a moment I found myself amazed that she had recalled the photos, as if she should not have done so. As I repeatedly returned to Vita and engaged Catarina and her neighbors, the travails of these persons gained form for me, as did the mental readiness by which they are assumed to be out of cognition.

Oscar, the chief caretaker, yelled from a distance, "What's up, João?" Along with Clóvis and Alencar, he was one of the few left to care for the abandoned. Oscar had gained weight. "Thank God, I keep healthy." He was very proud that his doctor had not yet prescribed antiretroviral treatment for him. His family was well too, he said.

Catarina continued: "I come here to the pharmacy every day, because I am the last one to be bathed."

The non sequitur sounded strange. She then pointed to the new building in which the women slept and explained that volunteers prepared their beds and helped them shower. She was proud that she could still wash her hair, which was getting very long. Catarina hinted that she was having erotic dreams every night but did not say more.

I gave Catarina a new notebook. She said that she felt well when she wrote. It was proof that she could still use her hands and create something with them: "I am happy that I can maneuver the pen and that I am able to transmit something." What the other abandoned individuals in Vita find in the objects they hold, Catarina finds in writing. How to bring her poetic imagination into the space of ethics?

I told Catarina that I had listened to the tapes of our previous conversations and had transcribed them.

"And the medical records?" She wanted to know: "Did you read them? Were they useful?"

Yes, I said. I mentioned some of the findings and asked whether she recalled anything in particular from the Caridade Hospital.

"I remember all those women laughing loud, very loud. And when we had recreation, we were put in line, and our names were called to kick a ball."

Catarina, I thought, was always trying hard to avoid becoming part of a stereotyped, gendered order, whether in the household, in the mental asylum, or in Vita. When I asked about her friends Lili and India, she referred to them as "bed neighbors." She complained that the older women were spreading rumors about her and Clóvis.

Catarina was looking at Adriana's ring: "It's beautiful . . . the wedding ring. It is the two."

Adriana gave her the ring to examine.

And your writing—I went back to it—what comes to mind when you write?

"That I don't forget what I thought was important."

What makes a word important?

"Because . . . these words were not used very much. . . . So I thought carefully so as not to forget them."

Thinking is caring for the words. It gives a new value and use to the unused words. I asked Catarina whether one word led to the other, but she said that it did not and spoke of an impersonal agency behind the words, always in the past tense: "It is not that one word led to the other. . . . It was that one remembered. One recalled a word that was not much used in the dictionary, perhaps it was not even in the dictionary, and then I wrote it."

The writing is a thoughtful effort to recall, to make the unused word human.

Why wasn't the word in the dictionary?

"One had never taken the word and written it down."

Why do you call it a dictionary? I asked the same question I had asked the year before, when I first saw her writing.

Again, Catarina emphasized her labor: "Because it is a work of mine, a work that I do."

I wanted her to explain the difference between a dictionary and a book.

"In the book, the story is already written; and in the dictionary, I must write it, I must make the story. Do you get it?"

The dictionary contains the lost words, disconnected from a plot. As dead objects, they give space to the lived aspect of the word. I wanted to hear more.

"I must make the story in the dictionary. I must generate the idea of the story. Many times one copies a legend, copies from a book or a notebook."

Do you write for yourself or for someone else?

"I am writing this now. . . . Perhaps I am writing for you, I don't know."

Catarina had not said that before. This was a sign of immense trust.

After a silence, she continued: "Sometimes I think of an illness, of how it has been generated . . . and then I start to think that the illness has a cure. Then I write the name of the illness."

Her thinking traced a pattern: if one knows how an illness is generated, one may think of a cure.

Then the illusion of medical science appears (though it is followed by a question mark), embodied in her exchanges with Clóvis:

"So if one day there is a remedy for it, I think there will be donations, right? For there are always friends of Vita who donate medication to the pharmacy, and Clóvis treats the wounds there. . . . He gives injections and also pills."

Do you recall any particular illness?

"Rheumatism . . . and spasm, chronic spasm."

I wanted to know more about how Catarina was feeling, because I was arranging to bring a doctor to see her, to inquire what was happening with her physically, and to assess what could be done to alleviate the pain she described as constant.

"It is my illness. . . . It is painful, it aches down to my bones. Every joint aches, in the hips, the legs, the fingers . . . it is generalized."

Are you tired of talking?

"No."

Am I asking too much?

"No."

Clóvis came by. He looked worn out and said that Catarina was healthy now. She got involved in the conversation. "You gave me medication."

"Yes, didn't I?" he countered. And he tried to defuse her love story by presenting himself as a conscientious caretaker: "She fights with me all the time. She screams like a cat. I cannot treat any other female patient. And she gets jealous. She wants my sole attention. But she is not alone here." He added that he could no longer stand the rotten food and was looking to leave Vita for a nursing job in a geriatric house, this time paid. "There I can put my nurse diploma on the wall, and I can give my injections."

As Clóvis left to attend to other patients, Catarina turned to Adriana and advised, "You should stop with the pills. Then children can come."

A bit embarrassed, we agreed that it was time to think of having a child. Catarina told Adriana that she used to take a pill called Neovular.

Oscar came by and greeted us warmly: "We missed you. You are already part of our people." We also think of Vita and the people here, I replied.

I told Catarina and Oscar that I wanted to bring a doctor to examine her, and they both agreed.

Catarina used the conversation to foster her wish: "Oscar, will you take me to Novo Hamburgo to see my family?"

I intervened and told her that I would look for them.

As Oscar was leaving, Catarina repeated, "Clóvis is my boyfriend." She looked Adriana in the eye and said, "You are very thoughtful."

"We think of you," replied Adriana, and Catarina added: "I believe you. I have an immense trust in you both."

Lili, Catarina's roommate, came over, complaining that she was not feeling well but insisting, "I don't know why." A conversation ensued, and at some point Adriana asked Lili what had brought her to Vita. Lili repeated the things she had told me before, elements of her life code: "I didn't stay at home, I was always in the church. . . . I prayed." She used to go to church in Vita, she noted, but the church was no longer active. On Sunday afternoons, however, Pentecostals continued to organize a collective service in Vita's cement square, distributing candies and prayer cards, singing and praying into a microphone. "I always thought that I had to go to church, and now I am still here."

She then turned to Adriana and sadly asked, "Are you my daughter?"

"No."

Lili told us that she had conceived two daughters, Cristine and Valéria. "I took them to my father's house so that he would take care of them." She said that she was already sleeping in the streets at that time.

Why in the streets?

"Because I liked it."

I insisted on knowing what had happened in her home, why she left.

"I thought I had to go to church. . . . I don't want to talk about it. . . . But, truly, he didn't treat me well. My husband beat me, because I left and went to the church."

As I was translating to Adriana, Lili interrupted: "I don't understand. . . . I don't understand the language you speak."

Clóvis, who was nearby, had heard part of the conversation, and he confronted Lili, demanding that she tell "the real truth" about why she had been sent to Vita.

"I am telling the truth," she rebuked him.

"What did you do to your daughter-in-law?" Clóvis asked.

"She did something to me. . . . She got a knife and wanted to kill me."

"The story I know," said Clóvis, "is that she called your son 'daddy,' and you didn't like that."

"That's true. . . . She wasn't his daughter, I told her that. But it was not me who wanted to cut her."

Clóvis contradicted her: "I heard that you were cutting meat and then jumped over her with a knife."

We made a gesture asking Clóvis not to distress her further, and he left.

Lili said, "Today, I saw my son passing by the gate, but he didn't stop to see me."

"It's so difficult," Adriana responded.

Catarina then asked about Adriana's family.

Lili could not go that far and insisted: "Aren't you really my sister?"

And, as Lili kept looking at Adriana, Catarina added: "They are married, they are husband and wife."

Nothing is simple as the abandoned engage those who will listen to the limit. This was not an encounter in which unconscious wishes (intrinsic, in any case) are actualized, or one in which the anthropologists become stand-ins for previous psychic forms. Rather, a terrain was carved out by respect and trust—a terrain in which basic life problems played themselves out, and the agonistic management of time and meaning was expressed as a tie was sought.

Lili, Vita 2001

Lili, Vita 2001

Ataxia

I asked Dr. Luis Guilherme Streb, a long-time friend, to examine Catarina and possibly treat her. Two days later, he accompanied me to Vita.

Catarina was waiting for us in the pharmacy, where Clóvis was sorting medication—the surplus of donations to which Catarina had referred. The highly specialized medication made freely available by the federal government also finds its way into Vita. Clóvis told us: "I get lots of psychotropics and antiretrovirals. I separate the ones I can use here, and the others I send down to the pharmacy we created for people from the surrounding areas."

These antiretroviral medications did not go to Guido, a former inmate and now a volunteer, for he received full AIDS treatment and monitoring through SUS, the universal health care system. Some of the medications might go to individuals among the continuous flow of young people with AIDS who stop by Vita but are sent away or leave after a brief stay because of the inadequate food and conditions. Some of these young people go back to the streets, despite suffering from full-blown disease, because there, as one such person told me, "I earn money." Antiretrovirals were dispensed in an unregulated and irregular way to those in Vita's infirmary and recovery area who unofficially had AIDS. Several times, Oscar, Clóvis, and Alencar mentioned that Vita had approximately ten people with AIDS, but they could not point them out. With Catarina's permission and that of Vita's administration, Dr. Streb wanted to have her blood tested for the various infectious diseases that were circulating in Vita.

Psychiatric drugs abounded. "I work with heavy medication . . . haloperidol, chlorpromazine, levomepromazine, prometazine, imipramine," repeated Clóvis. Of the seventy people remaining in the infirmary, about forty were being heavily medicated. Dr. Streb specifically asked whether such medication was being administered to calm people down, but Clóvis denied this, speaking as if he were a psychiatrist: "I have patients with epilepsy, some schizophrenics, psychotics, and many people who are simply nervous." He turned off the radio, got chairs for us, and told Catarina, "Now you will talk to this doctor, and I will see a patient who was bitten by a dog."

As Catarina had her notebook open in her lap, the doctor asked about the last word she had written.

"CURSO."

Her "R" was opened up and written in a form similar to the letter "K."

"It's 'K' like in 'GEKAL' [general], in 'DINHEIKO' [money], and in 'CATAKINA.' "

And what does this word mean in your dictionary?

"Which word?" she replied.

"*Curso,*" the doctor smiled.

"People make *cursos* to learn a profession, and there is also *curso* for people who will get married and for baptisms. We participated in a baptism *curso.*" These courses are mandatory in Catholic parishes. Counselors and physicians come to advise couples about sex education, and, prior to a baptism, godparents are taught their religious duties.

Who is "we"?

"I and my ex-husband. We participated in a wedding course."

And what did you learn?

"I recall that the couples sat apart from each other in a big room and that the doctors were at the blackboard, teaching about the genitals. . . . And when they spoke of love, the couples, I could see, got closer to each other, the pairs, as it had to be, next to each other."

You too?

"We were already."

Catarina was speaking with great difficulty, often stopping to take a breath and to drink water, which also took much effort. The doctor began to gather the clinical signs he needed to make a diagnosis.

"My illness is not easy, doctor. Rheumatism and chronic spasm in the body. My joints ache, and my feet get swollen." Catarina recalled that when she arrived at Vita, she could still walk by holding herself against the walls. "Here, I went to the wheelchair and couldn't walk anymore."

Can you stand?

"Yes. But if I try to walk, I will fall."

Her basic lack of coordination, both in walking and in hand movement, left no doubt that she suffered from some form of ataxia. She was unable to stand upright with her eyes closed (the Romberg test), a classic sign of a dysfunction of the cerebellum. She also showed the Babinsky sign—that is, as the doctor irritated the sole of the foot, her toes curved upward. This altered reflex indicated that her spine was not providing adequate motor control. Her hands trembled as she tried to hold objects. She also showed evidence of nystagmus: her eyes could not stay fixed on the doctor's finger. Rather, they oscillated, another sign of degeneration in the cerebellum. Her "cavus feet" were a late development of this spinocerebellar disorder.

Asked whether other family members had similar problems with walking, Catarina listed several: "My deceased mother, an uncle, and an aunt. . . . My deceased grandfather Horacio, my mother's father, was also like this. He was in ruins at the end of his life. He was very old, though. He lived many years."

Catarina knew that her disorder was hereditary, that it was linked to the maternal side of her family, and that her grandparents' generation had lived longer. Whatever this disease was, it had expressed itself in her at a very young age and in an accelerated way.

Any general practitioner anywhere could have carried out this routine and simple exam. I was appalled that no one in the public health care system had thought to perform it, in spite of Catarina's constant complaints of pain in her legs and her obvious problems with walking. A technical explanation is that many doctors have stopped using clinical signs to diagnose, preferring to leave diagnoses to specialists and machines. It is more likely, however, that nothing was ever done for Catarina because she was a poor mental patient in the public health care system. As one local physician put it, "They are simply perceived as not worth examining for signs to treat."

Dr. Streb checked Catarina's dilated eyes and found ocular alterations, just as Dr. Daniela Justus had in 1994 during her failed attempt to have Catarina examined neurologically. Catarina's heartbeat was fine, as was her blood pressure. She also told the doctor that her menstruation was normal. In fact, she kept sporadic track of her cycles in the dictionary. Her loss of weight was a result of the canned food, she claimed. "I keep throwing it up."

As for her general mood, Catarina said, "I feel bad, without will." She mentioned that she was still taking vitamins: "I improve, and endure the day better." In fact, as I read in Clóvis's medication chart, he was giving her the antidepressant imipramine. When I inquired, he told me that the doctor who paid weekly visits to Vita had prescribed it, which I doubted. "The vitamins make things more legible. They affect my voice. When one wants to free the voice, they help to get it out," stated Catarina.

In spite of her lack of coordination, Catarina's legs were very strong, the doctor concluded after the general examination. "Yes, I think you can walk. Let's try?"

"I cannot."

"I think it is possible. . . . Let's try?"

After some hesitation, she agreed. Catarina supported herself on Dr. Streb and took a few steps forward.

"Who said that you couldn't walk?"

Then she tried to stand without any support.

She could, with some imbalance.

"What happened to my legs?" Catarina wanted to know.

"This inability to coordinate the movements is what we call ataxia. It is linked to a deterioration of the cerebellum. We will have to investigate which kind of ataxia this is," the doctor explained. "But if you train a bit every day, you might be able to walk a little."

"I don't think I can. . . . I will fall."

"And with a cane?" continued the doctor.

"I will fall over the cane."

We laughed.

Dr. Streb insisted, "Your legs are strong, Catarina."

"But if I fall, I will hurt myself."

I wondered about Catarina's sense of impossibility. At first, I thought that it spoke of her experience of medicine: closures for her. As her records showed, Catarina's physical deterioration was accompanied by medical practices that never addressed her clinical signs. Instead, she was given dangerously combined medications and was oversedated by doctors and family members. This sense that she could not walk might thus also be a chemical matter.

Then I thought of how Vita might be occasioning it. When we first met her in 1997, Catarina was pedaling an old exercise bicycle, in defiance of the immobility that came with this place. Vita creates so many conditions that force life not to be that dying ends up happening—how to exert one's will and not be resigned to this course?

Finally, I recalled the scene in which Catarina at first resisted her father's attempts to teach her the alphabet but eventually acquired this knowledge, "without which I wouldn't be a person." Between her desire to walk away from Vita, her acceptance of the impossibility of doing so, and the thought of all that happened to her was the openness of the character "K" in her rewritten name, CATAKINA. This character seemed to counter the finitude of the specific figures who had determined her exit from ordinary life. Yet how to literally sustain this openness and possibility, step by step?

Catarina mentioned that she had not slept well the night before.

"Were you thinking of this visit?" asked the doctor.

She acknowledged that she had been, and then she added: "I dreamed erotic dreams. I dreamed of men with women."

"Everyone has erotic dreams," replied the doctor, caught off guard a bit.

"It's natural," agreed Catarina. She then repeated the image of two: "Sex is for two. Love then comes and transmits something good to us . . . pleasure and desire."

How important is this for you?

"Oh, my, is it important! It transmits life. As time passed, I realized that things should be this way . . . and I began to think like this."

What do you mean?

"At times, I have a thought, and I let the thought carry me away. . . . Not always, because I need to do my work. . . . I work with thinking."

Thinking can be imaginative and a flight, but ultimately there is still the need to face the dead end and then *to work with thinking*—could this open something up? Around Clóvis, insisted Catarina, she had another history to draw from and a future to look toward. "On January first, it will be one year since Clóvis and I began dating. We are dating because we cannot leave . . . like two elderly people. But when desire intensifies, then we have a foamy bath."

Do you want to ask the doctor a question?

"Do I have hope? Hope to walk?"

"What do you think?" he replied.

"You are the doctor."

"As I told you, your legs have strength. The important thing is that you have hope. . . . Do you have hope?"

"I do have hope and courage."

"That's the most important thing."

The doctor then explained that her ataxia was most likely hereditary and that it had no cure, but that one could work to delay its expression, with physical exercises and so forth.

She then asked for pain relief, a muscle relief gel called Doutorzinho ("Little Doctor"), which she knew was "good for rheumatism." The doctor said he would also give her Motrin.

She tried out another construction: "I've thought about doing something crazy, like getting pregnant."

What?

"To begin life in another place, Clóvis and I. . . . We could make a little shack. It's tough to be alone, and to wait for him if he were to leave." She knew he was going to leave Vita soon.

Oscar came by, and I asked him to take Catarina to a local health post for the blood test Dr. Streb had recommended. We said our farewells, and Clóvis led us to the car. He repeated that it was almost certain that he would get a job as a nurse in a geriatric house in the nearby town of Alvorada. He also wanted to exonerate himself of anything Catarina might have disclosed about their affair. "She is very depressed. A woman who loses her children. . . . This traumatizes a person. People here lack tenderness."

Dr. Streb and I spent some time talking about the examination. He repeated that Catarina's unsteady gait and inability to coordinate voluntary movements were a kind of spinocerebellar ataxia, "but the clinical definition of ataxic disorders is very difficult." He first hypothesized that it might be Friedreich ataxia, an inherited disease of the central nervous system that also leaves the feet deformed.[54] But, as we recalled Catarina speaking of the disorder among her maternal lineage, we doubted this hypothesis—the pattern of inheritance in Friedreich is recessive, that is, it needs the father's gene. The other initial hypothesis, far fetched, was Creutzfeldt-Jakob.

I was particularly happy to see that the ataxia classifications made very little, if any, reference to mental disorders. Dr. Streb understood Catarina's trajectory into Vita, "which kept taking verbs from her" but insisted on characterizing her thinking as "disaggregated and suffering from formal alteration." In contrast, I felt constantly challenged to find a way to listen to her voice, which had been displaced from these conventions and was attempting to claim experience in her own way and on her own terms.

At any rate, we were in the process of composing the biology of Catarina. The next move would be to get an MRI of her brain and wait for the blood test results. Meanwhile, I would find her family.

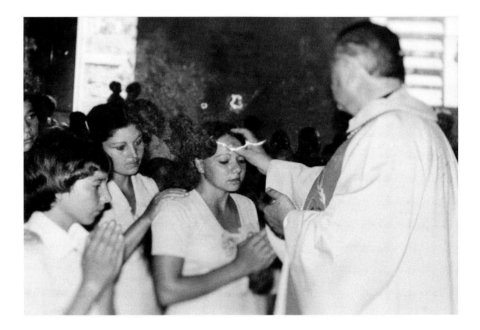

Catarina's first communion, at age fourteen

Catarina at seventeen, with her future husband

The civil marriage, when Catarina was eighteen

The wedding party

Twenty-one-year-old Catarina and her husband holding their second child

Her House

The next Sunday, I followed Catarina's clues into Novo Hamburgo's poorest districts. I drove around the dusty, narrow, and overcrowded alleys of the Santo Afonso district but could not find 999 Constituição Street.

I stopped at local businesses and at Pentecostal churches to ask people where the street was, with no success. At a gas station, I got a more recent city map. Although this map pointed me to Constituição Street, the street seemed to end with house number 747. I remember a turn and a bridge and more dark alleys, with people at the gates and windows wondering who the stranger was and what he wanted. No, nobody around knew of anyone like Catarina, the Gomes family, or the Moraes family.

I had gathered a few more addresses from Catarina's medical records. To my surprise, one of them led me into a rich neighborhood, closer to downtown. Beyond the dead end of Travessão Street, however, a cluster of wooden shacks sat on a large grassy field—a squatter settlement on city property. A bar connected the group of shacks. Dogs barked endlessly at each house. A man holding a baby told me that a Nilson indeed was living in one of the shacks, a pink house, where, according to the Caridade records, Catarina had once lived. "But there is nobody at home now." The man gave me his cell phone number and told me to call later. If Nilson was around, he would put me in contact with him.

That night I called. It turned out that the owner of the pink house was not Catarina's husband. "My name is Nilson Maurer. I am the other Nilson," he said. "I am married to Nilson Moraes's sister, Sirlei. You can call me Alemão [German]." He added that Anderson, Catarina's teenage son was visiting them, and that I was welcome to stop by.

A semblance. That was the first thing I heard about Catarina as I entered her former house and the world of her ex-family. "She was so beautiful in the wedding photos," said Catarina's sister-in-law, after I introduced myself and explained what had brought me there. The first memory was not the person but her apparition. "When Nilson first brought her photo home, I said, 'Father and mother, look, what a beautiful girl he got for himself.' Everybody agreed."

Catarina entered the new family unit as an appearance, as the property of a man, and as part of a domestic labor force. "When Nilson brought her home, she helped with everything, and now she is in this situation." In that world where semiliteracy is the norm, Catarina was also remembered for the form of her writing. "She had a beautiful handwriting; the way she connected the characters was so beautiful."

Today's paralysis could not be read in the past, Sirlei implied. "When I first laid eyes on her, one couldn't see she would have the problem she has today. She was a perfect person like us." To be counted as a person in the new family, Catarina had to be *like us*. No longer in that family's image, she was past. Alemão, however, suggested that the Moraes family had known something of Catarina's physical condition early on, recalling that "she was already dragging her legs a bit." This physical sign had not entered the initial recollection of Catarina's sister-in-law. "I didn't know her when she was single, but people say that she limped a bit," Sirlei excused herself.

Sirlei then associated Catarina with another disintegrating body: "Her mother also lost the legs and the hands." "One had to feed her"—a leftover body at the mercy of an impersonal pronoun and a certain moral obligation. A well-off uncle "is also like this," added Alemão. "I think this is hereditary." The onset of Catarina's limping seemed to be of great relevance, for her sister-in-law returned to it, dating its origin to Anderson's birth. This physiological sign also had an economic side: "She worked in a shoe factory. When she had Alessandra, she was still working, but they fired her because she began to fall there." Catarina was no longer work-able.

Anderson entered the conversation. "My uncles also have this problem. They have the legs like that." Nobody knew what the disease actually was, but Alemão had noticed a variation in expression: "it attacked her stronger than it did the brothers."

The fifteen-year-old Anderson was living with his father in the Boa Saúde district. He was studying at night, sixth grade, and was looking for a job. Alessandra was still living with their grandmother in the Santo Afonso district. Anderson told me that I had been close to finding the grandmother's house that afternoon—"the street ends, but the numbering continues to the left, after the bridge." Ana, the youngest sibling, was living "with her god-parents." Nilson, the children's father, had remarried and had a son with his new wife. He continued to work in shoe factories. His wife, I was told, was a maid and also helped out in a local bakery. She had three daughters from a previous marriage.

The TV was on, broadcasting the variety show *Fantástico*. Alemão and Sir-lei's two kids were running around, and several conversations were now taking place around the table simultaneously. The couple, who also worked in shoe factories, complained about the money they had to spend on child care. Like all the other workers in the shoe complex, they lived in constant fear of losing their jobs.

Sirlei again began to discuss Catarina's frequent hospitalizations, and her husband interrupted once more: "But she was not hospitalized only because of the legs. There were other problems. One day, she burned Nilson's cloth-ing and documents." In that local world, the word *(documentos)* also connotes male genitals.

Anderson said that he had witnessed it. "It happened in this house. Father came home, and she burned his things. That was long ago." As far as he could recall, "before suffering the attacks, she was normal. She cooked, she did everything in the house." Alemão added that she seemed to have intel-ligence. Anderson recollected a caring mother: "She woke me up at the right time to go to school, she helped me with homework. We had a normal life . . . until the problems began." But he could not recall precisely when it all began to fall apart.

"When Anderson was born, we began to see that it damaged her head. When Alessandra was born, it got worse," stated Sirlei. "It": something in Catarina, a child, an unknown disease, the experience of motherhood? Something worsened. Sirlei was now synchronizing Catarina's mental dis-turbances with the first expressions of her physical paralysis and with the ex-perience of motherhood. It was as if these things could not be teased apart.

As I listened to the inconsistencies in Sirlei's account of Catarina's deteri-oration, I thought that perhaps the human actions that had conflated these various occurrences needed to remain veiled. Catarina's condition had been constructed by the ways these various elements were brought together. In the end, Catarina was the equivalent of "it." The neutral pronoun "it" can stand for the contempt one has for a person.

"She went mad. In the middle of the night, she went to the streets and wandered. She had everybody preoccupied with her," recalled Sirlei. Alemão claimed that "she did not want to know her husband. No one could talk to her." The attacks "were not that frequent," he said, but when they happened, Catarina did not behave as she should have. She began to flirt with the other Nilson: "She sat next to me, talked to me, said that she liked me, began to say romantic things. But then, next day, she was normal."

"She went to the hospital in bad shape, but came back normal," Sirlei rushed to say, as if trying to defuse Alemão's description of a sexuality with the wrong object. Her husband, however, insisted on bringing dissonance into the conversation: "Normal, so to speak—she still had those problems with walking." "Yeah, but normal in her head," Sirlei rebuked him.

Alemão was linking Catarina's hospitalization and banishment from family life with her paralysis. He hinted about what should have remained unsaid: "The last time she was hospitalized, she couldn't walk anymore, so she had to stay there." Sirlei corrected his account by insisting that Catarina could stand on her own feet: "The last time we saw her, when we were leaving, she stood up from the chair and bade us farewell." In this image, Catarina had let the family go of her own volition.

"I thought that it was a family disease, that my grandmother also had it," said Anderson. For the child, "it" was not madness. Sirlei interrupted, saying that Anderson was too little when Catarina's mother died in 1988, "paralyzed in a wheelchair, here in this house." But Anderson remembered his grandfather, he said, and his mother pregnant. "He slaughtered a pig when we visited Caiçara. My father took us. Mom was pregnant with Ana."

The name Ana brought up a dramatic development in this new family complex. "When Catarina was hospitalized, they took the newborn to Dona Ondina, Nilson's mother. But then there was a fight with Tamara and Urbano, the godparents. They wanted to keep the child. They fought with the grandmother, and then Seu Urbano was able to—I don't know, we cannot say exactly how it happened. . . . But as far as we know, Seu Urbano made a deal with Nilson. Nilson is illiterate; he can only sign his name. They made a shady deal and took a paper there and forced her to sign, the poor woman."

Catarina?

"Yes. So that they could keep the child."

Did she know what she was signing?

"We don't know for sure. . . . But she was weak. . . . Now the girl has been legally passed on to them."

Sirlei reported that Urbano and Tamara did not want the siblings to visit each other. "They didn't let the girl call Catarina 'mom'—only 'auntie.'"

The absent mother had to be praised: "I remember the times Catarina lived alone with the kids, down there, next to my mom's. We could see the love she had for them. The little money she had, it was to go to the market to buy things for them." As the image of a self-sacrificing mother, Catarina still had value. But she had no money of her own, and her body was not working. "She separated from Nilson, she returned from the hospital. Then Nilson left her this house, and she exchanged it with Delvane. Then she went to the shack that was set on fire, went to the hospital, and did not return."

I was told that when they first arrived in Novo Hamburgo, Nilson and Catarina rented a room and then were able to convince Nilson's parents to migrate also. His parents bought the property at 999 Constituição Street, and Nilson and Catarina built a small annex there, as all his other siblings had done. This sort of familial grouping was common practice in Novo Hamburgo's working-class settlements.

Later, Nilson used his contacts at the city hall, where he worked, to obtain semilegal permission to squat on city property and build the house we were in. Even though it was never legalized as his property, the house had transaction value. Delvani, married to Nilson's sister, first lived with his in-laws and then built a shack nearby. When Nilson left Catarina, he made arrangements to occupy her house, which was more valuable, and had her move into the shack, where the mother-in-law would supposedly help her take care of the kids. This was the shack that burned down.

"When the house burned down, the family did not provide her with a new place. She lived with my mother. She was becoming crazy. . . . So many problems, poor thing, one can only go insane," said Sirlei. There was compassion now, even an understanding that there was a material and historical course to Catarina's condition, though contingent on her madness.

Catarina had said she wanted to know what people had written about her. Now I was discovering what people thought of her. She wanted me to find her family. I was bringing Catarina back. These people had responded with hospitality and information to my attempt to understand what had happened. And in the course of our interaction—amid dissonant recollections, dissimulations, hidden judgments, and moralities that protected their lives and interests—a common sense had been cracked open. Many relational, physiological, medical, and economic factors intersected and gave form to the belief that it would be impossible for Catarina to ever return.

How had this sense of impossibility emerged and evolved? It was neither a priori determined nor simply contingent, I thought. What were the specific situations and decisions through which it had all happened? I also found myself challenged to move beyond assigning blame, to find in Catarina's family the good she kept attributing to them, and to trace how their values and dispositions toward her had taken form.

Overall, I felt that these people saw me as a kind of emissary of the country's laws. In other words, they knew that by law they were legally liable to care for Catarina. As I learned from the Public Ministry in Porto Alegre, city attorneys have the power to subpoena family members of abandoned people and negotiate care or financial responsibility. But as Vita's history suggests, this happens in only a few cases, which then become emblematic of a supposed democratic state of human rights. The state then exists empirically as it restores family ties for some.

Brothers

That same night, Alemão and Anderson took me to see Altamir, Catarina's oldest brother. I would have had no hope of finding his place by myself. This was one of the roughest districts of Novo Hamburgo, chaotic in its squatting patterns.

Alemão was impressed with Altamir's gated property: a bike repair shop downstairs and a reasonably comfortable two-bedroom apartment upstairs. Altamir and his wife, Vania, had a three-year-old son, Eugenio. Her parents and several brothers had also migrated from the northwestern region of the province in the 1980s and lived nearby. Vania's brother, who owned a small store, had officially "hired" Altamir, allowing him to receive unemployment benefits now and then, which were used to expand the house. Vania worked in a shoe factory.

After introducing myself, I related what I knew of their family history through Catarina and mentioned that she always spoke very highly of her brothers. Her paralysis was the entry point of our discussion.

"This comes from the family," explained Altamir, using the expression "it is in the trunk of the tree." Their mother, maternal grandfather, and maternal great-grandfather "also had it," he said. "My mother had about ten siblings, and four or five had it. Some cousins have it, and others don't."

Vania linked "its" manifestation in Catarina to childbirth and labor: "It got to her when she had her last daughter, right, daddy?" Altamir did not follow that line of reasoning and mentioned that "it develops slowly." The symptoms were always the same: "The legs get shaky, more and more, and you walk as if you were drunk. Speech also gets slurred."

He then suggested a broken taboo as the root of the disorder. "People used to say that the root of this old trunk was marriage among cousins or brothers and sisters. I don't know if this is true; this is what I heard."

"It's a mystery," added Vania.

I asked whether anyone in the family had ever had a neurological exam.

"Once, my deceased father took my mother to a hospital in Porto Alegre, right, mummy? But nothing happened." I wondered whether Catarina's father had left her mother for another woman after realizing her physical problems and taking her in vain to Porto Alegre, where she was most likely treated as the poor are, with no specialized exams or procedures. I wondered about the identity of this disorder, its incidence, and the dynamics and strategies, both familial and medical, that had developed over time to manage it and that kept it unacknowledged. Altamir asked, "What is this blood problem that nobody knows about?"

"When Catarina lived with us," said Vania, "she was treated by the mental health people. Because there were times that she was very crazy, right, daddy? Crazy to run out, to escape, and all these things." After her shack burned down, Catarina moved from one brother's house to another. As I had found in the files of the Novo Hamburgo mental health service, these were the days when Dr. Gilson Kunz treated her.

"The doctor already knew her," Vania recollected. "It was not necessary to take her to the health services anymore. He gave us the medication. I went there myself and picked up the medication. After she was hospitalized, we never had to take her back to the doctor."

I wanted to be sure we were talking about the same doctor. "Yes, it was Dr. Kunz. When I went to see him, he knew of her. . . . He already knew which medication she had." To this day, I thought, this doctor does not know what he was prescribing or for whom. "I don't recall any neurological exam having been done. But it must have been done," added Vania. In her thinking, it seemed, good medicine existed to support a retrospective account in which all paths of knowing and care had been followed.

I asked again about the onset of Catarina's problems. Altamir described her as "normal" during their childhood. Vania then reintroduced the semblance of Catarina: "She was *very* normal. I remember the wedding photos." I wondered about this gradation of normality and what in one's life or interests determined its application to another family member.

Altamir said that they had grown up very poor, helping out on the plantation. Catarina was the eldest child. He was next, and two years later, Ademar—who also lived in the Santo Afonso district and repaired bikes—was born. Then came a sister, who was now paralyzed and lived in a nursing home in Ipiranga, and finally Armando, who lived next to Ademar and worked in a shoe factory. Altamir was the first to come to Novo Hamburgo, when he was eighteen years old, followed by Ademar. Altamir summed up the trajectory of his life: "I began working in shoe factories, gained some position and money, and opened my own repair shop. Then we married, right, mummy?"

Vania was still trying to answer my initial question. "Catarina passed through the health post, the general hospital, the Caridade. . . . The truth of her illness nobody knows." Simply put, the outcome of Catarina's passage through medicine and psychiatry had been *nonknowledge*, on several registers. First, Sirlei spoke as if the family had not known of Catarina's physiological deficiency before she entered their household. Second, Catarina was treated and medicated for something other than "it"—an "it" that remained unknown. Third, Vania, whose husband was beginning to show similar physical signs, looked back and saw Catarina as embodying something they all feared. And, finally, this family (and perhaps others) did not have medical knowledge of their condition and had devised ways to live with this unknown disease.

Vania was dominating the conversation. She commented that Armando was already limping, like the older brothers. "When they walk, you notice a difference. It's not normal." The immediate association was death, the mother who died in a wheelchair. I wondered what one had to have, own, or be to avoid the certainty of being cast out. "Catarina's children and Eugenio show no signs. Ademar's kids are also normal. I don't know if with time . . ."

The nonknowledge around this condition was visibly measured and had economic meaning; Vania speculated about whether the brothers would be able to work a few years from now. Altamir noted that when he stopped doing things, the difficulties with locomotion increased. His mind-set, he believed, could help to deter the disease: "One must not lose the will."

Vania brought the conversation back to Catarina, suggesting that some disorder other than the unknown disease had led her away from home. "Do you remember, daddy, you always told me that she escaped from home and that Nilson went after her?" But Altamir refused to attribute Catarina's mental condition to pathology. "This was due to the illness itself," he insisted. "I think that she revolted against the illness. I think that this provoked unhappiness in her." Her mood disorder was not a mental illness, so to speak, but a way to face the biological signs—or, perhaps, the ways they were handled domestically.

That is what Vania now speculated, for theories of causation focused on Catarina continued to change. "You are right, afterward she got even crazier. I shouldn't say crazy, for she knows what she is saying. Her daughter was given away, and she couldn't take care of the children anymore—all this had an impact on her. Then the children going from one house to the other—this weakens one's head." Catarina's motherhood was narrated in the past tense, in Alemão's words: "She had such a love for her kids."

As Catarina's ex-family members reasoned about her condition, they freely assembled a bricolage of etiology, unconcerned by contradictions. In the process, however, a constant theme crystallized: she was isolated and beyond treatment.

Vania recalled Catarina's last stay at the São Paulo Hospital. By then, no one was responsible for her. "It's complicated. I don't understand it well. She was hospitalized at the São Paulo. I think Nilson did it. She got better and came home, alone. When you least expected, she was coming home. She was discharged, obtained money at the bus station, and came home. She was so good in her head that she came home alone." It seemed that nobody expected her to come back. That nonplace she had in her family's mind and the indiscriminate medicating made Catarina crazy all over again, as she wrote in the dictionary: *louca da cabeça, louca da casa* (crazy in the head, crazy in the house).

As the conversation went on, they began to displace moral attention from Catarina to what had happened to her youngest daughter. Alemão again made the case that giving up Ana for adoption had been the "wrong thing." Altamir and Vania, however, were adamant that the child was well cared for and lived a rich life. Blood ties were not so meaningful. "The child is much better off than if she lived with her mother or grandmother. It couldn't be better. The stepmother likes her a lot. Ana has her own room; she has everything."

For Vania, the only problem is that they do not take the girl to visit Catarina. "Tamara told me Ana couldn't go to Vita, for it is a place for mad people. But I told her, if you think this will traumatize the kid, then take Catarina to spend a weekend with you." The most they consider are temporary measures to expunge the doubt of their morality.

Alemão insisted, "The girl is well off, but to change the name. . . . I don't agree." According to Altamir, "Urbano wanted the child." Vania whispered, so that Anderson might not hear, that the children's father was actually at fault. "You know, their father is an illiterate, a bum, the poor thing. . . . What can one say?"

Then the inevitable: how to speak of Catarina in Vita? Without my asking, Vania mentioned that "the last time we visited her in Vita, she was content and asked to see Ana." The phrase "the last time" minimizes how much time had passed since anyone had visited Catarina. Vita's oldest volunteers recall only a few visits to her, around 1996, just after she had been left there. But tonight's conversation, it seemed, had occasioned the thought of a brief return. "It's time for us to bring her here to spend a weekend with us," suggested Vania.

You grew up with her, I said to Altamir. Seeing what has happened to her, what comes to mind?

"It's tough, but what to do? If one brings her home, one also cannot do anything. And we have to work."

In the past three years, I have continued to work with Catarina's family. I have always been welcomed into their homes. And I have always been taken aback by the ease with which they speak of her. For Catarina, there is nothing to be done, I heard over and over again. That was common sense. The impossibility of doing anything to bring her back to social life was assumed rather than analyzed and acted on, I thought. Each one claimed that he or she had done all that was possible, to the limit.

An ordered realm existed in Catarina's exclusion. Who belonged in the house, who was worth medicine, who made money, and the gradation of acceptable normality—these were all key elements of the household's maintenance. The common sense that Catarina was physically unviable and mentally unsustainable had a value and validity for those who possessed it. And as Clifford Geertz has luminously written: "Here, as elsewhere, things [or humans] are what you make of them" (2000a:76). As Catarina was left all by herself, her relatives remained solid citizens looking for a position and a family life in a constantly changing social field marked by economic pressure and violence. In this dire context, how does one speak of the "evil" that is done and the "good" one must do? For Altamir and other family members, it was through a rhetorical question to which the unspoken answer was "nothing": "It's tough, but what to do?"

Children, In-Laws, and the Ex-Husband

The next day, I went to 999 Constituição Street. Anderson took me to meet his grandparents and his sister Alessandra. Ondina, the sixty-year-old matriarch, had her hair neatly tucked away in a bun, typical of women who belong to Pentecostal churches. She and her husband, Nestor, sixty-one years old, are professed "*crentes*, reborn Christians, baptized by the Holy Spirit in the waters."

Ondina told me that she had raised Anderson since he was two years old, Alessandra since she was six months old, and "the one that Urbano has" for three years. "Then they took her from me. When Anderson was twelve years old, his father took him." A twelve-year-old is a valuable family asset as a laborer. Alessandra helped her grandmother with household chores. The old couple emphasized living by God's word: "Once you listen to the Word, things get better. You normalize."

Like other family members, Ondina associated Catarina's breakdown with Alessandra's birth—more precisely, with her lack of womanly wisdom in dealing with that event. She claimed that Catarina "did not take care of herself." The old couple was still living in the countryside then, and Nilson and Catarina had stopped sending letters. "For a long time, I didn't get any news. I was very concerned. I contacted the factory where she worked, but she was no longer there. She had been hospitalized." Finally they reached Nilson, who begged his parents to come to the city and take care of the children while he worked.

At first, Ondina admitted, she was afraid of life in the city, but now there was no way she would return to the harsh agricultural life. Nestor proudly said that he immediately found work in a shoe factory. "All our kids came and found work. There, we were at the mercy of floods and drought; you couldn't count on a profit." Although the quiet and humble-looking man said that he had retired and received benefits, he still worked in the factory to increase the family income. For him, "the government is not solely to be blamed for the miserable monthly minimum wage."

Ondina described Catarina as "always hospitalized. She ran away from us." The aggressiveness that Nilson reported in Catarina's hospitalizations was also a constant in Ondina's account: "She was physical with me. She attacked me, and no one could control her." When I asked why, she replied that "Catarina's head maddened."

According to rumor, Catarina tried to pick up men, Ondina charged. "She didn't want to hear of Nilson anymore." No reference to Catarina's growing paralysis, but a hint, here and there, that she was not a good person: "She had bad sentiments toward others." Nestor softened the account a bit: "It was temporary. . . . She was extremely well, and then all of a sudden, something happened to her head, and she escaped."

Ondina saw a causality in Catarina's wanderings. "Because she escaped from Nilson, he lost the taste for her. He has always been an earnest and hard-working man. The last time she was hospitalized, he found another woman." In other words, it was clear that the hospitalization was a pretext for casting her aside; no return was expected. But when she did come back, "he abandoned her."

Ondina then mentioned something new. "Nilson exchanged the house. My son-in-law went to live there." That is, it was not Catarina who had been gullible. Rather, Nilson himself made the transaction, received some money, and left her the shack that later burned down. At every stage of Catarina's degradation, there was an economy.

For Ondina, Catarina's sheer existence then produced, "with no reason," suffering and danger: "I suffered with her here. When she got mad, she didn't want to know me. She got the knife and wanted to cut me. I didn't do anything to her." Ondina mentioned in passing that she was taking care of all the children, although Tamara and Urbano had removed Ana. "Now let it be," she said, and added, "Their father allowed it," suggesting her discontent with her son's handling of the adoption.

Catarina's last days in that neighborhood were Vita-like and self-imposed, according to Ondina. "She had nothing to eat. Nilson had to pay her a pension but was not doing it. How would I know that she had no food if I was not allowed in there? The neighbors told me that she would die of hunger, that she had no food. I took gas, flour, oil. But she didn't let me in."

But Ondina also stretched her story to the limit, claiming to have saved Catarina from death. "That same week, her neighbors' shack was set on fire, and it spread to hers. If not for me, she would have died. It was four-thirty in the morning. I jumped from bed and went screaming for help. My husband and I pulled her out of the flames."

The in-laws took her in for a month. "I treated her well but began calling on her brothers." Ondina and Nestor reported that even though none of the brothers wanted to help, they took Catarina to Ademar one day. "I told him, '*This is your blood, not mine.* It is your sister, you must support her.' . . . We did what we could, we rescued her from the flames." That is, they rescued both Catarina and her few remaining valuable possessions. "The first thing I thought was to get the gas tank out. She also had a refrigerator." When Ademar took Catarina in for a few weeks, he also took in her valuables.

There was something in Catarina's blood that people wanted nothing to do with. I asked them about her problems with walking. Ondina replied, "Yes, at that time, she was already holding herself against the walls. . . . When she got crazy, I don't know how she could walk from here to there. . . . I don't understand how these guys on the road never killed her."

And when did her locomotion problems begin?

The answer again was confused, mixing childbirth with a certain knowledge and denial of a disease Catarina's mother carried. "With Alessandra's birth. . . . I knew Catarina when she dated Nilson. . . . Her mom was already in a wheelchair then, and we told him, 'See, you will have a lump at home. Her mom already has this problem—perhaps it is from family, and she will have it too.'" But it was Nilson's choice, for "he didn't want a racy woman. . . . He just wanted her to be at home. So they got married . . . and all this happened. I never understood why she went mad and went into the world." Nestor leaked his view of the unknown disease: "It seems less severe among men."

Now that Catarina was gone, Ondina reasoned that she could not have kept a wheelchair-bound Catarina. "She likes me very much, and I also want her well-being. She is the mother of my grandchildren. I always treated her well. I think she thought that I was guilty that Nilson left her. But for me, he could live with her now and for the rest of his days. He kept hospitalizing her. He probably lost the taste for her."

Nestor's reasoning, however, resembled that of Altamir, Catarina's oldest brother: "I believe that she felt the disease. She thought that this had already happened to her mother. Her mom died in a wheelchair. She thought that would happen to her as well." Or perhaps Catarina knew what people did to those who had the disease. Ondina misheard Nestor and revealed that Catarina's tragedy was, after all, since the beginning, about her physiology: "Nilson was warned."

But then, I kept thinking, why did he choose her? What else did she have that was more important than her faulty body?

The answer was land.

I learned that from Nilson, the ex-husband himself, later that week.

I found Nilson at home one early afternoon, after he woke up from his rest after a night shift at the shoe factory. He lived on the other side of town, in the Boa Saúde district. His new house was under construction, in a squatter settlement in the outskirts, from which one could see farm fields. The thirty-six-year-old man was married to Lúcia, who looked much older than he did. They had their own son, Ricardo. Her hair up in a bun, she was also a Pentecostal, like Nilson's mother. Lúcia was knitting and sat by us, along with Anderson, throughout the conversation.

Nilson said that he was working two shifts a day, to save money for the construction of the house. He wanted to put Anderson to work. "Hopefully, I can get him to make gravel. One must put them to work when they are young. Then, when they grow up, they already have experience, know how to do a bit of everything, and can more easily find a better job. The earlier the better, because here in the city, if you are forty or fifty years old, the factories don't take you in. If you have not worked as a kid and have no experience . . . or if you wait to find a job until you are twenty or thirty, then you are lost."

Anderson showed me his drawings, cars from magazines and heroes from video games. "He wants to be an engineer. But in order to study, you must have money," said his father.

Like the others, Nilson spoke openly about Catarina. "It's all past," he stated. "It is not even in my mind." I asked him when Catarina's problems began, to which he replied, "After the premature birth of Ana." I told him that according to the Caridade records, Catarina was first hospitalized in 1988, four years before Ana was born. He agreed. (He might have simply forgotten, but I recalled Catarina saying that he had a tendency to lie.) At any rate, she had been escaping from home.

"I worked as a security guard at the city hall at night and left her at home. Then, once at midnight, people came, saying, 'Your woman is on the road.'

One day, we found her in the nearby town of Estância Velha. So I decided to hospitalize her." And this became routine. "It was a month at home and a month at the hospital."

Nilson then mentioned that Catarina had burned his clothes and documents, and he used this to make the point that she was not so much a mental case as a bad person. "That day, I was pissed off. I got home after work, and she took my clothing and documents and set them on fire. I told myself, this is no longer madness, it is evil. So I said now I will do something. I went to the judge to get a divorce. I left her the house and paid alimony and left. She exchanged the house, made money, and went to live next to my mother. We arranged a shack for her there."

His parents, however, had told me that he did not pay alimony and that in fact he had made some money by exchanging the house. Nilson's account of the divorce also contradicted Catarina's. In the medical records, she appeared to be the one asking for it. I also wondered why she kept saying that she wanted to sign the divorce papers.

"Finally," said Nilson, "the city hall took up the case, picked her up, and took her there."

To Vita?

"I don't know where. The last time I saw her was many years ago." In the end, she was a stray thing, to be picked up by the city's humane services, banished from one's view to a place one does not name.

"We met in Caiçara, in a dance hall. I was twenty and she was eighteen when we got married. Anderson was born there, and then we came to Novo Hamburgo. Two of her brothers were already here. We came in the hope of finding work, to improve our life, because in the countryside, you know . . . one year was good, the other year was bad. So we decided to sell the land and left."

Nilson explained that when he married Catarina, half the family's land was put in his name, as he assumed the care of her mother and her youngest brother. Nilson did not comment further on what had happened to the land, but he mentioned that he had brought the mother and brother-in-law along to the city. "The old lady was in a wheelchair. She lost her legs. We even had to feed her."

Nilson first found a job in a shoe factory and then was "fortunate" to get a job as a city hall security guard. "Life is better here in the city. There is work, there are doctors. You don't work if you don't want to. I have never been without a job. One company breaks down and another opens. The city is good, the country is bad. There, you have to buy on credit. Then, when you harvest, you are indebted to the store; and when there is no harvest, you have to sell an animal." I recalled Catarina's constant listing of words such as "debt" in her dictionary.

Nilson said that Catarina worked for a while, "but what I earned was enough for us all to live on. We never threw money away. My only vice was to smoke a cigarette now and then. She cooked, she did everything all right . . . but she had that mania to go into the world."

Nilson traced the onset of Catarina's problems not to the mysterious hereditary disease but to Catarina's mistreatment of her disabled mother. In this account, Catarina's mental disturbance was a result of guilt for domestic violence, for her *ruindade* (evil).

"After her mother died, she began saying things that didn't match with reality. She said that her mother appeared to her. She was very bad to her mom. Her mom required lots of patience; you had to feed her. She struck her mom in the face. I didn't like that. One day, my own mother took Catarina by the hair and prevented her from hitting her mom. But how many times she did that! We said, don't do that to the old lady, you don't know what will happen to you someday, what you will have to endure. . . . After her mom died, she began having problems."

Are you saying that she should be punished?

"Of course, if one does such a thing, it comes back to you. To do this to a sick mother!"

Nilson continued describing Catarina as restless and aggressive and himself as controlling the actions of the police and mediating hospitalizations: "When they found her wandering, they had to handcuff her. She jumped the police and fought with them, but they didn't put their hands on her without my presence. We tried to do things through conversation, in a civil mood, but it didn't work, so we had to handcuff her. So we put her into the police car, took her to the general hospital, and gave her a shot to calm her down. I hospitalized her six times in the Caridade and the São Paulo." Nilson suggested that he was able to use his city hall contacts to control and confine Catarina.

When she came back, what did she say?

"She said nothing. She stayed at home. For one month, things were all right, but then it all began again."

Did she undergo treatment at the local health post?

"She received medication. In Porto Alegre, they also gave her medication for the head. She didn't want to take it, though—she threw it into the toilet and flushed it down. All that medication. At home, she didn't continue her treatment. She didn't help herself. If she had only followed what the doctors told her to do . . ." In order to return home, Catarina had to self-medicate. But, as the records show, by this time she was more stigmatized and isolated from the family than ever. The issue of compliance gave them a pretext to wash their hands of her.

Nilson said that Catarina did not hurt the kids during her attacks. "She only escaped from the house and left them unattended. This happened quite often. She was so full of rage." He described a violent domestic realm: "She attacked me with a knife. When she was like that, I had to hide objects. It was worse when we forced her to come home. She screamed, so we had to give her an injection to calm her down. What an ordeal this was. If it were not for the help of the chief of the security guard, who today has my little girl. . . . At that time, he was the godfather. Without him, I would've had no help at all."

As Nilson told it, Catarina agreed to give the child away. "When the girl was in the hospital, the chief's wife talked to Catarina and said, 'Oh, you could give me the girl.' Then they spoke to me. She accepted, so I gave the girl to them. She is in good hands; they are well-off."

Nilson described Catarina's fraternal ties as ineffective. "My brothers-in-law never supported me. There was nobody to help. I had to leave my work and run after her. The city hall then pitched in. But the brothers never came to see whether we needed anything, and we had little children. One begins to lose strength, right? They had their houses and cars, but never came to visit, never said we will help to search for our sister. . . . That's what happened."

Catarina's family was to be blamed for her destiny, though she herself was not innocent, since she had refused to take medication. "They gave her the best medication in Porto Alegre. The problem was that she took them only while she was there. At home, she threw them away, and the same situation returned."

Did she tell you what happened in the hospital?

"No, she didn't remember."

For Nilson, Catarina had no memory.

And her difficulties with walking? I had to bring it up. Again, he spoke as though these things had no clear history or development. "She walked a bit shaky. I don't recall when this began. This comes from the family, from her grandfather, I think. She has an uncle who has the same problem. I don't know what this is."

Then he shifted to depict a delusional and guilt-ridden Catarina: "As I said before, I think she heard those voices because she injured her mom. The spirit comes down. Her mom said that Catarina would pay for her evil. The old lady cursed Catarina when she hit her. She got irritated, for the old lady was like a baby, very demanding."

When I later spoke to Ademar, Catarina's middle brother, he also mentioned that their mother had indeed been a very strong-willed woman, but he knew nothing of Catarina's alleged violence toward her. For Nilson, in any case, the fact that Catarina burned his documents marked the end. "There was no return."

When you think of her, what comes to your mind?

"I remember her way of talking . . . the echoes of her voice in my head."

What do you remember her saying?

"Her nonsense."

Catarina was outside familial common sense. As I spoke to her family members, I began to understand how an authoritative story occluding Catarina had been cobbled together out of incohesive frames and judgments. As Clifford Geertz points out, "common sense is not what the mind cleared of cant spontaneously apprehends; it is what the mind filled with presuppositions . . . concludes" (2000a:84). By empirically assessing how common sense is forged and conceptualizing deliberations over it, writes Geertz, one can see how culture is put together and better understand "the kinds of lives societies support" (93).

The more I learned about the interests and values of people once connected to her, and the medical and legal practices they employed, the more Catarina's disjointed writing made sense. Her family's actions were the missing verbs in her dictionary—the ones that made hers "a sentence without remedy." Catarina had become a leftover in a domestic world that was disassembling and reassembling in intricate interactions. She was the negative value, the unnecessary component of a migrant and urban poor culture. At the core of common sense are practices and attitudes toward death, real and imaginary. Catarina's abandonment speaks of what ties reality together and the forms of human life that are endorsed these days.

Adoptive Parents

The following week, I stopped at the Restaurante Tamara, next to the Novo Hamburgo city hall. The restaurant was run by Urbano and Tamara, the couple who adopted Catarina's youngest daughter, Ana. Once again, my fears of being turned away were unfounded. Like the other characters in Catarina's life, Tamara and Urbano were welcoming and talkative.

The couple belonged to an earlier generation of migrants who had arrived in the city in the 1960s. They were well-off economically. Urbano was still the chief of the municipal guard service (in charge of security for public buildings); he had been Nilson's boss for eight years. Tamara was in charge of the family business. Both struck me as self-confident as they recollected their "beautiful friendship" with Nilson and Catarina, her "crises," and the adoption of their girl.

References to their connections to the city's institutions punctuated the couple's version of what had happened to Catarina. The two were conscious of their difference from the *gentinha* (base, lower-class people), a term Tamara used to describe Nilson's extended family. "These are people who don't know how to control themselves. They drink a little bit and are already stabbing and shooting each other." According to Tamara, Nilson's mother, Ondina, "is worth nothing. Ask for her record at the police station. She has at least three charges against her." Tamara alluded to the incident that led to their formal adoption of Ana: "The old lady hit me and kidnapped the girl from me. But we put the police on her."

I mentioned that Nilson's parents were *crentes*.

"Now they say that they are believers. . . . But do you know of any convert who did not do something bad before? Tell me. X robbed, killed, and then enters the church and says, 'I am a new person.' "

Urbano depicted himself as a patron to the sixty-eight men who worked for him, most of them migrant workers. "The guards were like my sons. I got to know all of them and their families and cared for them." This tie was advantageous for all parties. The workers had a well-paid and honorable public service job and someone in a powerful position to help them navigate bureaucracies and more.

Here, city institutions are used for private and business purposes. Consider how Tamara managed to contribute to the family economy. In the early 1990s, she was a *sacoleira* (literally, bag lady), traveling to Paraguay and São Paulo to buy products, mostly clothing, which she subsequently sold in people's homes. The families of her husband's sixty-eight guards were her first clients. "We spent the weekends going into their homes and selling. . . . That's how I met Catarina. I listened a lot to her, and we established a very close relationship."

Soon, all city hall workers became their clientele. Tamara and Urbano opened a food stand next to the city hall and began serving meals. When the city hall moved to a new building, they were given the authorization to run a cafeteria for hundreds of civil servants. "Everyone in the city hall knows us. . . . They buy on credit." Again, Tamara used the expression, "We have a beautiful friendship."

As Tamara and Urbano recollected their "comradeship" with Nilson and Catarina, which had turned them into Ana's godparents and later her legal parents, I noticed that Tamara was getting most of the facts about Catarina's life wrong. For instance, she said that Catarina had come from the state of Santa Catarina (rather than from the northwestern region of Rio Grande do Sul), that she had willfully broken up her parents' marriage, that she had met Nilson in Novo Hamburgo, and that she had never worked. These misreadings of Catarina's past seemed to expose the general misunderstanding surrounding her existence and the current irrelevance of getting her account right.

As the conversation proceeded, I also saw that these misreadings contributed to modeling Catarina as "a difficult person," responsible for the breakdown of her own family and without resources of her own to make a future possible. In other words, in Tamara and Urbano's recollection, Catarina appeared largely in the negative. This lack, I thought, informs a unity of self, truth, and morality that they are daily negotiating, a transaction now being momentarily displayed to the anthropologist. By juxtaposing accounts, marking contradictions, locating fissures, and teasing out the various threads and actions that patterned Catarina in this enlarged family complex, I also felt that I was beginning to better understand how history happens and the unacceptable difference that Catarina was.

I did not need to ask many questions. Tamara talked compulsively, relating a ready-made account of Catarina, essentially a man's version of things. Catarina was a rebellious woman who was out of her mind—or, as Tamara conceptualized mental illness, "she was out of her little house" (*fora da casinha*). "I knew that she had that problem before I met her. I knew of her problem through my husband, who had heard about it from Nilson." While speaking of Catarina's "erratic temper," she often referred to Ana as "not being easy to deal with. She is giving us many problems. . . . She is truly from the same blood."

Tamara had seen her task as convincing Catarina to perform the duties of a proper housewife. "When we began going there to sell clothing, she opened herself up; she developed a deep trust in me. I always listened to her and told her not to be so rebellious and stubborn. But nobody could hold her back. She escaped from home, walked for one or two days on the streets, without direction, and took her shoes and clothing off. We got tired of finding her naked in the streets, saying that she was looking for her boyfriend named Valmir. Then, the next day, she was lucid."

Tamara repeated that Catarina "had a thing against her husband" and that she was even jeopardizing his life: "She didn't accept him at all. She didn't let him into the house, and once, after he broke in, she tried to kill him with a knife and a hammer."

Had Nilson done something to her?

"Nothing, nothing. . . . This was a thing from her head."

I mentioned that I had heard of Nilson hitting her. "If that ever happened," the couple agreed, "it was self-defense. She jumped at him first." Tamara then reversed the account she had given to the professionals at the House of Mental Health and said, "Catarina once hit Nilson with a chain."

Urbano added: "The entire municipal guard was in the streets searching for her. My men found her in the woods naked. Nilson had his defects—he drank and smoked pot at times—but overall he was a hard-working guy who provided for the house. She was always saying she wanted this guy named Valmir."

In Tamara and Urbano's account, Catarina was literally bare. They made no attempt to historicize or give meaning to her actions. In a later interview, Nilson contradicted the couple, stating that Catarina had always been well aware of what she was doing during her escapes and that she was never found naked in the streets. "She was always well dressed." Though versions of the story differed, Catarina remained the same thing: a mad and disposable organism, no longer vested in roles or values.

For Tamara, Catarina's craziness "came after she gave birth to Alessandra. It was a postpartum setback. Then she got this nonsense. . . . But this problem in the legs, this is hereditary. It comes from her mother. Her younger brothers are on the same path."

Catarina was described as having both a hereditary disorder, now also visible in her brothers, and a psychiatric one, made visible by Dr. Gilson Kunz and the rejected medication. "Dr. Kunz was treating her, but she threw the medication into the toilet. She had a crisis every six months or so." She was pharmaceutically noncompliant, and there was now the perception of a pattern—"every six months"—in the place of her actual experiences. As all other parties had put it, Catarina was beyond repair. What to do?

"After some time, the poor guy couldn't take it any longer." Tamara confirmed that when she first met Catarina, in the early 1990s, "her legs were already shaky, but no one thought that she would get to the stage where she is now." I asked how Nilson reacted to that. "He told us that even before Alessandra was born, Catarina's legs were already atrophying. Of course, he knew that she was like that, but this was of no importance."

Of no importance. After all, in the couple's account, Catarina could be blamed for the collapse of her household and ultimately for being abandoned. "She always expelled Nilson from home. If she is not with him today, it is because of what she did to him," said Tamara with a clear sense of gender rules. "Not that I defend him. I don't endorse his promiscuity, but as far as I know, he only got another woman after he saw that things would not work out with Catarina."

I told Tamara and Urbano that the records of the Novo Hamburgo House of Mental Health mentioned that they had taken care of Catarina and the newborn in their home for a while. "Catarina stayed ten days with me—not the baby, though. She was still in the incubator, for she weighed only 3.3 pounds." Tamara then described what sounded to me more like an elaborate plan to keep the baby than one to help Catarina recover.

Catarina had been sent home, and the ambulance came and took her to breastfeed the baby in the hospital. At the same time, her sister-in-law, Ademar's wife, died in childbirth. No one told Catarina about the woman's death, but she overheard conversations and took them to mean that her own baby had died. She refused to go back to the hospital, saying that people were hiding the terrible truth from her.

"Nilson called on me for help," said Tamara. "I told her that the baby was alive and took her to the hospital. I recall that she was already walking as if she were drunk, and she didn't want to breastfeed Ana. She gave her a bottle instead. She looked around as if she didn't know where she was, threw the baby on the bed, and left. The nurses and I agreed that she was *fora da casinha*" (out of the little house).

The pieces of Catarina's trajectory to Vita were coming together, as were the actions that had shaped it. "On the way home, I took her to Dr. Gilson Kunz at the Novo Hamburgo House of Mental Health." This part of Tamara's tale was an explicit statement of how people navigate the medical system available to them and become informal medical practitioners themselves. At the public heath service, the doctor confirmed that the problem was Catarina's nonadherence to treatment. Psychiatric drugs stood for a conjugal tie that no longer existed.

"The doctor told me that if the husband administered the medication, she would refuse and that there was no vacancy in the psychiatric hospitals. He said that the ideal would be if she could stay with somebody else until he could get her hospitalized."

Tamara decided "to keep her" and became a proxy psychiatrist herself. "Dr. Gilson instructed us on how to deal with her. If one dosage of the medication wouldn't help, then we should double the dosage." As I heard Tamara's story, I recalled what Simone Laux, the director of the Novo Hamburgo service, had once told me: "[Many times,] the psychiatrist is not for the patient. He works for the family."

For seven days, Catarina was okay, said Tamara. But then "she didn't eat, didn't sleep, and spent the whole night walking inside the house. . . . I had to lock all the doors. She was aggressive toward me. She entered my room and said that she wanted to take her baby, but in fact she wanted to take my four-year-old daughter. She pushed me and threw me against a wall. She was very strong. I got hurt, and I thought that I would not be able to handle that."

Contrary to what we might expect, Catarina's life was not managed at the margins but in the vortex of public institutions, psychiatry, law, and community. The rest of the story I heard was a condensation of the various mechanisms—call them, jointly, social psychosis—by which Catarina's exclusion gained form.

Visiting the health post was not working, so Tamara called Dr. Gilson Kunz at home. He saw Catarina in his private clinic. That is why we do not get the full picture in the records—and most likely it is why he told me he did not recall her. The doctor blended his public and private practices, just as Urbano and Tamara did business with the municipal infrastructure.

"She didn't want to stay at home. She only talked about divorce and wanting to kill Nilson—that's all she knew." Dr. Kunz sedated Catarina. Using Tamara and Urbano's city hall contacts, they made arrangements for an ambulance to take her to the São Paulo Hospital the next morning. To this story, then, add deceit. Recall that in the São Paulo records Catarina said that she had been told she was going to the maternity ward. Instead, she ended up back in the mental ward.

In Tamara's account, however, all is coincidence. "That same day, the hospital called the city hall to tell Nilson that the baby was ready for discharge, and he did not know what to do. I had already told my husband, 'Let's take this girl to our home, and when Catarina returns in good health, we will give the girl back.' For in general she was very good with the children. She took good care. The only problem was when she entered a crisis. Then she did not know what she was doing.

"We went to the hospital with Nilson. The social worker already knew of the situation. Nilson's family had also rejected the baby; she was all head, nothing much to hold. I said, 'Let's care for the baby. I will do this for Catarina. Poor Catarina, it's not her fault.'"

Even after Catarina returned from the hospital, they kept the baby, for "Catarina was too weak and fragile," explained Tamara. "Nilson called me, saying that she wanted to see the baby, and he told me that perhaps I could change Catarina's mind and that she would let us take care of the baby for a longer period. 'If it depends on me,' he said, 'I will give the baby to you. She is already yours.'"

Tamara was adamant that she "was only helping." Tamara and Urbano were asked to be Ana's godparents. After the baptism, the couple routinely took the girl for long weekends. "We cleaned her well," Tamara insisted, but Catarina always repeated, "You will bring her back, right?" These were the days when Catarina was often hospitalized, between 1992 and 1994, so the couple kept the girl throughout her hospitalizations. "The girl began to walk and speak at our home. We said, 'Call us uncle and auntie,' but she repeated, 'Mummy and daddy.' We never taught her that; she started calling us that on her own."

In the meantime, Nilson and his lover had a child of their own, a boy. Soon thereafter, Catarina and Nilson officially separated. As he was making a new life, she was withering. "They sold the house, and she went to live alone, and that was the end of it all. . . . She used to call me, saying, 'I don't have anything to eat.' " According to Urbano, Nilson at first paid some alimony to Catarina, who was responsible for Alessandra, the other daughter. "But after he was fired from the city hall, there was no more money for her." The nuclear family had been dismembered, and Catarina, as Tamara put it, "had nothing to eat anymore, had no money to pay for water and energy. I banked her for a whole year—utilities, clothing, food, even meat. Every Friday, I brought her groceries."

Tamara remarked on the plundering of Catarina: "The food I took to Catarina, the old lady, her mother-in-law took it away. Catarina's neighbors told me that. Her own mother-in-law. . . . Catarina also told me, 'Don't bring too many things, Tamara, for Ondina comes with bags and takes it home.' The old lady did this out of evil. They all have this evil. And Catarina was getting worse and worse."

Tamara asserted that it was a lie that Catarina had set the shack on fire, as Nilson had told the doctors during her last hospitalizations. "No . . . her neighbor's shack had a short circuit and began to burn down, and the flames hit her shack. She was doped with medication. She didn't die because a neighbor got her out." The mother-in-law had claimed that she saved Catarina's life.

The conversation went on for several hours. Urbano and Tamara then described in detail the entire legal process through which they adopted Ana. When the grandmother "kidnapped" the girl during a visit to Catarina, the powerful couple went to the police to report the event. "All the inspectors there know us, and two of our friends took up the case. They took us to the Juvenile Court, and the judge gave the inspectors a search warrant," Tamara stated.

Urbano corrected her, however, saying that it was not a real warrant, a comment that revealed the paralegality of the mise-en-scène that followed. "We had not yet filed a complaint against the old lady," he said, "but the inspectors scared the hell out of her, and she gave the girl back."

Nilson had already authorized the adoption. With Catarina absent, the couple managed to get a judicial order to keep Ana for four months until the adoption could be formalized. As Urbano put it: "We told the social worker to speed things up, for we were taking the child out of the mud into a better life." Tamara recalled that "on December 22, 1995, we got Catarina out of her shack and brought her to the judge. We had to carry her."

Urbano summarized the judicial pronouncement: "The judge explained it to them in plain language. 'As of today, Ana Moraes does not exist anymore. This is who she was. Today, she is being born again. Her name will change. From now on, you are not even relatives anymore.'"

Catarina hesitated and asked whether she would be able to see her daughter, Tamara acknowledged, and the judge noted that this would be up to Tamara and Urbano to decide, since Catarina would no longer have any tie to Ana. Urbano and Tamara reassured Catarina that "at any moment, if you want, you can see Ana, in our home, in our presence."

Throughout this long conversation, I was disturbed by the constant references to Catarina as irreversibly mad and maternally unfit. I tried to counter that image by mentioning her lucidity and intelligence. At one point, Tamara misread my comment as an endorsement of Catarina's supposed scheming personality.

"Yes, she was very smart; she had that sagacity. She was talking about the good, but behind it she was plotting something else. She was a good talker, but always took things in the direction she wanted. For example, I am talking to you here, but in the back of my mind, I am already thinking about taking the cassette of the tape-recorder so that you might not do anything with it. She schemed things. She was very stubborn and ingenious. Ana is just like that. You can't imagine how we suffer with her."

Here, Catarina is a surface upon which people project their own versions of events. With no meaning or reason attributed to her, she can be anything, good or bad, and the goodness or evil of others can be bestowed upon her. She circulates as an empty thing through which people who were once related to her confirm their moral, medical, and legal realities. In this space of business, so close to law and order, people's acts never have intention. Rather, it was Catarina who was evil and who plotted. That is how, I sensed, the uniformity of that worldview comes into existence and evil happens. Meanwhile, in a delirium recollected by Tamara and Urbano, Catarina uttered the name of a person, Valmir. I read this personal name as Catarina's desperate attempt to find some support in a relationship to someone who once existed and who was not part of the predatory world surrounding her.

Tamara kept talking about Ana. "She is full of revolt. She has everything, but is never satisfied. She is giving us problems. She already did a couple of bad things." The real hereditary problem that Catarina's offspring might carry was being coded as a moral disorder. And as I listened to the couple, I could not help but hear them dealing with the prospect of having adopted a daughter with a defect (now also visible in her uncles). It was as if they were using Catarina and the lack she had become to account for their own dissatisfaction with Ana.

"She is terrible, she takes things from others, she does not obey, she answers back. . . . We have taken her to a psychiatrist, Dr. Gilson Kunz," said Tamara.

The girl physically looked like Catarina, they told me, "and acts like her." Moreover, they were treating Ana as Catarina had been treated, even using the same doctor, who had helped transform what could have been a "mood disorder" into an irreversible condition. By speaking of and addressing Ana as "a bad girl," Urbano and Tamara set themselves up as the good ones, legitimately banishing any discussion of history and biology. In doing so, the couple nurtured their capacity to bracket affection from another "defective person" and potentially drive her out of the home on their own moral grounds. While people in Catarina's immediate and extended family by and large tried to explain away their actions or nonactions toward her, Tamara and Urbano openly displayed modes of subjectivity and morality that had been reworked through their encounter with Catarina—the living creature no one wanted anything to do with.

"To want my body as a medication, my body"

At a distance, there was sympathy for "the wounded stray dog" Catarina had become. "I think her situation is very sad," continued Urbano, "to have brothers, in-laws, children, and to be left abandoned like an animal. Being kicked from one side to the other, like a dog without an owner, asking for some food. That was her life; it was always like that."

What happened to the family ties?

"It is over. They have no love for anyone. Nilson's whole family is like that. They have a *ruindade* [evil]. They are very ignorant people."

And the brothers?

"They never looked out for her."

Why?

"Fear of having to care for her. She does not have any income, nothing. This helps keep her from being accepted anywhere."

In ancient Greece, every year two men—"true scum and refuse"—were chosen to be cast out of the cities, as part of the festival of the Thargelia (Harrison 1921:97). Initially, these individuals were seen as the remedy for a city suffering from famine or pestilence; later, they became the means through which cities prevented mischief (Le Marchant 1923; Girard 1996). These men were called *pharmakoi*, and, for them, there was no return to the city. Historians disagree over the ways in which they were chosen for this scapegoat role and whether they were actively killed or simply allowed to die (Harrison 1921:104, 105; Derrida 1981:132).

As I concluded this round of conversations with Catarina's brothers, ex-husband, children, in-laws, and friends, the plot to cast out Catarina became evident. She is, in a literal sense, a modern-day *pharmakos*. The handling of her defective body was at the heart of the various scenarios people empirically forged and in which they saw themselves with her through institutions such as medicine, city government, and law.

Consider Nilson's final words: "After we married, they told me the problems the family had. My mother's cousin said, 'Poor Nilson, he doesn't know what he has got his hands in.' She knew it. But she didn't want to say anything because she was a *crente*. I didn't believe it until I saw it. *Deus me livre* [May God free me from this]. . . . I got to know her relatives. An aunt of hers died of this problem, and so did some of her cousins. . . . I told myself, 'Ah, that's how it is . . . they will see.' "

These were revenge-laden words—as if through Catarina the man had taught them all a lesson. In retrospect, Catarina has meaning not as a person but as a representative of a collective and its pathology. Her growing social irrelevance took form around this medical unknown and its physical expressions, allowing Nilson now to read family ties as a retaliatory exchange.

And what are your plans? I asked the ex-husband.

"To make my life. To progress. I am content with my family now. This woman doesn't give me the problems I had before. A person must help herself. As I said, the doctor gave Catarina treatment so that the illness would not come back. It was just a matter of taking the medication, but she didn't help herself. . . . What has passed is over. One must put a stone over it."

Catarina is physically cast out, a stone set over her in life. As her story reveals, medical science has become a tool of common sense, foreclosing various possibilities of empathy and experience. Pharmaceutical commerce and politics have become intimate to lifeworlds, and it is the drug—the embodiment of these processes—that mediates Catarina's exclusion as a *pharmakos*. Both the empirical reality through which living became practically impossible for Catarina and the possibility of critique have been sealed up. As Catarina repeatedly told me: "They all wouldn't dialogue, and the science of the illness was forgotten. I didn't want to take the medication. . . . Science is our conscience, heavy at times, burdened by a knot that you cannot untie. If we don't study it, the illness in the body worsens."

In "Plato's Pharmacy," Jacques Derrida follows the term *pharmakon* as it stands for writing in Platonic philosophy. Acting like a *pharmakon*, both as remedy and as poison, writing is the artificial counterpart to the truth of things that speech allegedly can apprehend directly. According to Plato, argues Derrida, writing is considered "a consolation, a compensation, a remedy for sickly speech"—"writing is the miserable son" (1981:115, 143).

While living speech is conformity with the law, writing is a force wandering outside the domain of life, incapable of engendering anything or of regenerating itself: "a living-dead, a weakened speech, a deferred life, a semblance of breath. . . . It is like all ghosts, errant" (143). For Derrida, however, writing qua *pharmakon* is an independent order of signification. Operating as *différance*—"the disappearance of any originary presence"—writing is at once "the condition of possibility and the condition of impossibility of truth" (168).

The term *pharmakon* used by Plato has been overdetermined by Greek culture, Derrida points out: "All these significations nonetheless appear. . . . Only the chain is concealed, and to an inappreciable extent, concealed from the author himself, if any such thing exists" (1981:129). The contemporary philosopher sees a concealed connection between *pharmakon* as writing and *pharmakos*, the human figure excluded from the political body. Derrida thus brings to light the scapegoat figure of the *pharmakos*, which, interestingly, is absent from Platonic philosophical reflection. "The city body proper thus reconstitutes its unity, closes around the security of its inner courts, gives back to itself the word that links it with itself within the confines of the *agora*, by violently excluding from its territory the representative of an external threat or aggression. That representative represents the otherness of the evil that comes to affect or infect the inside by unpredictably breaking into it" (Derrida 1981:133).

The figure of the *pharmakos* in philosophical thought is quite pertinent, but the place kept by the death of the Other in households and in city governance also remains a key problem to be addressed. In speaking of Catarina as a modern-day *pharmakos*, I argue that her life and story are paradigmatic of a contemporary familial/medical/political structure that operates like the law and that is close to home. Pharmaceutically addressed, she was now the evil cast out, both subjectively and biologically. In the end, Catarina was a failed medication that, paradoxically, allowed the life, sentiments, and values of some to continue in other terms.

When I told Catarina that I had found her family, she pleaded with me to take her for a visit so that she could see the children. She also wanted to reenter the world of law and money, claiming that she needed to get her worker's ID and her bank card. She and Nilson had separated "from bed, house, and city," but she had to go back to sign the divorce papers; she insisted, "I have never signed them." I later learned that all this was true. Her cards were still in the possession of Tamara; Nilson, citing Catarina's madness and functional disability, had convinced the judge to sign the divorce papers for her.

I had always refused to engage in discussions of whether or not Catarina knew what was going on with her. As I read her medical records, many of the signifiers of her dictionary made sense; and, after working with her ex-family, I understood more about the history of the materials and thoughts to which she clung. As a *pharmakos*, Catarina had a formula and a language unique to her mutation and desire. The ethnographic engagement helped to illuminate both the juxtaposed contexts and techniques that placed her outside the house and the city and her altered inner life processes—the patient of a larger and deadly set of forces, yet with agency and struggles unique to her.

For Catarina, thinking was work and a matter of staying alive. As the ethnographic work unfolded, the life of her mind was becoming less of a puzzle to me. I was increasingly drawn to the human capacity unleashed through Catarina's work and found myself taking on the following question raised by Hannah Arendt: "Could the activity of thinking be among the conditions that make people abstain from 'evildoing' or even actually 'condition' them against it?" (1981:5).

Oscar agreed to take Catarina to see her family the day before Christmas. Vita's van was available, and I learned that every year one or two inhabitants were given the present of a visit home. This is more or less how the job of the social worker at Vita had been redefined—the main task was no longer to reconstruct the identity of the abandoned and try to create life possibilities for them, as I had been told in 1997, but to bring in funds for the new, and increasingly empty, buildings. As Oscar himself admitted, "Truly, they don't care about what happens in here. They need Vita to have an existence for the outside world." He said this to suggest the existence of corruption and diversion of funds, but the conversation ended at that.

I returned to the light pink house where Catarina had once lived. Alemão was alone with the kids. I told him that Catarina badly wanted to visit, to see her children. He promised to contact Altamir and Vania. He was straightforward with me: "The truth is that nobody wants her."

The next morning, Vania, Altamir's wife, anxiously called Oscar. She saw no problem with a visit, but stressed that they could not take care of Catarina in the long run. "I have my husband, and his problem is getting worse day after day." Among other things, the family was clearly afraid of the law—that is, of the unlikely appearance of the law in the form of an indictment by the Public Ministry. This is what haunts them, I thought, rather than the memory of Catarina or what had been done to her; this is what motivates and organizes the temporality of the castaway's return.

Oscar, Alencar, and Catarina spent the morning and early afternoon of December 24 visiting the homes of Ondina and Nestor, Altamir and Vania. The following week, I spoke at length with the three of them about that visit.

Oscar was euphoric. He had lost his way while trying to find the house, as I had. But he resorted to the police, who escorted Vita's van to the address of Catarina's in-laws. "You should have seen the reception she got. I had to bite my tongue. The in-laws, her daughter, friends of the family gathered and hugged her. . . . What a warm reception it was." They also told Oscar how much they had cared for Catarina in the past and that they had no material or human resources to take care of her now.

The family prepared a good lunch for all. "Catarina's eyes were glowing with happiness, and she told them about dating Clóvis." To Oscar, this was her fantasy, and he reiterated his approach: "People comment, but until I see it with my own eyes, I cannot blame anyone." I understood; he needed Clóvis's help. Moreover, it was clear that whatever was happening between Clóvis and Catarina was consensual. She wanted to tell her former family that she had a man and a future. The van then went off to Catarina's brother's house.

Oscar agreed that this was a very complicated situation. It was impossible to characterize these people as evil and simply assign blame to them. An entire economic and social structure was changing, and "when the person doesn't produce anymore," added Oscar, "what to do?" He remarked that he still saw cases in which family members care for a diseased person at home, and he asked what my wife and I would do if we had a diseased relative to look after. "It's always a difficult decision to make. If it is already difficult for people who have money, then what to say of people who have to work full time?" he reasoned. "Therefore, there are places like Vita. If people were not here, they would be in the streets. This is the social reason."

I told Oscar I thought of the destiny of the abandoned as a kind of photographic negative; if developed, it showed the human forms of life that the transactions of family, medicine, and state institutions were engendering these days. Oscar went further, saying that he saw this social reason being transmitted to the next generation. "If one could do research with their children . . . could one see if this generates a new psychic condition?"

The visit, at any rate, "was a Christmas gift for Catarina." Oscar said they were also well received at Altamir's. Inspired by our conversation, Altamir told the other siblings present that Catarina's problem was neurological. Someone replied, "So she is not mad?" This discussion took place in front of her, as if she could not hear. For me, this episode displayed both the frames for her absence and the forging of it. But for Oscar, seeing the physical signs of disability exhibited by the brothers convinced him that they were unable to care for Catarina. He mused, "After this visit, she will be tranquil for a year now."

Alencar did not see things in such a unified or accommodating way: "They received us out of obligation. It was dissimulation, masked." The façade was one of attention and joy, but as a "worldly man, who has seen much in the streets," said Alencar, they were truly conveying the message "we have nothing to do with this." In his view, people use whatever they can to get rid of the problem person. "The earlier they discharge the person as mad, the better for them. . . . That's Vita. Then they cry, saying they don't have the right conditions, that there is illness at home, and so forth. They invent thousands of excuses to get rid of the problem. If they do this in the family, what about a person they don't know?"

His diagnosis was acute and based on his own experience of broken ties with his own family. "The sentimental tie they had for her died. For another person, they try to say that it exists; but as an outsider, you feel the opposite." Alencar said that he and Oscar had fulfilled their obligation: to take Catarina back to witness that death of affection.

He elaborated further on how this death was integrated into people's mannerisms and superficiality, creating a play of appearances: "Catarina tried to demonstrate affection, but her own daughter . . . the way she looked at her mother with no empathy. . . . I was kind of shocked. I've seen many things in the world, but a daughter staring like that at her mom. . . . We know when a person is forcing it. . . . They want to pass as good persons. But there is no affection. They dissimulate and live their own way."

For the family members, the death of affection sanctioned the expulsion of Catarina. This void, and the hope that it would be otherwise, now provided the foundation for her daily existence in Vita. "Love is the illusion of the abandoned." Her writing was the spelling out of this condition. In Alencar's view, she wanted to return to confirm that this was not so, "but then she feels this death and does not want to open it up." She is left only with the killing. That is what I heard in his sore recollection of the visit.

Catarina described the trip as "worthwhile." "We were well treated. My mother-in-law made lunch, and my sisters-in-law were there, too." Then she corrected herself, saying, "My *ex*-mother-in-law and *ex*-sisters-in-law . . . *for they are no longer.*" She had presented herself as belonging to another man. Catarina then explained that she had gone there "mainly to see my daughter Alessandra. She is already of my height. Anderson was not there."

How was it, seeing your daughter?

"I felt something good inside. But Alessandra, she was very . . . it seemed that she had a strong urge to get running, to go and stop a fire. I thought that there would be time left . . . " She did not finish the sentence. Then she mentioned that "Delvani and Nina were there, too." They were the ones who took Catarina's house and whose shack caught fire with her inside.

And how was it with your brothers?

"My brother Altamir is a little ill. . . . He was concerned with me. He is very concerned with the work, with the debts. He wants to pay that debt."

A fraternal concern is said to still exist, but it now lags behind other forms of indebtedness. She then shifted her account to existence in Vita and what she saw as the realm of the possible: "Yesterday, there were worms in the meat. I cannot take this anymore. If I get pregnant, I don't want to stay here."

After her brief return to the world from which she had been banished, the fantasy of a pregnancy, to which Catarina had alluded in previous conversations, became her vision of another body and future. I asked her to pause and think this through, but she did not hear me and continued talking about a salvific child and blood renovation. "I am paralyzed here. After five months of pregnancy, I will walk normally again. My blood, my blood from menstruation will all go to the child. And then my blood will be new as well."

This fantasy has acquired such symbolic value for Catarina because she has such a lack of ties, I thought.

I told her that a pregnancy would not solve her health problem.

She disagreed. "Yes, it will. Because then the world will pay attention. The innocent has more force, and all will support."

She wanted to say, as I understood, that the ataxia was not all she was. She was more than that and death. "I must have health in the body's torso. . . . It is only in the legs that I am ill."

She added that she now wrote her name as KATKINA.

"There, in Novo Hamburgo, it is Catarina. Here, it is Katkina." In her dictionary, she had taken up this new name along with Clóvis's family name: Katkina Gama.

Why did you invent this name?

"I will be called this now. For I don't want to be a tool for men to use, for men to cut. A tool is innocent. You dig, you cut, you do whatever you want with it. . . . It doesn't know if it hurts or doesn't. But the man who uses it to cut the other knows what he is doing."

She continued with the most forceful words: "I don't want to be a tool. *Be-*

264 | The Family

cause Catarina is not the name of a person . . . truly not. It is the name of a tool, of an object. A person is an Other. . . . Katkina, Daiana are names of persons. Alessandra, I think it is. It might exist, but not under the power of . . . Alessandra and Anderson are siblings. My daughter is Alessandra, and I want her to sign Daiana."

Why?

"There was love between us, and that is gone. . . . And now in order to begin a family . . . to generate a new family, this is what I wanted."

She then said that her name "had been" and that she didn't want to be Moraes either, her husband's family name: "My uncle used to say, *'Moraes, quem não morreu não morre mais'* " (a Moraes who hasn't died yet won't die). Catarina was playing with the surname Moraes—which in Portuguese sounds like the combination of the verb *"morrer"* (to die) and the adverb *"mais"* (more)—suggesting that it stood for her personal destruction. The confused and painful recollection of her marriage and the fantasy of a pregnancy with the man who medicated her were basically all there was for her: "Because I try to revive." Threadbare lines of hope.

Everyday Violence

Adriana and I went to bid Catarina farewell. She was weeping. "For I have to be here the whole time."

She continued to write profusely. It was a way of keeping her mind open, she said, a way of seeing a little past the situation. "It's a work. . . . It has a beginning and an end."

If you were to write a story, Catarina, what would it be?

"The story of the three little pigs."

Again, the animal appeared in her imagination. I asked why.

"A cousin told us this story when we were kids."

And if you were to invent a story?

"Then I would invent . . . the story of the seven little guinea pigs from India."

Who are they? What do they do?

"After they are washed, they run under the table and stove to hide . . . and they are cozy together in a corner."

In speaking of animals, Catarina engages the human warmth she longs for.

And if it were about people, what story would you write?

"If it were a story about people, it would be a western. . . . A story of people shooting at each other . . . killing . . . and the others having to bury the dead."

Is there any other possible story?

"This is the beginning and the end."

Infirmary, Vita 2001

Cobrinha, Vita 2001

New building, Vita 2001

Part Five

BIOLOGY AND ETHICS

Pain

Catarina's magnetic resonance image (MRI) revealed the atrophy of her cerebellum. Her blood exam indicated no infectious diseases. The Waaler-Rose test indicated an autoimmune disorder, validating, in some ways, her claim of rheumatism (the most common clinical manifestation of autoimmune disorders). The specificity of Catarina's ataxia was not yet known.

Most of my work with Catarina and her brothers over the course of 2001 and 2002 involved attempts to diagnose their condition and to see what, if anything, could be done to improve the quality of their lives. As biology became the subject of inquiry, my attention turned to the question of how environmental dynamics (social and technical issues such as migration, economic pressure, domestic violence, the death of affection within families, and the pharmaceuticalization of relational breakdowns) might have influenced Catarina's gene expression, immune depression, and, ultimately, the course of her dying.

Catarina was in total pain when we met on August 4, 2001. "In the legs . . . my ankles feel broken . . . torn . . . the bones in the hip, too." Dr. Streb had visited her and left pain relief medication. "I felt a little improvement. It alleviated a bit in the legs." But, as always, the medication had been discontinued.

Clóvis had quit his volunteer job as Vita's nurse, and his departure had a significant emotional impact on Catarina.

"It was tough," she said. "He used to comb my hair. . . . There was nothing bad between us. He did my hygiene. I will not deny that we made love in the pharmacy and in the bathroom. He was dear to me. He made plans for both of us. He said he would find a house for us." She was adamant that "it was true." Catarina then blamed Oscar, claiming that he had not let her leave with Clóvis and that he was plotting "to control the pharmacy himself."

The fact is that Catarina no longer had direct access to the pharmacy and its goods. While I was visiting Vita, I made a long-term arrangement with Oscar to be sure she would be cared for. I also brought Catarina the pain relief creams she wanted. She later told me that Gilberto, the new volunteer who supervised her, used the creams for himself.

Alone, Catarina kept writing, though with much effort, for the pain in her arms was intense. Her notebook was now filled with references to Alemão, the new nurse who used an old manual to guide his dispensation of medicines. Alemão told me that his sister ran a "lucrative geriatric house." He wanted to recover from his alcoholism and join her. Alemão said that Catarina flirted with him and had sent him a love letter. In her notebook, there were several valentine hearts with her name and Clóvis's name erased.

According to Oscar, whom I met later that day, Clóvis had left to work in a Vita-like institution in nearby Alvorada. "But after getting his first paycheck, Clóvis got drunk and fought with the administrator, who then fired him." He was living on the streets. "We asked the captain, but there was no way he would let him come back. There is a rule that a person who leaves can only return after one year."

Oscar also noted that Clóvis's departure had been a big blow to Catarina, although he dismissed their affair as gossip. "He helped her. Other residents said they were having sex. . . . These people have rotten minds and think nothing constructive."

But did you talk to him about this?

Oscar again voiced his policy: "No. I only speak when I see. How can I punish someone if I have not seen the act?" Oscar simply preferred not to see. Help was now scarcer than ever, for the recovery area had fewer inmates and potential volunteers for the infirmary. Construction of a new infirmary wing with larger bathrooms continued, but there were no plans to change the overall precarious level of care. This time, Oscar spoke more candidly and, with a mixture of indignation and fear, suggested that the new construction was simply a façade to divert money to private enterprises.

When I returned to Catarina, I asked whether she and Clóvis had said good-bye.

"No. . . . Because I went to the doctor to operate on a tumor . . . long ago. . . . I went in the morning and came back later that day, and he was gone."

Catarina deployed a familiar explanatory grid to account for the abandonment she was again facing: a disease, a clinic, a doctor, an operation to remove her from a relationship or the illusion of it. The recurrent theme of this destiny involved a man exchanging women, the idea of not being a man's woman anymore: "I heard that Clóvis had another woman. . . . So be it." To change the subject, I opened the notebook she was writing to a random page and read it aloud. It turned out to be a continuation of the same topic:

I am not obligated to surrender my child
Not according to my law
And this is moral

What do you mean?

"That one is not obligated to give up one's child for somebody else to raise, if one does not want to. Moral is to do the right thing, or not."

And who decides what is right?

"Reason decides."

Catarina did not accept my inference that reason changes according to people's interests. She thought of herself as the embodiment of reason and explained that reason did not necessarily belong to "those who are the Incredible Hulk, who are always in the battle ring, those who have more force than others. At times, reason can come from those who are very weak but who keep thinking. One must be sensible, and then reason comes."

So, in your life, you feel that people did not respect your reason?

"Their conscience is burdened, and they want to say that they are the law . . . that nobody takes their flour . . . nobody puts the hand in the flour of the house."

Another law of the house, a new economy she could not use to mix and make something.

And how did you keep your mind sensible?

"I don't have the first word. I don't want to have the definite word. . . . I *try* to speak the truth."

Catarina then said that she did not know whether she would be able to keep writing. "Too much pain." She wept. "It's difficult. Only the head works. The rest, very little."

Human Rights

Catarina's body was withering away, and her neighbors in Vita were dying. During these last visits in 2001 and 2002, I made further contact with Porto Alegre's public health administration and the province's Human Rights Commission to report on this work and to see what could be done about such relentless neglect.

In 1998, the city administration discovered that thirty-four people had died in the Santa Luisa geriatric house, a clandestine business that charged for the care of elderly, disabled, and mentally ill people. This prompted the city to increase its inspection efforts. In the following years, city officials raided more than two hundred of these services, and, after long and arduous judicial battles, a few of them were closed.

"But the fact is that the judges always give the owners one last chance to legally comply with the new sanitation laws," said Jaci Oliveira, the health professional in charge of the city's work with the elderly. Many of these services reinvented themselves to meet some minimum standard of sanitation and care. They now have a "good façade of an infrastructure," as Oliveira put it. "There is food, but it is very bad, and there is no attempt to enhance people's remaining physical and social capabilities. They are made ever more dependent."

Many of these clandestine businesses of care are now moving to the nearby towns of Viamão, Canoas, and Alvorada, where they can escape public health and building code inspections. As Marcelo Godoy, the director of the city's division of public health inspection, explained to me: "When these houses liquidate themselves, the owners put everything, including the people, on a truck and roam the city until they successfully circumvent inspection and land somewhere else."

Oliveira has entered dozens of these institutions, and her description of them was scathing. The services have a gender bias toward women who come mostly from working poor and middle-class families, for they are seen as "less trouble" and as potential volunteer labor who "eventually might help to care for others."

Medication rather than medical care is the norm for those who are cast away. "The initial issue is to tame them. The routine practice is to dope the person for a week or two when she comes in, to make her compliant, and to present this compliant person to the family, who is then relieved that she has adapted to the new environment." The owners of these houses do not believe that they are doing evil, said Oliveira. "They say that they are keeping the institution running and under control and that, with medication, the person will be less aggressive toward herself and thus suffer less." In sum, there is no interest in keeping the patients lucid, in respecting them, or in treating them as citizens who have a life, "because their lives begin to end there."

Oliveira is quite vocal about the limits of political intervention. "Our action is mostly symbolic, and that is important, but negligence is the norm. The political discourse is that 'yes, we will change things.' The intentions are good, but things have not changed. We are a public institution of power, and we went as far as we could go. But we are now faced with a sense of impotence, that we are fighting something much bigger. . . . Where does this all begin? I think we must place this reality we uncovered in a larger context." The context that fosters such negligence remains, argued Oliveira— "the meager political value of the elderly, the lack of public policy, and the pervasive destructuring of families. We have not been able to address the unknown of the equation: legal practice and morality."

Public prosecutors and judges, Godoy stated, "are not our best partners." Despite the best political intentions of city officials, human rights standards are rarely enforced. Godoy and Oliveira told me about a geriatric business they wanted to close and recalled how, in this process, the city became the defendant in the case. After several frustrated attempts to reform the Santa Clara House, city inspectors raided the place and found elderly and disabled people left to themselves, "without any one caring for them, with no food, and filthy . . . expired medication next to insect repellents, disposable needles being reused." A week after issuing a notice of eviction, city representatives were called by the judge, who cited them as the problem. The judge sided with the owner and, in court, chided Oliveira and Godoy: "You are too strict. You must give her another chance. You are taking her livelihood away from her. You must consider what will happen with these people if this house closes."

Simply put, the victims do not have the same rights as the owner. "The owner has the right to have her business, and she can even mistreat the people who pay her to be cared for, and she will not be indicted," Oliveira asserted. "I told the judge, 'There is no way to talk to you, sir, for it is a matter of value.'" The few prosecutors who took up such human rights abuses were removed from their positions. As for the families, Godoy noted, "they end up finding places to dispose of the unwanted relative at the lowest possible cost—their demand fuels the supply. And we, the municipal administration, are supposed to regulate not state policy but this economy."

I was allowed to rummage through the archives of the city's public health inspection service, where I found several reports of human rights violations against Vita, filed by former residents. I also learned from city hall officers that these reports were not being investigated, given the political clout of Jandir Luchesi, Vita's patron and state representative. Apparently, politicians unofficially sponsored several such businesses of care: these businesses were part of the officeholders' intricate political base, which claimed to fight poverty with charity. These institutions solved immediate problems of locals and of people living in the interior, thus strengthening the politicians' base of appeal. I was told that Vita could not be shut down because, ostensibly, it helps to maintain the surrounding city district by, for example, providing medication and clothing. Moreover, Godoy added, "looking at the larger picture, Vita is not in as critical a state as other institutions."

In a move described as "clever" by the city's public health director, Vita never registered itself as a health care institution for the elderly, making it impossible for the city to inspect it or to deliver any form of human and material aid to Vita. The institution was receiving large sums of money through regional and national funds reserved for the philanthropic and pastoral work that was replacing former state institutions for the disenfranchised. According to Oscar, the use of these funds was never audited, and Vita's political ties were enough to keep the auditors out. "Philanthropic these places are not," Oliveira asserted. "The government gives them money not to do the work itself, and the administrators keep the money to themselves."

Letting people die brings in more money and donations, as Oscar implied: "The infirmary is the heart of Vita. Why do you think that donations come in? On the radio, Luchesi does not say that there are drug addicts here. He says that there are grandpas and grandmas and disabled people who need basic help and food. It is the abandoned who are still able to reach sensitive people." In spite of this machinery, Oscar kept thinking of pragmatic and simple alternatives for improving care. He often said that it would be easy to train volunteers; to pay for a full-time nurse; to get the city to assign a doctor to Vita; to offer a more balanced diet, with less canned and rotten food; and to set up recreational activities for the abandoned—all to no avail.

Value Systems

I returned to Vita the next day, August 5, 2001. Catarina was trying hard to write. Words were interspersed with references to Brazilian *reais* and American dollars. The currency of her writing and of our work together, I thought, was always related to her wish "to go to Novo Hamburgo," as she again asked me that morning. "To see the little ones." She also wanted to get her documents back, she said: "I would like to go myself and get the documents from the judge, to get my certificate of birth, worker's ID, my bank card. Take me in your car to Altamir's house, or to Ademar's—he lives in Santo Afonso."

Honestly, Catarina did not address me as her savior. At the most, I was a vector by which she might reenter the world of law and affection. She used to trace this wish to the moment in which she could have taken charge of life without her husband. At the time of her divorce, living alone, overmedicated, and with difficulty walking, she did not manage to get to court, and the judge ended up signing the divorce papers for her. She also continually remarked that she had to stop at a local bank to withdraw her savings, which, as she once reported, she had allowed Nilson to access. "I wanted nothing to do with him."

Catarina was well aware that, other than allowing a symbolic visit, her brothers would not help her. The value she sought had to do with the tie itself. Even though her brothers, ex-in-laws, and children had become the persons they now were, she wanted the recognition that a family tie confers. This reasoning somewhat explained to me the ethics that guided Catarina's recollection of the past: her thinking was not determined by the good or evil directed at her. From the distance of her thinking, she saw beyond blame, to the possibilities and closures that ties engender.

There was silence.

What are you thinking?

"People trying to stick needles in others. . . . But what do they have to do with me? I have my own thinking. I don't let them go in. Their voices. They want to manipulate me and put things in my head. I weep because . . . "

The sentence remained unfinished. And I asked whether she wanted to keep talking.

"It does good to me. It does not lower me. I am a free woman, free to talk whatever I want to. My mouth is an open game. My game is not closed. It does not have gates."

We spoke for a little longer, until it was time to go.

"You will not forget to come back . . . right?"

I won't forget, I told her.

———

I tried to get Catarina transferred from Vita into Casa da Vida (House of Life), an exceptional city service that treats and cares for homeless people, "citizens burdened by mental suffering." Casa da Vida was founded in the early 1990s by the city of Porto Alegre, when it had to find a place other than the street for fifty-three patients discharged by the São Paulo Psychiatric Hospital. When I visited that August, it housed twenty and provided all kinds of workshops and therapies (occupational and psychoanalytic—it is explicitly "nonpsychiatric"). Casa aims for family and community reintegration, and indeed most of the initial fifty-three patients have been socially integrated—only two have died.

The director was interested in Catarina's case, but she said that it would be impossible to take her in. Casa's policy excluded people in wheelchairs. "We have no way to give personalized care to the physically disabled." She made the case that even though aggression was quite rare among the residents, "if Catarina were hit, she would not be able to defend herself. We cannot expose her to this risk." The director regretted the result of this policy. "Unfortunately," she said, "I don't have any other place to recommend." I left thinking that, as a model service, Casa da Vida will always have success stories to tell, of people who will walk out of the institution and back into a community and family so rarely in place.

———

Catarina's son, Anderson, helped me out as I continued to work with that extended family. Still unemployed and out of school, the young man was happy that his father allowed him to be my research assistant during August 2001. He and his sister urged me to take them to Vita to visit with Catarina, and all the responsible adults agreed.

It was not easy. When I picked the kids up, Ondina, their paternal grandmother, gave Alessandra five packages of cookies for Catarina. An uncle, one of Nilson's brothers, accompanied the kids. When we arrived and got out of the car to go to Vita's infirmary, Alessandra grabbed only two packages of cookies for her mother; she ate the remaining three on our drive home. The visit made clear the value assigned to Catarina and the impossibility of a family reunion, even amid wishes that everything could be different.

I was content, however, that her children saw Catarina writing as we approached. Clumsily, they hugged. And Catarina told them, "It's better to dedicate my time to the pen now that I can no longer walk." Anderson said that he had stopped studying, and Alessandra reported that she was repeating the sixth grade as well as helping her grandmother with household chores. I left them alone to talk.

Watching from a distance, I saw many silent moments, while Leonildo crawled on the cement floor, yelling with all his force: "O devil, eat shit!" That day, Iraci told me that the poor man called on the devil because "he cannot leave Vita." Then I noticed that Anderson was writing something on his mother's hand. As I approached, I saw that he had written his name, and Catarina was now writing hers on his right palm. Alessandra asked for the same gesture, and after a while we left.

On our way back, the kids said that, compared to Vita's other residents, "she is not that bad." As Anderson put it: "I thought that she might have worsened even more. But for me, she is normal. For me . . . I don't know much of her condition. . . . You are the one who does the research. She had difficulty talking. Before, she said the correct words. Now it takes longer; the words don't come out of her mouth."

Both siblings admitted that they felt bad entering Vita. "But what to do? To see her, we must enter there. To see all these poor people, those loud voices and mad laughs." Hesitant, Anderson mused, "One wonders if one day one will end up like that."

He then added that during the visit Catarina had asked him to take her to Novo Hamburgo: "She wants so much to come to Novo Hamburgo. I said that, unfortunately, I couldn't do that. I don't have a car, and I am not of driving age." Again, he voiced his desire to get a good job and perhaps then bring his mother to live with him. But life had continued without her, and nobody wanted to—or, in his words, "could"—take care of her. "My grandmother did what she could, and she now has diabetes. My father has a new family; my uncles work."

When I talked to Catarina about the visit, she said that she had enjoyed it and that the children had promised to come back. She thought they were well but was concerned about Anderson dropping out of school. As for their mind-set, she sadly noted, "Too decorative." She meant staged.

Gene Expression and Social Abandonment

In all my meetings with Altamir (born in 1967) and the other two brothers, Ademar (born in 1969) and Armando (born in 1975), they never inquired about how Catarina was doing. Even my descriptions of how often and how dearly she spoke of them did not seem to evoke a response in kind.

They were very preoccupied with their own physical states. Following my last visit, the oldest brother, Altamir, who had more education and was economically better-off than his siblings, decided to seek a medical diagnosis of his ailment. He went to a well-known private neurologist in Novo Hamburgo, who performed a brain scan—"he said my cerebellum is shrinking"—and lured Altamir into a very expensive sham treatment. "One can hardly get a specialist through SUS," Altamir observed.

His experience was emblematic of the routine workings of private medicine, which the working poor and middle class often pay for in a quest for truth and hope. "I had to pay every time I went to see him. Cash. After I took the MRI back for him to see, he prescribed Sirgen, an injection, as well as Citoneurin and gingko biloba." Even though Altamir mentioned the family history of disease, the specialist claimed that he could treat the symptoms of atrophy. "This was a lot of money. I had to take one Sirgen shot every two days. This amounted to almost nine hundred *reais* [three hundred U.S. dollars] per month."

After two months of treatment, Altamir returned to the doctor, who gave him another round of the same medication, which did not help at all. He went back again the following month, and the doctor insisted that he had to keep complying and repeat the dosage. "For the doctor, I was improving.

But for me, who was living it, I didn't feel any difference. Nothing had changed."

After one more visit, the neurologist told Altamir, who had exhausted all his savings, to see a geneticist. "He gave me the name of a clinic in Novo Hamburgo, but one had to pay, and we had no more money. We looked for the university hospital in Porto Alegre, but it is hard to get an appointment there." This medical incident ended with the medication being passed on to Ademar, the middle brother, who had little money and was monitoring Altamir's progress for his own information, since they shared the disease. "Ademar took some of my injections, but they had no effect on him either."

All three brothers were eager to meet with me and Dr. Streb, who had already examined Catarina. We got together on Wednesday, August 14, 2001, and went to Porto Alegre for the medical examinations. We spoke at length about each brother's individual history, disease experiences, and some of our hypotheses about their ataxia. We also reconstructed, to the best of their sparse knowledge, the family tree of the disease. Like Catarina, all three brothers had signs of ataxia and slurred speech (their Romberg tests were positive, and they showed evidence of the Babinsky sign and nystagmus), though their symptoms were less advanced. Their MRIs also revealed cerebellar atrophy, with the most occurring in Altamir and the least in Armando. In comparison, Catarina had the most degenerated cerebellum of the four siblings. All these symptoms were markers of a spinocerebellar disorder that only genetic testing could verify.

The brothers knew—and we reiterated the point— that, given the genetics of their condition and the current state of medicine, there was most likely no cure. Nonetheless, they wanted to investigate what, if anything, could be done to slow the progression of the ataxia and whether they would be eligible for disability entitlements. "This is very important for us," they repeatedly asserted. "This is a disease that is killing. If we don't inform ourselves, we will soon be in a wheelchair. The sooner we know, the better; the more information, the better."

We made available to them all the information we gathered then and at subsequent specialized appointments. Given their social status and the vagaries of SUS, they likened this opportunity to "divine grace." Our work together, they implied, could at least halt the cycle of family denial and medical passivity vis-à-vis the disease that was costing them too much physically and emotionally.

The brothers' accounts revealed gendered and subjective patterns in the lived experience of their shared disease. Family secrets and anecdotes of this unknown disease point to the existence of unconsidered social practices and an embedded moral economy that, given the local state of science and medicine, determine the humanity of the afflicted as well as the course of their dying. Through the brothers' search for a diagnosis, Catarina's condition was being verified and a *biological complex* disassembled.

Altamir recalled that he first noticed changes in his movements when he was twenty-seven or twenty-eight years old, several years later than Catarina's onset, which had occurred in her late teens or early twenties. What accounted for this difference in the time of onset? In the past two years, Altamir had retreated to his repair shop and home, his symptoms publicly interpreted as the gait of a drunkard. He was adamant that his cognitive functions remained intact.

But there was a new constant anxiety. The lack of a cure and the many relatives who had already died from the disease made Altamir think that he was "living the last days of my life, of a normal life. In a while, I won't be able to walk anymore. This is the reality. Of course, one changes a lot. The thought that something is not well is always there." To surrender, however, would be "the worst," he added. His wife, Vania, strongly agreed: "We have to keep rolling on." They were already thinking of building an annex to their house, and Vania seemed to support Altamir unconditionally. Neither of them wanted to know whether their son, Eugenio, had "it." But, should the signs appear, they would find a way of dealing with it, they asserted.

Ademar also owned a bike repair shop. He lived in the poorest and most crime-ridden corner of the Santo Afonso district, where most of the unemployed resort to home business, thus fueling "too much competition." Given his condition, Ademar had even fewer job orders—"people say I am drunk," he admitted. Ademar's first wife had died while giving birth to their first son, at the same time Catarina had Ana. He remarried and had three boys with his new wife.

He was extremely anxious and made it clear how much he welcomed this help, for he desperately wanted to retire and receive disability benefits. With his initial symptoms and Altamir's medical initiative, he saw a window of opportunity. Through me, he thought, he would be able to find his way to a specialist who might provide a diagnosis that would allow him to collect disability. For him, illness was becoming "a form of work" (Petryna 2002:82).

He said that he had first noticed changes in his body two years earlier. "Now I see a difference month after month. It is always worse." To his great distress, he was now "forgetting things." Ademar wept, lamenting the mockery directed at him. "I endure a lot of difficulty, humiliation, shame. The other day, I went to the hospital to visit my son, who was ill, and the security guard said I couldn't go in because I was drunk. It cut me up inside. I told him that I had a family problem, but he replied, laughing, 'I know what you have.'"

According to Vania, Ademar's condition had worsened as he became increasingly concerned with retirement and with guaranteeing his family's future. Comparing the course of the disease in Catarina and her brothers, some hypotheses came to mind: for all four, the definite appearance of the ataxia seemed to be linked to the family's economic concerns, which were particularly sharp. These concerns were in turn linked to relational and affective states that certainly could have sped up the expression of the disease. But their experiences were distinctive: Catarina's disease had been made invisible when she became a mental case and the family's castaway, whereas the men saw themselves and were seen as deteriorating physically, but not mentally. They were supported by their spouses and new families and had the possibility, if they worked hard, of obtaining disability benefits.

I inquired further into their history. In 1986, Altamir and Ademar had been the first to leave the rural provinces in search of jobs in Novo Hamburgo's shoe factories. Nilson, Catarina's ex-husband, was left in charge of the family's land and animals. When Catarina's father left her mother, who was already showing signs of the disease, their property was split in half. It seems that, in order to avoid taxes, a shady agreement was reached in which close relatives were made part owners of the property. Another agreement stipulated that Nilson would take care of the ailing mother and Armando, the youngest sibling, in exchange for having the rest of the mother's property placed in his and Catarina's name.

As Altamir put it, "Cattle, land, plows, cart . . . all just for him to care for our mother, who is now deceased. At that time, Catarina was well. Nilson began selling off the cows and the tools. He threw it all away." The brothers have no qualms about accusing Nilson of opportunism, overspending, and being "dumb"—that is, unable to make money. "When everything leaves and nothing comes back, it ends," one remarked. The close relatives apparently took advantage of the situation and, in the end, took over the property. "No one signed anything," said Altamir. "We were already in the city. Nilson sold it off, the cousins took it over, we have nothing. It all ended."

The brothers no longer drew from a fraternal tie to account for Catarina. They had migrated from a world where that mattered, at least for Catarina, but since she had been given to Nilson and the young couple lost the family's land, the brothers no longer felt any obligation to her. That is the economic and gendered texture of their current morality, I thought, beyond the domain of the blood tie. Also, the development of ataxia in the family was entangled with patterns of spousal separation, the abandonment of women with the disease, and predatory claims to land and goods. After the Gomes' property disappeared, Nilson and Catarina migrated to Novo Hamburgo, bringing along their first child as well as the diseased mother and her own young son.

Ademar, who was able to study only until the third grade—"for when father left, I had to help mother on the plantation"—was even more frank than Altamir: "It was tough. We came to work here. Left everything to Nilson, and then afterward when Catarina became *ruim* [worse], he left her. I think that when she had things, he was with her—and after she became worse, he abandoned her."

Both the brothers and Nilson refer to Catarina as *ruim*, which means "bad," either in the sense of physically degraded or "evil." The verb used with *ruim* assigns the meaning. For the ex-husband, Catarina "was" *ruim*: she was an evil person. For the brothers, she "became" *ruim*: her condition worsened. At stake is the choice of a moral and biological "essence" whose historical constitution ethnography in this longitudinal form reveals.

It is important to mark the distinctions among these "essences." In the ex-husband's interpretation of Catarina as essentially evil, she is solely responsible for her own abandonment, and not even a utilitarian ethics can be evoked: she is paying for her evil actions (such as hitting her disabled mother and burning her husband's documents), she failed to adhere to her pharmaceutical regimen, and she is simply outside the domain of rational thought. In the brothers' account of Catarina as gradually becoming worse, there is room for a kind of historicity of the physical signs and for a maternal linkage, though not for ongoing relationships.

For instance, the brothers associate mother and sister: "When our mother came to the city, she was already in a wheelchair. In Catarina, it began earlier than in our mother. We were grown up when our mother stopped walking. But with Catarina, no. . . . Her kids were very small, and she had already become much worse *[bem ruim]*. We don't remember much of this. But we can see that nature is getting weaker and that the disease is beginning earlier and earlier." It seemed that as Catarina became increasingly like their deceased mother—read: biology—it became possible to leave her behind. An unspoken order or economically motivated common sense developed over time around this unknown disease, making possible the unbinding of the family and informing memory and morality. This biological complex, as it were, is more consequential to one's humanness and the course of life than the tie Catarina continues to live by.

Armando is the quietest of the brothers. The twenty-five-year-old works the night shift in a shoe factory; the shift premium allows him to earn an additional half of a minimum monthly salary. When I visited, he had just been robbed at gunpoint in his shack, which adjoins Ademar's house. "One is not the same person after that," he observed. He told me that, according to Novo Hamburgo's main newspaper, some 75 percent of the homes in that district had been robbed in the past year or so. The paper had shown the photograph of a house with a sign asking robbers, "Please, spare us—in the past week, we had two break-ins."

Altamir mostly spoke for Armando, describing him as a good, hard-working kid who did not take drugs. Armando had also studied only until the third grade: "I stopped because I had to take care of my mother. I was ten years old. Catarina and Nilson went to work on the plantation. I had to stay with her." The development, productivity, and life chances of this child were determined by the social course of his mother's paralyzing disease. I wondered about the impact that this repeated male abandonment of women with the disease had on reproductive choice.

Armando's speech was slurred, but he commented that he suffered "more from the loss of equilibrium." He was proud that he could still play soccer, and he credited his occasionally depressed mood to discrimination in the factory: "I take it lightly, but one feels it inside." He smiled as he spoke of his fiancée-to-be. "We have been dating for some time. I like her. She accepts one the way one is."

To my surprise, Ademar and Altamir abruptly interjected their own assessment, as if they had the authority to do so, saying that "Armando's relationship will depend on the disease. If it worsens, it will be difficult to continue." As the brothers increasingly focused on the medical issues in the family disease, diagnostics seemed to become a new relational technology that could affect family and reproductive arrangements. Vania told me that she had not known about the disease before she married Altamir. She also said that after Ademar had his first son, old Gomes, his father, had warned them to have a blood exam, which they never did. "It must have been something that a doctor told him," Vania speculated. "But I never considered that. Altamir had no problem, and I didn't know his people."

The brothers could not precisely date the onset of their mother's ataxia. All accounts suggest, however, that she might have been in her late twenties and that her husband was aware of her disability. Even though the children saw their mom getting sicker, Altamir recalled, there was never an open conversation about it in the household. An apparent unknown and a dissimulation to keep the disease off everyone's mind: "Our father knew about it . . . but the parents didn't speak openly about it. We kids all looked well. . . . Nothing appeared. . . . They thought that nothing was going to happen to us, so they hid it."

In fact, new affective, relational, and economic arrangements were being plotted and realized around the visible carrier of the disease. The husband left his wife (who had most likely given him a "faulty" lineage) for a younger and healthier woman (with whom he had other children). Altamir himself caught them in the act: "I found my father in the grain storage, making love to another woman." Ademar added that the parents' separation left them all with an immense sense of helplessness: "When I was a kid, at night I always wondered who would take me to the doctor in the city if I became ill." Interestingly, the children continued to see their father on a daily basis, since they all worked on the same plantation. Until they left for Novo Hamburgo, the children saw their father depart from work every night for his new home and family.

Dissimulation and distancing mechanisms seemed central to the culture assembled around the person with the unknown disease in this context of poverty. Even though one could argue that the mother had tried to deny the signs of impaired locomotion to herself and others as much as possible, the brothers could not recall the point at which her ataxia was no longer deniable. Most telling, they could not even recall the exact date or year of her death, as though it had all been part of some murky distant past, suitably far from one's own destiny. A temporal and affective distance had been established.

This was a means, I thought, of dealing with the overwhelming presence of the disease in daily life. After all, the children's identifications, both domestic and public, had been recast by this apparent unknown. There was no way to avoid seeing the past in front of them: their father had become their co-worker in the fields, and as he joined his new family, they returned home to their paralyzed mother. Given the geographic and economic constraints and survival needs, distancing devices were put in place, allowing everyday life to continue. Thus, face-to-face encounters at work and in the village became supposedly disaffective and nonmoral interactions, rather than the sources of dispute, guilt, and accusations of liability they might have been.

Later, after their disabled mother died, their father attempted to recast his

authority by trying to influence his son's fatherhood—in the name of protection. That lineage, it seemed, had to be discontinued. Nilson and the
brothers did just what the father had done: they changed their lives by making a second family. Ademar and Nilson both had new families, and Altamir
always praised his extended family of in-laws and kept an amicable distance
from Ademar and Armando. All of these men had, to some degree, cut themselves off from their blood family, so to speak. Recall Nilson saying that
Catarina was not even in his thoughts.

This was an intricate story. Only by listening to all parties, recurrently and
over time, by juxtaposing deceptions with finally revealed thoughts, was it
possible to access the underlying plot to cast Catarina out. While Catarina's
cerebellar degeneration remained medically invisible, she became increasingly unfit for the home. Familial and new medical interventions, accumulated with failures to act or nonactions, created a logic of their own. People
now had a medically legitimated fabulation of the mad and evil woman,
which stood in place of the family tie.

The narrative that formed around Catarina had no evident agents and,
after some time, no one was responsible for her any longer. Catarina, however, wanted the family tie, for, as I came to understand, she was the embodiment of the destructiveness of the biological culture that made the act
of letting die socially legitimate. In reinstating the tie, she thought there
might be values left that could rescue her from Vita.

Someone who had been completely absent from the brothers' recollections was a sister—not Catarina but Terezinha. In one of our earlier conversations, Catarina had in passing alluded to a younger sister, but she and
the other family members had never said anything about her. As the doctor
and I asked the brothers about other relatives with the disease, they mentioned her. "We don't know much. She had polio and was left with a defect
in her leg. One leg is shorter than the other. We don't know if it is or if it is
not the disease." She was now living in a nursing home in Ipiranga, the big
city next to Caiçara, where the family once owned their land.

I gathered more information from Vania, who recalled that Terezinha had
once worked as a maid in Porto Alegre and that she had a daughter, who was
now cared for by a grandmother. Terezinha had been able to retire, using
that money to pay for her institutional care. According to Vania, "she is like
Catarina. Once, she visited us. She does not walk without holding herself
against the walls. She also had difficulty in speaking." Overall, however,
Vania deemed her "a good and normal person." But Altamir replied, "She
was never so normal. She had polio when she was five years old."

There is a gradation of normality linking mental and physical deterioration that is applied solely to the women of this family who, in the end, are no longer mothers. For example, when I told the brothers things Catarina had recalled from their life in common, they stopped me several times and asked, "So, she does recall?" Both Catarina and Terezinha are unknowing parts of their past. The younger sister had fared better than Catarina. Left to her own devices since an early age—and given her unquestionable lack of physical value—she had most likely found ways to work only for herself. But I kept wondering why Catarina had never mentioned her.

On another visit to Vita later that year, I was astonished to learn the place that sister occupied in Catarina's experience. As we were again engaged in reconstructing the chronology of her exclusion, I asked her when the problems with her ex-husband began.

"He broke glasses on the table and betrayed me by having sex with my sister." At that time, before Ana's birth, Catarina alleged, he already had another woman. "So I banished him. . . . I told him to go with his woman . . . with Rosa."

All the legal documents and institutions Catarina had mentioned in the many volumes of the dictionary came to mind: the symbolic order in which she had constituted her existence no longer had value, and, as her body was deteriorating, she could be incestuously replaced by the sister inside her own house. Nilson was a free man, and I wondered how much this incident represented the revenge he had mentioned to me earlier.

"Terezinha came to visit. I was ill at that time . . . and she told me it happened." As Catarina told this part of the story, she gasped: "Terezinha—I walked through the field, the avenue. . . . I left home . . . and went to get milk for Anderson and Alessandra."

Did you confront Nilson?

Her response had been a wish to cut into his flesh. "He broke the table, and I got a skewer. . . . I wanted to skewer him like one does with meat. He got a skewer himself and also wanted to cut me. It was an ugly fight. I was pregnant with Ana. He then got the revolver and aimed at me . . . but he didn't shoot."

I asked Catarina directly whether she thought Nilson had known that she would become disabled like her mother. Her response was confused, oscillating between a knowledge of the plot and a fantasy of a hospital cure.

"If he did . . . he had conditions to give me shelter and comfort. . . . But he didn't want to give it to me. So I left and wandered. . . . He disgusts me."

And why did he hospitalize you?

"To cure me."

Of what?

"I had problems . . . and the nurses gave me injections, long needles. . . . I don't know which problem I had, I don't recall."

Maybe you had none, I said.

"No, I had. . . . I recall the many women there. They laughed so loud."

Family Tree

I was fortunate enough to be in the south of Brazil when the brothers had two visitors: Seu Núncio, an elderly and distant relative who had been a friend of their grandfather; and Neusa, Catarina's youngest maternal aunt. I was called to meet with them to gather further information on the family tree of these large and poor households.

The brothers had not been able to specify their ethnicity—they referred to themselves as *brasileiros*. Seu Núncio described the family as very light-skinned, commenting that "they looked like gringos"—that is, not black or Indian but of European descent. Most likely Portuguese, I thought.

Seu Núncio had migrated to the region of Caiçara around 1945, in search of land. Like many others, including the brothers' grandfather, he took advantage of a government plan to agriculturally colonize that northwestern region of the province: "We got some acres of forested land and start-up money. . . . The poor ones were the ones who went there. We cut the trees down, had to kill wild animals, and so it began."

The second generation was unable to keep the land, however. These small farmers were left without incentives, and the province's agriculture became ever more focused on soybean and tobacco production. The farmers either sold their nonprofitable land or exchanged it as payment for previous debts, as Nilson and Catarina had been forced to do. Landless, many would find a future in the government-subsidized shoe industry, in places such as Novo Hamburgo.

Others, including Neusa and her children, migrated further north to new settlements in the province of Paraná, which in the 1970s began recruiting farmers and workers for its internal development. Four of Catarina's mother's six siblings went to that province and have, in their own ways, prospered. In addition, as Neusa elucidated, they have taken along the unknown and mutating disease and its social forms.

Seu Núncio was adamant about the changing nature of the disease. "I met their grandfather Horacio when he was already surrendering. He was tied to a bed and died at an old age. He must have been some seventy years old. He was of a stronger nature. Next, his daughter Leontina died, then his son José died . . . and then in the late 1980s, Ilda died." Ilda was the mother of Catarina and the three brothers. Horacio's children all died in their late forties or early fifties, said Núncio. "But now the disease is killing younger. From seventy to fifty to thirty years old. . . . That's what I see." He was referring to Catarina and to the four children of Ilda's oldest sister, who had died in their thirties, wheelchair-bound. Seu Núncio noted that, earlier, "there was no knowledge"; only recently had he learned that "it was a problem in the head, in the brain."

Neusa was in her mid-fifties and considered it fortunate that she and her children had no signs of the disease. She was also amazed at how early the disease was now appearing. Her grandfather had died at the age of seventy-three. As Neusa recalled what had happened to her siblings during the course of the disease, I realized that there was a substantial time between the onset of the disease, which was marked by slight losses of equilibrium, and the moment this became visible to others. No one seemed to have a clear recollection of the onsets. But everyone knew when "the legs didn't help anymore."

That time frame was a period in which much dissimulation and negotiation over visibility and domestic productivity took place, and family ties and affections were recast. According to Neusa, the disease appeared in the oldest sister, Geni, "when she was forty-five to fifty years old," suggesting not necessarily a later onset but rather that her family configuration had allowed her to live a "normal and healthy life" longer, as the ataxia progressed.

Taken together, these eight siblings had more than fifty children. The high incidence of the ataxia among uncles/aunts, siblings, and their children did not halt procreation. In fact, the opposite seemed to be the case. I wondered how this was linked to an economy of care developed within that period of gradually visible onset. Leontina, another of Catarina's aunts, "got ill when she had Lena." Just as in Catarina's case, people often spoke of the onset of the disease in connection to giving birth.

As the work unfolded, it became increasingly evident how Catarina's trajectory resonated with that of other women in her immediate and extended family. The aunt whose story resembles Catarina's most, Neusa offered, was

Nair. "Like Catarina, she became an invalid. But the dying is slow." When I heard that, I could not help but think of Vita as a place where dying, for people like Catarina, is sped up. Neusa emphasized the role of Nair's husband in driving her mad and taking her motherhood away: "Nair's husband left her, and she became like an animal. She even went mad. The husband gave her daughter away."

According to Neusa, these tragedies were induced by a male *ruindade* (evil, baseness). The term *ruim*, so often used to describe Catarina and her condition, was here turned back onto male action during the time between the disease's onset and its social visibility. Neusa then spoke of Ilda, Catarina's mother: "When she had Ademar, she already did not control the legs well. . . . When the kids were small, their father got a lover. What ended Ilda, like Leontina, was his *ruindade*."

As I listened to Neusa's account, I noticed that among the men in the family who died "with problems in the legs," most likely related to the cerebellar and bodily degeneration, their conditions were always shrouded in mystery. José, for instance, had a problem in his foot when he was young and, because of medical malpractice, began to limp. Later, when he was in his thirties, Neusa remembered, "the same foot was bitten by a snake, and he couldn't walk anymore." For men, it seemed, this biological complex could produce positive results, protecting male honor and guaranteeing productivity and procreation. José had three children. Oscar, younger than Ilda, was said to have worked on the tobacco plantations until he was forty years old. As a result of chemical poisoning, reasoned Neusa, he "had a problem in his spine" and was able to officially retire. But, she added, in his last days, he also "walked like a drunk."

Neusa brought the conversation back to Catarina, "the poor thing," by saying, "Nilson was *ruim* to her." Altamir pitched in, agreeing that Nilson did many things wrong, "provoked her and made her get ever more out of herself, wandering and not making sense anymore." In every account, something always exempted one from maintaining any tie to her. Altamir continued: "She didn't like the way Nilson acted, and that began to put things in her head. She had no exit, had to stay with him . . . had to stay at home, care for the kids, and then she went mad."

Ademar agreed that Catarina's "mental weakness" was "because" of Nilson. "He betrayed her. . . . I think that when she began showing problems in her legs, with walking, that's when he began to look for other women. . . . All this weighs in the scale." Ademar spoke fondly of the younger Catarina as hard-working and caring. "Until she had the setback, she was a one hundred percent person. She worked hard on the plantation . . . took care of cattle, pigs, chickens. She was always normal, had good humor, didn't forget a thing. We fought a little, but it was nothing. . . . This was when she was single. . . . Then she got married, had Anderson. . . . With Alessandra onward, she had problems, and with the last ones, there were more problems."

I asked Ademar whether people realized that she was inheriting her mother's disease. "I think some people realized that," he replied. As I pushed further, he admitted that by 1988, when their mother died and Catarina was first hospitalized, one could already see the onset.

Nilson had asserted that Catarina was now paying for her *ruindade*, for hitting her disabled mother. I asked her relatives how she got along with her mom. Both Altamir and Ademar acknowledged that their mother was very "bossy, even in the wheelchair," and that, "of course," sometimes they fought "because this disease leaves one very nervous and agitated," in Ademar's words. But he denied that Catarina hit their mother: "Sometimes they argued. My mom didn't speak things in the right way. . . . She was very direct."

Altamir added that in fact Catarina did not get along well with their deceased father. "They didn't bond, for he had another family." Neusa alleged that in spite of his lack of aid to the family, the father still physically abused Catarina well into her teen years. "Catarina was a smart and nervous kid. She rebelled when she saw her mother in that condition. Her father had no patience to talk to her, and he hit her. Once, I heard him bragging in public, 'I got that big one and spanked her.'" Catarina was fifteen years old at the time.

Ademar resumed his recollection of how Catarina had been cast out. "Nilson took her to several doctors, the local health post, the mental health service, the Caridade. . . . One didn't see much improvement. It only worsened." At that moment in his account, the ataxia and Catarina's mental condition were conflated in the narrative of "it" worsening. Catarina's mind, her marriage, and the family's economic situation all deteriorated in the same proportion. "Their things were ending. . . . When Nilson lost his job, it worsened even more." But as the story continued, the future held different outcomes: For Catarina, dying. For Nilson, a new family.

Without her children, with no property to her name, no longer walking straight, referred to as "mad," Catarina was brought to the brothers by her mother-in-law. "She said that she wanted to stay with us," recalled Ademar. "She had no more direction; the things she spoke didn't match. I kept her for a week, but we couldn't take care of her. . . . We had to take her to the bathroom and all these things. Then she spent a week at Altamir's. For a few weeks, she was back and forth." The brothers then spoke to a local Pentecostal pastor, who told them about Vita. "Vita is a society—I don't know how to explain it," said Ademar. They went to Vita and negotiated with Zé das Drogas. "He said okay, you can bring her. So we left her there."

———

Catarina's overall condition was now worsening much more quickly. It was very difficult to understand her, and her writing was truncated, with fewer verbs, and almost illegible, I feared. "At night, I have this burning anguish . . . to leave running," she told me. "It is quite horrible. I think it is my impossibility. I want to go to Novo Hamburgo . . . and I am not able to. Then I get this anguish. I roll in bed and think. . . . Then I see that I am weeping." The abandonment: "I cannot pass my desire, my pleasure to anyone."

I offered to contact her brothers to arrange another visit, if she wanted. She said yes, but added, "They have no cell phone. It is not worthwhile to try to call them." She was afraid that they would say no. She asked me to put her in my car and take her there right away, but I replied that I could not. "They don't use the phone," she insisted. Enraged, she threw the notebook on the floor and wept.

After a long silence, our conversation resumed. She then revealed what was really at stake and spoke of being the family's shame: "Of course, they are ashamed of me . . . and will not want to receive me at their homes. They will be ashamed of all they did to me before. They didn't want to accept me before . . . and now that I cannot walk, now they don't accept me in the wheelchair." She insisted that, though they were ashamed, the brothers still "wanted" her. In making this claim, Catarina restored affectivity and responsibility to the brothers. Through claims like this, the abandoned in Vita reinscribe themselves onto their ex-families.

The visit with Catarina's brothers happened while Neusa, the aunt from Paraná, was still there. She had also expressed a desire to see Catarina.

Afterward, the return to Vita was difficult, as always. Having seen that no one wanted her to stay, Catarina was now faced with the effort it took not to entirely believe this reality. According to Alencar, who took her there, "it was the same coldness of the previous visit, a cold business." According to Oscar, such amputations of a family member had happened in earlier times, "but it was hidden. Today, people do it in the open and don't give a damn. Now it is normal." For both volunteers, today's families are automatically and directly responsible for the mental condition of people like Catarina. After leaving the castaways in Vita, as they cross the gates back to their lives, "they themselves become other persons."

A Genetic Population

At first glance, Catarina was just one more lost life in Vita, part of an indigent population with whom the country and its people had become accustomed to coexisting, a population that was so often placed out of sight and thought. But as this inquiry progressed, I began to see Catarina and her family as embodying a specific genetic population that had been made medically and socially invisible, just as her neighbors in Vita most likely embodied other kinds of biological and social processes that made them into human leftovers. Technologies of genetic testing are making certain people newly visible, and, in some measure, they are restored to themselves.

After our August 2001 work, the brothers continued their quest for diagnosis and were finally seen by the genetics team of the university hospital, considered one of the ten best in the country. Given the information we had gathered, Dr. Streb and I were also trying to come up with a possible diagnosis. One day, while searching for scientific studies of spinocerebellar ataxias in Brazil, I came across a reference to something called Machado-Joseph disease, commonly found among descendants of Portuguese-Azorean immigrants to the country. When I next phoned Altamir, in November 2001, he said that he had inquired further into the family's history and had confirmed their Portuguese ancestry. The three brothers had molecular testing done at the university hospital, and the results revealed Machado-Joseph.

Machado-Joseph disease (MJD) is a multisystem degeneration of the central nervous system (Jardim et al. 2001b:899; Coutinho 1996:15). Inherited as an autosomal dominant disease (Jardim et al. 2001a:224), it was first reported in North American families of Portuguese-Azorean ancestry (Jardim et al. 2001b:899; Sequeiros 1996:3–13). On the island of Flores in the

Azores, one out of every hundred inhabitants has the disease, one in forty carries the gene, and one in twenty is at risk for the disease (Coutinho 1996:20). This is the highest known prevalence of any hereditary ataxia in the world.

The gene associated with MJD is located on chromosome 14q32 (Jardim et al. 2001a:224; 2001b:899). MJD is characterized by a progressive cerebellar ataxia, affecting an individual's gait, limb movements, speech articulation, and swallowing. A Machado-Joseph patient shows, among other signs, alteration of voluntary movements, cramps and numbness, contorted hands and feet, squinting, loss of weight, and sleep disorders (Jardim 2001b:899; Coutinho 1996:15–22).

As I further studied Machado-Joseph, I was increasingly awed by how in touch Catarina was with the embodiment of the disease—and shocked by the extent to which this understanding had never found credibility or even a place in her medical treatment. Later, I was also extremely happy when I heard from Dr. Laura Bannach Jardim, one of Porto Alegre's leading geneticists, who has seen hundreds of MJD patients, that "there is no mental illness, psychosis, or dementia linked to this genetic disorder. In MJD, your intelligence will be preserved, clean and crystalline." Of course, biopsychiatrists could argue that Catarina may have had two concomitant biological processes going on. But for me, the identification of MJD was a beacon in the overwhelming disqualification of her as mad, a beacon that shed light on the historicity of her current condition.

After the diagnosis, Altamir said sadly, though without despair, "The doctors have set it right." He used the verb *"desenganar,"* which in this context literally meant that the doctors had used "truth" to undo a misunderstanding. *Desenganado* most commonly refers to a person for whom nothing can be done. As Altamir summarized: "It had to do with the DNA. It is hereditary. . . . It is not because of marriage between relatives. It is irreversible, and there is no cure. With this diagnosis, we can now retire." They had all been treated extremely well, he commented, and had been offered follow-up services such as psychological counseling, physical therapy, and speech therapy, to improve the quality of their lives.

Altamir continued working in his bike repair shop. He did not retire right away, intending to pay more into social security for a year or so in order to ensure a higher retirement income. He and his wife stayed close and soon finished their house remodeling. They did not immediately avail themselves of the hospital's quality of life services, citing the difficulty of getting to Porto Alegre every week for therapy sessions.

They preferred to keep things as they were, it seemed, not wanting to normalize the disease too much. As Vania put it: "We will roll on as long as we can." Their major concern was the future of Eugenio, their only child. "The doctors told us that there was a fifty percent chance that he would have the disease. He is fine. We will just go on as if this didn't exist." This past year, Vania stopped working in the shoe factory in order to help care for her mother, who had suffered a stroke.

Immediately after getting the official diagnosis, Ademar and Armando were able to get disability status, and they retired. Economics first. Ademar was happy with the money he was making, three times the monthly income he would have earned at his repair shop. "I never made that much in my whole life." He believed that his future care was guaranteed, along with his family's welfare after his death. Ademar was very close to his boys, who helped him to move around, making sure he did not fall.

Although he was happy with the benefits of retirement, one could see in Ademar a constant agony, a mixture of anger and guilt. Anger, because he tried in every way he could to leave behind what he called that "curse"—and now "it is all back"; guilt, for possibly transmitting the disease to his children. He continued to repair bikes on the side and preferred not to undertake any kind of special therapy, which was also Armando's choice.

Armando, the youngest brother, began spending most of his time at home, with Ademar's family. He suffered from serious depression when his fiancée left him. At one point, Altamir and Vania had met with a university geneticist and asked her whether it was okay to tell Armando's fiancée about Machado-Joseph. The geneticist advised them that such a disclosure should be Armando's prerogative. But, as the story goes, Vania decided to tell the young woman herself, which prompted her to leave Armando.

Until the diagnosis, people in this extended family had dealt with the disease through elaborate practices of nonknowledge and dissimulation, which had various social and affective outcomes. This culture of the disease is not discontinuous with the technology and medical ethics that now make MJD visible. In the encounter between these cultures and diagnostics, away from the clinic with its standards of bioethics, family members strategize over one another's destiny (particularly with regard to reproduction) and settle accounts concerning their own fates. Armando seemed to be the object of a new moral operation: Vania, who remained with her diseased husband and who had a child at risk, used the diagnosis to disconnect another woman from a possibly similar situation. Armando, whose childhood and educational opportunities had been limited by the social and economic consequences of his mother's disease, became the first to have his plans for a family of his own disrupted by the medical form of the disease, at least for the time being.

—

In August 2002, I worked with Dr. Laura Jardim, director of the Machado-Joseph research division at the university hospital, where the brothers had been seen. In complete contrast to my experience with public psychiatry, here I found an excellent interdisciplinary service (geneticists, neurologists, biologists, bioethicists, psychiatrists, and psychologists), solid laboratory infrastructure, and surprisingly comprehensive vision and patient care, in no small part owing to Dr. Jardim's direction. Trained as a neurologist, with a PhD in genetics, Dr. Jardim showed a rare understanding and sympathy for Catarina's story.

Overall, these were insightful and caring professionals who practiced good science and medicine (with publications in the most prestigious international medical journals). Their inability to offer either a cure or medications to experiment with, it seemed to me, made them even more sensitive to the subjective travails of patients as well as to various social, economic, and relational aspects of health. At the forefront of their practice as medical scientists was an exchange agreement: just as they needed the research patients, the patients and their families needed the best care they could provide, beyond hope of cure, care that basically is never available to the general public outside research institutions.

"We give them the truth, but the truth with support," Dr. Jardim told me. After a diagnosis of Machado-Joseph, the medical professionals tell patients what can be done and reassure them that services will be available whenever they need care. Patients are referred to physical therapy, which helps to preserve some equilibrium and to avoid falls. Speech therapy helps to preserve their ability to take in food, which is very important to prevent aspiration pneumonia, one of the main causes of death.

Patients also have continual neurological monitoring and are checked for depression. All too often, noted Dr. Jardim, depression is taken as inevitable by doctors who see these patients. "But we try to change that mentality. Even though I understand that it is normal for these patients to be depressed, I also know that this is not good for them, for they will be even more incapacitated and will suffer more."

Dr. Jardim was the first to describe a Machado-Joseph case in the province. Although this form of ataxia had been entirely absent from local neurological accounts, she discovered a cluster of patients who exhibited it in the late 1980s, when she began carrying out neurological evaluations on lysosomal diseases and needed a control group. "I was surprised that all of a sudden I had this group of volunteers with the same kind of ataxia—nine families, large and poor families, with many cases, and without any specific diagnostics, for we had no molecular exam at that time."

Since the development of the polymerase chain reaction (PCR) technique, there has been a boom in the discovery of genes that cause various forms of spinocerebellar ataxias (nineteen forms to date).[55] Soon after the gene for Machado-Joseph was discovered, in 1994, Dr. Jardim opened an outpatient clinic to specifically investigate the disease. As far as the medical team could tell, this was the dominant type of ataxia in the state—90 percent of the ninety families now enlisted in the service have MJD. This is only a "convenience sample," Dr. Jardim explained. "These are just people who come to us, mostly from the greater Porto Alegre area. Our lab is always packed, and there is no way we can advertise the service. MJD has become the largest genetic disorder studied by our department." The reason for this "abundance," she noted, was "a founder effect: Porto Alegre was founded by Azorean immigrants in the mid-1700s."

Dr. Jardim related the "neurological invisibility" of MJD in the state not only to a lack of genetic knowledge but also to a lack of historical accounting for Azorean immigration to the province. The immigrants were apparently fleeing a famine on the islands of Graciosa and São José. Although the two thousand families doubled the population of the province upon their arrival, they were basically left on their own, without the subsidies they had been promised as part of a colonization plan.

"There is no concern for preserving these roots," Dr. Jardim worried. "We don't have well-kept archives of this ancestry. We speak of it, but it is not part of our official history or tradition. Instead, we have forged a rather different beginning here in the state, focused on our Central European ancestry, the German and Italian immigrants who came in the course of the nineteenth century, as if only Indians and slaves were here earlier."

Biology is helping to rewrite this history. Dr. Jardim's team noticed that Brazilian patients of Portuguese descent have an earlier age of onset (thirty-four years of age on average) than Portuguese and Azorean patients (forty and a half years) (Jardim 2001a:224). Since local registries reported that the immigrants came mostly from the island of Graciosa, where the average age of onset is also said to be close to forty, the Porto Alegre team began to work with the hypothesis of a local gene mutation.

With new technology available, Tatiana Bressel, a biologist on the team, traced the Machado-Joseph gene in thirty-five people of this cohort back to affected populations in the Azores. The study revealed not gene mutation but the fragility of local historiography: all thirty-five cases could actually be traced back to the island of Flores, where the average age of onset is around thirty-four. "The registers we have are wrong. Since the beginning, these people have been treated as a subclass of no interest," stated Dr. Jardim.

It is only an association but a truly uncanny one: the genetic population Catarina belonged to has so many striking resemblances both to her own history of migration, displacement, and mistreatment and to the invisibility that enveloped her biology. Dr. Jardim described the average patients in her genetic cohort and their family dynamics in this way: "Most of our Machado-Joseph patients come from and have large families, more than five siblings or children, and they are very impoverished families. But this disease comes from long ago, and their ancestors have been impoverished before them. Very few social and economic resources are available to them.

"They are stigmatized by neighbors and other relatives as alcoholics and as nonproductive, both men and women, independent of their age. Then they retreat into the home to avoid suffering social marginalization. They stop working and then have no ability to take care of themselves. Another family member has to be mobilized for care, so at that moment at least two persons are not producing for the family. They really have no means to accumulate wealth and need more people in the household, which might partly explain their high reproductive rates.

"These are very depressed families, people who have a cloud over their heads, a sword of sorts: when will this happen to me? There are many cases of suicide, and there is an intergenerational network of blame, recrimination, and damage. In spite of this, they are tied to one another."

What happened to Catarina over time also uncannily resembled the destinies of most women in Dr. Jardim's sample. "From the gender and affective perspective," she said, "one sees that husbands commonly abandon their wives with the onset of the disease, whereas women usually stay and care for their men. Even though it might sound clichéd, we see that women are more concerned with the children's future. Men, no. Their reaction is one of repulsion and rejection. They project a sense of betrayal and anger for having married someone who didn't tell them that they would bequeath this to their children."

As I related some of Catarina's trajectory, which so closely resembled this general pattern, Dr. Jardim agreed with my assessment: "Yes, the signs of the disease were out there, and for some reason, it was convenient not to see." From her own experience, Dr. Jardim affirmed the existence of a cultural realm of risk assessment prior to and now coexisting with a scientific approach to the disease. "What we bring them that is new is the knowledge of the gene and the form of inheritance. . . . But the family history of the disease is so evident, so flagrant, that members already know who is at risk. So, in fact, we are not bringing news to them."

Exactly. As I explained my archaeology of Catarina's condition to Dr. Jardim and her team, I described my identification of particular ways in which the disease was handled, how the physical signs of Catarina's illness had been tinkered with to the point of familial and medical invisibility. In hindsight, her destiny seemed an ordinary thing in local family and labor regimes as well as in medical practice. As her biology was never investigated, she ended up the subject of these interactions—as if she were an ex-human. Catarina's version of what had happened to her, as well as the story of how the progression of her disease had been accelerated by various relational and technical processes, no longer existed, for she was "truly" outside reality—with the exception of her dictionary and now this ethnographic account.

In discussions with the genetics team, I expressed my interest in how environmental factors (particularly relational and affective states) influence gene expression.[56] Even though local scientists tended to associate the environmental explanation with a patient's coping mechanism, said Dr. Jardim, their empirical evidence and research prevented them from dismissing social stressors as triggers of the disease's onset and acceleration. There is, for example, a significant variation in time of onset among the patients Dr. Jardim oversees: "We have cases that started at twelve years of age and cases that started at sixty. The literature even reports cases of onset at the age of seventy." Patients with MJD survive on average from fifteen to twenty years after the onset, most of them dying in wheelchairs or bedridden.

Dr. Denise Albuquerque, the resident in genetics who was treating Catarina's brothers, said that the pattern of increasingly earlier manifestation of the disease "is quite common." Dr. Jardim explained, "There is a worsening of the condition as generations pass, as a result of gene mutation. We call this phenomenon 'anticipation,' and we have learned that paternal transmission is more likely to provoke earlier onset in offspring." With this tendency, one could expect an ever earlier manifestation prior to reproductive age, which would then hypothetically make the gene disappear in the population. This tendency is offset, however, by the gene's transmission tendency, which is higher than 50 percent.

"It is actually closer to seventy percent," Dr. Jardim added. "This is a preliminary scientific finding, but we actually see it empirically." This is indeed new medical knowledge, and the ethical and care dilemmas abound: "When we tell patients about the transmission rates, we settle for the lowest end of the spectrum of truth to prevent total despair."

Scientists have firmly established that the graver the mutation, the more it anticipates the disease. And while the gravity of the gene mutation can account for 60 percent of the probability of earlier onset, the unknown 40 percent remains. "So, seeing the person's genome, we could project a likely time of onset, but not with total certainty. There are protective factors that postpone the onset in some individuals, in spite of the gene mutation. These can be genetic or environmental factors." Among siblings, continued Dr. Jardim, "the age of onset is almost always the same."

How, then, to explain Catarina's early onset of the disease (late teens) and, for example, Altamir's (late twenties)? Such variations might result from "environmental reasons, social and psychological stressors, even issues related to a difference in personality. Who knows? We will continue searching for an answer to this question. We know that environmental influences are embodied, but we don't know how to get to them. We don't have the instruments to study how the history of the subject influences her own life."

The various sociocultural and medical processes in which Catarina's biology was embedded, I thought, pointed to the materiality and morality of this "unknown 40 percent"—in other words: *the social science of the biological mutation.* I was happy that there was room in this local scientific milieu to openly consider these social, relational, economic, and technical variables. Not only were the genetic researchers and I producing a broader and more complex understanding of Catarina's condition, but this collaborative process held potential for generating a science that could address some of the environmental unknowns and unconsidered values and practices that affect the actual course of biology and of dying.

To this, Dr. Jardim responded: "At the peak of her suffering, they were dismembering her. . . . This dying flesh is all that remained." Rather than being the residue of obscure and undeveloped times, Catarina's condition was part of a regularity, forged in all those public spaces and hazy interactions where a rapidly changing country, family, and medicine met.

The social exclusion and physical deterioration of Catarina and others like her gain language in inner lives that are as desperate as they are creative. Dr. Jardim told me about a patient who was also inventing a language as he was "incarcerated in a dying body." A farmworker, the young man first came to the service in his early twenties. His disease progressed quickly, and by the time he was thirty, he could no longer walk or speak.

"He got a typewriter and, with a single finger, wrote me three pages," she recounted. "They were the most moving thing I ever read. He invented ways to condense words in letter characters and said that, in spite of his body, he had an interior life, like any other person; that he desired to love a woman, although he was incarcerated; and that he wanted a machine that could show words on a large screen so that others could see his attempt to communicate. Our patients are persons who are locked in a black box, who are seen as deteriorated when they are not. They are thinking through their suffering, sadness, and desire.

Dr. Jardim and the residents remarked that patients develop strong ties to the service. They usually bring in more family members and have recently pushed forward the idea of an association of patients, families, and friends. Even though the MJD test is not a medical test, for it involves no clinical management, the relatives of affected persons are increasingly asking for it. "We are faced with the individual's right to know whether she has inherited it or not and with her reasons, relational and economic, for choosing what to do with this knowledge." The new ataxia-detected population, the "convenience sample," is a relatively small subestimate of a larger, invisible ataxia population. It is within this larger context that predictive testing has come into public use. Dr. Jardim's skepticism concerning the ability of geneticists and their technologies to effect change is illuminating: "Sometimes we presuppose that we and technology change the future of people. . . . I don't know whether we do that."

Forty persons at risk for MJD, relatives of individuals in the "convenience sample," recently asked to be tested. To guarantee each subject's autonomy, the service allows only adults to be tested, and only after they have been carefully screened and interviewed. "We do a pre-test for depressive and anxiety manifestations and also address hopelessness. In some cases, the whole team, along with the psychiatrist and the bioethicist, meets with the test subject. Then we collect blood. When the lab results come back, we keep them sealed and call the person. If the person comes for the meeting, we open the results; if not, they remain sealed.

"Only twenty so far have wanted to know the results. Some seventy percent of them were carriers of MJD. We do a regular follow-up on these people, to check their experience of anxiety and depression; to make sure that we have not altered them; and, if we have, to determine how we can then best intervene."

The reasons why people undergo testing are multiple. A few look for the guarantee of a possible retirement. In most cases, however, Dr. Jardim stated, people want diagnostic truth in order to make decisions about relationships. One young woman, for example, broke up with her boyfriend to avoid exposing herself to the suffering her adulterous father had inflicted on her disabled mother. Others want "to be able to make sound economic decisions about family land and assets." One semiliterate married woman used the test results for just such a reason, deciding not to sell a piece of land and choosing to invest some of her money in her children's account, in order to guarantee the family's future if her husband refused to care for her.

Here, we have glimpses of how the culture of the disease has endured, how it is actualized in the testing technology. These are tragic, affective, economic, and ultimately ordinary forms that "biosociality" takes in local worlds, where biotechnology coexists with entrenched inequality.[57] In the process, the groundlessness of universalistic bioethical imperatives is revealed, for they too are vectors for certain uses of technology and ideals of personhood that keep triage in place. "As scientists," added Dr. Jardim, "we are here daily faced with the insufficiency of our knowledge and our powerlessness to alter things."

A Lost Chance

After my August 2002 visit to Vita, I told Dr. Jardim about Catarina's current state: that her speech was now seriously impaired; that she complained of intense pain in her legs and arms; that she was no longer able to sit in the wheelchair, because she was too likely to fall out and hurt herself; that she had problems swallowing food and was losing weight—all common signs of deterioration associated with Machado-Joseph. Given Vita's strong push to let the *abandonados* in the infirmary die out, I was afraid that the few years she still had left would be cut short.

Given the inadequate staffing at Vita, Catarina had also developed ulcers on her back because she was not being moved often enough from the bed to the sofa, where she was passing her days. In addition, I again found that the pain relief medication prescribed by Dr. Streb and the anti-arthritis creams Catarina had requested had not been given to her. I was horrified to learn, upon reviewing the residents' medication charts, that she was being given the antibiotic amoxicillin—for no reason whatsoever—a regimen that could only further weaken her immune system and make her more vulnerable to illnesses such as pneumonia.

I knew that if something happened to Catarina, she would most likely be taken to a general hospital and simply left to die—a common fate for many residents of Vita's infirmary. I told Dr. Jardim all this because I wanted her to see Catarina and, if possible, to provide her with continued care.

Dr. Jardim was very moved and said that she would love to see Catarina and make her part of their service. There was an obstacle, however. She explained that new provincial and municipal legislation no longer allowed specialized medical services to schedule appointments freely. As of August 1,

2002, a new system required patients to have a referral from a local health post before seeing a specialist. After seeing the specialist, they would be referred to a central base, which would, if necessary, place them further in the medical system. The intent was to introduce equity of access to a system that favored informal networks, but in practice it meant limiting access to scarce specialized services and making research such as Dr. Jardim's impossible.

"We have filed complaints and asked the province and the city to make exemptions for research sites like ours," she explained. "We want to conduct exams of siblings or cousins of our patients and are unable to do so. They must also go through the new bureaucracy, and what we are seeing is that now we even have some open slots, whereas we used to be booked five months in advance. Patients are lost in their attempts to get the referrals."

Dr. Jardim and her colleagues were furious that they had lost the ability to do even "the minimum." Although they praised attempts to increase governmental attention to public health in these neoliberal times, the legal and bureaucratic means by which changes were being carried out were actually limiting the access of patients to specialized care, which was in turn leading to lower hospital expenses. Rather than creating better networks of access and expanding specialized services, the alternative Workers' Party administration produced the appearance of a quantifiable and immediate equity—a result needed more for reasons of political continuity than for public health. "I would very much like to see Catarina and help her, but . . . "

I was in awe. Fourteen years after entering the maddening mental health world, Catarina was so close to finally being treated for the disease she had. But it seemed that she would again be a leftover, this time in the name of social ethics. We did not give up, though. Dr. Jardim asked me to contact the local health post used by Vita and direct them to her; she would see whether they could enter the appointment into the computer system.

That same day, I went to Vita and explained to Catarina what I had discovered at the genetics department about her condition. She was happy about the possibility of being seen by the geneticists. First, Oscar sought a referral from the local health post—in vain. They told him to come back to talk to a superior the next day.

The next day, we both returned to this poorest of places, where multitudes of young women and children were lining up for care, referrals, vaccines, or medications. The chief nurse told me that her superior was in a meeting at the city hall and that dozens of people were ahead of Catarina in line for a genetics referral (as if all the demands were equal and could be channeled through the same service). But she added that she understood the gravity of the situation and would write a protocol to speed things up. She advised me to call the next morning, which I did. I was told that Catarina's file would be sent to the city's ethics committee and that in one of their next meetings they would decide whether or not to proceed with her referral.

This was supposed to be justice and ethics in action. We saw it as another lost chance.

Part Six

THE DICTIONARY

MI CANETA

ENTRE MEUS DEDOS
É TRABALHO MI
CONDENADO
A MORTE
EU NUNCA CONDENEI
I TENHO PODER O
PECADO MAIOR PENA
PENA SEN SOLUÇÃO
O PECADO MENOR
QUERER SEPARAR
MI CORPO DA MI ESPIRITO

"Underneath was this, which I do not attempt to name"

One of Czeslaw Milosz's last books opens with a poem called "This" (2001:663). The praise of being has been a protective device, says the poet as he looks back at his life on paper. Underneath his writing has always been that ordinary experience of abandonment and people's lack of response to it. The thought, day and night, that the body's needs, desire, and voice make no difference, which signifies Milosz's work, is literally the material of Catarina's writing.

> If I could at last tell you what is in me,
> if I could shout: people! I have lied by pretending it was not there,
> It was there, day and night.
>
> Only thus was I able to describe your inflammable cities,
> Brief loves, games disintegrating into dust,
> earrings, a strap falling lightly from a shoulder,
> scenes in bedrooms and on battlefields.
>
> Writing has been for me a protective strategy
> Of erasing traces. No one likes
> A man who reaches for the forbidden.
>
> I asked help of rivers in which I used to swim, lakes
> With a footbridge over the rushes, a valley
> Where an echo of singing had twilight for its companion.
> And I confess my ecstatic praise of being
> Might just have been exercises in the high style.
> Underneath was this, which I do not attempt to name.

This. Which is like the thoughts of a homeless man walking in an alien city in freezing weather.

And like the moment when a tracked-down Jew glimpses the heavy helmets of the German police approaching.

The moment when the crown prince goes for the first time down to the city and sees the truth of the world: misery, sickness, age, and death.

Or the immobile face of someone who has just understood that he's been abandoned forever.

Or the irrevocable verdict of the doctor.

This. Which signifies knocking against a stone wall and knowing that the wall will not yield to any imploration.

Largely incapacitated and at the margin of other people's experiences, Catarina spent her time in Vita assembling words that gave form to her being both at the present time, so as it is, and as it has been. Since my first encounter with Catarina in 1997, when she was pedaling an exercise bicycle, I felt that her subjectivity both expressed and channeled the tension she sensed of the personal, the domestic, the medical, and the public, fused in her body. This tension found a way into her writing. "The letters in this notebook turn and un-turn." In all, from December 1999 to August 2003, when I last saw her, Catarina wrote twenty-one notebooks, which composed her dictionary. Two of them were thrown away by the volunteer nurses; the others I kept for her. "This is my world after all."

Although Catarina's external functions were almost dead, she retained a puzzling life within her body. She refused her own erasure and ceaselessly wrote. Her seemingly disaggregated words were in many ways an extension of the abject figure she had become in family life, in medicine, in Brazil. All her efforts to constitute herself as daughter, sister, woman, worker, lover, wife, mother, patient, and citizen were deemed worthless. Her notebooks were filled with elements that compose the ordinary world she no longer inhabited—birth certificates, worker's IDs and voting cards, debts, prescriptions, shops, commodities and brands, local politicians and political parties, Christian prayers, family trees and names, caresses and feelings of tenderness.

Abandonment was all she had left—Vita was even in the vita-mins that were supposed to remedy her. As nothing organized her value any longer, Catarina was left to produce identifications all by herself. Her subjectivity was the constant struggle against the intertwining of biology and social death—writing helped her to draw out the best of herself and made "this" endurable: "I put my thoughts into words. When I have a pen in my hands, I am able to think the little letters, characters I will draw . . . and from the characters I form words, and from the words I form sentences, and from the sentences I form a story."

I studied all the volumes of the dictionary and discussed the words and associations with Catarina. In her writing, I found clues to the people, sites, and interactions that constituted her life. There was also a free pulsing of verse that first eluded and then slowly began to shape the terms of my own inquiry and cognition. As I juxtaposed her words with medical records, family versions and worries, I was able to identify those noninstitutionalized operations that ensured Catarina's exclusion and that are, in my view, the missing verbs to her scattered words. "I give you what is missing."

I found great joy in listening and talking to Catarina and considered it a stimulating challenge to relate the fragments of her story and the cryptic words in her dictionary to the world. As I investigated where she had come from and what caused her physical deterioration, I also helped Catarina to reenter, if only briefly, the worlds of family and medicine and the possibility of citizenship. "Ethics," says Michael M. J. Fischer in commenting on this work, "resides in the receptivity to the face of the other, to the voice and call . . . through the other, of the other's other, a horizontal transcendence . . . these worldly relationships." It is "the love of anthropology," as Veena Das puts it: "I allow the knowledge of the Other to mark me" (1998:193).

Throughout my work with Catarina, I did some theorizing that helped me to understand, to a point, the intertwining of family complexes and social reality with her genetic heritage and present existence. The idea of *social psychosis*, for example, was a way to bracket the madness ascribed to Catarina and to bring into view the relations that existed between her subjectivity and social, familial, and medical identifications. Archival research and the ethnography of her kin and of the local health care system exposed the malleable social form that the family has become—a key means and material of sociopolitical intervention and manipulation. Catarina's experience revealed profound fractures in the symbolic reordering of kinship as well as in monetary and medico-scientific realities that were presented as the desirable norms. Her presumed madness was intimately related to changing political and labor regimes as well as to pharmaceutical forms of knowledge and care that were embedded in nets of relatedness, intimacies, and betrayals. Social psychosis thus encompasses the manner in which diagnosis and treatment of various mental and affective disturbances fluctuate in concert with political and economic forces and the dying of social ties.

This is not to say that mental disorders are basically a matter of social construction, but rather that such disorders *do* take form at the most personal juncture between the subject, his or her biology, and the intersubjective and technical recoding of "normal" ways of being in local worlds. Hence, mental disorders also implicate those people claiming to represent common sense and reason, and it is their responsibility to address their embroilment in the unfolding of the disorders.

The concept of Catarina as a *pharmakos* helped me further understand how psychiatric diagnostics and treatments are integrated into a domestic "dramaturgy of the real" and how family members use them to assess human value and to legitimate the disposal of persons considered unproductive or unsound. Psychopharmaceuticals mediate abandonment both through the scientific truth-value such medications bestow and the chemical alterations they occasion. They work as moral technologies through which families and local medical practitioners do the triage work of the state. Here, bodies, inner lives, and new forms of exclusion are entangled in large-scale processes and shifting grounds of knowledge and power, science and money. And the domestic and public display of these entanglements, the reversal of ties and values, the uncertainty of limits, the instability of characters and experiences, and the anxieties created indicate the mutation of mental universes and the emergence of new laws of perception and action even in the face of an ingrained sameness.

While analyzing how and why people and institutions no longer took it to be in their best interest to address Catarina and her words, I also explored the ways in which social and medical practices affected her life. The discovery of Machado-Joseph was key in discrediting the categorization of Catarina as mad, and it helped to explain the development of her condition. In my work with her extended family, I found, for example, that social abandonment and an early onset of the disease were quite common among women. Affective, relational, and economic arrangements were plotted and realized around the visible carriers of the disease, and these gendered practices ultimately accelerated dying. I used the idea of the *biological complex* to think about how such environment-gene interactions affected Catarina's health.

Tensions between marginality and centrality, visibility and invisibility, encompassment and abandonment were constantly present and endlessly renewable in the field and coexisted within the same social figures and spaces. I tried to integrate these core paradoxes and tensions in my theorizing— first, in relation to the exclusion of the society of bodies in Vita and the life of the socially dead; then, inside the economy of the family itself; and, finally, in relation to the gendered differences in the visibility of the genetic disease in Catarina's family and in the overall genetic population to which the family belongs.

The concept I worked with the most hesitantly was that of the *ex-human*. I used this term neither to posit an abstract condition nor to upset and generate a response coded in our now familiar language of human rights. One of the main problems in human rights discourse is the a priori assertion of an irreducible common humanity that should provide the basis of our interactions and our social organizations. In the face of that assertion, the term "ex-human" helped me to make relative the claims of a generic humanness and to think about the contingency and pervasiveness of the forms of human life I found in Vita.[58] Catarina often referred to herself as an "ex," declaring "I am an ex-wife," or stating that she was no longer related to "my ex-family." She spoke of life in Vita as being outside the bounds of justice, and the concept of the ex-human helped both to analyze and illuminate the fact that this condition is generated in institutions and exchanges that are supposed to constitute and nurture humanness.

The ethnography of Vita makes it painfully clear that there are places in the present, even in a state founded on the premise of inviolable human rights, where these rights no longer exist, where the living subjects of marginal institutions are constituted as something other, between life and death. Such places demonstrate that notions of universal human rights are socially and materially conditioned by medical and economic imperatives. Vita also reveals the extent to which a certain kind of human rights discourse—the sort that generates "model programs" in restructuring states and economies— in practice works by a logic of exclusions; and it confirms that public death remains at the center of various social structures, animating and legitimating charity, political actors, and economic strategies.

But I have always worried that in representing the condition of the *abandonados* through such a philosophical-sounding term as ex-human, I might generate a distance and thus unintentionally participate in discursive regimes that ultimately miss the paradoxes and dynamism involved in letting the Other die. It is the fundamentally ambiguous being of the people in Vita that gives the anthropologist the opportunity to develop a real human critique of the machine of social death in which they are caught.

A human form of life that is no longer worth living is not just bare life—language and desire continue. And as I listened to and excavated what had made Catarina's voice "posthumous," a life force—often gaining form in the figure of the animal and related to libido, belonging, and opposition to a death drive—emerged to rework thought, social relations, and family life. Ethnography became the missing nexus between the real of Catarina's body and the imaginary of its mental and relational schemes, between the abandoned and the family, the house and the city, individuals and populations in Vita.

Many of her dictionary entries seemed to be raw poems. I translated some of them and have placed them in the form of stanzas in this part of the book. They are in the order I found them; the books are assembled chronologically. *Literality is the force of Catarina's work.* Her words are disjointed objects. What ties them together is the constant effort to address the unspeakable of the ordinary. I have tried, to the best of my ability, to render into English Catarina's usage of words and the sense of the lived experience they carry—what had been, dying in Vita, and the desired. What follows is only a small part of the abundance of writing in her many volumes. As I began to disseminate Catarina's dictionary among friends and colleagues, her words began to take on a life of their own as they carried her thinking into new contexts and possibilities.

Catarina remarked that other people might be curious about her words, but she added that their signification was ultimately part of her living: "There is so much that comes with time . . . the words . . . and the signification, you will not find in the book. It is only in my memory that I have the signification. And this is for me to untie. So many words that have to be deciphered. . . . With the pen, only I can do it. . . . In the ink, I decipher."

Catarina refused to be an object of understanding for others. "Nobody will decipher the words for me. I will not exchange my head with you, and neither will you exchange yours with mine." In order to carry out this work, "one must have a science, a light conscience." Not burdened by guilt, "one needs to put one's mind in place."

We might face Catarina's writing in the same way we face poetry. She introduces us to a world that is other than our own, yet close to home; and with it, we have the chance to read social life and the human condition, both hers and ours, differently.[59] To engage with her life and writing is also to work on oneself. "I am writing for myself to understand, but, of course, if you all understand, I will be very content."

As Catarina expressed the knots, the truths and half-truths of what was happening to her, her body experienced—along with hunger, spasms, and pain—uncontrollable desires, an overflow unthinkable in terms of common sense. While exposing Vita as a place of total annihilation, she also created a new letter, a character that, as mentioned earlier, resembled a "K." In her words: "It is open on both sides." With "K," she created a distance and wrote a new name for herself, "CATKINI." In the dictionary, she constantly placed this name in relation to those of others she met in Vita, such as Clóvis and Luis Carlos, or people she had known in the past, such as Valmir. They are counterparts to the null, the place of leftover into which she has been cast.

Unlike the Poet, Catarina refused to be consigned to the impossible, and she anticipated an exit from Vita. It was as difficult as it was important to sustain this anticipation: to find ways to support Catarina's search for ties to people and the world and her demand for continuity, or at least its possibility. Out of this intricate ethnographic tension emerges a sense of the present as embattled and unfinished, on both sides of the conversation and of the text.

Book I

I offer you my life

Dead alive
Dead outside
Alive inside

Divorce
Dictionary
Discipline
Diagnostics
Marriage for free
Paid marriage

Operation
Reality
To give an injection
To get a spasm
In the body
A cerebral spasm

Maimed statue
Birth certificate
Catarina and Anderson
To present it in person
Policeman
Electoral officer
Eye to eye
Machine
To make meaning

Documents, reality
Tiresomeness, truth, saliva

Who contradicts is convicted

Cerebral spasm
Corporal spasm
Rheumatic
Paralyzed

Frightened heart
Emotional spasm

With L I write Love
With R I write Remembrance
Inside your and my heart

Sweet blood
Sugar in the blood
Perfume
Smell
And science
I seduce you

[1999]

Book II

The pen between my fingers is my work
I am convicted to death
I never convicted anyone and I have the power to
This is the major sin
A sentence without remedy
The minor sin
Is to want to separate
My body from my spirit

To want my body
As a medication
My body

Invalid in the legs
Rheumatic in the head
Paralyzed in the arms
Disjointed wrists
Broken feet
Pain
Spasm

Catarina is subjected
To be a nation in poverty
Porto Alegre
Without an heir
Enough
I end

Woman
Servant
The servant of God
I served the penis
And departed
I served a man
My father
I am needy
I am legal

Sacred family
The tree that does not produce good fruits will be cut
and thrown into the fire
Man and woman leave father and mother to become one flesh

Partial contract of goods
Partial marriage

Divorce
Religion
Public registry
The separation of bodies

Marriage certificate
Civil register
Document
Personal data

Blood of menstruation
Lubricates the blood of the mother
The blood of the egg goes to the child
In the gestating womb
Judah men killed a goat
To save themselves
With the blood of the unknown animal

A knot in the intestines
A medical error
A fight
A knife in the belly

Premature
Born out of the schedule
Out of time, out of reason
Time has passed
The baby's color changes
It is breathless
And suffocates
The mother of the baby

Asylum
Laboratory
Pharmacy
Pharmacist
I and the cure

Conscience is the enemy
It attacks

In the calendar of my life there is no holiday

To make peace with time
The hours, minutes, and seconds,
With the clock and the calendar

To be well with all
But mainly with the pen

I make love in my mind to scare the cold

I am vain and proud
I have dollars
A secret love
In a box
On the tip of my fingernails

My spirit of love nobody can catch

I am in no hurry
We have to acquire it
What is for me
Is kept in the safety box
Brazilian safety box
Sample

Copying the scenes, the gestures, and the words
He succeeds at the expense of others

What an important thing
An ant carrying an elephant

Foam bath
Snow white
Baptism in the shower
Meal
Mermaid
Pubic hair, breasts
Half human
Half fish

The dresser prepares the bed
Thinking of the person who will sleep there
Delinquent, he takes desire from the mattress
And says that it is the dream of Catarina

When men throw me into the air
I am already far away

The diseased does not get the pen
I am not ill

My love
How wonderful it was to dream about you
Last night
I slept a little and dreamed about you
You appeared smiling, extending your hand toward me
Suddenly, in less than a minute, you transformed

Nobody is accountable anymore for the exact time
What will become of the world?

Nothing is dead
It is over
I don't want to stay here
I want to live with my children
When my brothers arrive
I want to leave this place
I don't want to be cheated by God the third time
To be the cross of each one of the actors

Brazil
Africa
Germany
Used clothing
Dead desire
Fainted pleasure
Blood-sucker
Lifeless

Catarina cries and wants to leave
Desire
Watered, prayed, wept
Tearful feeling
Fearful, diabolic, betrayed
My desire is of no value
Desire is pharmaceutical
It is not good for the circus

[2000]

Book III

To feel love
Lonely love
To follow desire in solitude
That's the illusion of the abandoned

I shall not pay a debt I didn't incur
I don't deserve to suffer for a crime I didn't commit
Rheumatism

Democratic God
Brazil
Brazilian
Baby
P. Pai [Father], Partido [Party] [the father who has departed]
T. Trabalhadores [Workers]

Pleasure and desire
Are not sold or bought
But they have a choice

Clóvis Gama
Catieki Gama
Alessandra Gomes
Ana G.
To restart a home
A family

Se goza gozo
Enjoyment enjoys itself

[2000]

Book IV

I like the ways I am
The ways I know myself
I like myself

Desire
Kissing
From beginning till the end
I feel pleasure
Pleasure to have life in my blood
Glory, hallelujah
Saint Catarina

The king asked to marry one of your daughters
We don't give our daughters for gold or silver
Nor for the blood of the lizard

I know because I passed through it
I learned the truth
And I try to divulge what reality is

My father was ashamed to have committed me to a white devil
He only told this to my brothers

What I was in the past does not matter

Catarina Inês
The name of a horse
Catarina Inês
The name of tools
Useful to men
Tools that are part of everyday work

Of love there is nothing
Only emptiness

One woman offers herself on a tray
The other woman cannot alter her footsteps
Offered, she fucks in the unknown
With horses
In front of the elderly
Sassá
The paralyzed woman does not offer herself on a tray
A woman must keep a secret

João Biehl
Reality
Catkini

Give me this chalice and I will drink its precious liquid
Animal desire

Calligraphy
Grammar
Who said that if I were to die they should place a child in the coffin?

I don't deserve to be in a wheelchair
Let's go to the field and plant,
My love

I am not obligated to surrender my child
Not according to my law
And this is moral

My cross is very heavy
That's why no man wanted to stay with me
To be alone is also enjoyable
Man is not the solution

The father who does not accept the child
All he touches becomes garbage
The woman who does not like the child
She does not honor her name

There is no exit in my road
You are waiting for me to get ill
To take over my home
Don't you dare try to control my studies
The desire of the father is blindness

Gilberto did it to India
Clóvis ties Ana Paula so that we can finish it
I didn't want it
To become a mannequin
A sample woman

There is no place to put me
I am forced to stay here
For I cannot move
I hope to be how I was before

The pain in my legs and hips
My children are distant from me
In another country

Forget that I exist

[2000]

Book V

Words used in the dictionary
Questioning
The civil judge
Notaries
The legal judge
The commitments of God's law
The honor of men's words
To produce
Progress
Prosecutor
Judge of desire
Sticky mucous

Medical records
Ready to go to heaven

I left my wife with the children in her arms
And was bewitched by another woman
This woman, a lost soul
Bewitched me with her smile
And placed my soul in the hell of life
I was all in the sacred home
Today I find myself with the soul lost

Ulcer: Nilson
Cyst: Clóvis
Hernia: Luiz Carlos

Take me to bed
Touch my body
Make my desire
May the angels say
Amen

[2000]

Book VI

The force of will
Of good will
Not to injure
But to kill the hunger
And not your brother
The force to do good
In the moment of weakness

I don't know how to pray
She lives with her hands open

The queen of the alphabet
The princess of words
The token of vowels
A, e, i, o, u
I divorced the man

My son will take me out of here
My brothers will come to take me to live with them in Novo Hamburgo

Die death
The medication is no more
The nurse is no more

I want to auction my heart

Surgery without pain
In the name of love

Look at Catarina
Without blindness
Pray
Prayer
Act of repentance
Sexual act
Jocastka
There is no tonic for Catkini
There is no doctor for any one
Altamir, Ademar, Armando
Anderson, Alessandra, Ana

Men raise children in captivity
Indian woman, never forget me
Hold it, cowboy
My blood cannot stay imprisoned
In the care of the woman who sleeps
With feminine and masculine blood

I am like this because of life

The letters in this notebook
Turn and un-turn
My hands
I did this calligraphy
Catkina
I baptize you, my dictionary
In the name of the father, the son, and the spirit of love
Amen
The future of our children
The dance of science

[2001]

Book VII

Sweeping
Running
Maria lame, who lamed?
Where is the stone?
The stone is in the woods
Where are the woods?
Map
Ocean
With the ox
Where is the ox?
Eating wheat
Where is the wheat?
Made bread
Where is the bread?
Priest ate it
Where is the priest?
Praying the mass
Where is the mass?
I enter through one door and the fool leaves through another door
It is you who answered

I need a father
To cover me with a blanket at night

I have two workers' IDs
One I did in the city hall of Caiçara
The other I did in Novo Hamburgo

Businessmen
They make love to each other
For a new pair of shoes

Everything has a limit
I already gave my heart

Not slave
But housewife
Wife of the bed
Wife of the room

Wife of the bank
Of the pharmacy
Of the laboratory

The abandoned are part of life

Don't grab my fingers and toes, I beg you
Let me go, Gilberto
If not, I will have to use the blade
It cuts on both sides

We announce the death of Jurema's leg
She wrote my name on a yellow ribbon
And asked that it be buried
I have nothing to alleviate the suffering of my hand

Vote for vote
Christ for Christ
Photo for photo
People for people
Lottery for lottery

[2001]

Book VIII

Dictionary
Social study

Chronic spasm
Encroached rheumatism
Generational rheumatism

I leave the question in the air
Is it worthwhile to make my life a misfortune?

Human body?

[2001]

Book IX

Sin will not leave paradise
Even if forgiveness exists

Judge of human rights
Judge of human beings

Traffic laws
Laws of the human body
Conviction laws
Work-related laws
Laws of the patient
Forcefully tied to the bed
Lawyers
Divorce

I was already the powder of flower
All ate me as bread
I was already a small potato
And spoke with others under the earth
I became a grain of sugar
Sweet as much as I want

I am a free woman
To fly
Bionic woman
Separated

[2001]

Book X

Crazy in her head
Crazy in her house

I will leave the door of the cage open
You can fly wherever you want to

Desire
That's my illness

My ex did everything to get medication

The best medication is the most recent
When Clóvis put me to work in the pharmacy
I was the official
Old Juju was the first to feel the expired medication
The lost effect

I don't want a feast
I just want to leave Vita

[2001]

Book XI

I want to recover alone
Without my sacred family

I didn't kill and didn't steal anything from anyone

I owe nothing
I pay nothing
Supermarket
Past debt
Inflammation
Infection of the heart
Precious pus

Dollars
Real
Brazil is bankrupted
I am not to be blamed
Without a future

Money
Live pharmacy
In the middle of the book

In order for us to be Brazilian citizens
The documents must be in our hands

Nobody wants me to be somebody in life

I dueled
It's not pain
It is pain against pain
The castration of the bull
My Christ
Resurrection
I pull myself backward
To the time Clóvis was here

[2001]

Book XII

Glimiton
Vaccine against the poison
Of insect bite
It is better to prevent than to remedy the poison
Snake, scorpion
Poison, vaccine
Catarina, Catieki
Contemporary spirit
I am not a nurse on call

I am not the daughter of Adam and Eve
I am Little Doctor [an over-the-counter medication]
Catieki

I need to change my blood with a tonic
Medication from the pharmacy costs money
To live is expensive

I wouldn't want to be Christ, the Lord
Nor would I want to be a singer who lives from songs
I just wanted to be the common man who walked on his own feet

I am Catieki
Neither scientific Arno
Nor Catkicia
Not even Catarina

Catieki rots
The frame of the bed

Woman looking at the pussy of another woman
Inspecting the pussy
I bought a fruit bowl from my brother

Chief nurse
Jo Castka
Caridade Hospital
Catieki
Catarina, nature

I want to leave and never again be treated by the state
By the women of this city
By Jandir Luchesi
Death sentence
Here I am being expelled
I don't have my body for business
I am not a slave
I do what I can do

I prefer death a thousand times
Than to endure leftovers

Trenches
Locked in captivity
People go hungry
They want us to be a bag of misery
And say that Catarina is a whore
Sacrilege
Skull
Burying place
Miracle
Hole
Mystery
Catieki

I tried
The effect of the medication
No
Expired medication

In the shelter of my cold arms
Catieki
Saint who protects the world

This is my world
After all
Tiresomeness dries one up
And then it all begins again
My delinquent world
I have no affair with the executioner

[2001]

Book XIII

Two women living under the same blanket
Eating from the same pan
Man is shameless
Accumulates women
He thinks that it is the old times
I prefer revenge
I don't accept two pussies filling the same air

I prefer my goods to the objects of others
I prefer to live my whole life or to live with nobody
I want what belongs to me

Catieki
Underneath
Forgetfulness
Reason: operation

The color of the sin
Sin has no color
For the one who sins does not confess

Forgotten neurons
Aged cranium
Expired brain

Pharmacist
Offers the cure
Doesn't want my head
It governs my life

It is not scripture
It is not promise
It is not you who will judge me

[2002]

Book XIV

Tenderness
Caresses
Love
Fuck
Relation
Professor of English, French, Japanese
Language
Head
Brain
Neurons
Cranium
Scalp
Forefront
Neck
Real
Dollar
Consortium
Rheumatism
Divorce
Spirit of love

Novo Hamburgo city hall
Constitution district
Rotting in life
Mother moon
Clóvis
Alemão
Luiz
Brazilian
Treatment
Recovery
Woman
Business
Divorced
She herself
House
Furniture

I give you what is missing

[2002]

Book XV

Catieki
The pen's ink

A b c d e f g h i j l m n o p q r s t u v x z
Complaint
Self-trial
Judicial audience
Punishment
Daily faces
Diagnostics in the blood
A bonfire
Burning in my heart

A deodorant
A box of soap

A suntan lotion
A cream for the skin
You give me pleasure

Pharmacy
Laboratory
Marriage
Identity
Army
Rheumatism
Complication of labor
Loss of physical equilibrium
Total loss of control
Govern, goalkeeper
Evil eye
Spasm, nerves

Juvenile judge
Public prosecutor
Human judge

In the United States
Not here in Brazil
There is a cure
For half of the disease
I will go with João

[2002]

Book XVI

I am a sedative
A couple's bed

Heir
Treasure
Fortune
Sole daughter

Sole son
Future
Catieki
Cakina
Catakina
To get the secret
Credit card

I threw a lemon that, ripe, fell into a glass

Driver's license
Pregnancy card
Worker's ID card
Brazilian universal institute
Catarina's institute

I will go to Novo Hamburgo
To get respect
I am out

[2002]

Book XVII

Our love needs a key

Informatics
Clóvis Gama
Catieki Gama Gomes
Reality
Pleasure, love, desire
Calm life
Imported car
In the shelter of your arms
Clóvis in my thoughts
Delicious, we are

If I stay
For love
I will not cry

Valmir, Clóvis, Christ
Catarina's pain
Don't teach me betrayal

Even or uneven
City hall or mayor
Catakina or Clóvis

Bodily spirit
Christian soul
Spirit of money
Good spirit of love
Spell: notary, office, Jesus Christ, to frighten
Mentally ill
Mental health
Ill in the head
To dress
Forgetfulness
Thought

Vitamin provokes
Get out, get out
Go, go
Don't do little with me
I only go with the much

Saint Catieki
Altamir
Armando
Ademar
Loyal
House, car, land
Documented

Genetics clinic
Novo Hamburgo's general hospital
Caridade Hospital

Catieki
Catakina
To throw all the blood away
Mentally ill
Mental health
There is no money

To make love
I love too much
Public registry
Marriage certificate
Dame Catarina
Field, song, time
Lotto
Caridade Hospital

I govern myself
I am neither coordinator nor volunteer
I don't get anything but critiques
By will or by force I shall stay
Friends, I want what is
Brother, bed, home
To notarize the divorce certificate

A treatment to join the fingers and toes,
To join the feet and bones
To cover the wounds
Jesus Christ
Nailed through his feet
Rheumatic
I was hit by him

Without knowing
If it does not exist
I, woman
It is not just you, man
If it is not possible to live
Woman you don't have
In the world I am not even woman
Now I want to make your step

This is my world
My lover
My point
I gave myself, and gave and gave and gave
I know myself
That I gave myself
And after all one passes
One starts it all, all again
I

I want to go
Nobody
I spend the whole night weeping
How many tears of pain
In agony
In this valley of tears
I want to go

[2002–2003]

Book XVIII

My life begins at forty

Policeman of the future
Robocop
Man made of tin
I cannot walk
Alone
Seated in a wheelchair
No pleasure
I do nothing

The will of thought practices the good
The person who took knife and fork and four photos to the cemetery
Needs the will of memory
Tools are lacking

Dead death
Death dead
To love, loved
Dead
Baptism
School graduation
First communion
Marriage
Divorce
Adult
Male judge

A b c d e f g h I j l m n o p r s t u v x z
WKZ
Ana
Memory
To translate words

Breast milk
Against children's disability
Chocolate, strawberry
Breast milk
I got peace and a book
In my hands
From Pastor Oscar
India's heart fainted
Heart accelerates and stops
Ana Gomes
Alessandra Gomes
Anderson Gomes
The owner of Catarina
Luiz Carlos
Owner of the bank
Catakina
Real bank
Caiçara
Director of the bank
Madame of the savings bank
A deposit of trust
Federal savings bank of Novo Hamburgo

Provincial savings bank of Novo Hamburgo
Saint Catieki
Clothing store
Divorced from bed, table, and bath
State house
Country
Catakina Inês
Daughter of Dario and Ilda Gomes,
who was the daughter of Horacio Pinheiro

I decide over my child
I don't want to take it to death

Tupã Guarani
I am true to the ink of the pen
Mother moon Tupã
Father sun Guarani
Ceretã
Play ball, boys
Play doll, girls
Bright moon
Moon darkness
Desired moon

[2003]

Book XIX

My historical diary

I don't bend myself for money
I don't do things because of others
I am an adult person

Saint Catieki
Lula democratic production
I am a working party
Menstruated, pure, normal

Natural chocolate
Indian, black, white
Polish, Japanese, German, Brazilian, Argentinian
Milk
Calligraphy
Letters
Calendar
Catakina Inês

Mystery, miracle, mysery
Miserable
Relentless rheumatism
Muscles, bones, blood, nerves tied up

A child wants to come to the world through my love

Only because I cannot walk I have to stay in the stone age
here in Porto Alegre
Our voice makes contact with the infirmity and becomes imperceptible

Voice
I, you study
We
Voice
He
They
Personal pronouns

Portuguese
Professor João Biehl
Home professor
Language
Untruth
Truth
Millennium
Reality
Real
Reais

Soul
Child reasoning
Reasoning of being human
Reasoning of objects
Judge of the law

Angel Anderson gets a fish in the river
Pharmaceutical candy bar
Headache
Delirium
Catarina
Desire out of time

Not another time
A chance is over

I, who am where I go, am who am so
[2003]

Catarina, Vita 2001

"A way to the words"

I received a phone call from a euphoric Oscar, asking whether I was the one who had arranged the surprise visit to Vita by Catarina's daughter Ana and her adoptive parents. No, I had not done this; I was also surprised. Oscar reported that Catarina was very happy—"they even brought her fruit."

Before leaving Brazil in early September 2002, I contacted Tamara and Urbano and asked them about the visit. "It's sad to see a person in that kind of misery," they said. "There are so many people who could take care of her, her in-laws and brothers. I would never let a part of my family be in such a situation," Tamara avowed. In spite of the conditions at Vita, the couple felt that "we should still be thankful to God that places like this exist, that at least take these people in. Otherwise, they would be in the streets and dead."

I asked why they had taken Ana there. Urbano spoke first, conveying a psychological and moral obligation: "We decided to take the girl there so that in case Catarina died, Ana would not be able to blame us for never taking her to see her mother." Tamara added, "At first, they didn't recognize each other. . . . The girl was frightened. . . . She did not want Catarina to touch her."

Tamara then explained the true motive behind the visit. The girl had become delinquent, Tamara claimed, and had stolen one of her rings. In the convoluted account, it was not clear whether the girl had intended to steal or was simply trying to identify with her adoptive mother through the ring. Ana was physically punished, and Tamara told her, "You should thank God that we took you out of the mud to raise you. You were rolling in the backyard amid chickens and pigs. And I picked you up at the entrance of the pigsty. You must understand that we only want the best for you. . . . What you did is wrong, and if I let this pass, you will do worse things." The visit to Catarina was the culmination of this moral castigation. Seeing Catarina was a way of letting Ana know "where she came from and where she was heading if she did not change. On the way back, in the car, she didn't say a word, but I am sure that this is inscribed on her mind."

In early October 2002, I got an email from Dr. Laura Bannach Jardim from the university hospital with the good news that the genetics service had been able to bypass the new public health bureaucracy, which would allow her to continue scheduling her own patients. Catarina would finally be seen for the disease she actually carried. I called Oscar to make sure that he would drive Catarina to the appointment.

Later, with Catarina's consent, I talked to the doctors who examined her and confirmed the presence of Machado-Joseph disease. They judged that Catarina was "completely lucid, knew of her condition, past and present, and presented no mental or other pathology." They scheduled a visit with a neurologist and told her to return to the service in a few months to make arrangements, contingent upon her willingness, to begin physical and speech therapy. She was also invited to participate in the first meeting of an emergent association of Machado-Joseph patients and families.

On Catarina's way out of the genetic consultation, a striking coincidence occurred—her sister-in-law Vania, married to Altamir, happened to be entering the office. She was there to get documents confirming her husband's condition so that he could initiate his disability claim. What an irony, I thought: Catarina had now been publicly recognized as having a genetic diagnosis by the same person who had once procured antipsychotic drugs for her at the local health post.

The two women spoke at length. Catarina was told that she would soon be a grandmother; her son, Anderson, was expecting a child with a fifteen-year-old girl. I later asked Catarina how she responded to this piece of news, and she said, "It's the renewal of the blood. There is always room for a new life."

The fall of 2002 also brought Clóvis back to Vita and into Catarina's life. Oscar desperately needed help in the infirmary and got the captain's permission to bring him back. Clóvis was in charge of caring for the "grandmothers," the elderly women who got welfare benefits and thus resided in a separate room, where they received slightly better care. And since "Catarina had a strong affection for Clóvis," he was also put in charge of her daily care.

After a few weeks, however, Oscar began noticing a few odd things. One early morning, he found Catarina out of her wheelchair on the patio.

Strangely, Clóvis was not regularly feeding her with the special food that we were providing for her. Finally, in early December, after taking a day off, Clóvis returned to Vita completely drunk. That afternoon, Oscar broke into the pharmacy and found Clóvis and Catarina having sex. The next morning, "I told him to leave things as they are and go, and I wouldn't tell anyone." Oscar said that he never raised the issue with Catarina, "for she is so needy, wanting affection, and there was no need to hurt her further."

I went back in January 2003 to visit Catarina. Vita seemed so desolate. The smell of urine and feces was overwhelming; there were flies everywhere. Because of lice, everyone's head had been shaved. In the previous month, the electricity had been shut off, explained Alencar, who along with Oscar kept things at least minimally running. "Upon the request of Representative Luchesi, the state intervened and paid the bill."

I also learned that at least eight people had died of tuberculosis in the fall, including Tranca, the black woman who had always stood at the gate, year after year, holding her two dolls. Only after these people died (some 15 percent of the infirmary's remaining population) did the nearby hospital send a medical team to investigate. They asked Oscar to select a group of people to be tested, and the exams revealed four additional cases of tuberculosis. Those individuals began treatment. We do not know how many cases were missed, but, according to Oscar, who is used to this spectacle of medicine, constructed invisibility, and selective care, "this problem is now solved."

What I had seen emerging over the years was now completely instituted. People in the infirmary were allowed to die, and the recovery area had also drastically reduced its operations, housing only fifteen men. The new buildings were empty, and none of the promised medical, dental, or social care was in place. I felt that Euclides da Cunha's description of Brazil's modernization in the early 1900s as "the construction of ruins" (1976) was still quite appropriate for this contemporary world. The fewer activities and people inside, "the fewer problems they have," I was told. "Now we have buildings, but people don't eat bricks." Moreover, "after some time, the buildings are torn down again. They want visitors to get the impression that there is always some construction going on; that helps to bring in money."

Oscar was proud that he had been able to avoid taking antiretrovirals for HIV and that he had returned to his Pentecostal church. "I settled my ideas, and now I am a lay pastor." He had been dissuaded from beginning his own Vita-like institution. He then made the case to Vita's administrators that he needed to be paid to continue running the infirmary—a job that literally no one wanted. "They don't want to know what is going on in here." Oscar now receives a minimum monthly salary along with housing, utilities, and food. "Where else could I find such conditions for my family and myself?" His payment is actually the pension of one of the grandmothers. "The institution has all the welfare cards of the patients. So the captain gave me one of these cards and said that when this person dies and there is another one that I care for, I will get that person's pension."

Vita's key managers had used the institution to their advantage and had moved up the political ladder and away from the place, I was told: the captain became a major in the police and had a thriving personal security business; Dalva, his wife and Vita's absent social worker, was a city representative from Luchesi's political party; Luchesi himself became the state's most widely supported federal representative in the last elections.

There was no investment or vision for the place, beyond what it had become. The few men in the recovery area now refused to volunteer or help in the infirmary. In the process, Oscar had become the infirmary's mayor, its social worker, philanthropist, pastor, pharmacist, driver—in other words, he was the institution itself. He brought his wife in to help with dispensing medication. Aided by Alencar, he was beginning to train a new group of addicted men, who, instead of going to the recovery area, were "rehabilitating" in the infirmary.

As Oscar put it: "The captain opened up a few spots that I can administer. The triage is with me now. I bring the men in and teach them. I tell them my testimony, how my life changed, from taking drugs and being in prison to fulfilling my mission to care." Oscar was making religion the basis of the infirmary's work: he also mediated the religious conversion of his closest aides such as Alencar, banned smoking, and brought in his Pentecostal friends for regular worship services.

Discontinuity of care remained the norm. Oscar knew that his new workforce would "recover," and then "in three months, they are no longer here." He also made special arrangements with some of the families of the infirmary's inhabitants. People paid him a little to give their relatives better food (such as yogurt and fruit), providing him with additional steady income. One could say that a family geriatric house was in business in Vita, as such houses were throughout the city.

As for Catarina, the family had not contacted her. But, according to Oscar and Alencar, "her whining has calmed down." They insisted on reducing her enduring desire to live elsewhere to a childlike affect: "This emotional bribery does not work with us." Oscar then commented on the genetic consultation. "The doctor drew the explanation on a paper for us. Her case is irreversible. The brothers suffer from the same thing. She already has much difficulty swallowing. We are already giving her mashed food."

I insisted that her quality of life could be improved, to which Oscar replied that, if possible, he would take her once a week for physical therapy. I told him that after the neurological evaluation, some specific treatments might be found to alleviate Catarina's muscular pains. Oscar mentioned the "nice coincidence" of Catarina meeting her sister-in-law outside the geneticist's office. History was being rewritten through this genetic diagnostics, I said. Her claims, past and present, of the problems in her legs were now scientifically validated, and the family could not so easily dismiss her as mad—for, after all, she was now being seen by the same doctors who treated the men in the family.

"I don't know, João. I sincerely think that you are taking this case very far. As I see it, you want to go to the root of the problem, so that in the future it might be possible to detect these things in persons before the disease speeds up. . . . There is nothing else that can be done. This is good work, beautiful work, for you are predicting the future, and perhaps other people can benefit from this."

Given that the irreversibility of Catarina's fate had now been medically certified, Oscar asked me what to him was the most obvious question, although to me it seemed the most violent: "Do you still want to keep helping with money to buy special food for her?"

Oscar, I said, of course. It is the minimum we can do. We must sustain her life. To make sure that irreversibility did not become Catarina's final value, I told Oscar that after her April genetic consultation, she would receive paperwork entitling her to a disability pension and that the genetics team would help out with it. He promised to follow up on all these plans involving Catarina and brought her to the pharmacy.

It was so sad to be unable to discern most of what Catarina was saying on this visit. She nodded that she was, overall, doing fine. She recollected what had happened since we last met: Clóvis's return, which she had written about profusely in one of the three new volumes of her dictionary; the appointment with the genetics team; the encounter with her sister-in-law; the pains in her joints, womb, and hips, "one pain connected to the other pain"; and the continual desire to be elsewhere.

"When Clóvis was here, he gave me vitamins. . . . I want you to take me to my brothers." She wept profusely.

Catarina then told Oscar, who was listening to us, that she wanted to take a vitamin injection "to become stronger."

"She has been wanting this for a month." Oscar rebuked her with a dismissive tone: "I want you to understand that I cannot medicate you because you want it. It is only if the doctor wants it, and it's me who has to take you there to the hospital. The doctor must prescribe it."

Catarina knew that this would not happen, so she ended that exchange by declaring, "I have live blood."

She then shifted the subject to becoming a grandmother and to the very ordinary fabric of existence from which she was removed.

"There is always room for one more life in a mother's heart." Catarina told me that she had known Eliane, the mother-to-be, "since she was a child." Eliane had been her daughter's best friend, who had played with Alessandra and Anderson when they were kids. The young woman's parents were "simple and good people. Like everybody there, they also make shoes at home."

Catarina then moved from that world back to the world of medicine, where she wanted to be a doctor, "to discover something of the head, of the brain, and limbs. . . . But then I would have to study." The knowledge of the impossibility is always there, but it does not prevent her from voicing the hope for a cure, "to heal many people who have rheumatism."

Catarina, you have something to help people that most doctors do not have. Very few people have the ability to think the way you do, and you have the words for it.

To which she replied, "I know. I am a judge of the law."

It is true, Catarina, you are a judge of the law.

"I have the capacity to struggle. My memory, the book of memories, is my diploma. . . . You gave the notebooks for me to write, and I filled them."

I told her that I had studied all the volumes of her dictionary, translated some of the poems, and placed them in this book.

"I am a teacher of languages . . . English, French, Japanese, and Portuguese . . . "

And the language of Catarina, I said.

"Yes." She was exhilarated. "The language of Catarina. . . . I write, and you give a way to the words . . . in all possible ways."

All possible ways, in her words.

"I am part of the origins, not just of language, but of people"

I returned to Vita at the end of August 2003 and saw Catarina one last time. For the first time in so long, her physical condition seemed to be improving. She had gained weight, and it was possible to understand her speech again. Oscar kept his promise and made sure that Catarina was regularly taken to the genetics service for medical check-ups and for speech therapy—she had had twelve sessions over the past three months.

"I did exercises with my mouth," explained Catarina. "I can swallow better now, I eat two plates of food. . . . Doctor Tatiane treated me so well."

I told Catarina that I would get a report on her medical condition from Dr. Jardim at the university hospital and that we would initiate procedures to get her a disability pension. Catarina showed me two more volumes of the dictionary. In spite of much pain, she kept writing, and she wanted to make sure that I could read her writing, which I could.

Oscar participated in that last conversation, telling us that he was fighting in court to obtain expensive hepatitis C medication from the city government. He was afraid that delay in treatment would influence the expression of AIDS, which he had been able to keep under control for five years. All Oscar wanted now was "to build my house" in the village around Vita. A package of cement and sets of bricks made him the happiest of men.

When reflecting on the work we had done and the awareness we had gained over the years, Oscar turned to Catarina and said, "I came to see myself in you." Catarina recalled the many little fights she had had with Oscar, "but that's part of living." He replied, "We acquire experience through familiarity." Catarina hoped to get out of the wheelchair, she said, and she began to weep. "I need to go to Novo Hamburgo, to get my documents. Another person cannot get them for me. . . . I want to go home."

What stayed in my mind as I left that day was Oscar saying, "They don't have the right to be persons. That's all they want, and people want to take this possibility away from the human being."

And then Catarina said: "I am part of the origins, not just of language, but of people. . . . I represent the origins of the person."

—

On September 15, Oscar called to say that Catarina had passed away.

The women in the room told Oscar that during the night Catarina had called for her mother many times and then had fallen silent. The next morning, she was found dead.

By chance, Dr. Jardim had called Oscar that morning to follow up on Catarina's treatment, and Oscar told her the news. She was positive that Catarina could not have died from complications from Machado-Joseph disease and requested an autopsy.

The autopsy revealed that Catarina died as a result of intestinal bleeding (*trombose hemorrágica intestinal*). This condition occasions what doctors call "acute abdomen," with intense pain and high fever. "If this was the case, she must have been in agony for several hours, without any assistance or treatment. Oh, my God, what a sadness," stated Dr. Jardim when she learned the results of the autopsy.

The morning Oscar called me, he had already talked to family members, and they decided to forego burying Catarina in an unmarked temporary grave for indigents, which is how most people in Vita are buried. "At least the family will take the dead body home," said Oscar.

Urbano and Tamara, the adoptive parents of Catarina's youngest daughter, took care of the funeral in Novo Hamburgo's public cemetery. The whole family showed up, the children, the ex-husband, the brothers and their spouses, the in-laws, and extended kin.

Catarina was buried in her mother's grave, together with her remains.

In memory of Catarina

Acknowledgments

I want to express my deepest gratitude to the people of Vita for allowing me to spend time with them and for their invaluable help in creating this book. My indebtedness to Catarina is immeasurable. I so much wanted Catarina to read the outcome of our work together, to see herself emerge from these pages, and to find another ending. As I think of her passing away, I like to recall what my son, Andre, now almost three, recently told us as we were looking at the brightly colored painting *Vincent's Room* (1889)—the empty chairs and bed, various images and clothing hanging on the walls, a mirror, and the utensils next to the window, which is opened inward. Andre suddenly asked: "Where Van Gogh go?" Caught by surprise, my wife, Adriana, and I threw the question back at Andre: "Where *did* Van Gogh go?" He then found a wonderful way to express the capacity of things and people to continue (at least, that is how we took his words): "Here," said Andre, with a smile, pointing to himself and to us as we faced the artwork. I hope that this book does justice to Catarina's life.

Among Vita's residents, I also want to specifically thank Iraci, India, Lili, Osmar, and Sassá for sharing their stories and their hope that things might be otherwise. I honored the desire of these people and Catarina to be known by their real names in this book. All other names of informants and institutions have been changed to protect privacy and confidentiality (unless otherwise requested). I am grateful to Vita's administrators and volunteers for allowing me to chronicle their work and everyday life in the institution and for the critical dialogue that ensued. It gives me great pleasure to acknowledge the help of the volunteer whom I have called Oscar. He has generously engaged with this research since its beginning, and I cherish his insightfulness and kindness.

Outside Vita, I thank the many people—family and friends of Catarina—who welcomed me into their homes and shared their memories and thoughts. Health professionals and human rights activists in various provincial and municipal institutions were invaluable in helping me to understand Vita's imbrication in broader political, medical, and social terrains. The staff of the several medical institutions in which Catarina was treated facilitated archival research, and Laboratórios Serdil provided technical support. I enjoyed spending time with and learning from the health professionals at the Casa de Saúde Mental in Novo Hamburgo, and I am deeply appreciative of their social consciousness and work. Among the numerous health professionals, social scientists, and activists who helped this study to gain form, I want to specifically mention two: Dr. Luis Guilherme Streb and Dr. Laura Bannach Jardim. Each of them played a pivotal role both in the research process and in the care of Catarina, and I am privileged to count on their wisdom and friendship.

My extended family in southern Brazil provided support throughout field research and writing. I want to especially thank my mother, Noemia Kirschner Biehl, for her kind help and for the values and sentiments that she and my father, the late Fernando Oscar Biehl, stand for. The support of my brother, Fausto Henrique Biehl, and of my sister, Alide Marina Biehl Ferraes, and their families, as well as that of Ruben Kirschner, Margarida Arend, Regina Dhein, and the Petryna family is immensely appreciated.

I have had the good fortune to carry out this project with a wonderful artist and friend, Torben Eskerod, and I am forever thankful for the time and creativity he dedicated to this book.

Distinguished teachers have fundamentally informed this book. I am deeply grateful to Paul Rabinow for his acumen and advice and for engaging with this study since it began. The work of Nancy Scheper-Hughes has also been an immense source of inspiration, and I owe a debt of gratitude to her and to Paul Rabinow for helping me find a destination in anthropology. I also thank Arthur Kleinman and Byron Good for their mentoring, their insights, and their engagement with this project both during fieldwork and in the writing process. The works of Veena Das and Michael M. J. Fischer have also been extremely influential, and I am grateful for their scrupulous and generous engagement with this stufy. The thinking of Lawrence Cohen and Stefania Pandolfo has also helped to shape this inquiry; my thanks go to them. The mentoring and friendship of Robert Kimball have been essential, and his many readings of the manuscript, his always illuminating comments, and his support are wholeheartedly appreciated.

My work and life have been greatly enriched by the conviviality and intellectual stimulation of Princeton University's Anthropology Department. I thank my colleagues James Boon, John Borneman, Isabelle Clark-Deces, Hildred Geertz, Carol Greenhouse, Abdellah Hammoudi, Rena Lederman, Alan Mann, Gananath Obeyesekere, Ranjini Obeyesekere, Lawrence Rosen, and Carolyn Rouse for their support and for critical comments offered in the course of discussions. The wisdom and care provided by our administrator, Carol Zanca, are formidable; and I want to thank her, Mo Lin Yee, and Gabriela Drinovan for their kindness and help.

I have had the distinct pleasure of working with superb graduate students over the last few years. There are a few whose help has been particularly important: Leo C. Coleman, Alexander Edmonds, Christopher Garces, William Garriott, Michael Oldani, Eugene Raikhel, Jan Whitmarsh, and Jessica Zuchowski. Thank you. The undergraduate students in my medical anthropology courses became engaged with the book's materials and, with great care, helped me find a way to tell the story. I am particularly grateful to Matthew Goldberg, Ann Kelly, Steven Porter, and Amy Saltzman.

A postdoctoral fellowship from the National Institute of Mental Health at the Departments of Social Medicine and Anthropology at Harvard University allowed me to carry out work in 1999 and 2000. Ethnographic research and photographic work were made possible by the Crichton Fund (Harvard's Department of Anthropology) and by the Committee on Research in the Humanities and Social Sciences and the Program in Latin American Studies of Princeton University. Membership at the Institute for Advanced Study during 2002/2003 was invaluable in bringing this project to completion, and I want to thank the faculty, colleagues, and staff of the School of Social Science. Torben Eskerod was generously supported by a research grant in photography from the Erna and Victor Hasselblad Foundation.

I profited greatly from discussion and argument as I presented my work-in-progress to the Department of Social Medicine of Harvard University; the Program in Science, Technology, and Society at the Massachusetts Institute of Technology; the Department of Anthropology at the University of Chicago; L'École des Hautes Études en Sciences Sociales in Paris; Haverford College; the Department of Anthropology and the Program for the Study of Women, Gender, and Sexuality at Johns Hopkins University; and sessions of the annual meetings of the American Anthropological Association. I am struck by the intellectual intensity and generosity of the many scholars who engaged with this work over the years, including Jeremy Adelman, Abigail Baim-Lance, Ariane Brusius, Robert Desjarlais, Joseph Dumit, Didier Fassin, Robson Freitas, Mary-Jo Delvecchio Good, Stephen Greenblatt, Clara Han, Albert O. Hirschman, Sarah Hirschman, Peter T. Johnson, Fábio Moraes, Sylvia Nassar, João Gilberto Noll, Tor G. H. Onsten, Christina Paxson, Kaushik Sunder Rajan, Amèlie O. Rorty, Claude Rosental, Aslihan Sanal, Denise Saper, Lucia Serrano, Burton Singer, Bhrigupati Singh, Michael Walzer, Susann Wilkinson, and Gerson Winkler.

Sections of Part One appeared in a 2001 article in *Social Text* 19 (3): 131–149; portions of several other chapters appeared as an article in *American Ethnologist* 31 (4):475–496 in 2004. I am grateful for the editorial guidance of Arvind Rajagopal and Virginia Dominguez, to the readers of both journals for their suggestions, and to Linda Forman. HarperCollins granted permission to reprint the poem "This," by Czeslaw Milosz (reprinted from Milosz's *New and Collected Poems, 1931–2001* [New York: Ecco, 2001], 663).

I have been most fortunate to work with Stan Holwitz at the University of California Press, and I thank him for his trust, encouragement, and editorial guidance at every step. Also at the Press, I am grateful to the book's reviewers for their comments and suggestions and to Mary Severance, Mary Renaud, Randy Neuman, Hillary Hansen, and Nola Burger for their fine work.

My unending gratitude and love goes to Adriana Petryna who, with all her brilliance and care, has been essential to the creation of this book, and to our son, Andre Biehl, for all the possibilities he opens up for us.

Princeton, December 2004

Notes

1. It is estimated that fifty million Brazilians earn less than a dollar per day. For official data on inequality in Brazil, see the Web site www.ibge.gov.br. See Ferreira and Barros 1999 for an overview of urban poverty in Brazil.

2. See Marcel Mauss's call for studies of "total facts" (1979:53), which consider the complex interaction of the social and the psycho-organic in specific settings and examine how this interaction engenders the moral. See also Michel de Certeau's work on everyday practices—their procedures, ambiguity, and creativity (1988).

   See also Arthur Kleinman's Tanner Lectures (1999) and his discussion of the anthropology of "local moral worlds."

3. Notable ethnographies structured around the life history of a single subject include those written by Shostak (1981) and Behar (1993) as well as Crapanzano's psychoanalytic portrait of Tuhami (1980). For a discussion of life history as a genre, see Fischer 1991; Bourgois 1995; Panourgiá 1995; Pandolfo 1997. See also Desjarlais's recent book on "sensory biographies" (2003).

   For a discussion of doing anthropology "at home," see Peirano 1998; Das 1996.

4. According to Nancy Scheper-Hughes, ethnography is challenged to identify the "political economic order that reproduces sickness and death at its very base" and to listen to, collect, and inscribe the histories of lives "whom the state hardly thinks worth counting at all" (1992:30).

5. Veena Das argues that "for Wittgenstein . . . philosophical problems have their beginnings in the feeling of being lost and in an unfamiliar place, and philosophical answers are in the nature of finding one's way back" (1998:171).

6. As George Marcus points out, "Life histories reveal juxtapositions of social contexts through a succession of narrated individual experiences that may be obscured in the structural study of processes as such" (1998:94). Following the plot of life histories can help one to identify the multisited character of local experience and

thus capture some of the density of a locality. See Devereux's discussion of inter-subjectivity and method in social science (1967).

7. For ethnographically grounded accounts of self and experience drawing on theo-ries of ritual and religion, see Hammoudi 1993; Csordas 1994, 2002; Nabokov 2000. Ochs and Capps (1996) review the expansive literature relating notions of the self to practices of narration, while Desjarlais (1994) and Chatterji (1998) discuss how far such ideas can be carried in interpreting the lives and words of the mentally ill. See Appadurai's discussion (1996) of media, migration, and self-fashioning. See Pandolfo 1997 and Cole 2001 for a discussion of practices of memory in postcolo-nial contexts. An influential narrative of the "modern self" can be found in Taylor 1989 (see Rose 1998, however, for a Foucault-inspired reinterpretation of this his-tory). Two recent collections of ethnographic essays (Greenhouse, Mertz, and War-ren 2002; Holland and Lave 2001) focus on the contemporary condition, examin-ing selfhood and identification in the contexts of crisis and drastic social change. Loïc Wacquant (2004) elaborates on the body as tool and vector of knowledge.

8. While the literature on colonialism and its aftermath is far too extensive to sum-marize in a note, important analyses on the border between anthropology and his-tory include work by the Comaroffs (1991, 1997) and Stoler (2002); see also the volume *From the Margins: Historical Anthropology and Its Futures*, edited by Axel (2002). A reader edited by Guha (1997) serves as a useful introduction to subaltern studies. See Bhabha 1994 on Fanon and the postcolonial prerogative.

9. In 1924, Freud wrote a short paper in which he stated that the outbreak of psy-chosis was the result of a conflict in the relation between the ego and its environ-ment—both the loss and the substitution of reality were at stake. Two steps are dis-cernible in psychosis, he argued: the first tears the ego away from reality, "a severe frustration by reality of a wish, a frustration which seemed too unendurable to be borne"; the second tries to make good the loss of reality by creating "in a lordly manner a new reality which is no longer open to objections like that which has been forsaken (1959b:279). The fantastic world of psychosis is constructed after the pattern of the impulses in the unconscious, Freud asserted, and attempts to set itself in place of external reality.

In this explanation, *reality as such* is not questioned. And this is where my main disagreement with Freud's approach to psychosis lies: in his noncritical attitude toward what counts as reality. This lack of critique is quite striking if one sets it against the insightful thoughts citizen Freud produced during the time of war, pic-turing "a world that has grown strange" (1957b:275). Was foregoing a critique of the plasticity of reality—the fabrication of its institutions and truthfulness and the mental tinkering that goes with them—the price Freud was willing to pay in order to garner scientific status for his concepts and techniques, which were mostly aimed at treating neurosis?

Philosophers Gilles Deleuze and Felix Guattari think so, and they take it personally: "How is it possible that the schizo was conceived of as the autistic rag, separated from the real and cut off from life? . . . Freud doesn't like schizophrenics. He doesn't like their resistance to being oedipalized, and tends to treat them more or less like animals. They mistake words for things, he says. They are apathetic, narcissistic, cut off from reality, incapable of achieving transference; they resemble philosophers—'an undesirable resemblance'" (1983:17, 23). Indeed, Freud ended his paper "The Loss of Reality in Neurosis and Psychosis" by giving psychosis away to future scientists of the mind: "Elucidation of the various mechanisms in the psychosis . . . is a task for a special psychiatry which has not yet been undertaken" (1959b:280).

See Ruth Benedict's discussion of anthropology and the abnormal (1959).

10. See Felman 1987:156.

11. In an early clinical monograph titled *The Family Complexes* (1989a), Lacan elaborates on how individual subjectivity is shaped by social structures. See also Lacan 1979. For a detailed discussion of truth production, subjectivity, and ethics in the works of Lacan and Foucault, see Biehl 2001a, 1999a.

12. Philosopher Ian Hacking follows Foucault in the view that subjects are constituted in and by the mechanisms of knowledge and power and the ethical templates in which they are entangled and which generate the potential for individual experience. Hacking has identified scientific and technical dynamics that mediate processes by which "people are made up" (1990:3; 1999). Categories and statistical counting engender new classifications within which people must think of themselves and of the actions that are open to them, Hacking notes (1990:194). As classes of people have their various ways of being in the world normalized, this process also has consequences for how we conceive of others and think of our own possibilities and potential (1990:6). See also Hacking's study of "transient mental illnesses" (1998) as well as Rose 2001.

13. For anthropological studies of schizophrenia, see Corin 1998; Corin and Lauzon 1992; Corin, Thara, and Padmavati 2003; Jenkins 1991; Jenkins and Barrett 2003. Ellen Corin, for example, elaborates on how psychotic patients rework cultural and social frameworks in their "positive withdrawal" from reality.

14. Translations of non-English sources are mine unless specifically noted otherwise.

15. In the *Magic Mountain*, Thomas Mann (1996:31) writes: "If the times respond with hollow silence to every conscious or subconscious question, however it may be posed, about the ultimate, unequivocal meaning of all exertions and deeds that are more than exclusively personal—then it is almost inevitable, particularly if the person involved is a more honest sort, that the situation will have a crippling effect, which, following moral and spiritual paths, may even spread to that individual's physical and organic life."

16. For a general review of the Fernando Henrique Cardoso administration, see Lamounier and Figueiredo 2002.

17. In the early 1990s, anthropologists began to follow the production of new bioscientific knowledge and the making of biotechnologies, inquiring into their multiple deployments and their interactions with old and new forms of power relations and ethical models (Rabinow 1999; Rapp 1999; Strathern 1992). Paul Rabinow (1996a), for example, notes a dissolution of the traditional social domain and the emergence of new forms of identity and moral reasoning around the technical possibility of the literal remodeling of life (what he calls "biosociality"). The recent work of anthropologists Veena Das (1997, 1999), Arthur Kleinman (1999), Allan Young (1995), Nancy Scheper-Hughes (2000), Margaret Lock (2002), Lawrence Cohen (1998), and Adriana Petryna (2002), among others, shows how medical and technical interventions affect—sometimes for better, sometimes for worse—the etiology, experience, and course of disease. The appearance and distribution of disorders such as drug-resistant tuberculosis and AIDS are also closely correlated with poverty and social and technological inequality. They are "pathologies of power" (Farmer 2002), mediated by biological, social, technical, and political–economic mechanisms. Concrete biological phenomena are thus intertwined with environmental conditions that are part of a larger context. And it is in this complicated web that the individual's life possibilities take shape.

18. See Luiz Fernando Dias Duarte's study of "nervousness" among the urban poor in Brazil (1986) and his discussion of physical-moral processes. See also Nancy Scheper-Hughes's study of the impact of shifting domestic economies on family ties and mental illness in rural Ireland in the 1970s (2001); and Scheper-Hughes and Lock (1987) on the "mindful body."

    For an overview of anthropological work on the body, health, and medicine in Brazil, see the volumes edited by Leibing (1997, 2003).

19. For a cross-disciplinary elaboration of the concept of "social suffering" in various contexts, see the contributions to these three edited volumes: Kleinman, Das, and Lock 1997; Das et al. 2000; Das et al. 2001. See also the volume on social suffering edited by Bourdieu et al. (1999) and Herzfeld's critique of the anthropology of suffering (2001).

20. On the symbolism of the animal, see Geertz's essay on the Balinese cockfight (1973). Singer 1975 focuses on animals and ethics. For historical and contemporary debates over the human/animal boundary in science, see Haraway 1989; Daston and Park 1998; Creager and Jordan 2002. Giorgio Agamben also explores the relation of human and animal (2004).

21. On the anthropology of human rights and violence, see Jelin 1994; Wilson 2000; Scheper-Hughes and Bourgois 2004. See also Lyotard 1991 on "the inhuman."

22. See Donzelot 1980 for an argument regarding families as the means and the object of government. On more recent transformations in family and kinship practices, as well as shifts in their interpretation, see the volume of articles edited by Franklin and McKinnon (2001); also see Finkler 2001. On domestic economies

and "modern subjectivity," see Collier 1997 and Ortner 2003; on the politics of kinship and caring, see Borneman 2001. Judith Butler addresses issues of kin and belonging in a philosophical mode in *Antigone's Claim* (2002), while Strong (2002) reads Butler in light of the anthropological tradition of kinship studies.

23. Eskerod (1997, 2001) is part of a group of artists (Struth 1994; Ruff 2001; Dijkstra 2001) who have put aside the tendency of much recent photography to simply de-construct representations (for example, Sherman 1997) and taken up the challenge "to restore our attachment to physical things" (Richard Sennett, quoted in Struth 1994:91).

24. On Benjamin and photography, see Sontag 1977; Cadava 1997.

25. For a review of Brazilian welfare policies since the 1930s, see Oliveira and Teix-eira 1986. For critical reviews of current social policies developed by the Brazilian state, see Laurell 1995; Fiori 2001; Lamounier and Figueiredo 2002. See Hoffman and Centeno 2003 on persistent social inequality in Latin America.

26. On parallel developments in other Latin American states, see Paley 2001; Alvarez, Dagnino, and Escobar 1998. Edelman (2001) reviews the broader anthropologi-cal literature on social movements.

27. See Michel Foucault's Collège de France Lectures from 1974–1975 on the "ab-normal" (2003). For an overview of anti-psychiatry debates and movements, see Laing 1967; Scheper-Hughes and Lovell 1987. For interpretations of psychiatry in the United States and Western Europe, see Goffman 1961; Lunbeck 1994; Luhrman 2000; Rose 1998, 2001. See Sue E. Estroff's seminal ethnography, *Mak-ing It Crazy* (1985). Freire Costa (1976) presents an interpretation of psychiatry in Brazil. On new taxonomies of mental illness and psychopharmaceuticals and their clinical and social implications, see Young 1995; Healy 1999. On imaging tech-nologies and new regimes of personhood, see Dumit 2004.

28. In *The Human Condition*, Hannah Arendt argues that in the contemporary world political action has been replaced by a primary focus on the control of natural life. The *homo faber* has given way to the *homo laborans*, the being concerned with phys-iological existence and mass consumption. This happens within the fabric of Christian societies: the fundamental belief in the sacredness of life has survived and has been transmuted through science and technology. "The only thing that could now be potentially immortal, as immortal as the body politic in Antiquity and as individual life during the Middle Ages, was life itself, that is, the possibly everlast-ing life process of the species mankind" (1958:321).

These insights found their way into Michel Foucault's concept of *biopolitics*, and they are helpful concepts for reflecting on how natural life has been taken as an ob-ject of modern politics: "If the old right of sovereignty consisted in killing or let-ting live, the new right will consist of making live and letting die. . . . The new right will not cancel the first, but will penetrate it, traverse it, change it" (1992:172). Rather than focusing on confinement and bodily discipline (Foucault 1979), biopolitical regimes work with the notion of population as a biological problem and human beings as part of the species as the struggle against mortality and for productivity ensues. "Modern man is an animal whose politics places his existence as a living being in question" (1980a:143).

But biopower is not all-encompassing in its life mobilization, and, in Arendt's words, there is a striking "loss of human experience involved" (1958:321). Anthropological studies show the diversity and unevenness of biopolitical operations (Petryna 2002; Rabinow 1999; Rapp 1999). The "governmentalization" of biological conditions must be understood on a continuum with the experience of death (Biehl 1999b, 2004; Cohen 2002; Fassin 2001; Scheper-Hughes 2000). See Veena Das and Deborah Poole's comparative discussion of biopolitics at the margins of the state: "The indeterminacy of the margins not only allows forms of resistance but more importantly enables strategies of engaging the state as some kind of margin to the body of citizens" (2004:30). See also Rose 1996 on the refiguring of neoliberal forms of governance.

29. See Biehl 2004. Adriana Petryna (2002) has coined the term "biological citizenship," as she chronicled the travails of people claiming status as Chernobyl victims in Ukraine's political and economic transition.

30. Following Arendt and Foucault, philosopher Giorgio Agamben states that the original element of sovereign power in Western democracies is "not simple natural life, but *life exposed to death*" (1998:24). "The ban is essentially the power of delivering something over to itself, which is to say, the power of maintaining itself in relation to something presupposed as nonrelational. What has been banned is delivered over to its own separateness and, at the same time, consigned to the mercy of the one who abandons it—at once excluded and included, removed and at the same time captured" (109–10).

On slavery and social death, see Patterson 1982; on colonialism and the politics of death, see Taussig 1986; on "necropolitics," see Mbembe 2003. On political violence and memory, see Klima 2002.

31. Veena Das and Renu Addlakha argue that the domestic, "once displaced from its conventionally assumed reference to the private, becomes a sphere in which a different kind of citizenship may be enacted—a citizenship based not on the formation of associational communities, but on notions of publics constituted through voice. The domestic sphere we present, then, is always on the verge of becoming the political" (2001:512).

See Carol Greenhouse's discussion of "empirical citizenship" (2002) and Aihwa Ong's discussion of "cultural citizenship" (1996).

32. Lawrence Cohen (2002; see also Cohen 1999) speaks of the phenomenon of "bioavailability," in which certain bodies, mostly poor and female, are made available for procedures such as organ transplantation, which will enhance the lives of others. Such a marking of bodies is made possible not only by new technologies

but by the moralities forged in their junction with new political-economic and social realities.

33. See Hannah Arendt's discussion of thinking and ethics in her book *The Life of the Mind* (1978).

34. See Lacan's linguistic treatment of psychosis (1993a); see also Pandolfo 1997. For a discussion of dreams and affects, see Rivers 1922 and 1923.

35. See Agamben's reflection on "subjectification and desubjectification" in the experience of concentration camps (1999). In my work with people in Vita, I did not find them totally robbed of the ability to react subjectively, and I began to think of their complex subjectivities as ethnographic alternatives to "philosophical figures" such as those articulated by Agamben ("homo sacer" [1998], "Muselmann" [1999]) in his effort to account for contemporary ethics. See also Caruth 1996.

36. According to Veena Das (2004:25), mental illness must be understood in the context of people's "refusal to accept the normatively normal": "I offer the idea that the illness resides in the network of relations, in the movement over institutions, and that the pathology is struggling to find an environment in which it could reestablish new norms."

   On "psychosomatic," see Kleinman and Becker 1998; Wilson 2004. See also Lutz 1985.

37. In their longitudinal study of symptom management in several poor neighborhoods in Delhi, Veena Das and Ranendra Das found illness to be ordinarily conceptualized as a "relational testing ground" and an "experiment with life." The individual's negotiation for health within "local ecologies of care" recasts illness categories, kinship textures, and patterns of social exclusion and inclusion (Das and Das forthcoming).

38. Not until 1992, after the passage of the province's Psychiatric Reform Law, were patients required to sign a consent form. In extreme cases, doctors themselves had to write a letter to the Public Ministry to request hospitalization.

39. See Goldberg (1994:51): "Such a situation constructs a pattern of individuation that is common to all. For the external observers, all patients have the same face, vague and inexpressive, behave the same way, and have the same disease. We ask if there isn't a regulatory disease produced by the institution itself that masks the expressiveness of each patient?"

40. The following portrait of the national and regional psychiatric reform effort draws from Moraes 2000.

41. *Diário Oficial/RS [Rio Grande do Sul]* 1992:1.

42. See Lawrence Cohen's discussion of how neuropsychiatric diagnostics work as new technologies of the person in Indian households (1998).

43. See Pitta in Goldberg 1994:155. In sum, these are the principles underlying CAPS's services: the weakening of biomedical authority; the shift of care from the

control of the body to the control of temporality and subjectivity; the linking of illness and labor regimes; the destigmatization of madness and the cultivation of respect for difference; the recasting of family ties; and the invention of "life possibilities."

44. On violent deaths in Brazilian psychiatric hospitals, see the volume *A instituição sinistra* (Vinicius 2001).

45. Currently, Brazil is among the eight biggest pharmaceutical markets in the world (Bermudez 1992, 1995). In 1998, some fifteen thousand drugs were being sold in the country, with sales reaching 11.1 billion dollars (Luiza 1999; Cosendey et al. 2000). See also Ministério da Saúde 1997, 1999; Yunes 1999.

   For a review of the anthropology of pharmaceuticals and pharmaceutical practices, see Geest, Whyte, and Hardon 1996; Nichter and Vuckovic 1994. See also Ferguson 1981 on pharmaceutical medicine and medicalization. On the social life of pharmaceuticals in Brazil, see Leibing 2003; Ferreira 2003.

46. Ian Hacking draws on Fleck's notion of "styles of reasoning" in his work on "making up people" (1999). See also Young 1995.

47. As Charles Melman puts it: "One no longer hears what the other says, but only what one has the habit to hear" (1991:62).

48. See Rabinow's discussion of the concept of "dispositive" (1996a).

49. The House of Mental Health is currently located in downtown Novo Hamburgo. Catarina had been treated at the old headquarters on Pátria Nova Street, a building that was closed down in 1996, after two fires and a flood (Moraes 2000).

50. On the "war machine," see Deleuze and Guattari 1987.

51. In an 1875 report, the Ministry of Agriculture and Commerce praised São Leopoldo as an exemplary settlement, to be copied everywhere if the country were to modernize its economy and society: "There, the German race has been working for the Empire. . . . The Brazilian people must be further lightened with new European blood, intelligence and the fever of progress. . . . With the ending of slavery and the productive birth of a free labor force, a beneficial moral revolution is taking form in the country. In this great laboratory of the present . . . the state's strong hand must continue to be wielded" (Souza 1875:420). For Germany, which had little success in colonial annexation of territory, the nineteenth-century settlements in South America and Africa became a testing ground for a different kind of cultural and economic imperialism (Frobel 1858; Williams 1989; Fabian 2000). By fostering German communities in isolated enclaves that were somewhat independent of the host country, Germany was opening up specific sites from which it could import raw materials and food as well as creating markets for the export of consumer goods, technologies, and other investments.

52. This brief historical sketch draws from oral narratives I collected among some of Novo Hamburgo's elderly.

53. In the mid-1970s, city officials created a Division for Health and Social Assistance to deal with the growing problems of the laboring poor: lack of adequate housing, sanitation, unemployment, alcoholism, and so forth. As usual, it was more a façade than a true intervention (Moraes 2000).

54. For a general introduction to the medical studies on ataxia, see Harding and Deufel 1993.

55. See Paul Rabinow's account of the invention of the polymerase chain reaction (PCR) (1996b). This technique provides an extremely sensitive means of amplifying small quantities of DNA and generating unlimited copies of any DNA fragment. It is extremely useful in detecting hereditary diseases.

56. Carol Ryff and Burton Singer (2001) explore the ways the cumulative wear and tear of lived experience—"allostatic load"—affects disease-health outcomes.

57. On "biosociality," see Rabinow 1996a. On the social and ethical impact of biotechnology and testing, see Rapp 1999. See Farmer 2002 for a discussion of biotechnology and structural violence.

58. According to Paul Rabinow (2003:30): "Observing, naming, and analyzing the forms of anthropos is the logos of one type of anthropology. How best to think about the arbitrariness, contingency, and powerful effects of those forms constitutes the challenge of that type of anthropology, understood as *Wissenschaft* or *science*. To place oneself amidst the relationships of contending logoi (embedded as they are within problematizations, apparatuses, and assemblages) is to find oneself among anthropology's problems."

59. See Vincent Crapanzano's discussion of "imaginative horizons" (2004).

Bibliography

Abers, Rebecca. 2000. *Inventing Local Democracy: Grassroots Politics in Brazil.* Boulder: Lynne Rienner Publishers.

Adorno, Theodor. 1982. "Freudian Theory and the Pattern of Fascist Propaganda." In *The Essential Frankfurt School Reader*, edited by Andrew Arato and Eike Gebhardt, 118–137. New York: Continuum.

Agamben, Giorgio. 1998. *Homo Sacer: Sovereignty and Bare Life.* Stanford: Stanford University Press.

———. 1999. *Remnants of Auschwitz: The Witness and the Archive.* New York: Zone Books.

———. 2004. *The Open: Man and Animal.* Stanford: Stanford University Press.

Almeida-Filho, Naomar de. 1998. "Becoming Modern after All These Years: Social Change and Mental Health in Latin America." *Culture, Medicine and Psychiatry* 22 (3): 285–316.

Alvarez, Sonia, Evelina Dagnino, and Arturo Escobar, eds. 1998. *Cultures of Politics/Politics of Cultures: Re-Visioning Latin American Social Movements.* Boulder: Westview Press.

Amarante, Paulo. 1996. *O homem e a serpente: Outras histórias para a loucura e a psiquiatria.* Rio de Janeiro: Fiocruz.

Appadurai, Arjun. 1996. *Modernity at Large: Cultural Dimensions of Globalization.* Minneapolis: University of Minnesota Press.

Arendt, Hannah. 1958. *The Human Condition.* Chicago: University of Chicago Press.

———. 1978. *The Life of the Mind.* New York: Harcourt Brace.

Asad, Talal. 2003. *Formations of the Secular.* Stanford: Stanford University Press.

Axel, Brian Keith, ed. 2002. *From the Margins: Historical Anthropology and Its Futures.* Durham, N.C.: Duke University Press.

Bachelard, Gaston. 1994. *The Poetics of Space*. Boston: Beacon Press.

Bastian, Ernestine Maurer. 1986. "Internatos para pessoas idosas: Uma avaliação." *Revista Gaúcha de Enfermagem* 7 (1): 123–131.

Beck, Ulrich, and Ulf Erdmann Ziegler. 1997. *Eigenes Leben: Ausflüge in die unbekannte Gesellschaft, in der wir leben*. With photographs by Timm Rauter. Munich: Verlag C. H. Beck.

Behar, Ruth. 1993. *Translated Woman: Crossing the Border with Esperanza's Story*. Boston: Beacon Press.

Benedict, Ruth. 1959. "Anthropology and the Abnormal." In *An Anthropologist at Work: Writings of Ruth Benedict*, 262–283. Boston: Houghton Mifflin.

Benjamin, Walter. 1979. *One-Way Street, and Other Writings*. London: New Left Books.

Bermudez, Jorge. 1992. *Remédios, saúde ou indústria? A produção de medicamentos no Brasil*. Rio de Janeiro: Relume Dumará.

———. 1995. *Indústria farmacêutica, estado e sociedade: Crítica da política de medicamentos no Brasil*. São Paulo: Editora Hucitec e Sociedade Brasileira de Vigilância de Medicamentos.

Bhabha, Homi. 1994. "Interrogating Identity: Frantz Fanon and the Postcolonial Prerogative." In *The Location of Culture*, 40–65. New York: Routledge.

Biehl, João. 1995. "Life on Paper: A Trip through AIDS in Brazil." With Jessica Blatt. Study document. Rio de Janeiro: Instituto Superior de Estudos da Religião.

———. 1997. "Photography in the Field of the Unconscious." In *Ansigter*, by Torben Eskerod, 10–15. Copenhagen: Rhodos.

———. 1999a. "Jammerthal, the Valley of Lamentation: *Kultur*, War Trauma, and Subjectivity in 19th Century Brazil." *Journal of Latin American Cultural Studies* 8 (2): 171–198.

———. 1999b. *Other Life: AIDS, Biopolitics, and Subjectivity in Brazil's Zones of Social Abandonment*. Ann Arbor: UMI Dissertation Services.

———. 2001a. "Technology and Affect: HIV/AIDS Testing in Brazil." With Denise Coutinho and Ana Luzia Outeiro. *Culture, Medicine and Psychiatry* 25 (1): 87–129.

———. 2001b. "Vita: Life in a Zone of Social Abandonment." *Social Text* 19 (3): 131–149.

———. 2002a. "Biotechnology and the New Politics of Life and Death in Brazil: The AIDS Model." *Princeton Journal of Bioethics* 5:59–74.

———. 2002b. "Cultura e poder no tempo dos mucker." *Jahrbuch 2002*, Institut Martius-Staden 49:162–181.

———. 2004. "The Activist State: Global Pharmaceuticals, AIDS, and Citizenship in Brazil." *Social Text* 22 (3): 105–132.

Boltanski, Luc. 1999. *Suffering and Distance: Morality, Media, and Politics*. Cambridge: Cambridge University Press.

Borneman, John. 2001. "Caring and Being Cared For: Displacing Marriage, Kinship, Gender, and Sexuality." In *The Ethics of Kinship: Ethnographic Inquiries*, edited by James Faubion, 25–45. New York: Roman and Littlefield.

Bosi, Maria Lucia. 1994. "Cidadania, participação popular e saúde na visão dos profissionais do setor: Um estudo de caso na rede pública de serviços." *Cadernos de Saúde Pública* 10 (4): 446–456.

Bourdieu, Pierre, et al. 1999. *The Weight of the World: Social Suffering in Contemporary Societies*. Stanford: Stanford University Press.

Bourgois, Philippe. 1995. *In Search of Respect: Selling Crack in El Barrio*. Cambridge: Cambridge University Press.

Boutté, Marie I. 1990. "Waiting for the Family Legacy: The Experience of Being at Risk for Machado-Joseph Disease." *Social Science and Medicine* 30 (8): 839–847.

Butler, Judith. 1997. *The Psychic Life of Power*. Stanford: Stanford University Press.

———. 2002. *Antigone's Claim: Kinship between Life and Death*. New York: Columbia University Press.

Cadava, Eduardo. 1997. *Words of Light: Theses on the Photography of History*. Princeton: Princeton University Press.

Caldeira, Teresa. 2000. *City of Walls: Crime, Segregation, and Citizenship in São Paulo*. Berkeley: University of California Press.

———. 2002. "Paradox of Police Violence in Democratic Brazil." *Ethnography* 3 (3): 235–263.

Cardoso, Fernando Henrique. 1998. "Notas sobre a reforma do estado." *Novos Estudos do CEBRAP* 50:1–12.

———. 1999. "Inaugural Address, 1995." In *The Brazil Reader: History, Culture, and Politics*, edited by Robert M. Levine and John J. Crocitti, 280–288. Durham, N.C.: Duke University Press.

Caruth, Cathy. 1996. *Unclaimed Experience: Trauma, Narrative, and History*. Baltimore: Johns Hopkins University Press.

Chatterji, Roma. 1998. "An Ethnography of Dementia: A Case Study of an Alzheimer's Disease Patient in the Netherlands." *Culture, Medicine and Psychiatry* 22:355–382.

Cohen, Lawrence. 1998. *No Aging in India: Alzheimer's, the Bad Family, and Other Modern Things*. Berkeley: University of California Press.

———. 1999. "Where It Hurts: Indian Material for an Ethics of Organ Transplantation." Special issue, "Bioethics and Beyond," *Daedalus* 128 (4): 135–165.

———. 2002. "The Other Kidney: Biopolitics beyond Recognition." In *Commodifying Bodies*, edited by Nancy Scheper-Hughes and Loïc Wacquant, 9–30. London: Sage.

Cole, Jennifer. 2001. *Forget Colonialism? Sacrifice and the Art of Memory in Madagascar*. Berkeley: University of California Press.

Collier, Jane Fishburne. 1997. *From Duty to Desire: Remaking Families in a Spanish Village*. Princeton: Princeton University Press.

Comaroff, Jean, and John Comaroff. 2000. "Millennial Capitalism: First Thoughts on a Second Coming." *Public Culture* 12 (2): 291–343.

Comaroff, John L., and Jean Comaroff. 1991. *Of Revelation and Revolution*. Vol. 1, *Christianity, Colonialism, and Consciousness in South Africa*. Chicago: University of Chicago Press.

———. 1997. *Of Revelation and Revolution*. Vol. 2, *The Dialectics of Modernity on a South African Frontier*. Chicago: University of Chicago Press.

Comissão de Direitos Humanos. 2000. *O livro azul*. Porto Alegre: Assembléia Legislativa do Estado do Rio Grande do Sul.

Constitution of the Federative Republic of Brazil. 1988. Available online at www.mercosul.co.kr/data/consti-brazil.htm.

Corin, Ellen. 1998. "The Thickness of Being: Intentional Worlds, Strategies of Identity, and Experience among Schizophrenics." *Psychiatry* 61:133–146.

Corin, Ellen, and G. Lauzon. 1992. "Positive Withdrawal and the Quest for Meaning: The Reconstruction of Experience among Schizophrenics." *Psychiatry* 55(3): 266–278.

Corin, Ellen, R. Thara, and R. Padmavati. 2003. "Living through a Staggering World: The Play of Signifiers in Early Psychosis in South India." In *Schizophrenia, Culture, and Subjectivity: The Edge of Experience*, edited by Janis Hunter Jenkins and Robert John Barrett, 110–144. Cambridge: Cambridge University Press.

Cosendey, Marly Aparecida, J. A. Z. Bermudez, A. L. A. Reis, H. F. Silva, M. A. Oliveira, and V. L. Luiza. 2000. "Assistência farmacêutica na atenção básica de saúde: A experiência de três estados Brasileiros." *Cadernos de Saúde Pública* 16 (1): 171–182.

Coutinho, Paula. 1996. "Aspectos clínicos, história natural e epidemiologia na doença de Machado-Joseph." In *O teste preditivo da doença de Machado-Joseph*, edited by Jorge Sequeiros, 15–22. Porto: UnIGene.

Crapanzano, Vincent. 1980. *Tuhami: Portrait of a Moroccan*. Chicago: University of Chicago Press.

———. 2004. *Imaginative Horizons: An Essay in Literary-Philosophical Anthropology*. Chicago: University of Chicago Press.

Creager, Angela, and William Chester Jordan, eds. 2002. *The Animal-Human Boundary: Historical Perspectives*. Rochester, N.Y.: University of Rochester Press.

Csordas, Thomas. 1994. *Embodiment and Experience*. London: Cambridge University Press.

———. 2002. *Body/Meaning/Healing*. New York: Palgrave.

Cunha, Euclides da. 1976. *Um paraíso perdido: Reunião dos ensaios amazônicos*. Petrópolis: Vozes.

Das, Veena. 1996. *Critical Events: An Anthropological Perspective on Contemporary India*. New Delhi: Oxford University Press.

———. 1997. "Language and Body: Transactions in the Construction of Pain." In *Social Suffering*, edited by Arthur Kleinman, Veena Das, and Margaret Lock, 67–91. Berkeley: University of California Press.

———. 1998. "Wittgenstein and Anthropology." *Annual Review of Anthropology* 27:171–195.

———. 1999. "Public Good, Ethics, and Everyday Life: Beyond the Boundaries of Bioethics." Special issue, "Bioethics and Beyond," *Daedalus* 128 (4): 99–133.

———. 2000. "The Act of Witnessing: Violence, Poisonous Knowledge, and Subjectivity." In *Violence and Subjectivity*, edited by Veena Das, Arthur Kleinman, Mamphela Ramphele, and Pamela Reynolds, 205–225. Berkeley: University of California Press.

———. 2004. "Mental Illness, Skepticism, and Tracks of Other Lives." Manuscript.

Das, Veena, and Renu Addlakha. 2001. "Disability and Domestic Citizenship: Voice, Gender, and the Making of the Subject." *Public Culture* 13 (13): 511–531.

Das, Veena, and Ranendra K. Das. Forthcoming. "Pharmaceuticals in Urban Ecologies: The Register of the Local (India)." In *Global Pharmaceuticals: Ethics, Markets, Practices*, edited by Adriana Petryna, Andrew Lakoff, and Arthur Kleinman. Durham, N.C.: Duke University Press.

Das, Veena, and Arthur Kleinman. 2001. "Introduction." In *Remaking a World: Violence, Social Suffering, and Recovery*, edited by Veena Das, Arthur Kleinman, Margaret Lock, Mamphela Ramphele, and Pamela Reynolds, 1–30. Berkeley: University of California Press.

Das, Veena, Arthur Kleinman, Margaret Lock, Mamphela Ramphele, and Pamela Reynolds, eds. 2001. *Remaking a World: Violence, Social Suffering, and Recovery*. Berkeley: University of California Press.

Das, Veena, Arthur Kleinman, Mamphela Ramphele, and Pamela Reynolds, eds. 2000. *Violence and Subjectivity*. Berkeley: University of California Press.

Das, Veena, and Deborah Poole. 2004. *Anthropology in the Margins of the State*. Santa Fe: School of American Research Press.

Daston, Lorraine, and Katharine Park. 1998. *Wonders and the Order of Nature, 1150–1750*. New York: Zone Books.

De Certeau, Michel. 1988. *The Practice of Everyday Life*. Berkeley: University of California Press.

Décima Conferência Nacional de Saúde—SUS. 1996. Final Report: "Construindo um modelo de atenção à saúde para a qualidade de vida." Brasília. Available online at www.datasus.gov.br/cns/cns.htm.

Deleuze, Gilles. 1988. *Foucault*. Minneapolis: University of Minnesota Press.

———. 1995. *Negotiations*. New York: Columbia University Press.

Deleuze, Gilles, and Felix Guattari. 1983. *Anti-Oedipus: Capitalism and Schizophrenia*. Minneapolis: University of Minnesota Press.

———. 1987. *A Thousand Plateaus: Capitalism and Schizophrenia*. Minneapolis: University of Minnesota Press.

Derrida, Jacques. 1981. "Plato's Pharmacy." In *Dissemination*, 61–171. Chicago: University of Chicago Press.

———. 1998. "'To Do Justice to Freud': The History of Madness in the Age of Psychoanalysis." In *Resistances to Psychoanalysis*, 70–118. Stanford: Stanford University Press.

Desjarlais, Robert. 1994. "Struggling Along: The Possibilities for Experience among the Homeless Mentally Ill." *American Anthropologist* 96 (4): 886–901.

———. 2003. *Sensory Biographies: Lives and Deaths among Nepal's Yolmo Buddhists*. Berkeley: University of California Press.

Devereux, George. 1967. *From Anxiety to Method in the Behavioral Sciences*. The Hague: Mouton.

Diário Oficial/RS [Rio Grande do Sul]. 1992. Vol. 51, no.152. August 10.

Dijkstra, Rineke. 2001. *Portraits*. Boston: Institute of Contemporary Art.

Donzelot, Jacques. 1980. *The Policing of Families: Welfare versus State*. London: Hutchinson.

Duarte, Luiz Fernando Dias. 1986. *Da vida nervosa nas classes trabalhadoras urbanas*. Rio de Janeiro: Jorge Zahar.

Dumit, Joseph. 2004. *Picturing Personhood: Brain Scans and Biomedical Identity*. Princeton: Princeton University Press.

Edelman, Marc. 2001. "Social Movements: Changing Paradigms and Forms of Politics." *Annual Review of Anthropology* 30:285–317.

Edmonds, Alexander. 2002. "New Bodies, New Markets: An Ethnography of Brazil's Beauty Industry." PhD diss., Department of Anthropology, Princeton University.

Eribon, Didier. 1996. *Michel Foucault e seus contemporâneos*. Rio de Janeiro: Jorge Zahar Editor.

Escorel, Sarah. 1999. *Vidas ao léu: Trajetórias da exclusão social*. Rio de Janeiro: Editora da Fiocruz.

Eskerod, Torben. 1997. *Ansigter*. Copenhagen: Rhodos.

———. 2001. *Register*. Copenhagen: Ny Carlsberg Glyptotek.

Estroff, Sue E. 1985. *Making It Crazy: An Ethnography of Psychiatric Clients in an American Community*. Berkeley: University of California Press.

Fabian, Johannes. 2000. *Out of Our Minds: Reason and Madness in the Exploration of Central Africa*. Berkeley: University of California Press.

Fanon, Frantz. 1963. *The Wretched of the Earth*. New York: Grove Press.

Farmer, Paul. 1999. *Infections and Inequalities: The Modern Plagues.* Berkeley: University of California Press.

———. 2002. *Pathologies of Power: Health, Human Rights, and the New War on the Poor.* Berkeley: University of California Press.

Fassin, Didier. 2001. "The Biopolitics of Otherness: Undocumented Foreigners and Racial Discrimination in French Public Debate." *Anthropology Today* 17(1): 3–7.

Felman, Shoshana. 1987. *Jacques Lacan and the Adventure of Insight: Psychoanalysis in Contemporary Culture.* Cambridge, Mass.: Harvard University Press.

Ferguson, A. E. 1981. "Commercial Pharmaceutical Medicine and Medicalization: A Case Study from El Salvador." *Culture, Medicine, and Psychiatry* 5 (2): 105–134.

Ferreira, Francisco, and Ricardo Paes de Barros. 1999. *The Slippery Slope: Explaining the Increase in Extreme Poverty in Urban Brazil, 1976–1996.* Washington, D.C.: World Bank.

Ferreira, Mariana K. Leal. 2003. "Atração fatal: Trabalho escravo e o uso de psicotrópicos por povos indígenas de São Paulo." In *Tecnologias do corpo: Uma antropologia das medicinas no Brasil,* edited by Annete Leibing, 81–112. Rio de Janeiro: Nau Editora.

Ferreira de Mello, Ana Lúcia Schaefer. 2001. "Cuidado odontológico provido a pessoas idosas residentes em instituições geriátricas de pequeno porte em Porto Alegre, RS: A retórica, a prática e os resultados." Master's thesis, Programa de Pós-Graduação em Odontologia da Faculdade de Odontologia da Universidade Federal do Rio Grande do Sul, Porto Alegre.

Finkler, Kaja. 2001. "The Kin in the Gene: The Medicalization of Family and Kinship in American Society." *Current Anthropology* 42 (2): 235–263.

Fiori, José Luís. 2001. *Brasil no espaço.* Petrópolis: Vozes.

Fischer, Michael M.J. 1991. "The Uses of Life Histories." *Anthropology and Humanism Quarterly* 16 (1): 24–26.

———. 2003. *Emergent Forms of Life and the Anthropological Voice.* Durham, N.C.: Duke University Press.

———. Forthcoming. "Implicated, Caught in Between, Communicating with the Mildly Cognitively Impaired: Toward Generative Anthropological Figures." In *Technologies of Perception and the Cultures of Globalization,* edited by Arvind Rajagopal. Minneapolis: University of Minnesota Press.

Fleck, Ludwik. 1979. *Genesis and Development of a Scientific Fact.* Chicago: University of Chicago Press.

———. 1986. *Cognition and Fact: Materials on Ludwik Fleck.* Edited by Robert S. Cohen and Thomas Schnelle. Dordrecht: D. Reidel.

Fleury, Sonia. 1997. *Democracia e saúde: A luta do CEBES.* São Paulo: Lemos Editorial.

Fonseca, Claudia. 2000. "Child Circulation in Brazilian Favelas: A Local Practice in a Globalized World." *Anthropologie et Sociétés* 24 (3): 53–73.

———. 2002. "Anthropological Perspectives on Problematic Youth." *Reviews in Anthropology* 31 (4): 351–368.

Foucault, Michel. 1972. *The Archaeology of Knowledge and the Discourse on Language.* New York: Harper Torchbooks.

———. 1979. *Discipline and Punish: The Birth of the Prison.* New York: Vintage Books.

———. 1980a. *The History of Sexuality.* Vol. 1, *An Introduction.* New York: Vintage Books.

———. 1980b. *Power/Knowledge: Selected Interviews and Other Writings, 1972–1977.* New York: Pantheon Books.

———. 1984. "What Is Enlightenment?" In *The Foucault Reader,* edited by Paul Rabinow, 3–29. New York: Pantheon Books.

———. 1992. *Genealogia del racismo.* Buenos Aires: Editorial Altamira.

———. 1997. "Psychiatric Power." In *Ethics: Subjectivity and Truth,* edited by Paul Rabinow, 39–50. New York: The New Press.

———. 1998. "What Is an Author?" In *Michel Foucault: Aesthetics, Method, and Epistemology,* edited by James Faubion, 205–222. New York: The New Press.

———. 2001. "Lives of Infamous Men." In *Power: Essential Works of Foucault, 1954–1984,* edited by James D. Faubion, vol. 3, 157–175. New York: Free Press.

———. 2003. *Abnormal: Lectures at the Collège de France, 1974–1975.* New York: Picador.

Franklin, Sarah, and Susan McKinnon, eds. 2001. *Relative Values: Reconfiguring Kinship Studies.* Durham, N.C.: Duke University Press.

Freire Costa, Jurandir. 1976. *História da psiquiatria no Brasil: Um corte ideológico.* Rio de Janeiro: Editora Documentário.

———. 1994. *A Ética e o espelho da cultura.* Rio de Janeiro: Rocco.

———. 2000. "Playdoer pelos Irmãos." In *Função fraterna,* edited by Maria Rita Kehl, 7–30. Rio de Janeiro: Relume Dumará.

Freud, Sigmund. 1957a. "The Sense of Symptoms." In *The Standard Edition of the Complete Psychological Works of Sigmund Freud,* vol. 16, *1916–1917,* edited by James Strachey, 257–272. London: Hogarth Press.

———. 1957b. "Thoughts for the Times on War and Death." In *The Standard Edition of the Complete Psychological Works of Sigmund Freud,* vol. 16, *1916–1917,* edited by James Strachey, 275–300. London: Hogarth Press.

———. 1959a. *Group Psychology and the Analysis of the Ego.* New York: W. W. Norton. First published 1922.

———. 1959b. "The Loss of Reality in Neurosis and Psychosis." In *Collected Papers,* edited by Ernest Jones, vol. 2, 277–282. New York: Basic Books. First published 1924.

Frobel, Julius. 1858. *Die Deutsche auswanderung un ihre culturhistorische bedeutung.* Leipzig: Franz Wagner.

Galvão, Jane. 2000. *A AIDS no Brasil: A agenda de construção de uma epidemia.* São Paulo: Editora 34.

Geertz, Clifford. 1973. *The Interpretation of Cultures.* New York: Basic Books.

———. 2000a. "Common Sense as a Cultural System." In *Local Knowledge: Further Essays in Interpretive Anthropology,* 73–93. New York: Basic Books.

———. 2000b. "The World in Pieces: Culture and Politics at the End of the Century." In *Available Light: Anthropological Reflections on Philosophical Topics,* 218–263. Princeton: Princeton University Press.

———. 2001. "Life among the Anthros." *New York Review of Books* 48, no. 2, February 8, 18–22.

Geest, Sjaak van der, Susan Reynolds Whyte, and Anita Hardon. 1996. "The Anthropology of Pharmaceuticals: A Biographical Approach." *Annual Review of Anthropology* 25:153–178.

Girard, René. 1996. *The Girard Reader.* Edited by James G. Williams. New York: Crossroad.

Goffman, Erving. 1961. *Asylums: Essays on the Social Situation of Mental Patients and Other Inmates.* Garden City, N.Y.: Doubleday.

Goldberg, Jairo. 1994. *A clínica da psicose: Um projeto na rede pública.* Rio de Janeiro: Te Corá, Instituto Franco Basaglia.

Goldstein, Donna M. 2003. *Laughter Out of Place: Race, Class, Violence, and Sexuality in a Rio Shantytown.* Berkeley: University of California Press.

Good, Byron. 1994. *Medicine, Rationality, and Experience.* Cambridge: Cambridge University Press.

———. 2001. "Le sujet de la maladie mentale: Psychose, folie furieuse, et subjectivité en Indonesie." In *La pathologie mentale en mutation: Psychiatrie et société,* edited by Alain Ehrenberg and Anne M. Lovell, 163–195. Paris: Édition Odile Jacob.

Good, Mary-Jo Delvecchio, and Byron Good. 2000. "Clinical Narratives and the Study of Contemporary Doctor-Patient Relationships." In *The Handbook of Social Studies in Health and Medicine,* edited by Gary L. Albrecht, Ray Fitzpatrick, and Susan C. Scrimshaw, 243–258. London: Sage.

Greenhouse, Carol. 2002. "Citizenship, Agency, and the Dream of Time." In *Looking Back at Law's Century,* edited by Austin Sarat, Bryant Garth, and Robert A. Kagan, 184–205. Ithaca, N.Y.: Cornell University Press.

Greenhouse, Carol, Elizabeth Mertz, and Kay B. Warren, eds. 2002. *Ethnography in Unstable Places: Everyday Lives in Contexts of Dramatic Political Change.* Durham, N.C.: Duke University Press.

Guha, Ranajit, ed. 1997. *A Subaltern Studies Reader, 1986–1995.* Minneapolis: University of Minnesota Press.

Hacking, Ian. 1990. *The Taming of Chance*. Cambridge: Cambridge University Press.

———. 1998. *Mad Travelers: Reflections on the Reality of Transient Mental Illness*. Charlottesville: University of Virginia Press.

———. 1999. "Making Up People." In *The Science Studies Reader*, edited by Mario Biagioli, 161–171. New York: Routledge.

Hammoudi, Abdellah. 1993. *The Victim and Its Masks: An Essay on Sacrifice and Masquerade in the Maghreb*. Chicago: University of Chicago Press.

Haraway, Donna. 1989. *Primate Visions: Gender, Race, and Nature in the World of Modern Science*. New York: Routledge.

Harding, A. E., and Thomas Deufel, eds. 1993. *Inherited Ataxias*. New York: Raven Press.

Harrison, J. E. 1921. *Epilegomena to the Study of Greek Religion*. Cambridge: Cambridge University Press.

Healy, David. 1999. *The Antidepressant Era*. Cambridge, Mass.: Harvard University Press.

Hecht, Tobias. 1998. *At Home in the Street: Street Children of Northeast Brazil*. Cambridge: Cambridge University Press.

Hertz, Robert. 1960. *Death and the Right Hand*. Glencoe, N.Y.: Free Press.

Herzfeld, Michael. 2001. "Suffering and Disciplines." In *Anthropology: Theoretical Practice in Culture and Society*, 217–239. London: Blackwell.

Hoffman, Kelly, and Miguel Angel Centeno. 2003. "The Lopsided Continent: Inequality in Latin America." *Annual Review of Sociology* 29:363–390.

Holland, Dorothy, and Jean Lave, eds. 2001. *History in Person: Enduring Struggles, Contentious Practice, Intimate Identities*. Santa Fe: School of American Research Press.

Jardim, Laura B. 2000. "Aspectos clínicos e moleculares da doença de Machado-Joseph no Rio Grande do Sul: Sua relação com as outras ataxias espinocerebelares autossômicas dominantes e uma hipótese sobre seus fatores modificadores." PhD diss., Programa de Pós-Graduação em Medicina, Clínica Médica, Universidade Federal do Rio Grande do Sul.

Jardim, L. B., M. L. Pereira, I. Silveira, A. Ferro, J. Sequeiros, and R. Giugliani. 2001a. "Machado-Joseph Disease in South Brazil: Clinical and Molecular Characterizations of Kindreds." *Acta Neurologica Scandinavica* 104:224–231.

———. 2001b. "Neurological Findings in Machado-Joseph." *Archives of Neurology* 58:899–904.

Jelin, Elizabeth. 1994. "The Politics of Memory: The Human Rights Movement and the Construction of Democracy in Argentina." *Latin American Perspectives* 21 (2): 38–58.

Jenkins, J. H. 1991. "Anthropology, Expressed Emotion, and Schizophrenia." *Ethos* 19(4): 387–431.

Jenkins, Janis H., and Robert J. Barrett, eds. 2003. *Schizophrenia, Culture, and Subjectivity: The Edge of Experience*. Cambridge: Cambridge University Press.

Jornal NH. 1988a. "Ala psiquiátrica: Verba pode ser liberada hoje." September 5.

―――. 1988b. "Hospital psiquiátrico é prioridade para Helena." November 27.

―――. 1989. "Saúde mental." September 16.

―――. 1991. "Novo Hamburgo busca novas soluções para doente mental." May 28.

―――. 1992a. "Governo quer acabar com manicômios." April 26.

―――. 1992b. "Loucura é associada ao sucateamento social." May 11.

―――. 1992c. "Novo Hamburgo é exemplo . . . também no atendimento à saúde mental." June 27.

―――. 1994a. "Cai a internação de doentes mentais." March 31.

―――. 1994b. "Conferência de saúde possibilita intercâmbio." November 7.

―――. 1994c. "Novo Hamburgo realiza serviço ambulatorial." May 18.

―――. 1995a. "Posto atende até carências afetivas." June 11.

―――. 1995b. "Santo Afonso/Vila Marte: Bairro é o segundo em dimensão e problemas." June 11.

―――. 1997a. "Casa de Saúde concentra os remédios controlados." March 15.

―――. 1997b. "Miséria está entre causas do desespero." April 4.

Kehl, Maria Rita, ed. 2000. *Função fraterna*. Rio de Janeiro: Relume Dumará.

Kleinman, Arthur. 1981. *Patients and Healers in the Context of Culture*. Berkeley: University of California Press.

―――. 1988. *The Illness Narratives: Suffering, Healing, and the Human Condition*. New York: Basic Books.

―――. 1999. "Experience and Its Moral Modes: Culture, Human Conditions, and Disorder." In *The Tanner Lectures on Human Values*, edited by Grethe B. Peterson, vol. 20, 357–420. Salt Lake City: University of Utah Press.

Kleinman, Arthur, and Anne Becker. 1998. "Sociosomatics: The Contributions of Anthropology to Psychosomatic Medicine." *Psychosomatic Medicine* 60 (4): 389–393.

Kleinman, Arthur, Veena Das, and Margaret Lock, eds. 1997. *Social Suffering*. Berkeley: University of California Press.

Kleinman, Arthur, and Joan Kleinman. 1985. "Somatization: The Interconnections in Chinese Society among Culture, Depressive Experiences, and the Meanings of Pain." In *Culture and Depression*, edited by Arthur Kleinman and Byron Good, 429–490. Berkeley: University of California Press.

―――. 1997. "The Appeal of Experience; The Dismay of Images: Cultural Appropriations of Suffering in Our Times." In *Social Suffering*, edited by Arthur Kleinman, Veena Das, and Margaret Lock, 1–23. Berkeley: University of California Press.

Klima, Alan. 2002. *The Funeral Casino: Meditation, Massacre, and Exchange with the Dead in Thailand*. Princeton: Princeton University Press.

Kroeber, Theodora. 2002. *Ishi in Two Worlds: A Biography of the Last Wild Indian in North America.* With a new foreword by Karl Kroeber. Berkeley: University of California Press. First published 1961.

Lacan, Jacques. 1977. "On a Question Preliminary to Any Possible Treatment of Psychosis." In *Écrit: A Selection,* 179–225. New York: W. W. Norton.

———. 1978. *The Four Fundamental Concepts of Psychoanalysis.* New York: W. W. Norton.

———. 1979. "The Neurotic's Individual Myth." *Psychoanalytic Quarterly* 48 (3): 386–425.

———. 1980. "A Lacanian Psychosis: Interview by Jacques Lacan." In *Returning to Freud: Clinical Psychoanalysis in the School of Lacan,* edited by Stuart Schneiderman, 19–41. New Haven: Yale University Press.

———. 1989a. *The Family Complexes.* New York: W. W. Norton.

———. 1989b. "Science and Truth." *Newsletter of the Freudian Field* 3:4–29.

———. 1992. *The Seminar of Jacques Lacan. Book 7, The Ethics of Psychoanalysis, 1959–1960.* Edited by Jacques-Alain Miller. Translated with notes by Dennis Porter. New York: W. W. Norton.

———. 1993a. "On Mademoiselle B." *Revista da APPOA* 4 (9): 3–31.

———. 1993b. *The Seminar of Jacques Lacan. Book 3, The Psychoses, 1955–1956.* Edited by Jacques-Alain Miller. Translated with notes by Russell Grigg. New York: W. W. Norton.

———. 1994. *O seminário de Jacques Lacan. Livro 17, O avesso da psicanálise.* Rio de Janeiro: Zahar.

———. 1998. *The Seminar of Jacques Lacan. Book 20, On Feminine Sexuality: The Limits of Love and Knowledge, 1972–1973.* Edited by Jacques-Alain Miller. Translated with notes by Bruce Fink. New York: W. W. Norton.

———. n.d. "O sinthoma" (Seminar 23, 1975–1976). Manuscript.

Laing, R. D. 1967. *The Politics of Experience.* New York: Ballantine Books.

Lamont, Michèle. 2000. *The Dignity of Working Men: Morality and the Boundaries of Race, Class, and Immigration.* New York: Russell Sage Foundation; Cambridge, Mass.: Harvard University Press.

Lamounier, Bolívar, and Rubens Figueiredo, eds. 2002. *A era FHC: Um balanço.* São Paulo: Cultura Editora Associados.

Laurell, Asa Cristina, ed. 1995. *Estado e políticas sociais no neoliberalismo.* São Paulo: Editora Cortez.

Leibing, Annete, ed. 1997. *The Medical Anthropologies in Brazil.* Berlin: VWB.

———, ed. 2003. *Tecnologias do corpo: Uma antropologia das medicinas no Brasil.* Rio de Janeiro: Nau Editora.

Le Marchant, A. 1923. *Greek Religion to the Time of Hesiod.* Manchester, U.K.: Sherratt and Hughes.

Lock, Margaret. 2002. *Twice Dead: Organ Transplants and the Reinvention of Death.* Berkeley: University of California Press.

Loraux, Nicole. 2002. *The Divided City: On Memory and Forgetting in Ancient Athens.* New York: Zone Books.

Luhrman, Tanya. 2000. *Of Two Minds: The Growing Disorder in American Psychiatry.* New York: Alfred A. Knopf.

Luiza, Vera Lucia. 1999. "Aquisição de medicamentos no setor público: O binômio qualidade-custo." *Cadernos de Saúde Pública* 15 (4): 769–776.

Lunbeck, Elizabeth. 1994. *The Psychiatric Persuasion: Knowledge, Gender, and Power in Modern America.* Princeton: Princeton University Press.

Lutz, Catherine. 1985. "Depression and the Translation of Emotional Words." In *Culture and Depression,* edited by Arthur Kleinman and Byron Good, 63–100. Berkeley: University of California Press.

Lyotard, Jean-François. 1991. *The Inhuman.* Stanford: Stanford University Press.

Malinowski, Bronislaw. 2001. *Sex and Repression in Savage Society.* New York: Routledge.

Mann, Thomas. 1996. *The Magic Mountain.* New York: Vintage Books.

Marcus, George E. 1998. *Ethnography through Thick and Thin.* Princeton: Princeton University Press.

Martin, Emily. 1988. *The Woman in the Body.* Boston: Beacon Press.

Mattingly, Cheryl. 1998. *Healing Dramas and Clinical Plots: The Narrative Structure of Experience.* Cambridge: Cambridge University Press.

Mauss, Marcel. 1979. "The Physical Effect on the Individual of the Idea of Death Suggested by the Collectivity"; "The Notion of Body Techniques." In *Sociology and Psychology: Essays,* 35–56; 95–119. London: Routledge and Kegan Paul.

Mbembe, Achille. 2003. "Necropolitics." *Public Culture* 15 (1): 11–40.

Melman, Charles. 1991. *Estrutura lacaniana das psicoses.* Porto Alegre: Artes Médicas.

Mendes, Maralucia. 2000. "As doenças nervosas e a família no vale dos sinos." Report. Novo Hamburgo: Secretaria Municipal de Saúde.

Milosz, Czeslaw. 1991. *Beginning with My Streets: Essays and Recollections.* New York: Farrar, Straus and Giroux.

———. 2001. *New and Collected Poems, 1931–2001.* New York: Ecco.

Ministério da Saúde. 1997. *Farmácia básica: Programa 1997/98.* Brasília: Ministério da Saúde.

———. 1999. *Política nacional de medicamentos.* Brasília: Ministério da Saúde.

Moraes, Fábio Alexandre. 2000. "Abrindo a porta da casa dos loucos." Master's thesis, Programa de Pós-Graduação em Psicologia Social e Institucional do Instituto de Psicologia da Universidade Federal do Rio Grande do Sul, Porto Alegre.

Nabokov, Isabelle. 2000. *Religion against the Self: An Ethnography of Tamil Rituals.* Oxford: Oxford University Press.

Nichter, Mark, and N. Vuckovic. 1994. "Agenda for an Anthropology of Pharmaceutical Practice." *Social Science and Medicine* 39 (11): 1509–1525.

Nietzsche, Friedrich. 1955. *The Use and Abuse of History.* New York: Macmillan.

Obeyesekere, Gananath. 1990. *The Work of Culture: Symbolic Transformation in Psychoanalysis and Anthropology.* Chicago: University of Chicago Press.

Ochs, Elinor, and Lisa Capps. 1996. "Narrating the Self." *Annual Review of Anthropology* 25: 9–43.

O'Dougherty, Maureen. 2002. *Consumption Intensified: The Politics of Middle-Class Daily Life in Brazil.* Durham, N.C.: Duke University Press.

Oliveira, J., and S. F. Teixeira. 1986. *(Im) Previdência social: 60 anos de história da previdência no Brasil.* Rio de Janeiro: Vozes.

Ong, Aihwa. 1988. "The Production of Possession: Spirits and the Multinational Corporation in Malaysia." *American Ethnologist* 15 (1): 28–42.

———. 1996. "Cultural Citizenship as Subject-Making." *Current Anthropology* 37 (5): 737–762.

Ortner, Sherry B. 2003. *New Jersey Dreaming: Capital, Culture, and the Class of '58.* Durham, N.C.: Duke University Press.

Paley, Julia. 2001. *Marketing Democracy: Power and Social Movements in Post-Dictatorship Chile.* Berkeley: University of California Press.

Pandolfo, Stefania. 1997. *Impasse of the Angels: Scenes from a Moroccan Space of Memory.* Chicago: University of Chicago Press.

Panourgiá, Neni. 1995. *Fragments of Death, Fables of Identity: An Athenian Anthropography.* Madison: University of Wisconsin Press.

Patterson, Orlando. 1982. *Slavery and Social Death.* Cambridge, Mass.: Harvard University Press.

Paúl, Constança, Ignacio Martin, Maria do Rosário Silva, Mário Silva, Paula Coutinho, and Jorge Sequeiros. 1999. "Living with Machado-Joseph Disease in a Small Rural Community of the Tagus Valley." *Community Genetics* 2:190–195.

Peirano, Mariza G. S. 1998. "When Anthropology Is at Home: The Different Contexts of a Single Discipline." *Annual Review of Anthropology* 27:105–128.

Petry, Leopoldo. 1944. *O município de Novo Hamburgo.* Porto Alegre: A Nação.

Petryna, Adriana. 2002. *Life Exposed: Biological Citizens after Chernobyl.* Princeton: Princeton University Press.

Pont, Raul, and Adair Barcelos, eds. 2000. *Porto Alegre: Uma cidade que conquista.* Porto Alegre: Artes e Ofícios.

Povinelli, Elizabeth. 2002. *The Cunning of Recognition: Indigenous Alterity and the Making of Australian Multiculturalism.* Durham, N.C.: Duke University Press.

Rabinow, Paul. 1996a. *Essays in the Anthropology of Reason*. Princeton: Princeton University Press.

———. 1996b. *Making PCR: A Story of Biotechnology*. Chicago: University of Chicago Press.

———. 1997. "Introduction: The History of Systems of Thought." In *Ethics: Subjectivity and Truth: The Essential Works of Michel Foucault, 1954–1984*, vol. 1, by Michel Foucault, edited by Paul Rabinow, xi–xlii. New York: The New Press.

———. 1999. *French DNA: Trouble in Purgatory*. Chicago: University of Chicago Press.

———. 2003. *Anthropos Today: Reflections on Modern Equipment*. Princeton: Princeton University Press.

Raffles, Hugh. 2002. *In Amazonia: A Natural History*. Princeton: Princeton University Press.

Rapp, Rayna. 1999. *Testing Women, Testing the Fetus: The Social Impact of Amniocentesis in America*. New York: Routledge.

Rheinberger, Hans-Jörg. 1997. *Toward a History of Epistemic Things: Synthesizing Proteins in the Test Tube*. Stanford: Stanford University Press.

Ribeiro, Renato Janine. 2000. *A sociedade contra o social: O alto custo da vida pública no Brasil*. São Paulo: Companhia das Letras.

Rivers, W. H. R. 1922. "Freud's Psychology of the Unconscious." In *Instinct and the Unconscious*, 159–169. Cambridge: Cambridge University Press.

———. 1923. "Affect in the Dream." In *Conflict and Dream*, 65–82. London: Kegan Paul.

Rose, Nikolas. 1996. "The Death of the Social? Refiguring the Territory of Government." *Economy and Society* 25 (3): 327–356.

———. 1998. *Inventing Ourselves: Psychology, Power, and Personhood*. Cambridge: Cambridge University Press.

———. 2001. "Society, Madness, and Control." In *Care of the Mentally Disordered Offender in the Community*, edited by Alec Buchanan, 3–25. Oxford: Oxford University Press.

Rosen, Lawrence. 2003. *The Culture of Islam: Changing Aspects of Contemporary Muslim Life*. Chicago: University of Chicago Press.

Ruff, Thomas. 2001. *Fotografien 1979-Heute*. Cologne: König.

Russo, Jane, and João Ferreira Silva Filho, eds. 1993. *Duzentos anos de psiquiatria*. Rio de Janeiro: Relume Dumará.

Ryff, Carol D., and Burton H. Singer, eds. 2001. *Emotions, Social Relationships, and Health*. New York: Oxford University Press.

Scheper-Hughes, Nancy. 1992. *Death without Weeping: The Violence of Everyday Life in Brazil*. Berkeley: University of California Press.

———. 2000. "The Global Traffic in Human Organs." *Current Anthropology* 41 (2): 191–211.

———. 2001. *Saints, Scholars, and Schizophrenics: Mental Illness in Rural Ireland.* 20th anniv. ed., updated and expanded. Berkeley: University of California Press.

Scheper-Hughes, Nancy, and Philippe Bourgois. 2004. "Introduction: Making Sense of Violence." In *Violence in War and Peace: An Anthology*, edited by Nancy Scheper-Hughes and Philippe Bourgois, 1–31. Oxford: Blackwell.

Scheper-Hughes, Nancy, and Margaret Lock. 1987. "The Mindful Body: A Prolegomenon to Future Work in Medical Anthropology." *Medical Anthropology Quarterly* 1 (1): 6–41.

Scheper-Hughes, Nancy, and Anne M. Lovell, eds. 1987. *Psychiatry Inside Out: Selected Writings of Franco Basaglia.* New York: Columbia University Press.

Sequeiros, Jorge, ed. 1996. *O teste preditivo da doença de Machado-Joseph.* Porto: UnIGene.

Sequeiros, Jorge, and Paula Coutinho. 1993. "Epidemiology and Clinical Aspects of Machado-Joseph Disease." In *Advances in Neurology*, vol. 61, edited by A. E. Harding and Thomas Deufel, 139–153. New York: Raven Press.

Sherman, Cindy. 1997. *Cindy Sherman Retrospective.* Chicago: Museum of Contemporary Art.

Shostak, Marjorie. 1981. *Nisa: The Life and Words of a !Kung Woman.* Cambridge, Mass.: Harvard University Press.

Singer, Peter. 1975. *Animal Liberation: A New Ethics for Our Treatment of Animals.* New York: Random House.

Sociedade Brasileira para o Progresso da Ciência. 1998. *Jornal da Ciência.* São Paulo, November 20.

Sontag, Susan. 1977. *On Photography.* New York: Farrar, Straus and Giroux.

———. 2003. *Regarding the Pain of Others.* New York: Farrar, Straus and Giroux.

Souza, João Cardoso de Menezes. 1875. *Theses sobre colonização do Brazil—Projecto de solução às questões sociaes, que se prendem a este difícil problema—Relatorio apresentado ao Ministerio da Agriculture, Commercio e Obras Publicas.* Rio de Janeiro: Typographia Nacional.

Steiner, George. 2001. *Grammars of Creation.* New Haven: Yale University Press.

Stoler, Ann L. 2002. *Carnal Knowledge and Imperial Power: Race and the Intimate in Colonial Rule.* Berkeley: University of California Press.

Strathern, Marilyn. 1992. *After Nature: English Kinship in the Late Twentieth Century.* Cambridge: Cambridge University Press.

Strong, Thomas. 2002. "Kinship between Judith Butler and Anthropology? A Review Essay." *Ethnos* 67 (3): 401–418.

Struth, Thomas. 1994. *Strangers and Friends: Photographs 1986–1992.* Cambridge, Mass.: MIT Press.

Taussig, Michael. 1986. *Shamanism, Colonialism, and the Wild Man: A Study of Terror and Healing*. Chicago: University of Chicago Press.

———. 1991. "Reification and the Consciousness of the Patient." In *The Nervous System*, 83–110. New York: Routledge.

Taylor, C. 1989. *Sources of the Self: The Making of the Modern Identity*. Cambridge, Mass.: Harvard University Press.

Tenorio, F. 2002. "A reforma psiquiátrica brasileira, da década de 1980 aos dias atuais: História e conceito." *Histórias, Ciências, Saúde–Manguinhos* 9 (1): 25–59.

Tierney, Patrick. 2000. *Darkness in El Dorado: How Scientists and Journalists Devastated the Amazon*. New York: W. W. Norton.

Vinicius, M., ed. 2001. *A instituição sinistra: Mortes violentas em hospitais psiquiátricos no Brasil*. Brasília: Conselho Federal de Psicologia.

Wacquant, Loïc. 2004. *Body and Soul: Notebooks of an Apprentice Boxer*. Oxford: Oxford University Press.

Weber, Max. 1946. *From Max Weber: Essays in Sociology*. New York: Oxford University Press.

Williams, Brackette F. 1989. "Anthropology and the Race to Nation across Ethnic Terrain." *Annual Review of Anthropology* 18:401–444.

Wilson, Elizabeth. 2004. *Psychosomatic*. Durham, N.C.: Duke University Press.

Wilson, Richard A. 2000. "Reconciliation and Revenge in Post-Apartheid South Africa: Rethinking Legal Pluralism and Human Rights." *Current Anthropology* 41 (1): 75–98.

Young, Allan. 1995. *The Harmony of Illusions: Inventing Post-Traumatic Stress Disorder*. Princeton: Princeton University Press.

Yunes, J. 1999. "Promoting Essential Drugs, Rational Drug Use, and Generics: Brazil's National Drug Policy Leads the Way." *Essential Drugs Monitor* 27: 22–23.

Zelizer, Viviana A. 2005. "Circuits within Capitalism." In *The Economic Sociology of Capitalism*, edited by Victor Nee and Richard Swedburg. Princeton: Princeton University Press.

Zero Hora. 1991. "Nem as famílias querem cuidar dos doentes mentais." May 2.

Žižek, Slavoj. 1999. *The Ticklish Subject: The Absent Centre of Political Ontology*. New York: Verso.

Index

abandonados: abuse of, 61, 80; animalization of, 39–41, 64–66; citizenship of, 47, 56, 65–66, 103; deaths of, 63, 76, 103–4, 210; encounters with, 214–15; ex-humanness of, 85–90, 317, 360; families of, 8, 61, 77, 88, 118, 142, 234, 296; medical assistance for, 105; numbers of, at Vita, 209–10; personal possessions of, 41–42, 99; pharmaceuticalization of, 275; photographs of, 42–43; psychiatric cases, 79; psychiatry and, 148; radio broadcasts of, 37; recollections of, 76; and self-generated death, 60–64; sexual abuse of, 116–18; and sexuality, 116; social class of, 2; and social death, 52–53, 65–66; social function of, 64–66, 103, 276–77; social reintegration of, 279; and zones of abandonment, 4. *See also* Vita
accountability, 144–45
Addlakha, Renu, 372n31
Adorno, Theodor, 16
Agamben, Giorgio, 372n30
affect , 2, 16, 17, 66, 124, 127, 129, 142, 146, 152, 183, 186, 193, 196, 200, 205, 302, 316, 356; Freud on, 197
AIDS: state programs for, 4, 56; at Vita, 39, 56, 58–59, 60, 84, 104–5, 218
Akineton. *See* biperiden
Albuquerque, Denise (geneticist), 303
alcoholism, 1, 181, 184
Alencar (Vita volunteer), 105, 218, 261, 262, 296, 355, 356

allostatic load, 375n56
ambulatory services, 134, 174, 177–78
Amorin, Irineu (psychiatrist), 203
amoxicillin (antibiotic), 307
Amplictil. *See* chlorpromazine
Angela (Vita resident), 36
animalization. *See* dehumanization
anthropology: ethics and, 315, 370n17; research methods of, 19–20; and social psychosis, 106; and subjectivity, 10–12; types of, 375n58. *See also* ethnography
anti-asylum movement. *See* deinstitutionalization; psychiatric reform movement
antiretroviral medications, 218
Arendt, Hannah, 260
ataxia: childbirth as purported cause of, 293; and culture, 288–89; in Gomes family, 199–200, 220, 230, 236–37, 246, 255–56, 282–85, 292–96, 357; mutating nature of, 293; research on, 300–301. *See also* Machado-Joseph disease; Moraes, Catarina Gomes, ataxia of
Azores Islands (Portugal), 297–98, 301

Babinsky sign, 220
Bachelard, Gaston, 98
Basaglia, Franco, 131, 134
Bastião (Vita resident), 109–10
Benjamin, Walter, 42
benzodiazepine nitrazepam. *See* nitrazepam
"bioavailability," 372n32
"biological citizenship," 372n29

biological complex: Catarina and, 285–87, 289–91, 294–96, 316; definition of, 284; Gomes family and, 283–84, 294
biopolitics, 132–33, 142, 371–72nn28–30
biosociality, 306
biotechnology, anthropology and, 370n17
biperiden: Catarina medicated with, 127, 147, 157, 165, 167, 203, 205; and extrapyramidal symptoms, 192–94, 197; and medical practices, 147
Bittencourt, José Hamilton (nurse), 168–69
B., Mlle. (Lacan's patient), 157–58
Bomarech, Rosana (neurologist), 205–6
Bonfim Hospital, 201–2
Borde, La (France), 131
Borges, Nilton (psychiatrist), 164–66, 167–68
Brazil: citizenship in, 46–47; constitution of (1988), 47, 130, 132–33; economic boom years in, 172; health care in, 47, 105, 130–31, 144–45; homelessness in, 50–51; illiteracy in, 83; MJD in, 297–98; pharmaceuticalization in, 374n45; poverty in, 2, 49–51, 367n1; psychiatric reform movement in, 130–37; social death in, 52–53; social effects of globalization in, 21–23, 46–49; Tenth National Health Care Conference, 136–37; welfare system in, 46–47, 57; zones of abandonment in, 4
Butler, Judith, 16

Caiçara (Brazil), 123, 160, 244, 292
Canudos district (Brazil), 168, 178, 180, 183–84
capitalism, social effects of, 49–50. See also globalization; neoliberalism
CAPS (Centers for Psychosocial Attention), 134–36, 140–41, 174, 183, 373–74n43
carbamazepine (mood stabilizer), 204
Cardoso, Fernando Henrique, 21, 50
Caridade Psychiatric Hospital: Catarina hospitalized at, 95, 108, 146–50, 163, 169, 192, 199–204, 211, 243–44; Catarina's medical files at, 119, 123–24, 126–29; medical routine at, 164; neurologist lacking at, 201; Novo Hamburgo hospitalizations at, 180; pharmaceutical-

ization at, 106; rehabilitation impossible at, 182, 185; SUS funding cuts at, 140
Casa da Saúde Mental. See House of Mental Health
Casa da Vida (House of Life), 279
Catarina. See Moraes, Catarina Gomes
Centers for Psychosocial Attention. See CAPS
Chatterji, Roma, 125
chlorpromazine (antipsychotic): abundance of, at Vita, 218–19; Catarina medicated with, 153, 193–94, 200, 203, 205
Cida (Vita resident), 39, 66
Citizenship, 372n29; Catarina and, 14; domestic sphere and, 372n31; globalization and, 21–22; and health care, 144–45; psychiatry reform and, 132–33, 135, 136–37; social class and, 46–47; social death and, 52–53, 65–66, 142; at Vita, 56, 65–66, 103
civil rights, 130
civil war, civic life and, 176–77
Clóvis. See Gama, Clóvis
Cobrinha (Vita resident), 109
Cohen, Lawrence, 15–16, 370n17, 372n32
"Colonial Wars and Mental Disorders" (Fanon), 16
Comissão de Direitos Humanos (Human Rights Commission), 84, 139–40
common sense, 9–10, 239, 247, 258, 316
community, health care privatization and, 47–48, 130, 141–42
Conceição Hospital, 39
Conselhos Tutelares (Tutelage Councils), 59–60, 169
Constitution of the Federative Republic of Brazil (1988), 47, 130, 132–33
consumer culture, citizenship and, 21–22
Costa, Jurandir Freire, 135
Cunha, Euclides da, 355

Dalmadorm. See flurazepam
Dalva (social worker), 57–58, 60–61, 104, 356
Das, Veena: on anthropology and Otherness, 315; and biotechnology, 370n17; on citizenship and domestic sphere, 372n31; and illness, conceptualization of, 373n36; and subjectivity, 10; on Wittgenstein, 367n5
death: -in-life, 38, 43, 118; politics of,

63–64, 371–72n28; self-generated, 52–53, 60–64, 104. *See also* social death

dehumanization, 39–41, 64–66, 84, 97–98

deinstitutionalization: and Catarina's treatment, 82–83, 125, 175; and family, 47–48, 130, 135, 139–41, 173, 316; and the mentally ill, 47–48, 138–39; and pharmaceuticalization, 125, 131, 141; psychiatric reform movement and, 138–39, 152; and psychiatry, 124–25, 130–31. *See also under specific hospitals*

Deleuze, Gilles: on capitalism, social effects of, 49; and "machine," 169; National Health Care Conference and, 137; and schizophrenia, 88, 368–69n9; on space-times, 133; on subjectivity and becoming, 18

democratization, social effects of, 48–49

depression, MJD and, 300

Derrida, Jacques, 258–59

desire: Catarina and, 97, 99, 100, 101, 114, 115, 118, 198, 222; Lacan on, 198

Desjarlais, Robert, 88

diabetes, treatment for, 105

diazepam (hypnotic), 204

disability certificates, 139

Divided City, The (Loraux), 176–77

domestic economy, 8, 48

domestic violence, 179–86, 245–47

drug abuse programs, 1, 56, 58–59

drug economy, 48

drugs. *See* Moraes, Catarina Gomes, over-medication of; pharmaceuticalization; *specific drugs*

environmental dynamics, 271, 282–291, 303

Eskerod, Torben, 5, 35, 37, 42–43, 371n23

ethics: anthropology and, 20, 315, 370n17; bioethics, 299; biology and, 282–91; justice and, 309; language and, 24; medical ethics, 299; social life and, 10; and universals and exceptions, 24

ethnography, impact of, on Catarina, 209; of family life and medicine, 22–23; and life histories, 367–68n6; noninstitutionalized ethnographic spaces, 145; photography and, 42–43; and present human conditions 14, 319; research methods of, 19–20; and social death, 125, 367n4; of transition, 125; of Vita,

317; and ethnological ,17. *See also* anthropology

evil *(ruim /ruinande)*, 260; Caterina as, 286–87, 289; definition of, 286; males as, 294

ex-humanness: *abandonados* and, 90–91, 317, 360; Catarina and, 186,317–18; definition of, 24, 90; at Vita, 24, 52, 85–90, 317

family: and abandonment, 8, 61, 77, 88, 118, 142, 296; deinstitutionalization and, 47–48, 130, 135, 139–41, 173, 316; financial responsibility of, 234; and hospitalization, 126, 140–41, 182–85, 203–4; of House patients, 180–81; and mental illness, 95, 180–81, 185; and MJD patients, 302–3; and pharmaceuticalization, 96, 106–7, 141–42, 164–65, 185–86; as proxy psychiatrists, 125; psychiatrist and, 252; and psychosocial politics, 176–77; and rehabilitation process, 58; and social death, 21–22, 38–39, 41, 181–82; and social psychosis, 315–16; as state within the state, 185; Vita as, 59. *See also* Gomes family; Moraes family

Family Complexes, The (Lacan), 369n11

Fanon, Frantz, 16

Fenergan. *See* prometazine

Ferro, Rubem, 132–33

Fischer, Michael M. J., 315

Fleck, Ludwik, 148–49

Fleury, Sônia, 47

flunitrazepan (hypnotic), 200

flurazepam (hypnotic), 203

Foucault, Michel, 15, 137, 369n12, 371–72n28

Freire, Paulo, 83

Freud, Sigmund, 15, 16, 40, 185, 196–97; on psychosis, 368–69n9

Gama, Clóvis, 85; background of, 102–3; as caretaker, 108–10, 213, 214, 220; Catarina's relationship with, 99, 114–16, 210, 212, 222–23, 261, 271–72, 355; departure from Vita, 271–73; on pharmaceuticalization, 105, 218–19; return to Vita, 354–55, 357; on Vita administration, 104

Garcia Viato, Carlos (psychiatrist), 151

Geertz, Clifford, 9–10, 239, 247

Genesis and Development of a Scientific Fact (Fleck), 148–49

"geriatric houses": conditions at, 48; emergence of, 84; pharmaceuticalization at, 275; in Porto Alegre, 2, 48, 84; public intervention in, 139, 274–77; Vita as, 356; as zones of abandonment, 2

Germany, Brazilian settlements of, 374n51

globalization, social effects of, 21–23, 46–49. *See also* deinstitutionalization; neoliberalism

Godoy, Marcelo (public health professional), 139, 274–76

Goldberg, Jairo, 135

Gomes, Ademar (brother): ataxia of, 251, 283, 284–85, 287; on Catarina, 236, 247, 294–95; Catarina abandoned by, 282, 295–96; Catarina taken in by, 242; employment history of, 285; and MJD diagnosis, 299; on parents' separation, 288

Gomes, Altamir (brother), 98; ataxia of, 251, 282–84, 287; on Catarina, 235–37; Catarina abandoned by, 260, 263, 282, 295–96; Catarina's visits to, 261; employment history of, 285; and MJD diagnosis, 298–99; on Nilson, 294; on parents' separation, 288; on Terezinha, 289

Gomes, Armando (brother): ataxia of, 237, 251; and biological complex, 286–87; Catarina abandoned by, 282, 295–96; and MJD diagnosis, 299–300; Nilson and, 285

Gomes, Dario (father), 123, 287–88

Gomes, Eugenio (nephew), 235, 284, 299

Gomes, Horacio (grandfather), 293

Gomes, Ilda (mother) 123; ataxia of, 205, 232, 242–43; and biological complex, 286–87, 295; Catarina as caretaker of, 92–93; Catarina buried in grave of, 360; Catarina's abuse of, 295; death of, 205, 242, 288–89, 293; marital separation of, 288

Gomes, José (uncle), 293

Gomes, Leontina (aunt), 293

Gomes, Terezinha (sister), 236–37, 289–90

Gomes, Vania (sister-in-law), 354; on Catarina, 235–39; Catarina abandoned by, 260; and Gomes family ataxia, 284, 285, 287, 299; on Terezinha, 289

Gomes family: ataxia in, 199–200, 220, 230, 236–37, 246, 255–56, 292–96, 357; and biological complex, 316; Catarina abandoned by, 18, 155, 164–67, 203–4, 295–96; Catarina's reentrance into, 14; ethnicity of, 292, 297. *See also specific family members*

Good, Byron, 17–18

Gross, Mariane (journalist), 83–84

Guattari, Felix, 88, 368–69n9

Hacking, Ian, 369n12

haloperidol (antipsychotic): abundance of, at Vita, 218–19; Catarina hospitalized under influence of, 202; Catarina medicated with, 113, 127, 147, 153, 157, 165, 167, 200, 205; and extrapyramidal symptoms, 192–94, 195–96; and medical routine, 147

health care: for AIDS cases, 105; privatization of, 21–22, 47–48, 130, 141–42; public access to, 308; state and, 132–33, 144–45. *See also* Sistema Único de Saúde; universal health care system

Hertz, Robert, 37

homeless: Catarina as, 214; psychiatric reform and, 49; state assistance to, 50–51, 279; and zones of abandonment, 4. See also abandonados

hospitalization: as abandonment, 203–4; compulsory, and civil rights, 130; criteria for, 126, 134, 373n38; family and, 126, 140–41, 182–85, 203–4; patient reaction to, 373n39; pharmaceuticalization vs., 183–84; psychiatry reform and, 140–41, 152, 173–74; of schizophrenics, 182–83; and subjectivity, 373n39. See also deinstitutionalization

House of Life (Casa da Vida), 279

House of Mental Health (Casa da Saúde Mental): care culture in, 169–70; Catarina treated at, 163–69, 175–76, 177, 192, 205, 236, 251–52; establishment of, and deinstitutionalization, 173–74; families of patients at, 180–81; female clientele in, 179–85; as model mental health service, 172–78, 183; objectives of, 174; patients referred to, 168; pharmaceuticalization at, 175; rehabilitation at, 182;

relocation of, 374n49; services offered at, 177–78; and social domain, 174–75; triaging at, 178

human rights, 19, 23, 39, 52, 274, 276, 317

Human Rights Commission (Comissão de Direitos Humanos), 84, 139–40

imipramine (antidepressant): abundance of, at Vita, 218–19; Catarina medicated with, 108, 200, 203, 204, 220

incest, 290

India (Vita resident), 75, 76, 80, 211–12

Iraci (Vita resident), 76–77, 80, 280

Jardim, Laura Bannach (geneticist): and Catarina's treatment, 307–9, 354, 359–60; on MJD and mental illness, 298; MJD research of, 300–306

Jornal da Ciência, 51

Jornal NH, 168, 173

Justus, Daniela (psychiatrist): Catarina treated by, 201, 203, 220; on family and pharmaceuticalization, 185; on hospitalizations, 203; on schizophrenia, treatment for, 127–28, 182–83

Kleinman, Arthur, 10, 15, 42, 370n17

Kleinman, Joan, 42

Kunz, Gilson (psychiatrist), 192; Catarina diagnosed by, 87, 199–200; Catarina hospitalized by, 169, 199, 202; Catarina's behavior with, 182; at House of Mental Health, 163–64, 175–76; medications prescribed by, 87, 204, 205, 236, 251, 252–53; and general hospital, 177

Lacan, Jacques, 16–17, 131, 157–58, 198, 369n11

language: Catarina and, 5, 9, 97, 358; and ethics, 24; language-thinking, 12, 86–87, 97, 212–13; and personhood, 86–87, 359–60; and social death, 88–91; subjectivity and, 10–12. *See also* Moraes, Catarina Gomes, dictionary of

"Language and Body" (Das), 10

Lauro (Vita resident), 64–65

Laux, Simone (psychologist): on CAPS services, 141; on Catarina as socially dead, 186; on female House patients, 179, 182; on psychiatrist and family, 252; on triage system, 140

levomepromazine (sedative): abundance of, at Vita, 218–19; Catarina medicated with, 127, 147, 150, 194; and extrapyramidal symptoms, 195–96; and medical routine, 147

life codes, 88, 214

life determinants, 145, 150

life histories, ethnography and, 6, 10, 367–68n6

Lili (Vita resident), 87–88, 112, 211–12, 214–15

Lima, Artur (psychiatrist), 194, 200

literacy, 50, 83, 135

Lock, Margaret, 370n17

Lomba Grande district (Brazil), 168, 178, 180

Loraux, Nicole, 176–77

love: God as, 112; sexuality and, 100–101, 109

Lucas (Vita resident), 64–65

Luchesi, Jandir (politician), 37, 56, 276–77, 355, 356

Luciano (Vita volunteer), 39–40, 64

Luis (Vita resident), 58–59

Machado-Joseph disease (MJD): and biosociality, 306; in Catarina, 354; and creativity, 304–5; definition of, 297–98; genetic population of, 301–2; in Gomes family, 298–300; mutating nature of, 303–4; and physiological deterioration, 307; research on, 300–301; and social exclusion, 302–3, 304–5, 316; testing for, 305–6. *See also* ataxia

magnetic resonance image (MRI), 271

Malinowski, Bronislaw, 15

Mann, Thomas, 369n15

Marcelo (Vita resident), 75–76

Marcus, George, 367–68n6

Maurer, Nilson ("Alemão"; sister-in-law's husband), 229–30, 231–32, 238, 260, 272

Maurer, Sirlei Moraes (sister-in-law), 229–34, 237

Mauss, Marcel, 15, 38

medical automatism/routine: Catarina as victim of, 149–50, 194, 201–6, 220–21, 236–37; pharmaceuticalization and, 147; in psychiatric hospitals, 164. *See also* pharmaceuticalization medical institutions: and abandonment, 77; deinstitutionalization of, 138–39; and mental illness, 95, 123–25; and social death, 38–39

medication. *See* Moraes, Catarina Gomes, overmedication of; pharmaceuticalization; *specific medications*

Mello, Lilian (nurse), 186, 204

Mendes, Maralucia (sociologist), 180, 183–84

mental health movement, 47–48

mentally ill, the: deaths of, 138–39; deinstitutionalization of, 47–48, 138–39; family and, 95, 180–81, 185; medical institutions and, 123–25; and patterns of normality, 373n36; pharmaceuticalization of, 105–7, 127–28; and psychosocial politics, 315–16; subjectivity and, 18; women as, 179–85; and zones of abandonment, 4. See also *abandonados*

middle class: globalization and, 48–49; private health care plans for, 130

migration, 48, 171, 271

Milosz, Czeslaw, 313–14

Miranda, Andreia (therapist), 184

Miranda, Osmar de Moura (Vita resident), 90

Mogadon. *See* nitrazepam

Moraes, Alessandra (daughter): birth of, 231, 240; Catarina abandoned by, 262–63, 264; and Catarina's divorce, 230; Catarina's visits to, 262–63; Catarina visited by, 280–81; and Nilson's affair, 92; taken from Catarina, 108

Moraes, Ana (daughter): adoption of, 232, 240, 246, 248, 254–56; birth of, 243, 251–52; and Catarina's divorce, 108, 231; Catarina unvisited by, 238–39; Catarina visited by, 353–54; godparents of, 253–54; heredity and mental condition, 250, 255–56

Moraes, Anderson (son), 229, 264; birth of, 244; on Catarina, 230–32; and Catarina's divorce, 108, 240; Catarina visited by, 279–81; as father-to-be, 354; marriage of, 358; Nilson and, 243; and Nilson's affair, 92

Moraes, Catarina Gomes: abandonment of, 1, 12, 77, 209, 229–56, 295–96; as anthropological subject, 11, 12–14, 19–20, 318; ataxia of, 219–23, 263, 271; autoimmune disorder found in, 271; and biological complex, 285–87, 289–91, 294–96, 316; "CATKINI", 319; children of, 153, 156, 161–62; death/burial of, 360; divorce of, 94–96, 161–62, 182, 244, 253–54, 259–60, 278; dreams of, 85–86, 222; as ex-human, 52, 85–91, 186, 317–18, 360; family of (*see* Gomes family; Moraes family; *specific family members*); family visits by, 259–64, 278–81, 296; family visits to, 239, 353–54; first love of, 153–54, 156, 160–61; former house of, 229–30; and fraternal tie, 278–79, 285–86; hallucinations of, 146, 152, 154–55, 157, 159–62; hospitalization history of, 123–25, 192 (*see also* Caridade Psychiatric Hospital; House of Mental Health; São Paulo Psychiatric Hospital); marriage of, 153, 155–57, 219, 244; medical examination of, 219–23; and MJD diagnosis, 302–3, 304–5; mood disorder of, 237–38, 250–51; MRI of, 271; personal possessions of, 77, 85; as pharmakos, 257–64, 316; pregnancy fantasy of, 263–64; as semblance, 229–30, 236; and sexuality, 97–101, 109, 111–16, 355; and social death, 20–21, 23, 186, 314–15; and social psychosis, 18, 315–16; spousal abuse, 161, 166; subjectivity of, 8–10, 17–18, 23–24, 109, 118, 137, 314–15. *See also* Moraes, Catarina Gomes, ataxia of; Moraes, Catarina Gomes, dictionary of; Moraes, Catarina Gomes, overmedication of

Moraes, Catarina Gomes, ataxia of, 219–23; deinstitutionalization and, 82–83; emergence of, 93; family abandonment and, 78–80, 230–33, 235–37, 246–47, 295–96; hereditary nature of, 93, 151–52, 153, 232, 235–36, 242–43; 246; and medical practices, 149–50, 201–6, 236–37; misdiagnosis of, 124–29, 153–54, 157, 165, 201–2; as MJD, 307, 354; nonknowledge of, 237; and pharmaceuticalization, 108, 149–50, 167–68, 202–6, 236–37; physiological deterioration, 12, 13–14, 192, 296, 357; as "rheumatism," 187–91; and symptom management, 189–91; treatment for, 307–9, 354, 357, 359–60

Moraes, Catarina Gomes, dictionary of, 321–50; and Catarina as pharmakos, 258, 260; as "dictionary," 72; family abandonment and, 247; language of, 358; new letters, 319; on paralysis, 82, 187–91; and pharmaceuticalization, 147–48; as poetry, 318–19; on political economy, 21; reasons for writing, 73, 212–13, 271, 313–14; recollections in, 5–8, 71–73; on separation of bodies, 78; signifiers in, 124–25; subjectivity and, 314–15

Moraes, Catarina Gomes, overmedication of: as abandonment, 96, 106–7, 148, 167–68, 199–206, 238, 252–53, 259; and ataxia, 220–21; Catarina's refusal of, 245–46, 251, 252; deinstitutionalization and, 125, 175; and dependency, 3–4; and extrapyramidal symptoms, 192–98; and family breakup, 164–65; for psychosis, 146–48; psychosocial politics and, 176–77; for schizophrenia, 127; and sexuality, 112–13; side effects of, 149–50, 307; and subjectivity, 8–10; Vita volunteers and, 5, 108

Moraes, Eliane (daughter-in-law), 358

Moraes, Fábio (psychologist): on cost of pharmaceuticals, 179; on families of House patients, 180–81; on House and abandonment, 177, 178; on House as model, 164, 169, 183; on House objectives, 174

Moraes family: Catarina abandoned by, 18, 155, 164–67, 203–4; Catarina's reentrance into, 14. *See also specific family members*

Moraes, Lúcia (ex-husband's second wife), 243

Moraes, Nestor (father-in-law), 240–43, 248–49, 261

Moraes, Nilson (ex-husband), 129; and biological complex, 290–91, 294; Catarina abandoned by, 92–98, 243–47, 254, 258; Catarina abused by, 161, 166; Catarina hospitalized by, 146, 155, 192, 204–5, 243–44, 245, 291; Catarina's aggressive behavior with, 169, 231, 241, 247, 250–51; divorce of, 94–96, 161–62, 164–65, 244, 253–54, 259–60, 278; employment history of, 244–45, 295; and Gomes family land, 243, 244–45, 285–86; hospitalization information provided by, 151–52, 155, 241; incest, 290; marriage of, 123, 153, 155–57, 219, 244; remarriage of, 241, 243

Moraes, Ondina (mother-in-law), 280; on Catarina, 240–43; Catarina abandoned by, 240–43, 254, 295; Catarina's children cared for by, 232, 240; Catarina's visits to, 261; religious beliefs of, 240, 243, 248–49

Moraes, Sirlei. *See* Maurer, Sirlei Moraes

Nadvorny, Nei (psychiatrist), 146
Nair (aunt), 293–94
National Health Care Conference, Tenth, 136–37
nation-state, discredited imaginaries of, 23, 40. *See also* Brazil
neoliberalism: market mechanisms, 47; psychiatry reform and, 130–37, 138; and psychosocial politics, 315–16; public health access and, 308; social effects of, 21–22, 48–49, 83; and state reform, 21. *See also* deinstitutionalization
Neozine. *See* levomepromazine
Neusa (aunt), 292–96
Nietzsche, Friedrich, 15
nitrazepam (hypnotic), 127, 147, 200
noninstitutionalized ethnographic spaces, 14, 145
Novo Hamburgo (Brazil): Catarina buried in, 360; Catarina in, 6, 93, 123, 153, 233, 244, 286; Catarina's family in, 210, 278–81; crime in, 287; Division for Health and Social Assistance, 375n53; historical background of, 171–72, 374n51; mental health reform in, 131, 136; mental illness in, 180; as model city, 172–78; working poor in, 375n53. *See also* House of Mental Health
Núncio, Seu (Gomes relation), 292–93

Obeyesekere, Gananath, 15
Oliveira, Jaci (public health professional), 84, 139–40, 274, 275–76
Ortiz, Ada (psychiatrist), 151–57, 160
Oscar (Vita volunteer), 14, 22, 46, 213; on abandonados and Vita donations, 276–77; on AIDS at Vita, 218; and AIDS cases, 104–5; on dehumanization, 39–40, 64; and Catarina's family visits, 260–62, 296,353; Catarina's relationship

Oscar (Vita volunteer) *(continued)*
with, 359–60; and Catarina's treatment, 308; and Clóvis's departure, 272–73; as infirmary coordinator, 38, 61–63, 78–79, 211, 355–57; and pharmaceuticalization, 106; on sexual activity at Vita, 272; on triage system, 104
Osvaldo (police captain), 56–57, 58, 60, 104
Other/Otherness: Catarina as, 257–64; death and, 40, 66, 142; ethics and, 315; family and, 183; language and, 10–12; psychosis and, 150; sexuality and, 100, 111–12; in Vita, 319
overmedication. *See* Moraes, Catarina Gomes, overmedication of; pharmaceuticalization; *specific medications*

paralysis. *See* ataxia; Machado-Joseph disease; Moraes, Catarina Gomes, ataxia of
Partido dos Trabalhadores. *See* Workers' Party
Pedro (Vita resident), 46
Pentecostalism: families of House patients and, 181; Moraes family and, 240, 243, 248–49; Vita and, 37, 59, 214; Zé das Drogas and, 1
personhood, 41, 53, 86–87, 359–60. *See also* dehumanization
Petry, Leopoldo, 171–72
Petryna, Adriana, 370n17, 372n29
pharmaceuticalization: of *abandonados*, 275; average cost of, 179; in Brazil, 374n45; deinstitutionalization and, 125, 131, 141; family and, 96, 106–7, 164–65, 185–86; globalization and, 22; hospitalization vs., 183–84; medical automatism and, 147; and mental illness, 95, 127–28; as moral technology, 8, 20; neurological side effects of, 149–50, 192–94, 197; in Novo Hamburgo, 175; and psychosocial politics, 176–77, 315–16; and social psychosis, 105–7; at Vita, 3–4, 5, 8–10, 102–4, 105, 218–19. *See also* Moraes, Catarina Gomes, overmedication of; *specific medications*
pharmakos: Catarina as, 257–64, 316; definition of, 257; writing and, 258–59
photography, 42–43, 116, 229–30, 371n23
"Physical Effect on the Individual of the Idea of Death Suggested by the Collectivity, The" (Mauss), 38

plasticity, 15–18, 368n9
Plato, 258–59
"Plato's Pharmacy" (Derrida), 258–59
police, 21, 50
Porto Alegre (Brazil): Central Prison of, 58; family responsibility for *abandonados* in, 234; "geriatric houses" in, 2, 48, 84, 139, 274–77; homeless in, 51; MJD in, 301; popular administration in, 82–83; public health inspection in, 64; Vita located in, 1. *See also* Vita
poverty: in Brazil, 2, 49–51, 367n1; capitalism and, 49–50; Catarina's family and, 288; lack of social mobility, 179–80. See also urban working poor
prometazine, 193–94, 202, 205, 218–19
psychiatric reform movement, 130–37; deinstitutionalization and, 138–39, 152; and hospitalization reduction, 173–74
psychiatry: *abandonados* and, 148; Catarina and, 18; deinstitutionalization of, 124–25, 130–31; family and, 252; pharmaceuticalization as alternative to, 128; and social death, 41
Psychic Life of Power, The (Butler), 16
psychosis: acute brief psychosis, 17–18; causes of, 368–69n9; misdiagnoses of, 194; MJD and, 298; pharmaceuticalization and, 105, 192–98; postpartum, 194; reactive, 153, 157–58; social, 18; subjectivity and, 16–17, 150; and medical science, 149
Psychosocial Attention, Centers for. *See* CAPS
Public Ministry, 61, 134, 141, 192, 373n38
public psychiatric institutions, 140. *See also* Caridade Psychiatric Hospital; São Paulo Psychiatric Hospital

Rabinow, Paul, 11, 375n58
rape, 116–18
Renato, João (psychiatrist), 129
rheumatism, and Catarina: misdiagnosis of, 124, 196; Catarina's belief in, 5, 71, 92–93, 187–90, 100, 194, 271
Ribeiro, Janete (mental health activist), 131–32, 133–34, 138–39, 141–44
Ribeiro, Renato Janine, 51
Rio Grande do Sul, 47, 130–31, 136
Rohypnol. *See* flunitrazepan
Romberg test, 220

Rückert, Luisa (psychologist), 184–85, 185–86
Ruschel, Flávia (social worker), 168
Ryff, Carol, 375n56

Santa Clara geriatric house, 275–76
Santa Luisa geriatric house, 274
Santo Afonso district (Brazil), 168, 178, 180, 183–84
São Paulo Psychiatric Hospital: *abandonados* at, 143; Catarina hospitalized at, 38, 95, 151–58, 166, 177, 192, 238, 253; Catarina's medical files at, 119, 123–24; Clóvis at, 102; deinstitutionalization at, 138–39, 173, 279; medical practices at, 164; Novo Hamburgo hospitalizations at, 180; SUS funding cuts at, 140
Sassá (Vita resident), 116–18, 210–11
Scheper-Hughes, Nancy, 15, 367n4, 370n17
schizophrenia: causes of, 368–69n9; epidemiological fading of, 144; and hospitalization, 182–83; misdiagnoses of, 127–29, 194; redefinition of, psychiatry reform and, 131; and medical science, 149
"Sense of Symptoms, The" (Freud), 196–97
sexual abuse, 80, 116–18, 181–82
sexuality, Catarina and, 97–101, 109, 111–16, 355
Silva, Inácio (psychiatrist), 192, 193
Silva, Patrícia (psychiatrist), 185
Singer, Burton, 375n56
Sistema Único de Saúde (SUS): AIDS treatment through, 218; establishment of, 47, 130; hospitalization funding cut by, 140; medical routine in, 220; and social death, 52; wait for MRI through, 203
social death, 317; *abandonados* and, 52–53, 65–66; "bioavailability" and, 372n32; in Brazil, 52–53; Catarina and, 20–21, 23, 186, 314–15; citizenship and, 56, 65–66, 142; dehumanization and, 39–41; ethnography and, 367n4; family and, 21–22, 38–39, 41, 181–82; language and, 88–91; personhood through, 41, 52–53; psychological effects of, 38; at Vita, 37–39, 41, 56, 65–66; zones of abandonment and, 20–21

social psychosis: definition of, 106; family and, 315–16; pharmaceuticalization and, 105–7
Sontag, Susan, 42
Souza, Valmir de (boyfriend), 153–54, 156, 160–61, 250, 255
Souza, Wildson (psychologist), 179–80, 184
state: and abandonment, 8; 132–33; and citizenship, 65–66; and exclusion, 144–45; family as medical agent of, 22, 185, 316; homelessness and, 50–51; mental health service as, 180; and social death, 21–22, 38–39; and Vita, 84, 143–44
Steiner, George, 86
Streb, Luis Guilherme, 218–23, 271, 283, 297
subjectivity: hospitalization and, 373n39; and identification, 137; language and, 10–12; mental health reform and, 136–37; plasticity and, 15–16; politics and, 16; psychosis and, 16–17, 150; sexuality and, 109; social control and, 131; social influences on, 369n11, 369n12; typical symptom and, 197; at Vita, 11, 23–24; zones of abandonment and, 23–24. *See also under* Moraes, Catarina Gomes
symptoms: extrapyramidal, medication as cause of, 192–94, 197; management of, 189–91; typical vs. individual, 196–97, 200. See also rheumatism

Tenth National Health Care Conference, 136–37
Thargelia, festival of, 257
"This" (Milosz), 313–14
"Thoughts for the Times on War and Death" (Freud), 40
"thought-styles" (Fleck), 148–49
Tofranil. *See* imipramine
Tranca (Vita resident), 355
triage: Catarina excluded by, 279, 307–8; citizenship and, 65–66, 145; family and, 316; at local health posts, 168, 175, 178; at public psychiatric institutions, 140; at Vita, 57–58, 104
Tutelage Councils (Conselhos Tutelares), 59–60, 169

unemployment, 46, 48, 179–80
universal health care system: Catarina and,
12–13; establishment of, 47; malfunctioning of, 46; and mental illness, 124;
partial privatization of, 21–22; and social death, 52–53. See also Sistema
Único de Saúde
Urbano and Tamara (adoptive parents):
Ana adopted by, 161, 246, 248, 254–56;
as Ana's godparents, 253–54; and Ana's
visit to Catarina, 353–54; Catarina
abandoned by, 232, 238, 248–56; and
Catarina's funeral, 360; Catarina taken
in by, 165–66, 192; family business,
248–49
urban working poor: globalization and, 21;
mental health care for, 13, 124; pharmaceuticalization and, 106, 141; private
health care plans for, 130

Valério (Vita resident), 39
Vanderlei (Vita volunteer), 35–36
Vera (psychiatrist), 202
Verinha (Vita resident), 116
Viola (psychiatrist), 204–5
violence, 48, 179–80
Vita (asylum): AIDS cases at, 39, 56,
58–59, 60, 84, 104–5, 218; Catarina at,
279, 296; citizenship at, 56, 64–66, 103;
conditions at, 2, 355–56; donations at,
276–77; ethnography of, 317; ex-
humanness at, 24, 52, 85–90, 317;
founding of, 1; human rights violations
at, 276; infrastructure improvement at,
5, 56–58, 209–10; legal definition of, 64;
management priorities at, 105–6; mission of, 35; organized crime at, 118;
personhood at, 41; pharmaceuticalization at, 3–4, 5, 8–10, 102–4, 105,

218–19; psychiatric cases at, 79; recovery area at, 5, 56, 118; recovery deadline at, 59; as rehabilitation service, 104,
139, 276; religion at, 37, 59, 214; repli-
cation of, 139; sexual abuse at, 80,
116–18; sexuality at, 100–101, 109, 116;
social death at, 37–39, 41, 56, 65–66;
state and, 84, 143–44; subjectivity at, 11,
23–24; triage system at, 57–58, 104; volunteers at, 37; as zone of abandonment,
1–2, 35–37. See also *abandonados*
Vó Brenda (Vita resident), 60–61

Waaler-Rose test, 271
wealth distribution, 46
welfare, citizenship and, 46–47
Winkler, Gerson, 1–2, 35
Wittgenstein, Ludwig, 367n5
women: and biological complex, 290–91,
316; mental illness and poverty, 179–85;
MJD and, 302–3
Workers' Party: consciousness-raising philosophy of, 83; and psychiatry reform,
130; public health access and, 308; and
public health inspection, 64, 139; and
social inclusion, 48

Young, Allan, 370n17

Zé das Drogas: as administrator, 36,
57–59; evicted from Vita, 56; on social death and personhood, 41; as
Vita founder, 1; on Vita's mission, 35,
36–37
zone(s) of social abandonment: *abandonados* directed to, 4; biopolitics and, 52;
personhood in, 41; and social death,
20–21, 41; and subjectivity, 23–24; Vita
as, 1–2, 35–37